PRINCIPLES AND PRACTICE OF MANAGEMENT

R.S.N. Pillai
M.A., M.Com., LL.B.
Professor and Head of the Commerce Department
Arignar Anna College, Aramboly
Kanyakumari

S. Kala
M.Sc., M.Phil.
Annai Velankanny College
Saidapet, Chennai

S Chand And Company Limited
(ISO 9001 Certified Company)

S Chand And Company Limited

(ISO 9001 Certified Company)

Head Office: D-92, Sector–2, Noida – 201301, U.P. (India), Ph. 91-120-4682700

Registered Office: A-27, 2nd Floor, Mohan Co-operative Industrial Estate, New Delhi – 110 044, Phone: 011-49731800

www.**schandpublishing.com;** e-mail: **info@schandpublishing.com**

Marketing Offices:

Chennai	:	Ph: 23632120; chennai@schandpublishing.com
Guwahati	:	Ph: 2738811, 2735640; guwahati@schandpublishing.com
Hyderabad	:	Ph: 40186018; hyderabad@schandpublishing.com
Jalandhar	:	Ph: 4645630; jalandhar@schandpublishing.com
Kolkata	:	Ph: 23357458, 23353914; kolkata@schandpublishing.com
Lucknow	:	Ph: 4003633; lucknow@schandpublishing.com
Mumbai	:	Ph: 25000297; mumbai@schandpublishing.com
Patna	:	Ph: 2260011; patna@schandpublishing.com

First Edition 2013
Reprint with corrections 2014, 2016
Reprints 2018, 2019, 2020, 2021, 2023

Reprint 2024

ISBN: 978-81-219-4149-5 **Product Code:** H8MAN48BMGT10ENAA13O

PRINTED IN INDIA

By Vikas Publishing House Private Limited, Plot 20/4, Site-IV, Industrial Area Sahibabad, Ghaziabad – 201 010 and Published by S Chand And Company Limited, A-27, 2nd Floor, Mohan Co-operative Industrial Estate, New Delhi – 110 044.

PREFACE

The book "Principles and Practice of Management" is one of the Management book out of several books available in book shops. We have been teaching the subject "Management" for the last several years to the students of Commerce and Management. Our aim is to provide a book to the students of management as well as the professionals. By keeping this view, we have tried to explain the basic issue of management which is required to everyone. While reading this book, the readers will have a clear idea of what management is all about, how to acquire managerial skills and how to manage an organisation.

The matter covered in this book has been drawn from several Indian and Foreign books and a number of articles published in management journals. This book has been specially written for management students and other professional courses. The managers of today have to be conversant with the principles and techniques of modern management for taking up a job effectively and efficiently. Keeping this in mind, the book has been planned and written. It explains the nature of management and the evolution of management theory from the traditional to modern application, it highlights the importance of planning function in the business enterprises.

The book has been written in a simple and self-learning style. Clarity has been given top priority throughout. Attempt has been made to narrate even the most tough ideas in a simple and easy-to-follow style. Key concepts and ideas in every chapter are highlighted in bold/italics. In fact, this is the uniqueness of this book.

We are thankful to the Management Team and the Editorial Department of S. Chand & Company Pvt. Ltd. for all help and support in the publication of this book.

AUTHORS

BRIEF CONTENTS

DETAILED CONTENTS

Concepts and Nature of Management

- Introduction
- What is management ?
- Definition of management
- Concept of management (meaning)
  - Management as an economic resources
  - Management as a group
  - Management as a process
  - Management as a discipline
  - Management as an activity
- Nature of management
- Importance of management
- Importance of management in India
- Principles of management
- Management - as a science or as an art
  - Management as an art
  - Management as a science
- Management is both a science and an art
- Management as profession
- Professionalisation of management
- Management and Administration
- Levels of management
- Managerial roles
- Managerial skills
- Management functions
- Case study - 1
- Review Questions

INTRODUCTION

Every organization requires management for its sustained success and survival. When we look at the existing organisations all over the world, we find that some are highly successful, some are striving hard for success, and some are unsuccessful. There are certain factors influencing their success. Managers in their organizations perform the functions of planning, organizing, staffing, directing and controlling for success. Every organisation, for example, a family, a college, a business enterprise, an army, a Government, a church, etc., is basically a group of people seeking to attain some common objectives.

Every human being has several needs and desires. But no individual can satisfy all his wants. Therefore, people work together to meet their mutual needs which they cannot fulfil individually. It is important that man is a social being as he likes to live together with other people. By working and living together in organised groups and institutions the people satisfy their economic and social needs. As said above, there are several types of groups - a business firm, a cricket team and the like. Such formal groups can achieve their goals effectively only when the efforts of the people working in these groups are properly coordinated and controlled. The task of getting results through others by coordinating their efforts is known as management. Management coordinates and regulates the activities of various members of an organisation.

Utilization of resources has been the most common and yet perhaps the most complex human activity ever since the dawn of civilization. Management is the process of utilization of resources in an effective manner in the today's dynamic environment. Management involves an organised effort to achieve the objectives. People work together in a group to achieve common objectives so the coordination of physical and human resources become necessary. Most of us are members of one organisation or the other - be it a college, a business organisation or a school. Each organisation, whether business or non-business, has a goal and needs effective management to achieve that goal.

WHAT IS MANAGEMENT ?

Simply speaking, management is what managers do. But the simple statement doesn't tell us much. A better explanation is that MANAGEMENT involves coordinating and over-seeing the work activities of others so that their activities are completed efficiently and effectively. We know that coordinating and over-seeing the work of others is what distinguishes a managerial position from a non-managerial one. However, this doesn't mean that managers can do what they want anytime, anywhere or in any way. Instead, management involves ensuring that work activities are completed efficiently and effectively by the people responsible for doing them or at least that's what managers aspire to do.

In the words of Stanley Vance, "Management is simply a process of decision-making and control over the actions of human being for the express purpose of attaining the predetermined goals. "The management is the part of executing the policies of an enterprise effectively and efficiently so that the predetermined goals of the enterprise may be attained. Management is related to the human activities of an enterprise. In the words of Henry L. Sisk, "Management is the coordination of all the resources through the process of planning, organising, direction and controlling in order to attain the predetermined objects. "The manager is the dynamic, life-giving element in every business. Without his leadership, the "resources of production" remain resources and never become production. For the quality and performance of its managers is the only effective advantage of an enterprise than a competitive economy can have.

DEFINITION OF MANAGEMENT

There is no universally accepted definition of management. Management experts have defined management differently. Management means "managing men tactfully to get the things done". The term "management" involves getting things done through others, and a manager is a person who accomplishes objectives by directing the efforts of other people. The definitions by some of the leading management thinkers are given below:

"Management is the art of getting things done through and with people in formally organised groups." — Harold Koontz.

"Management is the creation and maintenance of an internal environment in an enterprise where individuals, working in groups, can perform efficiently and effectively towards the attainment of group goals." — Koontz and O'Donnel.

"Management is a distinct process consisting of planning, organising, actuating and controlling performed to determine and accomplish the objectives by the use of people and resources." —George R Torry.

"Management is the coordination of all resources through the process of planning, organising, directing and controlling in order to attain stated goals." — Henry L Sisk.

"Management is the art of knowing what you want to do in the best and cheapest way." — F.W. Taylor.

"Management is that function of an enterprise which concerns itself with the direction and control of the various activities to attain the business objectives. Management is essentially an executive function; it deals particularly with the active direction of the human effort." — William Spreigel.

Management is managing people and other resources in the organisation and outside the organisation for achieving the mission and objectives of the organisation. It is nothing but managing people with tact and managing people achieving targets.

CONCEPT OF MANAGEMENT

The term 'management' has been interpreted in several ways: some of which are given below:

1. Management as an Economic Resources

This is the economists' view of management. Development of organisation depends upon the availability and effective utilisation of resources like men, material, capital, entrepreneurial ability, etc. Coordination of these resources is reflected in the end results of the organisation. As the organisation moves from lower to higher levels of management, there is need for research, development, innovation, etc. This can be done if the resources human and non-human, are effectively managed by the executives. Thus, the management viewed as a separate resource which largely determines the productivity of the organisation.

2. Management as a Group

Management is a group effort. An individual cannot manage the organisation. Managers at all level - top, middle and low, coordinate their efforts to establish organisational goals and frame policies to achieve them. The performance of organisation depends upon collective performance of its managers. Top managers, titled as chief executives, presidents, or vice-presidents of a company, are responsible for overall management of the enterprise. They lay company's plans and policies and integrate its working with the external environment. Middle level managers mediate between top level and lower level managers. They integrate company's plans and policies with the capacities of their subordinates, guide their subordinates and motivate them to excel in organisational performance. Lower level managers are also known as first-line managers. They directly instruct the employees to work according to company's plans and goals. Management as a group is defined as performing organisational tasks with and through others. "Management is defined as the process by which a cooperative group directs actions towards common goals."

3. Management as a Process

This is the practitioner's view of management. Process means a course of action or proceeding. It involves a series of steps to carry out an activity. "Management is the process of planning, organising, leading and controlling the efforts of organisation members and of using all other organisational resources to achieve stated organisational goals." The process defines management as a set of functions performed by managers regardless of their levels, aptitude and skills.

4. Management as a Discipline

Management, as a discipline, is viewed as a distinct field of study. Since importance of management is increasing, there is need for specialised institutions to impart the knowledge of management to people. Management is taken as a separate field of study. All over the world, many institutions offer specialised courses in management of business administration. Though management practices ideas from other fields of study as sociology, psychology, etc. It is a complete discipline in itself.

5. Management as an Activity

Activity means exercising some kind of action. Management as an activity can be understood in terms of actions performed by managers to achieve organisational objectives within the contraints of internal and external environment. Management as an activity is "the art of getting things done through people." - Follett. Management as an activity defines the role of managers. Empirical evidence has proved that managers perform roles which can be classified into three–Interpersonal roles or activities, informational roles or activities and Decisional roles or activities.

NATURE OF MANAGEMENT

The salient features which highlight the nature of management are as follows:

1. Management is Universal

The basic principles of management are universal. They apply more or less in every situation. The functions of management are performed by all managers. Wherever two or more persons are engaged in working for a common goal, management is necessary. All types of organisations, for example, family, university, army, government, etc. require management. Management is a pervasive activity.

2. Management is goal-oriented

Management is not an end in itself. It is a means to achieve certain goals. Management has no justification to exist without goals. Management goals are called group goals or organisational goals. The basic goal of management is to ensure efficiency and economy in the utilisation of human, physical and financial resources. The success of management is measured by the extent to which the established goals are achieved. So, management is purposeful

3. Management is Intangible

Management is an unseen or invisible force. It cannot be seen but its presence can be felt everywhere in the form of results. However, the managers who perform the functions of management are very much tangible and visible.

4. Management is a Social Process

Management is done by people, through people and for people. It is social process because it is concerned with interpersonal relations. Human factor is the most important element in management. According to Appley, "Management is the development of people, not the direction of things." It is the pervasiveness of the human element which gives management its special character as a social process.

5. Management is a multi-acted discipline

Though the management is a distinct discipline, it contains principles drawn from many social sciences like anthropology, psychology, etc. Much of the management literature is the result of the association of these disciplines. Due to this, management is also known as a "Behavioural Science."

6. Management is a continuous process

Management is a dynamic function and it has to be performed continuously. It is constantly engaged in moulding of the enterprise in the ever changing business environment. The cycle of management continues to operate so long as there is organised action for the achievement of group goals.

7. Management is purposeful

Management is a way to achieve certain end results, but without end results it would be directionless. All activities of management are goal oriented, the success of management is measured by the extent to which the desired objectives are attained. Group efforts in management are always directed towards the attainment of pre-determined objectives. These objectives are the final goals of any organisation towards which all the management activities are systematically and purposefully directed.

8. Management is a group phenomenon

Management involves the use of group effort in the pursuit of common objectives. People join in groups to achieve what they cannot achieve individually. Management is an activity whenever and wherever people come together to achieve some common goals.

9. Management is essentially an executive function

It deals with the active direction and control of the activities of people to attain predetermined objectives. Management is a technique by means of which the objectives of a human group are determined, clarified and accomplished. A manager does not do any operating work himself. He gets the work done by, with and through the people.

10. Management makes things happen

Managerial ability is distinctly different from technical ability. As we know, management is the art of getting things done through people. It implies that under given set of constraints or problems, how positive results can emerge, by taking well defined actions.

IMPORTANCE OF MANAGEMENT

There is no substitute for management in a modern organisation. As remarked by Peter F. Drucker, "Management is the dynamic, life-giving element in every business. Without it the resources of production remain resources and never become production." An organisation may have raw materials, machines, human resources, etc., but those can't produce want satisfying products unless they are efficiently managed. Management acts as catalyst which enhances the productivity of the various factors of production. Organisations stand or fall on the quality of their managements because sound management provides the following:-

1. Determination of objectives

The objectives of any organisation are laid down by the management. They are put into writing and communicated to all others in the organisation. No organisation can succeed in its operations unless its objectives are identified and defined. Management adapts the organisation to its environment and often shapes the environment to make it more suitable to the organisation. It also allocates resources, arbitrates disputes and provides leadership.

2. Achievement of group goals

A human group consists of several persons, each specialising in doing a part of the total task. Each person may be working efficiently, but the group as a whole cannot realise its objectives unless there is mutual cooperation and coordination among the members of the group. Management creates team-work and coordination in the group. It reconciles the objectives of the group with those of its members so that each one of them is motivated to make his best contribution towards the accomplishment of group goals.

3. Human development

Management is not simply the direction of things but the development of men. It improves the personality of people to raise their efficiency and productivity. A good manager serves as a friend and guide to his subordinates.

4. Efficient use of resources

Efficient management is the life boat of any developed business. The resources of the business may be identified and developed by the management. They can help in the efficient use of various resources and increase the productivity of the enterprise. The expert managers can lead the business towards growth and prosperity. Workers are trained as to what to do and how to do their jobs. Managers develop a spirit of mutual cooperation and sense of responsibility among workers. They make human efforts efficient and effective.

5. Economic growth

By bringing together the four factors of production, viz. men, money, material and machines, management enables a country to experience a substantial level of economic development. A country with enough capital, manpower and other natural resources can still be poor if it does not have competent managers to combine and coordinate these resources. Poor economic growth of many Asian countries very well illustrates this point. Drucker rightly observes that without management, a country's resources of production remain resources and never become production.

6. Development of the Nation

Efficient management is equally important at the national level. Management is the most crucial factor in economic and social development. The development of a country largely depends on the quality of the management of its resources. Capital investment and import of technical know how cannot lead to economic growth unless wealth producing resources are managed efficiently.

7. Stability

Management ensures the survival of an organisation in a fast changing environment. It coordinates the activities of different departments in an organisation and maintains team spirit among the personnel. Modern business operates in a rapidly changing environment. An enterprise has to adapt itself to the changing demands of the market and society. Management keeps in touch with the existing business environment and draws its predictions about the treads in future. It takes steps in advance to meet the challenges of changing environment. Changes in business environment create risks as well as opportunities. Managers enable the enterprise to minimise the risks and maximise the benefit of opportunities.

8. Fulfilment of social obligations

Sound management monitors the environment of business and makes necessary changes in business policies and practices so as to keep the consumers and workers to satisfy. In this way managers help an enterprise to fulfil its obligations towards different sections of society. Management balances and integrates various interests in group efforts.

9. Life-giving element

It is this element that coordinates current organisational activities and plans future ones. It arbitrates and provides leadership. It adapts the organisation to its environment and often shapes the environment to make it more suitable to the organisation. In a competitive economy, the quality and performance of the management determine the success of an organisation and they determine its very survival.

10. Meeting challenges

Management is the brain of any enterprise. All the policy decisions are taken by it. Management keeps itself in touch with the current environment and supplies foresight to the enterprise. It helps in predicting what is going to happen in future which will influence the working of the enterprise. It also takes steps to ensure that the enterprise is able to meet the demands of changing environment.

11. Balance between multiple goals

At a point of time, managers face multiple goals, all of which cannot be simultaneously achieved. Deciding about what is more important and what is less important so that scarce organisational resources can be optimally allocated to different organisational goals, is facilitated through management.

12. Free competition

Today's world is the world of intense competition. Effectively managed business firms outperform those which are not effectively managed and thus capture a bigger share of the market. Management helps firms to face competition in the market.

IMPORTANCE OF MANAGEMENT IN INDIA

The management is now regarded as a profession in our country. But the process of management in still to be developed much more than it has developed. The importance of management knowledge is not confined to business only, but it remains equally a vital input for economic development of the country. The rate and pace of economic development of any nation is greatly influenced by the quality and talent of management knowledge used. In every economy, resources are scarce and limited and it is only through their effective and efficient utilisation rate of economic development can be enhanced. To have a faster rate of economic growth, more emphasis is to be laid down on revolution of management knowledge in the country. It has been rightly stressed that the good quality of management is an important input not only for the success of the business but also for overall economic development of the country. Management has to play a more important role in developing countries, like India. In such countries, the productivity is low and the resources are limited. It has been rightly observed, "There are no underdeveloped countries. There are only under-managed ones". Management is the brain of any enterprise. All the policy decisions are taken by it. It helps in predicting what is going to happen in future which will influence the working of the enterprise. The importance of management becomes manyfold in India. India is an underdeveloped country, marching ahead on path of development and self-dependence.

The importance of management is increasing in India day by day, because of the following reasons:

1. The distribution of wealth is very imbalanced in India.
2. India is having the largest number of unemployed persons in the world.
3. India is facing the labour problems many times more than other countries.
4. The productivity of Indian industry is very low when compared with the productivity of the industries of developed countries.

5. India is a country which is regarded as one of the poorest countries in the world as above 40% of the population is still living below the line of poverty.
6. India is marching on the path of self-dependence through the rapid industrialisation and largely depends on the efficiency of management.
7. In India, we find only 13% of capital formation while the rate is as high as 30% in other countries.
8. The nature gifted all its resources to India but we could not exploit these resources fully.
9. The rate of scientific and technical development in India is very low.
10. India now a days is facing a huge problem of foreign indebtedness.

PRINCIPLES OF MANAGEMENT

Principle refers to fundamental truth about a concept that provides guide to action. Principles evolve in every field of knowledge, for examples, medicine, accountancy, engineering, etc. Management principles tell about administration of a business, that is, the way a business should run. Principles underlying the field of management help in evolving management theories and making successful managers. Principles serve as guide for management thought. The principles of management are vital to organise and manage the business.

Henri Fayol has suggested 14 principles of management in order to make the job of management more effective and efficient. They are given below:

1. Division of work

Division of work means specialisation. Each job and work should be divided into small elements and each element should be assigned to the specialist of the element. Fayol wanted division of work not only at factory level but at management levels also.

2. Authority and responsibility

Authority and responsibility are coexistent and they must go hand in hand. Authority should commensurate with responsibility. Fayol stressed that right and power to give orders should be balanced with the responsibility for performing the necessary functions.

3. Discipline

Discipline is a sine-qua-non for the proper functioning of an organisation. Members of an organisation are required to perform their functions and conduct themselves in relation to others according to rules, norms and customs.

4. Unity of command

According to this principle, one subordinate should get orders and instructions regarding his work only from one superior. It helps in maintaining discipline among employees, controlling their activities, fixing responsibility, etc.

5. Unity of direction

Each group of activities having the same objective must have one head and one plan. It will create dedication to the purpose and loyalty.

6. Subordination of Individual interest to general interest

The interest of the organization is above the interests of the individual and the group. According to this, in every work setting, each employee should sacrifice and subordinate his personal interest and goal for achieving the goals of the organization.

7. Remuneration

Remuneration should be fair and adequate. It should lead to the maximum satisfaction and include both type of incentives - financial as well as non-financial.

8. Centralisation

The relationship between centralisation and decentralisation of authority is a matter of proportion and optimum balance should be maintained according to the needs of organisation.

9. Scalar chain

Scalar chain means the hierarchy of authority from the highest executive to the lowest one for the purpose of communication. It states superior-subordinate relationship and the authority of superiors in relation to subordinates at various levels. The orders or communications should pass the proper channels of authority along the scalar chain.

10. Order

Order, in the conception of Fayol, means right person on the right job and everything in the proper place. This kind of order, "depends on precise knowledge of human requirements and resources of the concern and a constant balance between these requirements and resources."

11. Equity

Kindness and justice should be exercised by management in dealing with its subordinates. This will create loyalty and devotion among employees.

12. Stability of tenure of personnel

The management policies should provide a sense of reasonable job security. Stability of tenure helps to develop loyalty and attachment on the part of employees.

13. Initiative

It focuses on the ability, attitude and resourcefulness to act without prompting from others. Managers must create an environment which encourages their subordinates to take initiative and responsibility.

14. Esprit de corps

Cohesiveness and team spirit should be encouraged among employees. It is one of the chief characteristics of organised activity that a number of people work together in close cooperation for the achievement of common goals.

MANAGEMENT - AS A SCIENCE OR AS AN ART

The controversy with regard to the nature of management, i.e. whether it is an art or science is very old and has created a great confusion. Webster dictionary defines an art as "skill in conducting any human activity" and science as "any skill or technique that reflects a precise application of facts or principle". Management, as a science, would indicate that in practice, managers use a specific body of information and facts to guide their behaviours, but that management, as an art, requires no specific body of knowledge, only skill. The nature of management can be understood through its features. An important aspect that explains the nature of management is that management is viewed:

1. As an art
2. As a science
3. As a profession

Management as an art

What is an art ? Art is bringing about a desired result through the application of skills. It is concerned with the application of knowledge and skills. If a science is learnt, an art is practised. In other words, science is to seek knowledge and art is to apply knowledge. Thus an art has the following features:-

(*i*) It denotes personal skills.

(*ii*) It signifies practical knowledge.

(*iii*) It helps in achieving concrete result.

(*iv*) It is creative in nature.

(*v*) It is improved through practice.

Let us examine to what extent management fulfils the above requirements.

(*i*) *Personal skill:* Every artist has his own style and approach to his job. The success of different artists differ even when all of them possess the same technical knowledge or qualifications. This is due to the level of their personal skills. Management is personalised. The success of a manager depends on his personality in addition to his technical knowledge.

(*ii*) *Practical knowledge:* It is concerned with application of knowledge. Management does not merely mean the knowledge of principles of management rather than it is the application of this knowledge which makes it effective and useful. A person cannot become a successful manager simply by reading the theory and getting a degree in management. He must also learn to apply his knowledge in solving managerial problems in practical life.

(*iii*) *Result oriented approach:* Every manager applies certain knowledge and skills to achieve the desired results. He uses men, money, materials and machinery to promote the growth of the organisation.

(*iv*) *Creativity:* Art is always creative. Artist's creativity can be enhanced through training and motivation. Management is also creative. It requires managerial skills to foresee future, forecast the future, look for opportunities in the environment and exploit them gainfully. Managers also need to be creative for coordinating the human and non-human resources for achieving the practical results.

(*v*) *Practice:* Managers can expertise in the art of management through constant practice. The more they practice, the more they learn and become successful business-men.

On the basis of above discussion, one may conclude that management is an art of applying skill, knowledge, creativity, personal judgement and innovativeness to understand the behaviour of subordinates and application of suitable devices to allocate scarce resources over organisational objectives. Scientific principles and theories cannot always solve organisational problems.

Management as a science

What is science ? Science is an organised body of knowledge based on proper findings and exact principles. It develops a relationship between cause and effect and its findings apply in all the situations. The basic difference between an art and science is that art implies knowing how the application whereas science is concerned with knowing why. Any branch of knowledge can be called a science if it possesses the following characteristics:

(*i*) Cause and effect relationship

(*ii*) Universal application

(*iii*) Systematic body of knowledge

(*iv*) Scientific enquiry and investigation

(*v*) Test of validity

Let us examine to what extent management fulfils the above requirements.

(*i*) *Cause and effect relationship:* Science is a systematised body of knowledge pertaining to a particular field of enquiry. It is systematised in the sense that it establishes cause and effect relationship between different variables. There is a systematised body of knowledge. Principles and theories are now available in every area of management. For example, there are several principles to serve as guidelines for effective delegation of authority.

(*ii*) *Universal application:* The principles have universal applicability. They can be applied under different situations barring a few exceptions which can be logically explained. The principles are verifiable and lead to predictable results. Though not always true, management principles are universally applicable. The principles of 'Esprit de corps' - unity is strength is applied in almost every organisation and every situation. On this basis also management can be called a science.

(*iii*) *Systematic body of knowledge:* Management concepts and principles have evolved over a period of time and have systematised into well defined management theories being studied and practiced in most of the successful organisations. Management can, therefore, be rightly said a systematised knowledge. "Management science is a body of systematised knowledge accumulated and accepted with reference to the understanding of general truths concerning management."

(*iv*) *Scientific enquiry and investigation:* "A scientific method involves the determination of facts through observation." Repeated observations of similar facts and situations lead to certain generalizations which help in making predictions about what will happen in similar situations. While dealing with people in organisations, managers repeatedly observe the human behaviour, analyze their physiological and psychological needs and frame policies and devices that satisfy those needs.

(*v*) *Test of validity:* Validity of scientific principles can be tested at any time and any number of times. Every time the test will give the same result. Moreover, the future events can be predicted with reasonable accuracy by using scientific principles.

On the basis of above, management is undoubtedly a science. It contains a systematic body of knowledge in the form of general principles which enjoy universal applicability. However, management is not as exact a science, like Physics, Biology, Chemistry, etc. This is because management deals with people and it is very difficult to predict accurately the behaviour of living human beings. Management principles are universal but they cannot be expected to give exactly the same results in every situation. That is why management is known as a soft science. Management is a social science. It is still growing, with the growing needs of human organisation.

MANAGEMENT IS BOTH A SCIENCE AND AN ART

"Management is both a science as well as an art." It is a science because it has an organised body of knowledge consisting universal facts. It is known as an art because it involves creating results through practical application of knowledge and skills. Science teaches one to know and art to do. It cannot, however, be clearly defined as to when it is science and when an art.

As science, it is based on principles and theories, on the basis of which managers act, and as art, it deals with decision making process through application of practical and personal skills. The management begins where the science of management ends.

Art without science has no guide and science without art is knowledge wasted. Science (theory) and art (practice) are both essential for the success of management. Science provides the knowledge of management principles and art helps in skillfully applying those principles to solve managerial problems.

MANAGEMENT AS PROFESSION

What is a profession ? Profession means occupation in some branch of advanced learning, for example, medical profession. Is management a profession like the profession of law or medicine ? According to Mc Farland a profession possesses the following characteristics:

"(*i*) a body of principles, techniques, skills and specialised knowledge;

(*ii*) formalised methods of acquiring training and experience;

(*iii*) the establishment of a representative organization with professionalisation as its goal;

(*iv*) the formation of ethical codes for the guidance of conduct; and

(*v*) the charging of fees based on the nature of services."

Accordingly, on the basis of above, let us examine to what extent management fulfils the characteristics:

1. *Systematic knowledge:* Professionals base their decisions on certain principles. These principles grow out of specialised knowledge that a person acquires through formal education and training programmes.
2. *Learning and experience:* There exists institutions and universities to impart education and training for a profession. No one can enter a profession without going through the prescribed course of learning. For example, one must pass the Chartered Accountancy examination to practice accountancy profession.
3. *Representative association:* Every professional is guided by the norms laid by the association or council under which he exercises his profession. After attaining formal education in medicine, for instance, a doctor is registered under the Medical Council of India. The association or council establishes the standards of performance for the professionals.
4. *Ethical code of conduct:* There must be a suitable code of conduct or ethics. Every member of the profession is expected to observe the ethical standards laid down for that profession. Members who violate the code can be derecognised and disqualified from the profession.
5. *Dedication:* Though professionals practice their profession for making financial gains, they are guided by service motive more than financial motive. True professionals work with complete dedication, commitment and loyalty.

Management is a profession to the extent it fulfils the above conditions. Management, as we all know, does not possess all the above characteristics of a profession. Unlike medicine or law, management does not have any fixed norms of managerial behaviour. No minimum qualifications have been prescribed for managerial personnel. Further, the entry to managerial jobs is not restricted to individuals with a special academic degree only. No management association has the authority to grant certificates of practice or to regulate entry into management careers. The management associations have no legal right to enforce their code of conduct. According to Peter F Drucker, "management is a practice rather than a science or profession though containing elements of both. No greater damage could be done to economy and society than to attempt to professionalise management by licensing managers or by limiting access to management to people with special academic degree."

Formal education and training are becoming increasingly popular among managers. Several national institutes have been established for importing specialised knowledge and skills in management. Persons with formal education and training in management are given preference for filling managerial positions in industry and business. National-level association of managers have been formed in most of the countries. In India, All India Management Association has been recognised as a representative body of professional managers. A code of professional conduct has been formulated and there is increasing recognition of the social responsibilities of managers.

PROFESSIONALISATION OF MANAGEMENT

The professionalism implies that specialised knowledge will come into existence. Institutions will grow to provide the required specialised knowledge and skill. Management still remains a developing field, changes are taking place regularly in its nature, significance, importance, etc. In a modern society, professionalisation of management occupying an important position which has brought in new dimensions. Management is a universal process in all organized activity. It is not only the business enterprises that need management but all kinds of organizations need this vital force for integrating the scarce resources in an optimum productive relationship. All organizations whether a Government, hotel, bank, research institutions, etc. are purposive entities and achieve their objectives with limited resources. Management integrates these scarce resources in a productive relationship so as to achieve the organizational objectives with optimum efficiency and effectiveness.

The benefits of professional management are:

1. Professional managers will undoubtedly improve the working of business enterprises and make them more productive.
2. Professional managers will follow a specific code of ethics.
3. Professional managers will not only maximise firm's profits but also its image among the creditors, Government suppliers, competitions, etc.
4. In the competitive environment of today both at national and international levels, only professionally qualified managers can face competitions.

MANAGEMENT AND ADMINISTRATION

Management and administration are generally taken to mean as one and the same and are often used interchangeably. But there has been a controversy because of these two terms. Different authors on the subject have expressed conflicting opinion. Many experts make no distinction between management and administration while others, consider them as two separate functions. Three different views have been expressed by various authorities on the subject. According to the first, management and administration are different functions. The second view regards management as a generic term including administration which is considered to be a narrow function. The exponents of the third view do not make any distinction between the two terms and use them interchangeably. These three points of view are explained below:

1. Administration is different from management
2. Administration is a part of management
3. Administration and management are one.

Let us explain the above 3 points, in brief:

1. Administration is different from management

According to this viewpoint, administration is a higher level activity while management is a lower level function. *Administration* is a determinative function concerned with the determination of objectives and policies while *management* is an executive function involving the implementation of policies and direction of efforts for the achievement of objectives. This view is held by American experts on management.

Oliver Sheldon was the first person to make a distinction between management and administration. According to him, "*Administration* is the function in industry concerned with the determination of corporate policy, the coordination of finance, production and distribution, the settlement of the compass (structure), of the organisation, and ultimate control of the executive. *Management,* on the other hand, is the function in industry concerned with the execution of policy within the limits set up by administration, and the employment of the organisation for the particular objectives set before it. Administration defines the goal, management strives towards it."

2. Administration is a part of management

According to the European School of thought, management is a wider term including administration and organisation. This viewpoint has been propounded by Brech. According to him, "Management is the generic term for the total process of executive control involving responsibility for effective planning and guidance of operations of an enterprise. Administration is that part of management which is concerned with the installation and carrying out of the procedures by which the programme is laid down and communicated and the progress of activities is regulated and checked against plans. According to Kimball also hold similar view. "Administration is only an implementing agency while management is determinative."

3. Administration and management are one

Many writers like, Henri Fayol, William Newman, Chester Barnard, George Terry, etc. make no distinction between management and administration. According to Newman, management or administration is "the guidance, leadership and control of the efforts of a group of individuals towards some common goals." According to Fayol, all undertakings require the same functions and all must observe the same principles. In actual practice, the two terms are used interchangeably. Both management and administration are based upon the same set of principles and functions. It may be possible to make theoretical or conceptual distinction between the two.

In order to avoid any controversy, we can classify management into:

(*a*) Administrative management and

(*b*) Operative management.

Administrative management is primarily concerned with laying down policies and determining goals whereas *operative management* is concerned with implementation of the policies to the achievement of the goals. But both these functions are performed by the same set of people. According to Spriegal "At the higher levels, the managerial authority is concerned more with administrative management and less with operations." Every manager spends a part of his time in performing administrative management functions and the remaining time on operative management functions.

LEVELS OF MANAGEMENT

Management is a manifold activity. It is carried on at different levels of the organisation structure. The stages in the organisation where a particular type of function starts is called level of management. Thus, the term "Levels of Management" refers to a line of demarcation between various managerial positions in an organisation. Broadly speaking, an organisation has two important levels of management, viz., functional and operative. The functional level is concerned with the process of determining primary objectives, formulating basic policies, making vital decisions and controlling and coordinating activities of personnel. The operative level of management is related to implementation of plans and decisions, and the pursuit of basic policies for achieving objectives of the organisation.

According to levels, management or manager can be classified as follows:

1. Top level managers (Top management)
2. Middle level managers (Middle management)
3. Lower level managers (Lower management or First-line managers)

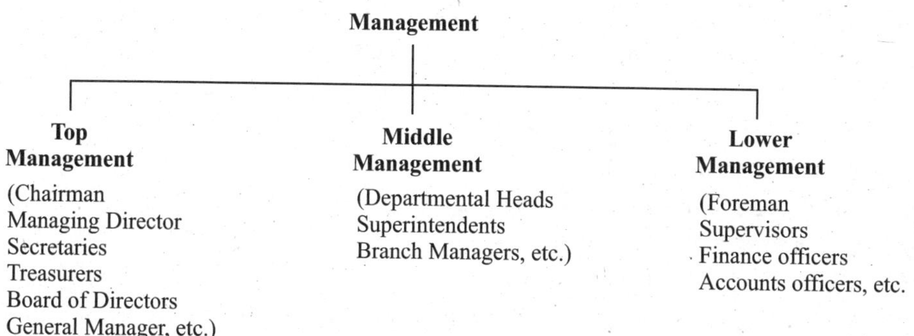

1. Top Level Management

The top level management is generally occupied by the ownership group. In a joint stock company, equity shareholders are the real owners of the company. They are in a large number, widely scattered and not interested in the management. They elect their representatives as directors, to form a board, known as Board of Directors, which constitutes the top level of management.

The major functions are:

(*a*) To formulate basic policies and providing direction and leadership to the organisation as a whole.

(*b*) To make a corporate plan for the entire organisation.

(*c*) To decide upon the matters which are vital for the survival, profitability and growth of the concern.

(*d*) To decide corporate goals.

(*e*) To make decisions on all matters.

(*f*) To design structure of the organisation.

(*g*) To select officials for the company.

(*h*) To maintain liaison with outside parties.

(*i*) To exercise overall managerial control, etc.

2. Middle Level Management

Middle level management consists of departmental heads which are generally classified under upper middle management, and sectional heads, area managers, etc. It is basically concerned with the task of implementing the policies and plans laid down by the top management.

The major functions are:

(*a*) To evaluate the performance of junior managers.

(*b*) To send progress report to the top management.

(*c*) Interpreting the policies of the top management.

(*d*) Motivating the personnel to achieve higher productivity.

(*e*) To coordinate with other departments.

(*f*) Reporting the feedback to the top management.

(*g*) Assigning duties and responsibilities to staff, etc.

3. Lower Level Management

It is the lowest level of management and thus has a direct contact with the workers. It includes supervisors, foremen, accounts-officers, etc. It is directly concerned with the control and performance of the operative employees. Lower level managers guide and direct the workers under the instructions from middle level managers. They devote more time on supervision of the workers and are responsible for building high morale among workers.

The major functions are:

(*a*) To plan day today operations of the business.
(*b*) To get the things done by the workers.
(*c*) To issue necessary orders and instructions.
(*d*) To assign work to the workers.
(*e*) To guide, assist and help the workers.
(*f*) To motivate and maintain a team spirit among them, etc.

MANAGERIAL ROLES

The role of managers differ from their functions. The functions describe what managers should do while roles describe what they actually do. A manager who occupies different positions in different situations plays different roles because people in each situation have different expectations of him concerning his functions. A role is an organised set of observable behaviour that is attributed to a specific position. As applied to the manager's job, a role would be viewed at the capacity in which a manager acts. For example a manager may act as a leader of subordinates, a spokes person of the organisation, or as a decision-maker. Thus a manager plays multiple role while performing his job.

Mintzberg has identified ten roles of a manager which are grouped into three categories - interpersonal, informational and decisional. That is, managers spend their time engaging in ten key activities or roles, falling into three categories, as said above.

Why organisations need managers ?

As a result of describing the nature of managerial work in terms of a set of ten roles, Mintzberg suggests six basic purposes of the manager, or reasons why organisations need managers:

1. to ensure the organisation serves its basic purpose - the efficient production of goods or services;
2. to design and maintain the stability of the operations of the organisation;
3. to take charge of strategy-making and adapt the organisation in a controlled way to changes in its environment;
4. to ensure the organisation serves the ends of those people who control it;
5. to serve as the key informational link between the organisation and the environment; and
6. as formal authority to operate the organisation's status system.

1. Interpersonal Roles

Figurehead: In this role, every manager has to perform some duties of a ceremonial nature, such as greeting the touring dignitaries, attending the wedding of an employee, taking an important customer to lunch and so on.

Leader: As a leader, every manager must motivate and encourage his employees. He must also try to reconcile their individual needs with the goals of the organisation.

Liaison: In this role of liaison, every manager must cultivate contacts outside his vertical chain of command to collect information useful for his organisation.

2. Informational Roles

Monitor: As monitor, the manager has to perpetually scan his environment for information, interrogate his liaison contacts and his subordinates, and receive unsolicited information, much of it as a result of the network of personal contacts he has developed.

Disseminator: In the role of a disseminator, the manager passes some of his privileged information directly to his key subordinates who would otherwise have no access to it.

Spokesman: A manager is also required nowadays, to spend a part of his time in representing his organisation before various *outside* groups, which have some stake in the organisation. These stakeholders can be government officials, labour unions, financial institutions, suppliers, customers, etc. They wield influence over the organisation. The manager must win their support by effectively managing the social impact of his organisation. Thus, he advises shareholders about financial performance, assures consumer groups that the organisation is fulfilling its social responsibilities and satisfies government that the organisation is abiding by the law.

3. Decisional Roles

Entrepreneur: In this role, the manager proactively looks out for innovation to improve his organisation. These days, it is not necessary for an organisation to grow bigger. However, it is necessary that it constantly grows better. This makes innovation an important function of a manager. Innovation means creating new ideas, which may either result in the development of new products or services, of finding new uses for the old ones. Thus, a salesman who can persuade Eskimos to purchase refrigerators to prevent food from freezing, is as much an innovator as the one who invents a new product.

Disturbance Handler: In this role, the manager has to work reactively like a fire fighter. He must seek solutions of various unanticipated problems—a strike may loom large, a major customer may go bankrupt, a supplier may renege on his contract, and so on.

Resource Allocator: In this role, the manager must divide work and delegate authority among his subordinates. He must decide who will get what.

Negotiator: The manager at all levels has to spend considerable time in negotiations. Thus, the president of a company may negotiate with the union leaders a new strike issue, the foreman may negotiate with the workers a grievance problem, and so on.

TEN MANAGERIAL WORK ROLES

Role	*Description*	*Examples*
Interpersonal Roles: *Interacting with people inside and outside the organisation*		
Figurehead	As symbolic head of an organisation, the manager performs routine duties of a legal or ceremonial nature.	Receiving official visitors, signing legal documents, distributing gifts to retiring employees.
Leader	Hiring, training, motivating and guiding subordinates.	Such activities involve formal authority.
Liaison	Interacting with other managers outside the organisation to obtain favours and information.	Keeping in touch with the external community and Government departments through meetings and phone calls.
Informational Roles: *Serving as a focal point for exchange of information.*		
Monitor	Seeks and receives information concerning internal and external events so as to gain understanding of the organisation and its environment.	Reading periodicals and reports about internal and external events so as to gain understanding of the organisation and its environment, changes in consumer's attitudes, competitor's plans, etc.

Disseminator	Transmits information to subordinates, peers and superiors with -in the organisation.	Calling staff meeting after a business trip, sending memo or reports and making speech to local groups.
Spokesperson	Speaking on behalf of the organisation and transmitting information on organisation's plans, policies and actions to outsiders.	Giving statements in Press, conversation with suppliers, making speech to local groups.
Decisional Roles: *Makes important decisions.*		
Entrepreneur	Initiating changes or improvements in the activities of the organisation.	Realigning subordinates' jobs, launching new project or products
Disturbance handler	Taking charge and corrective action when organisation faces unexpected crisis.	Resolving conflicts between employees, reacting to an insolvent customer, adjusting to strike at suppliers.
Resource allocator	Distributing organisation's resources like money, time, equipment and labour.	Approving budget, scheduling time for projects, awarding bonuses, etc.
Negotiator	Representing the organisation in bargaining and negotiations with outsiders and insiders.	Bargaining with trade unions, negotiating with an important supplier, entering into a lease agreement with the local authority, etc.

MANAGERIAL SKILLS

In modern business, the job of management has become very difficult. Several skills are required to manage successfully a large organisation in a dynamic environment. These skills of managers have been classified into four categories, namely technical, human, diagnostic and conceptual skills.

1. Technical Skills

Technical skills refer to the ability and knowledge in using the equipment, technique and procedures involved in performing specific tasks. These skills require specialised knowledge and proficiency in the mechanics of particular job. Ability in programming and operating computers is, for instance, a technical skill. There are two things a manager should understand about technical skills. In the *first* place, he must know which skills should be employed in his particular enterprise and be familiar enough with their potentiality to ask discerning questions of his technical advisers. *Secondly,* a manager must understand both the role of each skill employed and the interrelations between the skills.

2. Human Skills

Human skills consist of the ability to work effectively with other people both as individual and as members of a group. These are required to win cooperation of others and to build effective work teams. Such skills require a sense of feeling for others and capacity to look at things from others point of view. Human skills are reflected in the way a manager perceives his superiors, subordinates and peers. An awareness of the importance of human skills should be part of a manager's orientation and such skills should be developed throughout the career. While technical skills involve mastery of 'things' human skills are concerned with understanding of 'people'.

3. Conceptual Skills

Conceptual skills comprise the ability to see the whole organisation and the interrelationships between its parts. These skills refer to the ability to visualise the entire picture or to consider a situation in its totality. Such skills help the manager to conceptualise the environment, to analyse the forces working in a situation and to take a broad and farsighted view of the organisation. Conceptual skills also include the competence to understand a problem in all its aspects and to use original thinking in solving the problem. Such competence is necessary for rational decision-making.

Thus technical skills deal with jobs, human skills with persons and conceptual skills with ideas. These types of skills are interrelated. But the proportion or relative significance of these skills varies with the level of management.

4. Diagnostic Skills

Diagnostic skills include the ability to determine by analysis and examination, the nature and circumstances of particular conditions. It is not only the ability to specify why something happened but also the ability to develop certain possible outcomes. It is the ability to cut through unimportant aspects and quickly get to the heart of the problem. Diagnostic skills are probably the most difficult ones to develop because they require the proper blend of analytic ability with common sense and intelligence to be effective.

MANAGEMENT FUNCTIONS

Functions mean activity. Management functions mean activities performed by managers. There is no single list of functions acceptable to all. Various authors have classified these functions differently. But there is never complete agreement among experts on what functions should be included in the management process. However, Koontz and O'Donnell's classification of management functions is best of all and is accepted. According to them, "functions of management are planning, organising, staffing, directing and controlling."

There are two types of functions performed by managers. They are shown below:

Functions of Management

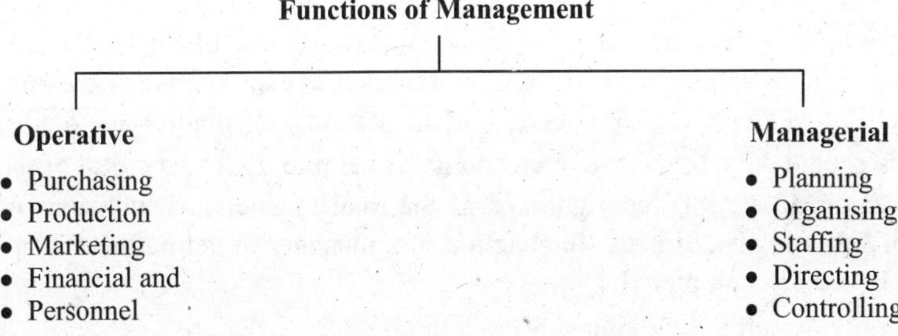

A brief description of managerial functions of management is given below:

1. Planning

Planning is an indispensable function of management determining the objectives to be achieved and the course of action to be followed to achieve them. It is a mental process requiring the use of intellectual faculties, foresight and sound judgement. Planning virtually pervades the entire gamut of managerial activity. This function is performed by managers at all levels. The managers at the top level in an organisation devote more time on planning as compared to the managers at the lower levels. It includes:

(*a*) Determination of objectives,

(*b*) Forecasting,

(*c*) Search of alternative courses of action,

(*d*) Drawing policies and procedures,

(*e*) Budgeting, etc.

2. Organising

Careful organising, like planning, helps in making efficient utilisation of human resources. It is a process of establishing working relationship among employees. The various activities are assigned to them, authority is granted to them, and they are brought in the relationship of superior and subordinate. This working relationship brings order and discipline with organisation. It includes:

(*a*) Determination of activities,

(*b*) Division of activities and its assignment,

(*c*) Fitting individuals to specific work,

(*d*) Delegating authority and fixing responsibility, etc.

3. Staffing

After planning and organising, the next logical function of management is to procure suitable personnel for manning the jobs. Since the efficiency and effectiveness of an organisation significantly depend upon the quality of its personnel, staffing has been recognised as a distinct function of management.

According to Harold Koontz and O'Donnell, "The managerial function of staffing involves manning the organisational structure through proper and effective selection, appraisal and development of personnel to fill the roles designed into the structure." It includes:

(*a*) Proper recruitment and selection of people,

(*b*) Fixing remuneration,

(*c*) Selection of suitable persons,

(*d*) Placement and orientation of employees,

(*e*) Training and development of employees, etc.

4. Directing

After plans have been made and the organisation has been established and staffed, the next step is to move towards its defined objectives. This function is also known as leading, motivating or actuating, etc. But whatever the name used to identify it, in carrying out this function the manager **explains to his people what they have to do and helps them to do it to the best of their ability**

According to Massie, "Directing concerns the total manner in which a manager influences the actions of subordinates. It is the final action of a manager in getting others to act after all the preparations have been completed."

Directing involves the following sub-functions:

1. *Communication:* It is the process of passing information and understanding from one person to another. A successful manager should develop an effective system of communication so that he may issue instructions and receive the reactions of the subordinates and motivate them.
2. *Leadership:* It is the process by which a manager guides and influences the work of his subordinates.
3. *Motivation:* Motivation means inspiring the subordinates to zealously work towards accomplishment and achievement of organisational goals and objectives.
4. *Supervision:* Managers have to personally watch, direct and control the performance of subordinates. In doing this they have to plan the work.

5. *Controlling:* The manager must ensure that everything occurs in conformity with the plans adopted, the instructions issued and the principles established. Thus the controlling function of management, involves the following elements:

The manager must ensure that everything occurs in conformity with the plans adopted, the instructions issued and the principles established. Thus, the controlling function of management, involves the following elements:

(*a*) Establishing standards of performance,

(*b*) Measuring current performance and comparing it against the established standards,

(*c*) Taking action to correct any performance that does not meet those standards.

CASE STUDY - 1

Mr. R.M. Jain joined the Fresh Foods Ltd. as a sales officer in 1995. Being an intelligent and hardworking man, he earned quick promotions and in 2010 he was promoted Sales Manager of the company. Soon after taking over as the Sales Manager, he issued an order that hence forth every order from dealers should be supplied against advance payment. The dealers who had enjoyed credit facility for the last 20 years felt cheated but they had no alternative as the company's products were selling like hot cakes.

Mr. R.M. Jain felt that there was no need for heavy advertising because the company was not able to meet the present level of demand. Therefore, he reduced the advertising budget to half of the previous level. He also scrapped the incentive bonus for salesmen.

QUESTIONS

1. Analyse the activities of Mr. Jain in terms of managerial functions.

2. Which of his activity was not a managerial function ?

3. Do you think the steps taken by him were right ?

REVIEW QUESTIONS

1. Define management and discuss the essential characteristics of the management.

2. "Management is getting things done through and with the people". In the light of this definition, give a concise.

3. Briefly discuss the scope of management.

4. Why the study of management in India is necessary ? Discuss the importance of management.

5. What do you understand by universality concept of management ?

6. Explain the principal functions of management.

7. Discuss whether management is a science or an art or both.

8. What do you understand by process of management ? Describe essential elements.

9. Discuss the various roles of management in brief.

10. Explain briefly the different principles of management.

11. Differentiate between management and administration.

12. Discuss the characteristics of management as profession.

13. Discuss the scope of management.

14. Describe the skills of a good manager.

15. "Management is an art as well as a science". Discuss.

Evolution of Management Thought

CHAPTER 2

- Introduction
- Pre-Scientific Management Era
- Classical (traditional) management Approach
  - Scientific Management (FW Taylor)
  - Administrative Management (Henri Fayol)
  - Bureaucratic Management (Max Weber)
- Behavioural (Neo-classical) Approach
- Modern Management Approach
  - Quantitative Approach
  - Systems Approach
  - Contingency Approach
  - Operational Approach
- Schools of Management Thought
  - Management Process School
  - Empirical School
  - Human Relations School
  - Decision Theory School
  - Quantitative Management School
  - Systems Approach School
  - Contingency School
- Pioneers of Management Thinkers
  - Peter Ferdinand Drucker
  - George Elton Mayo
  - Douglas Mc Gregor
  - Mary Parker Follett
  - C.K. Prahlad
  - Chester I. Barnard
  - Rensis Likert
  - Herbert A. Simon
  - Mc Kinsey's 7-S Approach
- Management Theory Jungle
- Case Study - 1
- Review Questions.

INTRODUCTION

Management has been practised in some form or the other since the dawn of civilisation. Management was unknown anywhere about two and a half centuries ago but now it is well known everywhere in every activity, and every enterprise - from small family business to multinational corporation. It is considered to be an important and part of life of every human being.

In the ancient times, there were groups of priests who directed and controlled people by virtue of their authority as the representatives of God. In Rome, the organization was supreme. The city of Rome was expanded into an empire with tremendous organizational skill and order. The scalar and delegation of authority principles made Rome a great civilization. The Roman Catholic Church was another example of effective application of management and organizational technique to fulfil religious objectives.

Despite ancient origins, very little conceptual and organised body of knowledge was developed in management till the end of 19th century. A systematic study and analysis of management as a science began in the 20th century after the Industrial Revolution. Since then management has developed as a distinct discipline and as a social science.

Management thought refers to the theories and principles that guide the management of people in organisations. Management theories are explanations of why a particular practice is effective or ineffective. These theories developed initially out of experience of practising managers. Management principles were based on practical experience of managers. As societies developed, practice of management started in all business and non-business organisations. With Industrial Revolution in the 18th century, a new era of Industrialisation came into existence. Use of both, machines and labour force increased. Need for integrating the two arose and, thus, the need for more comprehensive management was felt. With further advancement, business houses became so large that their financial requirements could not be met by the owners. They raised money from outside through shares and debentures. Since ownership became diverse and it was not possible for owners to manage their businesses, managers were appointed to look after business affairs. There was, thus separation of ownership from management and by the end of 19th century, management theory was recognised as a formal theory for managing business enterprises.

The schools of management thought are theoretical frameworks for the study of management. Each of the schools of management thought are based on some what different assumptions about human beings and the organisations for which they work. Since the formal study of management began late in the 19th century, the study of management has progressed through several stages as scholars and practitioners working in different eras focused on what they believed to be important aspects of good management practice.

Management theories can be classified into four main schools of thought.

1. Pre-Scientific Management Era
2. Classical or Traditional Management Approach
    1. Taylor's Scientific Management
    2. Fayol's Administrative Management
    3. Weber's Bureaucracy Management
3. Behavioural or Neo-classical Approach
    1. Human Relations Approach
    2. Behavioural Science Approach
4. Modern Management Approach
    1. Quantitative Approach to Management
    2. System Approach to Management
    3. Contingency Approach
    4. Operational Approach

PRE-SCIENTIFIC MANAGEMENT ERA

Pre-scientific management era refers to the period immediately preceding the Scientific Management Movement started by F.W. Taylor and others. A number of monumental examples of management can be traced, when we look back at recorded history. No important tools and techniques were available until end of the 15th century to solve organisational problems. The early contributors to the management (Pre-scientific management era) are discussed below:

1. Charles Babbage (1792 - 1871)

Babbage was a Professor of Mathematics at Cambridge University from 1828 to 1839. He visited many factories in England and France. He found that manufacturers were totally unscientific and most of their work was guess work. They relied upon old opinions instead of investigations and accurate knowledge. Babbage was the forerunner of Scientific Management. His work was closely related to that of Adam Smith (an economist), as he emphasised on work specialisation (dividing the work into various jobs) to increase managerial efficiency. He introduced methods to improve industrial productivity and perceived this could be done through work measurement, cost determination, bonus plans, profit-sharing, etc. His emphasis on the application of science and mathematics laid the foundation for the formulation of a science of management.

2. Robert Owens (1771 - 1858)

He was a textile entrepreneur and is known as the father of Personnel Management. His emphasis was not on the process of industrialisation or division of labour but on development of personnel. Robert Owens manage ' a group of textile mills in Scotland during 1800 - -1828. He carried out experiments and introduced many social reforms. He said employees are vital machines. He believed that workers should work because they want to work and not because they have to work. He believed and practised the idea that workers should be treated as human beings. He introduced new ideas of human relations, for examples, shorter working hours, housing facilities, education of children, provision of canteen, training of workers, etc. He is known as the father of personnel management. His ideas and philosophy may be considered as a prelude to the development of the behavioural approach to management.

3. Henry Robinson Towne (1844 - 1924)

He was the president of the famous "Yale & Towne" a lock manufacturing company. He took particular interest in the better management of business and applied his ideas successfully in his own company. Towne also served as the president of the American Society of Mechanical Engineers in 1889. He suggested organised exchange of experience among managers and an organised effort to pool the accumulated knowledge in the art of workshop management.

4. Charles Dupin (1784 - 1873)

He was an industrial educator in France. According to him, it was not enough for managers to possess technical knowledge for contributing to organisational output; they needed broader management skills to maximise industrial output. He emphasised more on management education than technical education.

5. James Watt (1796 - 1848) and Mathew Robinson Boulton (1770 - 1872)

They were incharge of the management of the Soho Engineering Foundry in Great Briton. Watt was incharge of organisation and administration. Boulton was administering sales. They developed several management techniques such as:

(*a*) Market research and forecasting;

(*b*) Standardisation of components and parts;

(*c*) production planning;

(*d*) Planned machine layout for better work-flow;

(*e*) Elaborate statistical records; and

(*f*) The provision of employee welfare schemes, etc.

CLASSICAL (TRADITIONAL) MANAGEMENT APPROACH

The classical approach offers a convenient framework for the education and training of future managers. It views management as distinct discipline based on certain principles. Another merit of this approach is that it focuses attention on what managers actually do, that is, functions of management. It highlights the universal nature of management. It provides a foundation for further research in management.

It is the oldest theory of management and is, therefore, called the traditional theory of management. The classical viewpoint is a perspective on management that finds ways to manage business organisations effectively. It is the first step towards the study of management as a distinct field of study. Three areas of study that can be grouped under the classical school:

(*a*) Scientific Management

(*b*) Administrative Management

(*c*) Bureaucratic Management

(a) Scientific Management

During the beginning of the 20th century, skilled labour was scarce in the United States which affected productivity. Management thinkers searched for ways to increase efficiency of workers to increase productivity by deleting or combining operations of work. It was then that scientific management theory was introdued by Taylor, who is also known as the father of Scientific Management.

Fredrick Winslow Taylor (1856 - 1915) started his career as an apprentice in a small machine shop in Philadelphia in 1875. In 1878, he joined the Midvale Steel Works in Philadelphia as a machinist and rose to the position of Chief Engineer in 1884. Later he joined the Bethelhem Steel Works. Throughout his career, Taylor was concerned with the problems of increasing labour productivity without putting under strain on workers. He has conducted several experiments and through his experiments he has developed a theory of management which was known as "Scientific Management". Taylor was assisted in the development of scientific management by many other pioneers like Henry L. Gantt, Harlow S Person, Harrington, Frank B Gilbreth, etc.

"Scientific management means knowing exactly what you want your men to do and seeing that they do it in the best and cheapest way". F.W. Taylor.

"The cost of scientific management is the organised study of work, the analysis of work into its simplest elements and the systematic management of the workers performance of each element." Peter F. Drucker.

Principles of Scientific Management (Taylor)

They are as follows:

1. Development of a true science for each element of a man's job to replace the old rule of thumb method.
2. Scientific selection, training and development of workers for every job.
3. An almost equal division of work and responsibility between management and workmen, management entrusted with the planning of work and workmen to look after execution of plans.
4. Close cooperation between management and workers to ensure that work is done in accordance with the principles of the science which has been developed.
5. Maximum output in place of restricted output.

Techniques of Scientific Management

Taylor developed several techniques, in addition to the above principles. They are:

(*a*) *Scientific work study:* Work study refers to the systematic objective and critical examination of all factors influencing the efficiency of operations to improve there on. This study includes Method study, Motion study, Time study and Fatigue study.

(*b*) *Scientific task setting:* Scientific planning of a task is the technique of forecasting and viewing ahead every step in a long series of separate operations - routing, scheduling, Despatching and follow up. Each step has to be taken in the right place, of the right degree and at the right time so that work can be done with maximum possible efficiency.

(*c*) *Standardisation:* Standardisation is the process of fixing well thought-out and tested standards of norms with a view to maximise efficiency of work.

(*d*) *Selection and training:* Proper selection and training on the basis of an objective criteria necessary to match the job and job-holder.

(*e*) *Differential Piece rate system:* He has suggested the use of differential piece rate system in order to motivate workers to produce maximum quantity.

(*f*) *Functional foremanship:* Taylor introduced and practised the concept of functional foremanship.

(b) Administrative Management

While Taylor is considered the Father of Scientific Management, Henri Fayol (1841 - 1925) is considered the Father of Administrative Management theory with focus on the development of broad administrative principles applicable to general and higher managerial levels. He was a French mining engineer turned a leading industrialist and successful manager. He wrote a monograph in French in 1916, entitled "General and Industrial Administration". Until this book was translated into English in 1929, little was known about him by the Western World. In his treatise, Fayol provided a broad analytical frame work of the process of administration. (He used the word "administration" for what we call management.). His perspective, unlike that of Taylor extended beyond the shop level and the physical production processes and was of a macro nature, covering the general administrative and managerial functions and processes at the organisational level.

His work can be found in business even today and therefore Fayol is aptly called the Father of Modern management Theory. Fayol's contribution to management can be classified into four categories:

(A) Activities of a Business

Fayol divided business activities into six groups:

(*a*) Technical	: It relates to production and manufacturing of goods.
(*b*) Commercial	: It relates to buying raw materials and selling or exchanging the finished goods.
(*c*) Financial	: It relates to search, acquisition and optimum use of financial resources.
(*d*) Security	: It relates to protecting human and non-human resources.
(*e*) Accounting	: It relates to (*i*) keeping accounts such as profit & Loss Account and Balance Sheet. (*ii*) Minimising costs, and (*iii*) Maintaining statistics.
(*f*) Managerial	: It relates to functions performed by a manager.

(B) Functions of Management

Fayol classified the following functions of managers or management.

(*a*) Planning	: To determine the goals of the organisation and devise a course of action to achieve them.

(*b*) Organising : To coordinate human and non-human resources of the organisation to put the plans into action.

(*c*) Commanding: To direct and guide the workers to perform their duties well.

(*d*) Coordinating : To synthesise and synchronise the resources and activities of the organisation to achieve the goals.

(*e*) Controlling : To ensure that plans are effectively carried out and discrepancies are checked.

(C) Abilities of managers

Fayol has identified qualities of a good manager which are shown below:

(*a*) Physical : Health and vigour

(*b*) Mental : Ability to analyse, interpret and arrive at conclusions.

(*c*) Moral : Willingness to accept responsibility, loyalty and dignity.

(*d*) General Education : Knowledge of overall affairs of the organisation.

(*e*) Special Knowledge : Knowledge of a specific activity - technical, commercial or financial.

(*f*) Experience : Knowledge gained over a period of time while working in a particular functional area.

(D) Principles of Management

Fayol listed fourteen principles of management based purely on his experience. He described these principles as flexible and not exhaustive. They can be changed according to situations. They were termed as indispensable for every business and non-business organisation. The word "Principles" was used by Fayol to describe their flexibility. In his words, "I prefer the word principles in order to avoid any idea of rigidity, as there is nothing rigid or absolute in administrative matters; everything is a question of degree. The same principle is hardly ever applied twice in exactly the same way, because we have to allow for different and changing circumstances, for human beings who are equally different and changeable, and for many other variable elements. The principles, too are flexible and can be adapted to meet every need; it is just a question of knowing how to use them".

These fourteen principles are as follows:

1. Division of work
2. Authority and Responsibility
3. Discipline
4. Unity of command
5. Unity of direction
6. Subordination of individual interest to general interest
7. Remuneration
8. Centralisation
9. Scalar chain
10. Order
11. Equity
12. Stability of tenure of personnel
13. Initiative
14. Espri-de-crops

(for explanation, see chapter 1.)

Critical Evaluation:

Scientific management has been criticised on the following grounds:

1. *Mechanistic approach:* The main criticism is that scientific management ignores the human element in production and is devoid of a human touch. It treats workers as factors of production and not as human beings.
2. *Unrealistic assumptions:* Scientific management is based on the assumption that people are rational and they are motivated by material gains.
3. *Exploitation of labour:* In the name of increasing efficiency, workers were forced to speed up affecting their physical and mental health. Specialisation and standardisation make the job dull and monotonous.
4. *Impracticable:* Many ideas of Taylor are said to be infeasible in practice. For example, planning cannot fully be separated from doing because these are two sides of the same job and are not different jobs.
5. *Narrow view:* Scientific management is quite limited in scope. Taylor focused attention completely on efficiency at the shop floor.

The principles and functions of management developed by Henri Fayol, got widespread applicability. Inspite of reformulation and expansion of management knowledge, these are found in every texts of management. Moreover, modern management theory to a large extent is based on these principles and functions therefore he is said to be father of modern management. Many management scholars have made the following observations regarding the contribution of Fayol. They observed that "the classical functions of management still represent the most useful way of conceptualising the manager's job, especially for management education and perhaps this is why still the most favoured descriptions of managerial work in current management textbooks.

Comparison of Taylor's and Fayol's theories

Taylor (Father of scientific management)	***Fayol (Father of principles of management)***
1. The theory studies management from bottom to top.	1. Management is viewed from top to bottom.
2. Improving productivity through work simplification and standardisation.	2. Improving overall administration through general principles.
3. Aim is to increase production at the shop level.	3. Aim is to increase overall production of the organisation.
4. The theory was designed as "Scientific management".	4. The theory was named as "General theory of administration."

Similaries:

The theories of Taylor and Fayol are similar to each other with respect to the followings:

1. Both of them - Taylor and Fayol - are found ways to increase production.
2. Both the theories are the basis to the study of management.
3. Management principles are important to industrial progress.
4. Both the theories are developed on the basis of practical experience of Taylor and Fayol.
5. They viewed organisations as independent units with very little or no interaction with the external environment.

(*c*) Bureaucratic Management

Max Weber (1864 - 1920) a German sociologist, made significant contribution in the fields of management, economics, philosophy and sociology. In the filed of management, his most significant contribution is his work on bureaucratic management. Bureaucratic management focuses on the ideal form of organisation. Max Weber was the major contributor to bureaucratic management. Based on observation, Weber concluded that many early organisations were inefficiently managed, with decisions based on personal relationships and loyalty. He proposed that a form of organisation, called a bureaucracy, characterised by division of labour, hierarchy, formalized rules, impersonality, and the selection and promotion of employees based on ability, would lead to more efficient management. Weber also contended that manager's authority in an organisation should be based not on TRADITION or CHARISMA, but on the position held by managers in the organisational hierarchy.

Important features of Bureaucratic management

(*a*) *Division of labour:* In a bureaucratic organisation, jobs are broken into smaller units where each person carries out a specialised task.

(*b*) *Standard rules:* Weber believed that the authority in an organisation should not be governed by the personal preferences of the employer but it should be governed by standard rules.

(*c*) *Scalar chain:* Each lower officer is under the control and supervision of a higher one. That is, orders and instructions flow from top to bottom and obedience flows from bottom to top.

(*d*) *Appointment on the basis of merit:* All appointments or selections are based purely on merit performance on the job.

(*e*) *Official records:* All decisions and activities of the organisation are formally maintained in official records and preserved for future reference.

(*f*) *Impersonality:* In this type of organisation, there is no room for emotions, sentiments and personal attachment. The employees have very formal and functional type of the personality.

Criticisms of Bureaucracy

Weber's concept of bureaucracy has a number of disadvantages and has been subject to severe criticism.

1. The over-emphasis on rules and procedures, record keeping and paperwork may become more important in its own right than as a means to an end.
2. Officials may develop a dependence upon bureaucratic status, symbols and rules.
3. Initiative may be shifted and when a situation is not covered by a complete set of rules or procedures there may be a lack of flexibility or adaptation to changing circumstances.
4. Position and responsibilities in the organisation can lead to officious bureaucratic behaviour. There may also be a tendency to conceal administrative procedures from outsiders.
5. Impersonal relations can lead to stereotyped behaviour and a lack of responsiveness to individual incidents or problems.

BEHAVIOURAL APPROACH (NEO-CLASSICAL)

The 'behavioural approach, bears to bring existing and new developed theories, methods and techniques of the relevant social sciences such as psychology, sociology, and anthropology upon the study of human behaviour. The pioneer of this school such as Gantt and M. Berg, reasoned that in as much as managing involves getting things done with and through people, the study of management must be centered around the people and their interpersonal relations. The advocates of this school concentrate on motivations, individual drives, group relations, leadership, group dynamics and so forth. This approach of management was evolved gradually over many years. It is based on strong conviction that successful management depends on manager's ability to understand work as well as people with different backgrounds, needs, values, perceptions and personality. Thus in this approach of management human factor remain central focus and high pedestal in organisation.

This approach can be studied into two phases, viz.:

(*a*) Human Relation approach

(*b*) Behavioural science approach

(*a*) Human relations approach

The Hawthorne experiments began in 1924 and continued through the early 1930s. A variety of researchers participated in the studies, including Claid Turner, Fritz J. Roethlisberger, and Mayo, whose respective books on the studies are perhaps the best known. One of the major conclusions of the Hawthorne studies was that:

- Worker's attitudes are associated with productivity.
- The workplace is a social system and informal group influence could exert a powerful effect on individual behaviour.
- The style of supervision is an important factor in increasing worker's job satisfaction.
- The studies also found that organisations should take steps to assist employees in adjusting to organisational life by fostering collaborative systems between labour and management.

According to the human relations school, the manager should possess skills for diagnosing the causes of human behaviour at work, interpersonal communication, and motivating and leading workers. The focus became satisfying worker needs. If worker needs were satisfied, wisdom held, the workers would, in turn, be more productive. Thus, the human relations school focuses on issues of communication, leadership, motivation and group behaviour. The individuals who contributed to the school are too numerous to mention, but some of the best known contributors include Mary Parker Follett, Chester Barnard, Abraham Maslow, Kurt Lewin, Renais likert, Keith Davis, etc. The human relations school of thought still influences management theory and practice, as contemporary management focuses much attention on human resource management, organisational behaviour and applied psychology in the workplace.

(*b*) Behavioural Science approach

Behavioural science and the study of organisational behaviour emerged in the 1950s and 1960s. The behavioural science school was a natural progression of the human relations movement. It focused on applying conceptual and analytical tools to the problem of understanding and predicting behaviour in the workplace. However, the study of behavioural science and organisational behaviour was also a result of criticism of the human relations approach as simplest and manipulative in its assumptions about the relationship between worker attitudes and productivity. The study of behavioural science in business schools was given increased credence by the 1959 Gordon and Howell report on higher education, which emphasized the importance to management practitioners of understanding human behaviour.

The behavioural science school has contributed to the study of management through its focus on personality, attitudes, values, motivation, group behaviour, leadership, communication and conflict, among other issues. Some of the major contributors to this school include Douglas Mc Gregor, Chris Argyris, Renais Likert, Ralph Stogdill, etc.

Comparison of Human Relations Approach and Behavioural Science Approach

Human Relation Approach	*Behavioural Science Approach*
1. It views the worker as 'a social man'.	1. It views the worker as 'a self-actualising man'.
2. Focus is on interpersonal relations	2. Focus is on group relationship.
3. It is based on Hawthorne experiments	3. It is based on application of behavioural sciences.
4. It emphasises on formal organisation structure.	4. It emphasises on comparatively a flexible organisation structure.
5. Techniques of self-direction and self control are applied to a limited extent.	5. Self-direction and self control are extensively used for increasing group efficiency.
6. Motivation and job satisfaction are major concepts.	6. Group dynamics and informal organisation are major concepts.
7. It lacks scientific vision to study human behaviour.	7. It provides scientific understanding of human behaviour.

MODERN MANAGEMENT APPROACH

Modern management theories indicate further refinement, extension and synthesis of all the classical and neo classical approaches to management. We have the following approaches to the modern management:

1. Quantitative approach to management
2. Systems approach to management
3. Contingency approach to management
4. Operational approach to management

1. Quantitative approach to management

This theory is also known as "Operations research theory", "Decision theory", or "Management science theory". It became an acceptable theory during World War II when Britain wanted to solve the problems of war. Coordination of different teams of scientists from several fields is one of the main characteristics of this school of management thought. This school utilizes all the scientific techniques and tools for providing a quantitative basis of managerial decisions. It believes that management is a logical process which can be expressed in terms of mathematical symbols and relationships. The main contributors to this school are Taylor, Gilbreth, Gantt, Joel Dean, Newman, Hicks, etc. It is based on the approach of scientific management. It offers systematic and scientific analysis and solution to the problems faced by managers. The quantitative approach aims at achieving high degree of precision, perfection and objectivity by encouraging the use of mathematical and statistical tools for solving complex problems.

QUANTITATIVE TECHNIQUES have become popular because of their wide application in several countries. LINEAR PROGRAMMING helps in input-output analysis and product mix. QUEUEING THEORY helps in inventory control, traffic control, telephone trunking systems and radio communications. SAMPLING THEORY helps in profit planning, inventory control and manpower requirement study. INFORMATION THEORY helps in data processing, systems design and organisation analysis. Nowadays, computers are being used in solving management problems.

The quantitative approach has provided sharp tools for rational decision making. The mathematical formulation enables practising managers to discover significant relationships that they could control. This approach provides a rational base for making decisions with precision and perfection. It has been widely used in planning and control.

Operations research is "the application of scientific methods of problems arising from operations involving integrated systems of people, machines and materials". It involves knowledge of inter-disciplinary research team to provide optimum operating solutions. "The quantitative management **view point focuses on the use of mathematics, statistics and information aids to support managerial** decision-making and organisational effectiveness". The branches of quantitative management are:

(*a*) Management science

(*b*) Operations management

(*c*) Management information systems

(*a*) *Management science:* "Management science is an approach that aims at increasing decision effectiveness through the use of sophisticated mathematical models and statistical methods". According to Hodgetts, "The quantitative school, which is also called "Management science school" consists of those theorists who see management as a body of quantitative tools and methodologies designed to aid today's manager in making the complex decisions related to operations and productions".

(*b*) *Operations management:* "Operations management is the function, or field of expertise, that is primarily responsible for managing the production and delivery of an organisation's products and services." Here, people use quantitative techniques of forecasting inventory analysis, statistical quality control etc., in areas such as inventory management, production planning, storing and selling the final products and similar areas in manufacturing units.

(*c*) *Management information systems (MIS):* "MIS is the field of management that focuses on designing and implementing computer-based information systems for use by management." Large amount of information is quickly processed to help managers in making useful business decisions.

2. Systems approach to management

The system approach to management is based on general system theory. Ludwig von Bertalanffy, a scientist who worked mainly in physics and biology, is recognized as the founder of general system theory. The main premise of the theory is that to understand fully the operation of an entity, the entity must be viewed as a system. A system is a number of interdependent parts functioning as a whole for some purpose. For example, according to general system theory, to fully understand the operations of the human body, one must understand the workings of its interdependent parts (ears, eyes, and brain). General system, theory integrates the knowledge of various specialised fields so that the system as a whole can be better understood.

Types of Systems

According to von Bertalanffy, the two basic types of systems are closed systems and open systems. **Closed systems** are not influenced by, and do not interact with, their environments. They are mostly mechanical and have predetermined motions or activities that must be performed regardless of the environment. A clock is an example of a closed system. Regardless of its environment, a clock's wheels, gears, and so forth must function in a predetermined way if the clock as a whole is to exist and serve its purpose. The second type of system, the **open system,** is continually interacting with its environment. A plant is an example of an open system. Constant interaction with the environment influences the plant's state of existence and its future. In fact, the environment determines whether the plant will live.

Systems and "Wholeness"

The concept of "wholeness" is important in general system analysis. The system must be viewed as a whole and modified only through changes in its parts. Before modifications of the parts can be made for the overall benefit of the system, a thorough knowledge of how each part functions and the interrelationships among the parts must be present. L. Thomas Hopkins suggested the following six guidelines for anyone conducting system analysis:

1. The whole should be the main focus of analysis, with the parts receiving secondary attention.
2. Integration is the key variable in wholeness analysis. It is defined as the interrelatedness of the many parts within the whole.
3. Possible modifications in each part should be weighed in relation to possible effects on every other part.
4. Each part has some role to perform so that the whole can accomplish its purpose.
5. The nature of the part and its function is determined by its position in the whole.
6. All analysis starts with the existence of the whole. The parts and their interrelationships should then evolve to best suit the purpose of the whole.

Because the system approach to management is based on general system theory, analysis of the management situation is a system of stressed.

Several pioneers have made significant contributions to the development of the systems approach. Notable among are Ludwig Von Bertalanffy, Stafford Beer, Kutz, R.L. Khan, R.A. Johnson, Resenz Weig, etc.

Subsystems. The parts that make up the whole of a system are called **subsystems.** And each system in turn may be a subsystem of a still larger whole. Thus a department is a subsystem of a plant, which may be a subsystem of a company, which may be a subsystem of a conglomerate or an industry, which is a subsystem of the national economy, which is a subsystem of the world system.

Synergy. Synergy means that the whole is greater than the sum of its parts. In organizational terms, **synergy** means that as separate departments within an organization cooperate and interact, they become more productive than if each were to act in isolation. For example, in a small firm, it is more efficient for each department to deal with one finance department that for each department to have a separate finance department of its own.

Open and Closed Systems. A system is considered an **open system** if it interacts with its environment; it is considered a closed system if it does not. All organisations interact with their environment, but the extent to which they do so varies. An automobile plant, for example, is a far more open system than a monastery or a prison.

System Boundary. Each system has a boundary that separates it from its environment. In a closed system, the **system boundary** is rigid; in an open system, the boundary is more flexible. The system boundaries of many organizations have become increasingly flexible in recent years. For example, managers at oil companies wishing to engage in offshore drilling now must consider public concern for the environment. A trend is that American communities are demanding more and more environmental responsibility from companies. For example, Santa Rosa, California, a city of 125,000, treats environmental violations such as "off-gassing" a waste product, that is, allowing it to evaporate into the atmosphere, as a potential criminal offense.

Flow. A system has **flows** of information, materials, and energy (including human energy). These enter the system from the environment as *inputs* (raw materials, for example), undergo transformation processes within the system (operations that alter them), and exit the system as *outputs* (goods and services).

Feedback. Feedback is the key to system controls. As operations of the system proceed, information is fed back to the appropriate people, and perhaps to a computer, so that the work can be assessed and, if necessary, corrected.

3. Contingency approach to management (Situational approach)

In simple terms, the contingency approach to management emphasizes that what managers do in practice depends on, or is contingent upon, a given set of circumstances - a situation. In essence, this approach emphasizes "if then" relationships. "If" this situational variable exists, "then" a manager probably would take this action. For example, if a manager has a group of inexperienced subordinates, then the contingency approach would recommend that he lead in a different fashion than if the subordinates were experienced.

In general, the contingency approach attempts to outline the conditions or situations in which various management methods have the best chance of success. This approach is based on the premise that, although there is probably no one best way to solve a management problem in all organisations, probably there is one best way to solve any given management problem in any one organisation. Perhaps the main challenges of using the contingency approach are the following:

1. Perceiving organisational situations as they actually exist.
2. Choosing the management tactics best suited to those situations:
3. Competently implementing those tactics.

The notion of a contingency approach to management is not novel. It has become a popular discussion topic for contemporary management thinkers. The general consensus of their writings is that if managers are to apply management concepts, principles and techniques successfully, they must consider the realities of the specific organisational circumstances they face.

Major contributors to this theory are Kast and Rosenzweig, Joan Woodward, Daniel Katz and Robert Kahn, James Thompson, Robert Lawrence, etc.

4. Operational approach

According to Koontz and O'Donnell, "The operational approach regards management as a universally applicable body of knowledge that can be brought to bear on all levels of managing and in all types of enterprises. At the same time, the approach recognises that the actual problems managers face and the environment in which they operate may vary between enterprises and levels, and it also recognises that application of science by a perceptive practitioner must take this into account in designing practical solutions." This theory has practical application today. "Since the activities of a manager are basic, the process school provides an excellent framework not only for the study of management using this fundamental approach but also for using valuable contribution offered by other schools of management. The goal is to take the best from what is available in management thought and work it into a single theory."

An important post-World War II outgrowth of the operational approach is operations management. Operations management, like scientific management, aims at promoting efficiency through systematic observation and experimentation. However, operations management tends to be broader in scope and application than scientific management was. Whereas scientific management was limited largely to hand labour and machine shops, operations management specialists apply their expertise to all types of production and service operations, such as the purchase and storage of materials, energy use, product and service design, work flow, safety, quality control and data processing. Thus operations management is defined as the process of transforming raw materials, technology, and human talent into useful goods and services.

Thus, the operational approach is an electric approach, that is, it takes the best from what is available in management thought and integrates it with the central core of process framework to build up a unified theory of management.

SCHOOLS OF MANAGEMENT THOUGHT

1. Management Process School: The chief contributors belonging to this school are Henry Fayol, J.D. Mooney, A.C. Railey, Lyndall Urwick, Harold Koontz, William Newman and Mc Farland. According to this school, management can best be studied in terms of the process that it involves. The proponents of this view believe in the universality of management principles. Essential features of process school are as follows:

1. Management is the study of functions of managers.
2. The functions of managers are the same irrespective of the type of organisation.
3. The conceptual framework of management can be built through an analysis of the process of management, viz.; planning, organising, staffing, directing and controlling are the core of management.

Benefits of Management Process Approach are:

1. Though knowledge of the functions/process makes one versatile in the art of management.
2. This approach recognises management as a distinct discipline. It is easy to understand and practice.
3. This approach recognises that management is universal irrespective of the types of organisations or the levels of organisations.
4. It integrates the knowledge of various disciplines to better management for a better tomorrow.
5. It is an aid to the professionlisation of management.
6. It provides flexibility and there is room for innovation, research and development.
7. It recognises that management is both art and science.
8. The elements of management and its principles are true even if a practising manager chooses to ignore them in a particular situation.
9. It provides a helpful and purposeful philosophy of management.
10. It involves the performance of functions by managers aiming at proper and systematic utilisation of resources.

The management process school has been criticised on the following grounds:

1. It ignores the multiplicity of organisational objectives.
2. This school adopts a mechanical approach to human behaviour.
3. This school ignores the influence of culture on management.
4. The so-called universal principles of management are not always truly applicable.

2. The Empirical School: The main contributors to this approach are Ernest Dale, Mooney, Railey, Urwick and others. This school believes that by analyzing the experience of successful managers or the mistakes, we somehow learn about applying the most effective management techniques. This school is also called as *customs school.*

It recoils from the theoretical approach to management which works on deductions and generalisations. The argument of this approach amounts to virtual rejection of the scientific management or its study as a set of principles and systems. The only generalisation that this school of thought would allow is what lessons history and actual happening may hold for practice in the future.

The main features of this school are:

1. Management is the study of managerial experiences.
2. The managerial experience can be passed over to the practitioners and students.

3. The techniques used in successful cases can be used by future managers.
4. Theoretical research can be combined with practical experiences.

3. Human Relations School: This school takes particular note of psychological factors underlying the human behaviour in organized groups under the given situation. It is based upon the fact that managing involves getting things done with and through people; therefore management must be centered on inter-personal relations. The range of thought in this school goes from (*a*) human relations and how the manager can understand and uses his understanding (*b*) the manager as a leader and how he should lead to (*c*) a study of group dynamics and inter-personal relationships.

The main thinkers subscribing to this school are Elton Mayo, Mc Gregor, Keith Davis and others.

The main features of this school are:

1. This approach draws heavily its concepts from psychology and sociology.
2. According to this school, management is getting things done through people, hence managers should understand human relations.
3. Motivation, leadership communication, participative management and group dynamics are the core of this approach.
4. Management must study inter-personal relations among people.
5. Greater production and higher motivation can be achieved only through good human relations.

The study of human relations is no doubt very important in management but it is not the complete study of the field of management. There are many other variables in management. The behaviouralists failed to give an integrated theory of management.

4. Decision Theory School: This school concentrates on rational decisions-the selection of a suitable course of action from various possible alternatives. This approach may deal with the decision itself or with the persons or organisational groups who make the decision and with an analysis of the decision process. *The scientific approach to decision making involves the following steps:*

(*a*) Defining the problem
(*b*) Collecting all relevant information
(*c*) Formulate/Search alternatives
(*d*) Examination of all the alternatives and the solutions
(*e*) Test the solutions
(*f*) Select a course of action
(*g*) Implement the action
(*h*) Evaluate the result of action.

The main features of this school are:

1. Management is essentially a decision making process.
2. The members of the organisation are decision makers and problem solvers.
3. Decision making is the central point in management.
4. For increasing the organisational efficiency, the quality of decisions is a prime factor.
5. Management information system and the process and techniques of decision-making from the subject matter of the study of management according to this school of thought.

The main contributors and thinkers belong to this school are **Chester Bernard, James March, Herbert Simon, Richard Cyert** and others.

Limitations:

1. Narrow and limited scope.
2. Does not take the total view of management.

5. Mathematical or Quantitative Management School: The contributors of this school see management as a system of mathematical models and process. This group believes that if management, or organisation, or planning or decision making is a logical process, it can be expressed in terms of mathematical symbols and relationships. This approach forces the analyst to define a problem area allow for the insertion of symbols for unknown data and follow logical methodology, which provides a powerful tool for solving complex problems.

The main contributors to this school are Richard Cyert, Russel Ackoff, William Churchman, etc.

Essential features of mathematical school are:

1. Management is concerned with problem solving and it must make use of mathematical tools and techniques for the purpose.
2. The different factors involved in management can be quantified and expressed in the form of models.
3. Operational research, mathematical tools, simulation and model building are the basic methodologies developed by this school of thought.
4. Management problems can be described in mathematical symbols.

Limitations:

1. Mathematical models cannot be a substitute for sound judgement. They are best tools of analysis.
2. Mathematics is at best a tool of management and cannot be treated as the whole area of management.
3. There are certain phases of management process, for instance, interpersonal relations, which cannot be expressed in mathematical symbols and formulae.

6. The System Approach School: This school of recent origin and developed in late 1960's. It is an integrating approach which considers the management in its totality based on empirical data. According to this approach, attention must be paid to the overall effectiveness of the system rather than the effectiveness of a sub-system in isolation from the other sub-systems. The main emphasis is on the interdependence and interrelatedness of the various sub-systems, from the point of view of the effectiveness of a large system.

The main contributors of this school are Kenneth, Boulding, Johnson, Churchman, etc.

Features of this approach:

1. A system has a number of sub-systems, parts and sub-parts.
2. The systems approach to management brings out the complexity of a real life management problem much more sharply than any other approaches.
3. It can be utilised by any other school of management school.

7. The Contingency School: This approach to management emphasizes the fact that management is highly practice oriented and action packed discipline. Managerial decisions, actions and initiatives are to be matter of pragmatism and not of principles. The environment of organisations and managers is very complex, uncertain, ever changing and diverse. It is the basic function of managers to analyze and understand the environment in which they function before adopting their techniques, processes and practices. The choice of approaches as also their effectiveness is contingent on the behaviour and dynamics of situational variables. There is no universally valid one best way of doing things. Management theory and principles tend to be deterministic. What is valid and good in a particular situation need not be so in some other situation.

Contingency approach has the following features:

1. Management action is dependent upon certain activities inside the system or sub-system as the case may be.
2. Organisational system should be based on the behaviour of action outside the system so that organisation should be integrated with the environment.
3. Because of the specific organisation-environment relationship, no action can be universal. It varies from situation to situation.

PIONEERS OF MANAGEMENT THINKERS

1. Peter Ferdinand Drucker

Drucker is more popularly known as the Father of Modern Management. He wrote extensively on subjects like economics, history, religion, education, management, etc. He is famous for his contribution in the field of management.

His contribution to management is discussed below:

1. Management is a profession

Managers are different from owners and possess specialised skills to perform the managerial tasks. He is thus considers management as a profession.

2. Management by objectives (MBO)

The credit for developing MBO goes to Peter Drucker who emphasized that performance of each job should be directed towards by the achievement of whole business objectives. MBO is also known by the names, Management Motivation, Management by Exception, Management by results etc.

"The system of management by objectives can be described as a process where by the superior and subordinate managers of an organisation jointly identify its common goals define each individual's major areas of responsibility in terms of results expected of him and use these measures as guides for operating the unit and assessing the contribution of each of its members."

3. Managerial skill

Drucker advocated that managers must have the following skills to make management effective:

(*a*) Skills to make effective decisions

(*b*) Skills to communicate in and outside the organisation

(*c*) Skills to make proper use of controls and measurements, and

(*d*) Skills to make proper use of analytical tools, that is, management sciences.

4. Organisation Structure

Rather than focussing on task-oriented or person-oriented approach to management, Drucker focused on organisation structure that is both task-focused and person-focused. He thus, advocates both scientific management and human relation doctrine.

5. Business objectives

According to Drucker, "There is only one valid definition of business purpose, *to create a customer.*" To manage a business is to balance a variety of needs and goals and a business enterprise by its very nature requires multiple objectives. Profit is essential for the survival and growth of business. It is indeed the ultimate test of business performance.

6. Management Development

Managers represent a business. There must be constant development of managers through training and development programmes. The prosperity of a business depends on its future managers. The demand for executives is steadily increasing.

7. Focus on business organisation

Among various institutions, the focus of management is on business institutions because efficiency of management can be judged through economic results that it produces and the most important economic institution is the business institution. Besides, management can also reform Government and society and promote values, customs and beliefs of the society.

8. Role of management

Drucker has stressed the role of management. According to him, "The manager is the dynamic, life-giving element in every business." Management is important not only for business enterprises but for all types of organisations. Drucker categorically stated that the developing countries are not underdeveloped, they are undermanaged. In his opinion, management is a discipline and a social function.

9. Decision-making

According to Drucker, "Whatever a manager does he does through making decisions. Management is always a decision-making process. There are two types of decision-tactical and strategic. Decision-making has five distinct phases: (*a*) Defining the problem, (*b*) Analysing the problem, (*c*) Developing alternative solutions, (*d*) Deciding upon the best solution, and (*e*) Converting the decision into effective action.

10. Key result areas

Drucker identified the following eight areas in which objectives should be set and performance be evaluated:

- Market standing
- Innovation
- Productivity
- Physical and financial resources
- Profitability
- Manager's performance
- Workers performance
- Public responsibility.

2. George Elton Mayo (1880-1949)

Elton Mayo was a professor of industrial psychology at the Harvard Business School. He published several books and papers. He served as the leader of the team which carried out the famous Hawthorne Experiments. These experiments were conducted in the Hawthrone plant of Western Electric Company in Chicago, from 1927 to 1932. Hawthrone Experiments may be classed into four stages:

(*a*) Illumination experiments - designed to assess the effects of illumination on employee efficiency.

(*b*) Test room experiments - designed to judge the influence of working conditions (duration of rest periods, length of the work week, wage incentives etc.) on worker performance. These were experimental in nature.

(*c*) Interviewing studies - undertaken to improve employee attitudes. These were psychological in nature.

(*d*) Observational studies - carried out to understand the factors influencing informal organisation of work groups. These were sociological in nature.

Mayo and his associates derived the following conclusions from Hawthrone experiments:

1. Physical factors do not materially influence worker's behaviour and performance.
2. A worker is not merely an economic man motivated solely by pay. He responds to the total work situation.
3. Psychological and social factors like sense of security, recognition, belonging, etc. exercise significant influence on productivity and performance.
4. Social norms and informal group determine the behaviour and efficiency of workers. Workers do not react as individuals but as members of a group.
5. An organisation is a social system much more than a formal arrangement or structure of functions. Human factor is the most important element in organisations.
6. Informal leaders exercise a greater influence than formal leaders (supervisor) on workers' attitudes and performance. However, supervisory climate is important in this connection.

The Hawthrone experiments led to a new image of the worker and the work place. Human factor became the focus of management theory and practice. There was remarkable change in the teaching and practice of management. Emphasis began to be placed on interpersonal relations and group behaviour.

3. Douglas Mc Gregor (1906 - 1964)

Mc Gregor's theory focussed on behavioural management. He contributed to management thought by developing theory X and Y. This theory helped managers in motivating their employees. Motivation is an important area of management to satisfy employees' needs and improve their performance at work. Mc Gregor's contribution to management is discussed below:

1. Theory X and Theory Y

These theories are explained in the Chapter on motivation. Mc Gregor emphasised that in order to create effective organisations, managers should advocate theory Y. They should adopt democratic styles of leadership, participative decision-making processes and general measures of supervision and control.

2. Professional managers

Mc Gregor emphasised on professionalisation of management. He felt that professional managers are more efficient in making decisions, solving problems and administering the organisation.

3. Self appraisal

Mc Gregor emphasised on self appraisal and evaluation rather than appraisal by superiors.

4. Management team

He focused on effective management team with the qualities of understanding mutual trust, support and agreement.

5. Cooperation

Management and labour union should cooperate rather than bargain with each other on labour-management issues.

6. Management responsibilities

Management has the responsibility of (*a*) increasing organisation profits, (*b*) keeping the labour satisfied, (*c*) renewing plant and machinery, and (*d*) maintaining productive efficiency. Satisfied and happy employees are more efficient and productive. He tried to implement his theories in real life situations when he was the President of the Antioch College, from 1948 to 1954.

4. Mary Parker Follett (1868 - 1933)

Mary Parker Follett was a political and social philosopher. At the age of 32 she began a career of public service in the Bostan area of USA. As a political scientist she examined the activities of several organisations in England and the United States. Her main interest was the psychological foundations of all human activity. She adopted a psychological approach to the problems of power, authority, conflict and control. Follett was a social worker and studied issues related to working conditions of employees. She believed in group behaviour and mutuality of interests between employers and employees.

Follett's contributions are summarised below:

(*a*) Constructive conflict

The best way to resolve conflict is not domination or compromise but integration. Under integration, individual differences are integrated to form a new opinion with which everyone is satisfied.

(*b*) Leadership

Leadership is the product of knowledge rather than of position. The role of a leader is to understand the importance of group activity and to integrate the efforts of all for serving a common purpose.

(*c*) Principles of coordination

Follett suggested four principles to achieve effective coordination: (*i*) Coordination in the early stages, (*ii*) Coordination by direct personal contact among the persons concerned, (*iii*) Coordination as a reciprocal relation of all the factors in a situation, and (*iv*) Coordination as a continuous process.

(*d*) Laws of the situation

One person should not give orders to another but should agree to take the orders from the situation. For example, the sales manager should not issue orders to production manager or vice versa. The two should analyse the market and take a final decision according to market requirements.

(*e*) Authority

The concept of final authority inherent in the chief executive should be replaced by an authority of function in which each individual has final authority for his own allotted task. Authority and responsibility go with function.

5. C.K. Prahlad

Prahlad's idea on management focus primarily on firm's core competence. Core competence is an organisational skill and capability which is not possessed competing firms. It is a bundle of skills and technologies that enables a company to provide a particular benefit to the customers.

Core competence is enduring strength of a company that its competitors cannot easily imitate or match. It can be a superior product design, technology, process engineering or any other capability that provides a lasting competitive edge.

Core competence does not relate to a particular product or business unit. It spreads to the complete product line and varieties in each product. Proctor and Gamble has a wide product line of food items, pharmaceuticals, cosmetics etc. In the line of cosmetics, it manufactures detergents, soaps, shampoos, etc. Its core competence is reflected in every product, it produces in all the product lines.

His ideas on competence help to achieve the following:

(*a*) Core competence is a bundle of skills and technologies. Core competence can be nurtured through collective learning of all people in the organisation.

(*b*) Core competence is the base for all products. Core competence does not reside in a single product or business unit. It requires leadership in a wide range of products or services.

(*c*) Core competence cannot be copied easily. It is very difficult and time-consuming to imitate a firm's core competence. By the time competitors copy, the firm has taken away the cream of the company.

(*d*) Core competence provides competitive edge. Core competence enables a firm to compete against its rivals.

6. Chester I. Barnard (1886 - 1961)

Chester Barnard's theory is based on social systems school of thought. It fills the gap between the traditional and modern theories of management. He defines organisation as "system of consciously coordination activities or forces of two or more persons." He mainly emphasised on the role of executives in business organisations.

His contribution to management thought is discussed below:

(*a*) Organisation

He has highlighted three characteristics of the organisation - (*i*) the persons are able to communicate with each other, (*ii*) they are willing to contribute to the action, and (*iii*) there is a common purpose.

(*b*) Formal and informal organisation

Barnard focused on co-existence of formal and informal organisations. He viewed informal organisations as means of promoting social interactions and through it, achieving formal organisational goals.

(*c*) Authority

Barnard introduced the acceptance theory of authority. He said that superiors have authority to command their subordinates only if it is accepted by them. Authority does not, thus, necessarily flow from top to bottom. A subordinate will accept the authority if: (*i*) He understands the communication, (*ii*) He believes that it is not inconsistent with organisational goals, (*iii*) it is compatible with his personal goal, and (*iv*) He can physically and mentally comply with it.

(*d*) Functions of the executive

Barnard has identified the following functions of an executive: (*i*) The maintenance of organisation communication, (*ii*) Securing essential services from individuals in the organisation, and (*iii*) Formulating and defining the purpose.

(*e*) Incentives

Barnard considered incentives as motivating forces to make people contribute towards organisational goals. He emphasised on the importance of both financial and non-financial incentives, like money, opportunities for growth, social interactions, participative decision-making, etc.

(*f*) Motivation

Barnard pointed out that financial rewards beyond the subsistence level are ineffective except to a limited number of persons. He stressed upon pride of workmanship, pleasant organisation, participation, opportunity for power, feeling of belongingness, and mutually supporting personal activities to motivate people.

(*g*) Leadership

Good managers have to be good leaders. Leadership qualities help managers to unify individual goals with organisational goals. They also integrate formal organisation structure with the informal one.

(*h*) Communication

Communication is an important means of telling people the purpose or objectives of the organisation. There should be formal, short and clear channels of communication so that quick and efficient transmission of information takes place throughout the organisation.

Barnard has a profound impact on management thought and practice. His main contributions have been his logical analysis of organisation structure and application of sociological concepts to management. The credit for analysing the socio-psychological and ethical aspects of management goes to him. Barnard is regarded as the spiritual father of the social systems school as he viewed organisation as a social system.

7. Rensis Likert (1903 - 1972)

Likert was a leading social psychologist. In 1948 he became the Director of the Institute of Social Research at the Michigan University (USA). He conducted extensive research in the field of leadership. His famous publications are New *Patterns of Management* (1961) and *Human Organisation* (1967). Likert believed that the traditional job-centered supervision was mainly responsible for low morale and low productivity. Therefore, he suggested the employee-centered supervision wherein maximum participations would be given to workers in the decision-making process. Likert is best known for his classification of management styles into four categories:

SYSTEM 1 (Exploitative autocratic): Leaders have no confidence in subordinates. Therefore, subordinates are given no participation in decision-making.

SYSTEM 2 (Benevolent autocratic): Management has condescending confidence in subordinates just as a master has towards a servant.

SYSTEM 3 (Participative): Leaders have substantial but not total confidence in subordinates. Employees are allowed to participate meaningfully in decisions affecting their lives.

SYSTEM 4 (Democratic.) : Leaders have full confidence in subordinates. Therefore participation is meaningful.

According to Likert, managers generally lean more heavily on the first two systems. His research revealed that system 4 leads to high productivity, low costs and better labour relations.

Likert treats an organisation as a complex system based on the principle of supporting relationship in which decision-making, leadership, motivation, communication and control move together. He applied behavioural sciences to explain managerial situations. His ideas have had a lasting impact on management thought and practice.

8. Herbert A. Simon

Simon advocated the social system school of management thought. He viewed organisations in their social and psychological context. His contribution is best known for decision-making though he has contributed to varied areas of management interests. Some of his contributions are summarised below:

(*a*) Decision-making

Simon's major contribution is in the field of decision-making. To him management means decision-making. He envisages three stages in decision-making process:

(*i*) Intelligence activity, the initial phase consisting of searching the environment to identify the conditions requiring decisions,

(*ii*) Design activity, involving finding and developing alternative courses of action, and

(*iii*) Choice activity, relating to selection of a particular course of action. Subsequently, March and Simon added the fourth stage, that is, review activity consisting of follow-up action for correcting deviations.

(*b*) Bounded rationality

Simon is of the view that man is not completely rational and does not insist on optimal solutions. Rather he has only bounded rationality and is satisfied with "good enough" solutions. As a manager, cannot maximise due to several constraints he seeks to take satisfying decisions.

(c) Authority

It is not the absolute power of managers to make decisions. It is a combination of instructions, suggestions and persuation.

(*d*) Communication

He suggests a strong system of formal and informal communication to enrich the contribution of social relationships to formal organisational goals.

(*e*) Influence

Simon examined in detail different components of influence mechanism. He suggests that a manager should efficiently utilise all forms of external influence.

9. Mc Kinsey's 7-S Approach

Two researchers - Thomas J. Peters and Robert H Waterman from the world famous management consultancy firm Mc Kinsey & Company of USA carried out extensive research. The main outcome of their research is a 7-S model. A brief description of this model is given below:

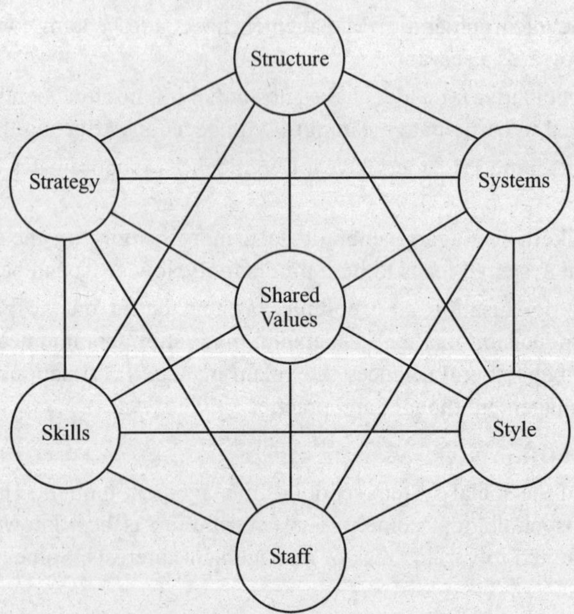

McKinsey 7.S Approach

1. Shared values

This variable is the central core of the model and is inter-connected with all the other variables. Shared values or super-ordinate goals refer to a set of values and aspirations that go beyond the conventional format statement of corporate objectives. These represent the fundamental values around which a business is built. They embody the mission of the organisation as determined by the values of the leader, market place compulsions, competitive actions, etc. For instance, the super-ordinate goal of Bajaj Auto is to be a leader in the two wheeler industry in India by offering the best scooter for Indian roads at the lowest price through economies of scale.

2. Strategy

It refers to taking a systematic course of action to allocate company's resources to achieve its objectives efficiently. Strategy is the determination of the purpose and the basic long term objectives of an enterprise and the adoption of courses of action and allocation of resources necessary to achieve these aims."

3. Structure

Organisation structure is "establishing effective behavioural relationships among persons so that they may work together efficiently and gain personal satisfaction in doing selected tasks under given environmental conditions for the purpose of achieving some goal or objective." It defines authority-responsibility relationships among positions to link the tasks of individuals and groups in achieving organisational goals.

4. System

System refers to all the rules, regulations and procedures, both formal and informal that complement the organisation structure. It consists of production, planning and control systems, capital budgeting systems, cost accounting procedures, training and development systems, performance evaluation systems etc. Changes, in strategy and structure often require changes in management systems.

5. Styles

Organisations differ from each other in terms of their style of working. The style of an organisation becomes evident from the pattern of actions taken by top management over a period of time and the reporting relationship. People in an organisation tend to emulate the style of top managers. According to the Mc Kinsey model, style is more than top management behaviour. It also includes the organisational culture which refers to the basic understandings shared by the member of the organisation one organisation may be open and friendly while the other may be aggressive and secretive.

6. Staff

Staffing refers to selecting people for specific organisational positions and developing in them the competence for effective performance. According to Waterman, staff implies the way organisations introduce young recruits into the mainstream of their activities and the manner in which they manage their careers. The Mc Kinsey study reveals that excellent companies take extraordinary care in moulding the young persons into future managers.

7. Skills

These are the distinctive capabilities of an organisation that make it different from its competitors. It represents organisation's strength that enables it to accept the environmental challenge and improve its competitive position. Organisation's strengths can be two types: (*a*) Common strengths and (*b*) Distinctive competencies. While the common strength is an organisational skill and capability possessed by other organisations also, distinctive competence is an organisational skill and capability possessed by a small number of competing firms.

The seven S's exhibit a complete philosophy of management. They cover the entire range of management functions:

1. Planning : Strategy and skills
2. Organising : Structure and shared values

3. Staffing : Staff
4. Directing : Style
5. Controlling : Systems.

MANAGEMENT THEORY JUNGLE

Over a period of time, such vast number of management theories have developed that one gets confused about the exact meaning of terms like management, organisation, authority, etc. Different terms have different interpretations and therefore, have vagueness in their understanding. Confusion over concepts of management and management theories made Koontz call this whole situation as the "management theory jungle."

One way of avoiding the management theory jungle is to consider management as situational. Managers should study and understand the given situation and select principles, techniques and styles that are most suited to the given situation.

CASE STUDY - 1

Mr. Naidu was a young officer in a nationalised bank in Chennai. He was approached by Mr. Datta, owner of a small textile plant, for a loan to renovate his plant. Naidu gave him a loan of ₹ 50,000. The bank's branch manager, who saw no future in textiles, was shocked at the loan transaction. He told Naidu to stay close to Datta until the money was paid back. Naidu stuck so close that he became Datta's financial adviser. The loan was repaid but Naidu became Datta's partner and resigned his bank job. Within six years, Naidu set up another textile plant and after two decades his textile unit became the second fastest growing textile company in the country. Naidu's management style was characterised by an emphasis on innovation and tight control. To his employees, Naidu was a friendly and highly visible boss. He always worked around the plant and called vast number of workers by their first names. He preferred to lead by example rather than telling people how to do their jobs.

However, Naidu committed a big mistake of not grooming a successor. Therefore, there was a vacuum at the top when he had a severe heart attack and died.

QUESTIONS

1. What were the qualities of Naidu as a manager ?
2. Did he consider management to be an art or science or both ?
3. Do you think Naidu was a successful manager ?
4. On which roles of a manager, Naidu laid maximum emphasis ?

REVIEW QUESTIONS

1. Discuss the Pre-scientific Era of Management thought.
2. Discuss the contribution of Henri Fayol.
3. Differentiate Taylor Vs. Fayol.
4. Explain human relation approach.
5. Discuss the modern approach to management.
6. Explain the contingency approach to management.

7. Explain quantitative approaches to management.
8. Differentiate human relation and behavioural science approach.
9. Explain the evolution of management thought.
10. What is meant by scientific management ?
11. Explain Fayol's contribution to management.
12. What is bureaucracy ? Discuss the bureaucratic organisation structure and point out its merits and demerits.

3
CHAPTER

Management Process

- Introduction
- Managerial and Operative Functions
- Functions of a Manager
  - Planning
  - Organising
  - Staffing
  - Directing
  - Controlling
- Nature of Management Principles
- Significance of Management Principles
- Qualities of a Manager
- Managerial Skills
- Case Study - 1
- Review Questions.

INTRODUCTION

Every organisation has some pre-defined objectives and the process which is adopted to achieve these objectives is called management process. Therefore, management process is primarily concerned with the important task of goal achievement. Thus, management process is identified as a set of functions performed by managers to accomplish organisational goal, that is, management functions explain the process of management. No business enterprise can achieve its objectives until and unless all the members of the unit make an integrated and planned effort. Management process, in general, is defined as a *series of actions or operations conducting to an end.* The knowledge of management revolves around management functions. The logic of the management process is that particular functions are performed in a sequence through time. In other words, whatever, functions are performed is called as management process.

According to Stanly Vance, *"Management is simply the process of decision making and control over the actions of human beings for the express purpose of attaining predetermined goals."* Functions mean activity and management functions mean activities performed by managers. There are two types of functions performed by managers. (*a*) Managerial functions and (*b*) Operative functions.

MANAGERIAL AND OPERATIVE FUNCTIONS

According to Koontz and O'Donnell's "Functions of management are planning, organising, staffing, directing and controlling." Management functions are closely interlinked and interwoven in character. All the managers have to perform certain functions in an organisation to get the things moving. But there is never complete agreement among experts on what functions should be included in management process. Generally speaking, the functions of management can be classified into two categories:

1. Operative functions - Constituting of *Purchasing, production, marketing, financial, personnel,* etc.
2. Managerial functions - constituting of *Planning, Organising, Staffing, Directing and Controlling.*

Managerial Functions and Sub-Functions

Functions	*Sub-Functions*
Planning	Forecasting, Decision -making, Strategy formulation, Policy-making, Programming, Scheduling, Budgeting, Problem-solving, Innovation, Research, etc.
Organising	Functionalisation, Divisionalisation, Departmentalisation, Delegation, Decentralisation, Activity analysis, Task allocation, etc.
Staffing	Manpower planning, Recruitment, Selection, Training, Placement, Compensation, Promotion, Appraisal, etc.
Directing	Supervision, Motivation, Communication, Leadership, Activating, etc.
Controlling	Fixation of standards, Recording, Measurement, Reporting, Corrective action, etc.

FUNCTIONS OF A MANAGER

The managers have a greater role to play in the modern business today. They have to apply the management process and its principles in order to achieve the objectives of business. Operative functions differ according to the nature and size of business. For example, there is no production function in a retail store. On the other hand, managerial functions are essential in all organisations irrespective of their nature and size.

Management process include the functions of management which are performed by managers to achieve the desired objectives. The functions broadly be classified, as shown above, into the following categories.

1. Planning
2. Organising
3. Staffing
4. Directing
5. Controlling

Thus the basic functions of modern manager, under managerial functions, are enumerated as under:

1. Planning

"Planning is selecting information and making assumptions regarding the future to formulate the activities necessary to achieve organisational objectives." Terry and Franklin. According to Koontz and Weihrich, "Planning involves selecting missions and objectives and the actions to achieve them; it requires decision-making, that is, choosing from among alternative future courses of action."

Planning involves the formulation of what is to be done, how, when, where it is to be done, who is to do it and how results are to be evaluated. It is the first essential function which is to be performed by a manager to determine what must be done by the member in order to accomplish the work.

Planning is the basic function of management that involves determination of objectives and devising ways and means to achieve those objectives. It fills the gap between where we are and where we want to go. In the course of analysis, it answers the basic questions of what to do, when to do, how to do and who is to do.

Planning is required for both business and non-business organisations. In business organisation, planning is required at all levels - top, middle and low; all sizes - large, medium and small; and all purposes - profit or non-profit.

The process of planning involves:

(*a*) The top management must lay down the objectives of the company.

(*b*) Relevant information relating to the objectives should be properly collected and classified.

(*c*) Development of the alternatives course of action and compare the alternatives in terms of objectives.

(*d*) He must adopt the one which has the highest probability of yielding the maximum benefit.

(*e*) Establishment of policies, methods, schedules, systems, procedures, standards, budgets, etc.

Planning is future-oriented and done in advance to achieve a goal in future. It has to be carefully done so that future uncertainties do not fail the plans. A manager is a person who works for the company to achieve the objectives and goals.

2. Organising

Once a manager has established objectives and developed plans to achieve them, they must design and develop a human organisation that will be able to carry out those plans successfully. According to Allen, this organisation refers to "the structure which results from identifying and grouping work, defining and delegating responsibility and authority and establishing relationship."

According to J.L. Massie, "Organisation is the structure and process by which a cooperative group of human beings allocates its tasks among its members, identifies relationships, and integrates its activities towards common objectives."

The process of organising involves:

(*a*) Division of the work into component activities;

(*b*) Assignment of duties to workers;

(*c*) Defining responsibility;

(*d*) Delegation of authority

(*e*) Grouping of activities necessary to obtain objectives;

(*f*) Establishment of structural relationship to secure coordination.

3. Staffing

Staffing means appointing people and placing them at the appropriate job. It is a managerial function of hiring people, placing them on jobs of their competence, training and developing them so that they perform their best at the respective jobs. A properly conducted staffing function helps managers to lead and control organisational activities. According to J.L. Massie, "The staffing function includes the process by which the right person is placed in the right organisational position."

The managerial function of staffing, a manager, embraces the following activities:

1. Forecasting of the number of personnel required.
2. Decide their qualification which is required.
3. Recruitment and selection.
4. Training and development of employees.
5. Performance evaluation of employees.
6. Take the decision relating to the issues like promotion, transfer, demotion, etc.
7. Prepare a compensation package plan.
8. Maintaining personnel accounts.

4. Directing

Directing is the managerial function of guiding, supervising, motivating and leading people towards the attainment of planned targets of performance. This function can be called by various names, "leading", "actuating", "motivating" and so on.

Directing functions of managers involve the following steps:

(*a*) Issuing orders and instructions,

(*b*) Supervising people at work,

(*c*) Motivation,

(*d*) Communication,

(*e*) Providing climate for subordinate's progress,

(*f*) Providing effective leadership.

5. Controlling

Henry Fayol states that "Control consists of verifying whether everything occurs in conformity with the plan adopted, the instructions issued, and the principles established. It has the object of pointing out weaknesses and errors in order to rectify them and prevent recurrence. It operates on everything: things, people, actions. Control involves:

(*a*) Establishing standards of performance,

(*b*) Measuring current performance and comparing it against the established standards,

(*c*) Taking action to correct any performance that does not meet those standards.

Control compels events to conform to plans.

NATURE OF MANAGEMENT PRINCIPLES

Principle refers to fundamental truth about a concept that provides guide to action. Principles evolve in every field of knowledge – medicine, engineering, accountancy, etc. Management principles tell about administration of a business, that is, the way a business should run. Principles underlying the field of management help in evolving management theories and making successful managers. Principles serve as guide for management thought. Management principles have evolved over years of experience and testing in organisations in both public and private sectors. They enable managers to carry their tasks effectively and achieve organisation objectives successfully. A study of management is advancing, new principles emerge and old principles are discarded or modified.

Principles of management are essentially operational in nature. They represent the distilled experience of managers in a wide variety of organisations. Most of these principles are applicable in all kinds of managerial situations. But they are not ready made solutions or formulae. In the words of Terry, "they are capsules of selected management wisdom to be used carefully and discreetly."

What proves effective in a given situation may fail to resolve another problem.

The management principles are characterised by the following:

1. **Universality:** Management principles are applicable in a wide variety of organisations - both business and non-business organisations.
2. **Dynamic:** Principles of management are not static. They change with the passage of time and with changes in the environment.
3. **Relative:** Management principles are not absolute and rigid. Rather they are relative and flexible.
4. **Human nature:** Management is concerned with the direction of individual and group behaviour. Individuals and groups differ in terms of their motives, attitudes, capacities and perceptions. Therefore, management principles cannot be applied uniformly in all cases.

SIGNIFICANCE OF MANAGEMENT PRINCIPLES

The following are the reasons to highlight the management principles:

1. **To increase efficiency:** A sound knowledge of the principles of management enables a manager to take more realistic view of organisational problems and their solutions.
2. **To simplify managerial work:** Management principles make the work easy and simple. Managers can perform complex managerial tasks on the basis of these principles and make sound business decisions.
3. **To develop management thought:** Management is a full-fledged field of study taught in Schools and Universities. Management teachings on the basis of management principles develop management theories and thoughts.
4. **To attain social goals:** The standard of living of the people in a society depends upon the quality of management. Development of management principles enables more efficient utilisation of human and material resources.
5. **Better performance:** Management as a discipline is taught to manage large sized business houses. Teaching and training managers on the basis of sound management principles helps them to perform better in all the functional areas.
6. **To increase productivity:** Management principles help to solve various organisational problems in a pre-defined manner. They guide actions appropriate to the situation. This results in efficient decisions and increase organisational productivity and profits.
7. **To improve research:** When management principles exist as the foundation of management thought, they provide scope for future research and improvement in the existing principles.

QUALITIES OF A MANAGER

An efficient manager must have the following qualities, in brief:

(*i*) A manager must be well educated and qualified.

(*ii*) He must have both general and specific education in business administration.

(*iii*) The manager must have the specific training for the job he is required to perform.

(*iv*) Management is a team of work. Head is a manager. He has to direct, supervise, guide and lead the efforts of the employees.

(*v*) He should have effective personality. He should have sound health, good manners and behaviours.

(*vi*) Managerial decision regarding planning, organising and selection of employees should not be based upon emotions but on the logical considerations.

(*vii*) The manager must know the work, he is assigned. It will be good, if he understands the jobs, he has to supervise.

(*viii*) The manager is self-confident about his decisions.

(*ix*) It is rightly said "honesty is the best policy" in the business.

(*x*) The manager should be technically proficient. His qualification, ability and experience must correspond to the needs of the enterprise.

(*xi*) He must accord human treatment to his subordinates. He must honour the emotional and psychological needs of employees.

(*xii*) He must be able to set up, organise and operate the functions successfully.

(*xiii*) He must have spirit of cooperation. Cooperation is reciprocal - two way traffic.

(*xiv*) He must have the capacity to judge and must be courageous.

(*xv*) He must have ability to teach others, which depends upon deep knowledge, mastery of language, clarity of expression, etc.

MANAGERIAL SKILLS

In addition to fulfilling numerous roles, managers also need a number of specific skills if they are to succeed. The most fundamental management skills are technical, interpersonal, conceptual, diagnostic, communication, decision-making, and time-management skills.

1. Technical Skills: *Technical skills* are the skills necessary to accomplish or understand the specific kind of work being done in an organisation. Technical skills are especially important for first-line managers. These managers spend much of their time training subordinates and answering questions about work-related problems. They must know how to perform the tasks assigned to those they supervise if they are to be effective managers.

2. Interpersonal Skills: Managers spend considerable time interacting with people both inside and outside the organization. For obvious reasons, then, the manager also needs ***interpersonal skills***—the ability to communicate with, understand, and motivate both individuals and groups. As a manager climbs the organizational ladder, he or she must be able to get along with subordinates, peers, and those at higher levels of the organization. Because of the multiple of roles managers must fulfill, a manager must also be able to work with suppliers, customers, investors, and others outside of the organization. Although some managers have succeeded with poor interpersonal skills, a manager who has good interpersonal skills is likely to be more successful.

3. Conceptual Skills: ***Conceptual skills*** depend on the manager's ability to think in the abstract. Managers need the mental capacity to understand the overall workings of the organization and its environment, to grasp how all the parts of the organization fit together, and to view the organization in a holistic manner. This allows them to think strategically, to see the "big picture," and to make broad-based decisions that serve the overall organization.

4. Diagnostic Skills: Successful managers also possess ***diagnostic skills***, or skills that enable a manager to visualize the most appropriate response to a situation. A physician diagnoses a patient's illness by analyzing symptoms and determining their probable cause. Similarly, a manager can diagnose and analyze a problem in the organization by studying its symptoms and then developing a solution.

5. Communication Skills: ***Communication skills*** refer to the manager's abilities both to effectively convey ideas and information to others and to effectively receive ideas and information from others. These skills enable a manager to transmit ideas to subordinates so that they know what is expected, to coordinate work with peers and colleagues so that they work well together properly, and to keep higher-level managers informed about what is going on.

6. Decision-making Skills: Effective managers also have good decision-making skills. ***Decision-making skills*** refer to the manager's ability to correctly recognize and define problems and opportunities and then to select an appropriate course of action to solve problems and capitalize on opportunities. No manager makes the right decision *all* the time. However, effective managers make good decisions *most* of the time.

7. Time-management Skills: Finally, effective managers usually have good time-management skills. ***Time management skills*** refer to the manager's ability to prioritize work, to work efficiently, and to delegate appropriately. As already noted, managers face many different pressures and challenges. It is too easy for a manager to get bogged down doing work that can easily be postponed or delegated to others.

CASE STUDY — I

The Ethical Company

Bharat Gears Limited, a medium sized unit manufacturing gears for two-wheelers, is located at Palampur near Rajkot. Its headquarters is in Mumbai and has been a family-owned enterprise of the Maheshwaris. The company was making moderate profits, and there was job satisfaction amongst the employees. The recent Gallop Survey showed employee satisfaction levels at 67 per cent. The average tenure of employees was five years, which was a matter of surprise to other companies in Palampur. It was common for employees in that area to search for greener pastures, once they had a little experience. Bharat Gears Limited has won the Best Ethical Performance Award by the State government for the last three consecutive years.

Balaji was a very satisfied worker at Bharat Gears. He was the first employee to join his unit and has completed twelve years of his service. An efficient worker, he had also been felicitated with the 'Best Employee Award' twice. Balaji was nearing 50 and his experience and enthusiasm kept other supervisors on their toes. Due to his performance, he had become a cherished and valued employee for the management and his peers alike. Aditya, Human Resource Manager, often took some important decisions after consulting Balaji.

One day, Balaji was working on the Gear Cutting Machine. It was a new machine, imported from Pfaff, Germany. Balaji did not have complete knowledge of the machine's functions. While working, a small slip near the meshed wires found his legs trapped inside the machine. The next moment, all he knew was a terrible pain. He was in a pool of blood. His fellow workers rushed to get him out. To the dismay of all, both his legs had to be amputated. Balaji's physical disability made him discontinue the job. He surrendered to his fate, and accepted that the mishap has happened due to his negligence. As per the rules in HR Handbook, within a week's time, the company gave him full compensation and paid towards all the medical expenditure. As a good gesture from the top management, he was allowed to stay in the staff quarters. Aditya Singh spoke to Balaji and assured him of a suitable job for his son Sameer, who was Balaji's only hope. Sameer was a young engineer working with Tanushree Cables at Vadodara. The company was humane in its attitude towards Balaji, one of its trusted and valued employees. Paresh, one workshop engineer in Bharat Gears, was looking for a change to another company. This fact was known to Aditya. Paresh, being close to the HR manager, had intimated him of his success at the final interview at Container Corporation of India, a public sector undertaking, which, he hoped, would give him greater stability. Aditya had promised the job to Balaji based on this premise.

After a month, Sameer presented himself before Aditya. The HR manager welcomed him and made him go through the selection process of Bharat Gears. He was satisfied with Sameer as an able and prospective candidate, who could easily fit into Paresh's shoes. He asked Sameer to contact him in a couple of days.

Meanwhile, he called Paresh and enquired as to when he was joining Container Corporation. Paresh's reply made him heavy on heart. Paresh quoted of a last minute rejection at Container Corporation due to medical grounds (though not important for the job, but PSUs had to comply) Aditya was now in a dilemma. He did not know what to answer to Paresh. He discussed this problem with a friend over the coffee table and ruminated late at night. When Sameer reported to the HR office, Aditya apologized about his inability to induct Sameer at present. Though he did not disclose the details to Sameer, he could make out that Aditya was in a fix. He was surprised because Aditya was the one for whom his father had high regard and trust. Aditya promised Sameer to give him first preference in Bharat Gears whenever next vacancy arose. For the time being, he requested Sameer to continue at Vadodara.

Sameer replied that he had resigned from Tanushree Cables after Aditya's assurance. Not only the job at Bharat Gears suited his profile better, it also made possible for him to stay with his handicapped father.

He reminded Aditya of the commitment he had given to his father. Due to his commitment, Balaji had asked Sameer to quit his job and report at Bharat Gears. Aditya was in a big trouble. His efforts as securing a job for Sameer in adjacent factories at Palampur did not yield any results. He felt guilty for not keeping his word. Aditya needed a solution so that he could do some justice with the old lieutenant of Bharat Gears—a motivated, cherished and valued worker who had met with an accident. Not finding a job for his son Sameer, who had left a good job due to his assurance, pricked Aditya's conscience.

QUESTIONS

1. What are the main issues in the above case ?
2. What are the lessons that we can learn from the case ?

REVIEW QUESTIONS

1. "Management is a distinct process, consisting of planning, organising, actuating and controlling performance to determine and accomplish objectives by the use of people and resources." Explain.
2. What is the concept of universality of management ?
3. "A manager plans, organises, staffs, directs and controls." - Discuss.
4. Name the various functions which constitute the process of management and discuss each of them briefly.

5. "The principles of management are universal. They apply to all situations." Do you agree. Give reasons ?
6. List and briefly describe the functions of management.
7. Define management process.
8. How managerial functions classified ?
9. Explain the principles of management.
10. What are the functions of management ?
11. Explain the qualities of a good manager.
12. How would you argue that management is important for all organisations ?
13. What are the skills which managers at different levels need to possess ?
14. How can organisations develop the competencies of their management ?
15. "Management is the art of getting things done through and with people." Comment and explain.

Social Responsibilities of Business

4

CHAPTER

- Introduction
- Meaning
- Growth of the Concept
- Nature of Social Responsibility
- Arguments for social Responsibilities
- Arguments against Social Responsibilities
- Profits and Social Responsibility
- Barriers to Social Responsibility
- Various Stakeholders and Social Responsibilities
- Conflicting Groups
- Davis Model
- Social Responsibilities of Bussiness in India
- Social Audit
- Objectives of Social Audit
- Benefits of Social Audit
- Ethics
- Definition of Ethics
- Objectives of Business Ethics
- Corporate Governance
- Benefits of Good Corporate Governance
- Need for Business Ethics
- Guidelines for Ethical Behaviour
- Benefits of Business Ethics
- Case Study - 1
- Review Questions.

INTRODUCTION

Social development is the main aim of any form of organisation all over the world. Therefore, business has certain responsibilities towards society. Managements are expected to follow the values of the society they work in. In India, everyone is competing for products and profits. But many organisations are not fulfilling their social responsibilities.

Social responsibility is a nebulous idea and hence is defined in various ways. Adolph Berle has defined social responsibility as the manager's responsiveness to public consensus. This means that there cannot be the same set of social responsibilities applicable to all countries in all times. These would be determined in each case by the customs, religions, traditions, level of industrialisation and host of other norms and standards about which there is a public consensus at any given time in a given society.

Society has become increasingly aware of the interdependence between business and its environment. Business organisations are no longer viewed as totally private bodies free to pursue their own goal. Instead they are increasingly expected to contribute to the betterment of society. Managers are no longer considered to have responsibility not only to the owners: rather managers increasingly held accountable for the social effects of their actions. As business firms grow in size and power, society expects more from them.

Social responsibility is an ethical or ideological theory that an entity whether it is a government, corporation, organisation or individual has a responsibility to society. This responsibility can be "negative", in that case it is a responsibility to refrain from acting or it can be "positive", meaning there is a responsibility to act.

MEANING

Public demands on private business have expanded greatly in recent years. Business enterprise was once expected to denote its efforts to producing and distributing goods and services as efficiently as possible and to make innovations and improvements in product and process with the ultimate objective of maximisation of profits. Now business is increasingly called upon to promote a variety of social purposes in addition to these long standing economic ones. The demands for social responsibility have provoked enthusiastic discussion and debate on what new roles, if any, business firms should play in the social system.

"Social responsibility of business refers to the obligation of businessmen to pursue those policies, to make those decisions or to follow those lines of action, which are desirable in terms of the objectives and values of the society." — Howard R. Bown

"Social responsibility is the personal obligation of every one as he acts for his own interests, to assure that the rights and legitimate interests of all others are not impinged." — Koontz and O'Donnell

The European Union defines corporate social responsibility as "A concept that an enterprise is accountable for its impact on all relevant stakeholders. It is the continuing commitment by business to behave fairly and responsibly and contribute to economic development while improving the quality of life of the work force and their families as well as the local community and society at large".

GROWTH OF THE CONCEPT

Although the subject "social responsibilities of business" in its present form and content has gained popular attention in recent years only, its origin can be traced back to the evolution of the concept of a welfare state. The changing image of business in recent years has lent further support to the idea of social responsibility. Some public opinion polls of the 1960s and 1970s in the United States have left the businessman disenchanted. These polls have revealed that the businessman is viewed as an individual who does not care for others, who ignores social problems, who preys upon the population, who exploits labour and who is a selfish money grabber.

Several forces have led to the development of the concept of social responsibility. Some of these forces are given below:

(*a*) **Consumerism:** Growing consciousness among consumers about their rights, establishment of consumer groups and consumer laws have given rise to the dictum "Consumer is the king". Businessmen have been forced to care for the interests of consumers.

(*b*) **Trade Unionism:** Growing power of trade unions and labour laws have led business to be concerned with labour welfare.

(*c*) **Public Opinion:** Public opinion and the threat of Government control has made businessmen to realise that the responsible behaviour is essential for the preservation of free enterprise. If business does not accept social responsibilities it would be forced upon by the Government.

(*d*) **Enlightened Self-interest:** The spread of education has led businessmen to be concerned with the quality of life. Many of them recognise that business is a reflection of social objectives and values and an agency for promoting them.

(*e*) **Professionalisation:** Separation of ownership from management in the large corporation has replaced "owner manager" by "paid manager". Ownership has become diffused in large companies. Managers having no stake in ownership tend to take a longterm and more responsible view of their role.

(*f*) **Trusteeship:** The trusteeship principle suggests that business managers should be caretaker of their property holding it in trust for the society as a whole. The more fortunate members of society should assist their less fortunate brothers.

Social responsibility implies responsibility to society beyond the basic economic responsibility of efficiency and profitability. As an economic agent of society, a business enterprise must use its economic power to protect and promote public interest and social values. *Social responsibility*, relates to current issues whereas *social responsiveness* is anticipatory in nature. A social responsive organisation is expected to anticipate changing or emerging social problems and respond to them.

NATURE OF SOCIAL RESPONSIBILITY

A socially responsible enterprise considers both the economic and social implications of alternative courses of action before taking any decision. It finds out and pursues an appropriate harmony between its economic and social goals. It is ready to forgo a commercially profitable opportunity if it is socially unacceptable. Enterprises may have to make decisions which may not be economically profitable but which contribute to their long-term viability and public image.

Social responsibility is not catering to the interests of society once or twice. It is continuously engage in social issues, if they want to survive and grow in the long-run. Though both business and non-business organisations should be responsible towards society, the focus is more on business firms to look after social interests.

Social responsibility is not just the obligation of top level managers. Managers at all levels are involved in discharging social responsibilities.

ARGUMENTS FOR SOCIAL RESPONSIBILITIES

Following arguments are offered in favour of social responsibility:

1. **A better society means a better environment for doing business:** Business can enhance its long-run profitability by making an investment in society today. Today's problems can turn into tomorrow's profits.

2. **Corporate social action will prevent Government intervention:** As evidenced by waves of antitrust, equal employment opportunity and pollution-control legislation, Government will force business to do what it fails to do voluntarily.
3. **Long-run Survival:** Firms engaged in social responsibility may suffer losses in the short-run but fulfilling social obligations is beneficial for long-run survival of the business-firm. Short-term costs are, therefore, investments for long run profitability.
4. **Helps in avoiding Government regulation:** A business organisation which does not assume social responsibility on its own shall be required to do so by the Government. To avoid excessive Government regulation and interference, the enterprises themselves become morally aware of the social responsibility.
5. **Improvement in public image:** A business firm that looks after the interests of society earns goodwill and a positive public image. Its goods and services are more readily acceptable to society than those of competitors.
6. **Creation of society:** Business is a sub-system of society. It draws support and sustenance from society in the form of inputs. Socially responsible behaviour is essential to sustain this relationship between business and society.
7. **Social power:** Social power and social responsibility must be balanced. When an institution's power grows, its responsibility grows accordingly. According to Davis, "In the long run those who do not use power in a manner that society considers responsible will lose it. This is the iron law of responsibility."
8. **Public image:** Adoption of social responsibility as an objective will help to improve the public image of business. A good public image is a valuable asset for business.
9. **Coalition:** A business organisation is a coalition of several interest groups or stakeholder, examples, shareholders, customers, employees, suppliers, etc. Business should therefore work for the interest of all of them rather than for the benefit of shareholders alone.
10. **Competence:** Business organisations and their managers have proved their competence and leadership in solving economic problems. Society expects them to use their competence to solve problems and thereby play a leadership role.
11. **Legitimacy:** It is in the enlightened self-interest of business to assume social responsibility. Social responsibility *legitimises* and promotes the economic objectives of business. Social responsibility is thus good citizenship as well as good business.
12. **The creation of a better social environment benefits both society and business:** Society gains through better neighbourhoods and employment opportunities; business benefits from a better community, since the community is the source of its work force and the consumer of its products and services.

ARGUMENTS AGAINST SOCIAL RESPONSIBILITIES

Arguments against social responsibility of business are given below:

1. **Burden on consumers:** If business deals with social problems, costs of doing business would increase. These costs will be passed on to consumers in the form of higher prices or will have to be borne by the owners.
2. **Misuse of responsibilities:** Acceptance of social responsibilities will involve diversion of precious managerial time and talent on social programmes. It may result in misdirection of valuable corporate resources.
3. **Business already has enough power:** Considering that business exercises powerful influence over where and how we work and live, what we buy, and what we value, more concentration of social power in the hands of business is undesirable.

4. **Profit maximization ensures the efficient use of society's resources:** By buying goods and services, consumers collectively dictate where assets should be deployed. Social expenditures amount to theft of stockholder's equity.
5. **Business is an economic activity:** It is for the Government to look after interests of the society through various social programmes. The prime responsibility of assuming social responsibility should, therefore, be that of the Government and not business enterprises.
6. **Transfer of social costs:** The costs related to social programmes are adjusted by business concerns in the following ways:
   (*a*) Increase in prices of goods or services;
   (*b*) Reduction in wages of workers;
   (*c*) Reduction in profits.
7. **Lack of social skill:** Professionally qualified managers may not have the aptitude for solving social problems. There are specialist social service organisations such as Government which can better deal with social problems.
8. **Cost-benefit analysis:** A social benefit programme where initial costs exceed the benefits may not be taken up by business enterprises even in the short run.
9. **Social cost:** The cost of social programmes would have to be added to the price of the product. Companies selling their products in international markets would be at a disadvantage when competing with companies in other countries that do not have these social costs to bear.
10. **Responsibility without power:** Business organisations possess only economic power and not social power. It is unjust to impose social responsibilities without social power.
11. **Improper role:** The proper role of business is to use its resources and energies efficiently so as to earn the best possible return on investment within the confines of law and ethics. Business should concentrate on economic performance leaving social service to other organisations.

PROFITS AND SOCIAL RESPONSIBILITY

Business firms are primarily economic institutions and if they fail to earn profits they will not survive for long. Successful economic activity is thus a firm's social responsibility. Some managers insist that profit maximisation is the road to social responsibility. They feel that by maximising profits they can create more jobs, pay more dividends, more wages, etc. Profits are the life of business enterprise but maximising profits should not be the ultimate objective of a business. Unless a company earns profits, it will not be able to discharge social responsibilities. Profit, the main economic goal, serves as a stimulant to hard work, initiative and risk-taking. An enterprise that earns economic surplus improves its capability to serve the society. Thus, profit contributes to public interest and social welfare.

In the short-run, expenditure on social action programmes may reduce the amount of profits. But in the long-run, such expenditure improves the socio-economic environment of business. For instance, when a business firm contributes to the education and health of the community, it can get more competent and healthy employees. Profits maintain the support of shareholders and creditors. Profits improve the firm's image. All social programmes involve costs that may be adjusted by organisation by increasing prices of products, lowering wages or reducing dividend rates. If the company pass the costs of social responsibilities to consumers in the form of higher price or workers by reducing their wages or shareholders by reducing dividends, the purpose of social responsibility gets defeated.

BARRIERS TO SOCIAL RESPONSIBILITY

A department which discharges social responsibilities may report lower profits than its counterparts. This attitude may not be acceptable to high level manager, unless social programmes are approved by him.

Lower profits because of social responsibilities may not be acceptable to owners or workers of the organisation. This is because of low dividend rates or lower wages to workers.

If employees of the organisation want to assume social responsibilities, high level managers may object it. Under this circumstances, employees may be forced to choose between personal growth and social growth.

According to Ernest Dale, "The manager sees himself as an arbiter among the many interests of publics' affected by the business: the stockholders, the employees, the local community, the suppliers and the customer. It is his duty to divide the return from the business equitably by providing a "fair return" to the shareholders, "fair" working conditions and pay for the employees, "fair prices" to the suppliers and customers and to make the business, in general, an asset to the local community and the nation".

VARIOUS STAKEHOLDERS AND SOCIAL RESPONSIBILITIES

The scope of social responsibilities of business is very wide. The responsibility is manifold and extends to all those who have a stake in business. The management of a business enterprise is responsible to different parties - shareholders, employees, customers, Government, Community, creditors, etc. Such responsibilities are briefly enumerated below:

1. Responsibilities towards shareholders

(*a*) A fair return on investment;

(*b*) Safety of investment;

(*c*) Fair and reasonable appreciation of capital;

(*d*) Regular and full information about working;

(*e*) Accurate progress of the firm.

2. Responsibilities towards employees

(*a*) Fair wages and salaries;

(*b*) Good and safe working conditions;

(*c*) Workers participation in decision-making;

(*d*) Trade union rights;

(*e*) Opportunities for education, training and promotion;

(*f*) Adequate service benefits, such as housing, medical facilities, insurance cover, retirement benefits, etc.

(*g*) Job security and safety.

3. Responsibilities towards customers

(*a*) Providing quality goods at reasonable price;

(*b*) Avoid unsafe products;

(*c*) Ensure regular and adequate supply of goods;

(*d*) Provide satisfaction to purchasers;

(*e*) Prompt and redressal of customer's grievances;

(*f*) True and fair information through advertisements;

(*g*) Avoid unfair and unethical practices, like black-marketing, adulteration, hoarding, etc.

(*h*) Provide for after-sale servicing;

(*i*) Achieve better public relations.

4. Responsibilities towards Community

It is an important responsibility of business to inform the community about company's policies and programmes. It is also to inform the community as to how the enterprise contributes to the welfare of the community.

(*a*) To make the best possible use of the society's resources;

(*b*) To provide maximum employment opportunities;

(*c*) To contribute to the upliftment of the weaker section of community;

(*d*) To keep the atmosphere free from all types of pollution;

(*e*) To refrain from anti-social practices;

(*f*) To develop good relation with community.

5. Responsibilities towards Government

(*a*) To abide by the laws of the land;

(*b*) To follow fair trade policies and practices;

(*c*) To pay taxes honestly;

(*d*) To discourage unhealthy practices, like bribing the Government officials for favours, etc.

(*e*) To avoid monopoly in business.

6. Responsibilities towards suppliers

(*a*) Provide accurate information regarding the firm;

(*b*) make prompt settlement of transactions;

(*c*) There is fairness in transactions.

CONFLICTING GROUPS

There arise situations that different groups want their returns to be maximised from business concerns. In short, the groups consisting of:

Owners want maximum profits;

Shareholders want maximum dividend;

Workers want high wages;

Consumers want good product at low price;

Community wants upliftment of social programmes, etc.

Balancing the demands of all the stakeholders become important for the manager and to see that these multiple demands do not affect the company's objectives. Manager, who is a rope-walker, to carry out the business activities in a manner that support all the stakeholders.

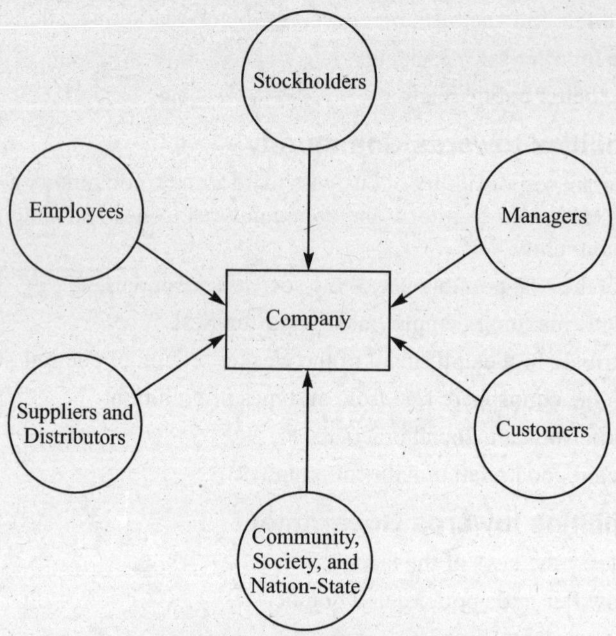

Types of Company Stakeholders

DAVIS MODEL OF SOCIAL RESPONSIBILITY

A generally accepted model of corporate social responsibility was developed by Keith Davis. Stated simply, Davis's model is a list of five propositions that describe why and how business should adhere to the obligation to take action that protects and improves the welfare of society as well as of the organisation:

1. Social responsibility arises from social power

This proposition is derived from the premise that business has a significant amount of influence on, or power, over, such critical social issues as minority employment and environmental pollution. This power necessitates the business concerns to assume social responsibility.

2. Two-way communication between business and society

Business concerns receive information from society regarding consumer's desire and they, in turn, send them information about their practices. Thus, the two-way communication between business and society makes it necessary for corporate world to assume social responsibility.

3. Cost-benefit analysis

Before taking up a social programme, business enterprises must consider its social costs and benefits and if the benefits outweigh the costs, the programme should be undertaken by them.

4. Passing social cost to consumers

This proposition states that business cannot be expected to completely finance activities that may be socially advantageous but economically disadvantageous. The cost of maintaining socially desirable activities within business should be passed on to consumers through higher prices for the goods or services related to these activities.

5. Expertise to solve social problems

Since managers have skills and competence to look after social needs and values, they must do so even if it lies outside their area of operations.

SOCIAL RESPONSIBILITIES OF BUSINESS IN INDIA

A few leading business houses have made significant contribution to the economic and social well-being of the country. But instances of adulteration, hoarding, black marketing, tax evasion and other anti-social practices are very common. The Government industrial policy states that if industry acquires an increasing sense of social responsibility Government can concentrate more on measures to help industry rather than to control it. In a mixed economy like ours, social responsibilities of business assume special significance. The main aspects of social responsibilities of Indian business are as follows:

(*a*) To make the best use of national resources so as to raise the level of national income and standard of living of the people.

(*b*) To create more and more employment opportunities for engineers, technicians and other skilled persons from educational institutions.

(*c*) To protect the national environment and ecological balance from all types of pollution.

(*d*) To contribute to the economic development of backward regions and weaker section of society.

(*e*) To recognise and respect social values, business ethics and cultural heritage.

(*f*) To cooperate with the Government in solving problems like illiteracy, over-population, monopoly, concentration of income and wealth, etc.

(*g*) To make the country economically self-reliant through export promotion and import substitution.

In India, a large number of companies like TISCO, DCM, Mafatlal Group, Hindustan Steel Ltd., Escorts Ltd., Godrej, Kirloskars, Reliance, etc. have accorded a place of importance to social action programmes. Corporate social responsibility is seen as a relevant constraint to business and a large percentage of managers assign a high place for social responsibility, responsibility with that of profit. However, the process of social commitment in India is somewhat different: like starting social trusts, anti pollution measures, starting family planning clinics, for the benefit of workers and residents, etc.

Recently, we have seen many progressive organisations in our country keenly playing a social role. In some of these organisations the approach has been to take up only *business-centric activities,* that is, which are directly relevant to their business. The guiding philosophy in these organisations is that social responsibility is good only if it pays. This approach benefits both the organisation and the stakeholder. Thus, ITC has been afforesting private degraded land to augment the supply of raw material for its paper factory. Similarly, Nestle which requires good quality milk for its dairy plant in Moga, Punjab has been providing farmers financial and technical assistance for constructing deep-bore wells, which, apart from affording enhanced irrigation and access to surplus crops, also improve the qualities of livestock's feed crop and milk yield. Companies like Cadbury India, Glaxo and Richardson Hindustan are helping farmers to grow crops which serve as raw materials for them. Lipton in Etah district of Uttar Pradesh has started veterinary hospital in the region from where it buys milk.

In this way they not only serve social causes but also strengthen their brands. In some other organisations the approach has been to take up such *philanthropic activities* in which they can make a difference. Thus, Indal, Gujarat Ambuja, Wipro, etc. are involved in community development work of building roads, running schools and hospitals and similar projects.

Tata Group: The Tata group of companies perform the following social activities:

(*a*) To promote higher education, it has established the JN Tata Endowment Scheme which awards scholarships to deserving Indians.

(*b*) Its articles contains provisions for social and moral responsibilities towards consumers, employees, shareholders, society and the local community.

(*c*) Tata Steel Rural Development Society was established that provides education, health care, family planning, irrigation, adult literacy, etc.

(*d*) It spends on basic infrastructure and disburses money through charitable trusts and reconstruction societies.

SOCIAL AUDIT

A social audit is a systematic study and evaluation of the organisation's social performance as distinguished from its economic performance. The term "Social performance" refers to any organisational activity that effects the general welfare of society. Social audit concept is gaining increasing attention. The use of an effective social audit is likely to encourage a careful cost-benefit analysis of corporate programmes for the benefit of society. It could also provide a means for measuring the result of a social programme. Both investors and social activists may then better evaluate the overall record of a firms' social involvement.

Social audit is also defined as "A commitment to systematic assessment of and reporting of some meaningful definable domain of a company's activities that have social impact." (Bauer and Fenn)

"Social audit, like financial audit, is an identification and examination of the activities of the firm in order to assess, evaluate, measure and report their impact on the immediate social environment" —Belkaoui

Social audit helps to determine the areas where the firm could be vulnerable to public criticism. Organizations can inform the public regarding their activities for society. The true picture of corporate accountability can be given to the society. Social audit may be measured in the areas of employment, production, consumer effort, consumer funds absorbed, payrolls, dividends and interest, environmental protection, etc.

Effective social audit is, however, difficult. No clear standards exist as to the activities to be included and there are no uniform standards for measuring results. Data collection about the effects of social problems may also be a problem. A few organisations have attempted to measure the costs and benefits of their social activities in formats similar to those used in financial reporting. The results of social involvement may be included in the company's annual report as well as social report.

OBJECTIVES OF SOCIAL AUDIT

1. It assesses the gaps between needs and resources available for local development.
2. It creates awareness amongst the company's stakeholders about the company's productive services.
3. It increases efficiency and effectiveness of the corporate development programmes.
4. It assesses corporate policy decisions, in the interest of its stakeholders.
5. It estimates the opportunity cost for stakeholder of not getting access to public services.

BENEFITS

Social audit offers the following advantages:

1. Enterprises know the extent to which they have been able to achieve their social goals.

2. It develops a sense of social awareness among all staff. In the process of preparing reports and responding to evaluations, employees become more aware of the social implications of their actions.
3. Data on social costs and benefits can be gathered to assess social performance of the enterprise. This helps in carrying out cost-benefit analysis of the social programmes.
4. It provides data for comparing the effectiveness of different types of programmes.
5. It helps in locating the potential areas for carrying out the socially productive programmes.
6. It provides data about the cost of social programmes so that the management can relate this data to budgets, available resources, company objectives, etc.
7. It provides information for effective response to external groups which make demands on the organisation.

Sachar Committee recommended the following information may be included in the social report:

(*a*) Amount spent on social development;
(*b*) Employment provided to public from SC and ST, handicapped, minority community, other weaker sections of society;
(*c*) Amount spent on pollution control;
(*d*) Contributions to National Relief Funds;
(*e*) Amount spent on public health, population control, adult literacy, etc.
(*f*) Contribution to import substitution and export promotion;
(*g*) Expenditure on cost reduction, etc.

ETHICS

Ethics distinguishes between good and bad. It is governed by a set of principles or code of conduct. Though ethical behaviour varies with individual preception, it is generally determined by socially accepted norms.

Business ethics refers to the application of ethics to business. To be more specific, business ethics is the study of good and evil, right and wrong and just and unjust actions of businessmen. Business ethics does not differ from generally accepted norms of good or bad. If dishonesty is considered to be unethical and immoral in society, then any businessman who is dishonest with employees, customers, shareholders, is acting unethically and immorally. If protecting others from any harm is considered to be ethical, then a company that recalls a defective and harmful product from the market is acting ethically. To be considered ethical, businessmen must draw their ideas about what is desirable behaviour from the same sources as anybody else. Businessmen should not try to evolve their own principles to justify what is right and wrong. Employees and employers may be tempted to apply special or weaker ethical rules to business situations but society does not condone or permit such an exception. People who are in business, are bound by the same ethical principles that apply to others.

Ethics may be defined as a theory of morality which attempts to systematise moral judgements and establish and defend basic principles. According to Garret, "ethics is the science of judging specifically human ends and the relationship of means to those ends. In some way it is also the art of controlling means so that they will serve specifically human ends." Thus, ethics is the science of human conduct, a study of right and wrong in human relationships.

According to Payton, ethics is said to be the science of morals, moral principles and recognised rules of conduct. The character of a man is expressed in terms of his conduct. Conduct of a person is a series of actions, which when taken together, can be termed as good or bad, right or wrong, moral or immoral. These right, wrong, good, bad, moral, immoral are termed as moral judgements. Moral judgement requires moral standards by which we judge human conduct. Thus, ethics can also be termed as the science of character of a person expressed as right or wrong.

Business ethics is the application of moral principles to business problems. However, ethics extends beyond the question of legality and involves the goodness or badness of an act. Therefore, an action may be legally right but ethically wrong. For instance, a village, far away from urban area, has a single provision store. The shop owner can charge any exorbitant price for his goods; though legally but not ethically.

DEFINITION

Wright defines, "Ethics is that branch of philosophy which is the systematic study of reflective choice of the standards of right or wrong by which it is to be guided and of the goods towards which it may ultimately be directed."

Webster defines ethics as "the discipline dealing with that which is good and bad and moral duty and obligation."

Hurley defines, "Ethics as a system of moral principles." Business ethics may be defined as a set of moral rules and principles to protect the interest of customers, employees, society, business unit and the industry as a whole.

Ethics is a belief that an action is right or wrong. Ethics has the following implication:

1. Ethical behaviour varies from person to person.
2. Ethics is involved in all business and non-business activities.
3. Ethics is not related to law. What is ethical may be illegal or vice versa.
4. Though depending on individual perception, ethics normally relates to behaviour within socially accepted norms.

OBJECTIVES OF BUSINESS ETHICS

The basic objectives of business ethics are:

1. Ethics studies human behaviour and makes evaluative assessment about them as moral or immoral.
2. Ethics establishes moral standards and norms of behaviour.
3. Ethics make judgements upon human behaviour based on these standards and norms.
4. Ethics prescribes moral behaviour and makes recommendation.
5. Expresses an opinion or attitude about human conduct in general.

CORPORATE GOVERNANCE

The term "corporate governance" is used to denote the extent to which companies run in an open and honest manner in the best interest of all stakeholders. The key elements of good corporate governance are transparency and accountability projected through a code which incorporates a system of checks and balances between all players, viz., Board of Directors, Auditors and Stakeholders.

BENEFITS OF GOOD CORPORATE GOVERNANCE

1. It creates overall market confidence and long-term trust in the company.
2. It leads to an increase in company's share prices.
3. It ensures the integrity of company's financial reports.
4. It maximises corporate security by acting as a whistle blower.
5. It limits the liability of top management by carefully articulating the decision making process.

6. It improves strategic thinking at the top by inducting independent directors who bring a wealth of experience and a host of new ideas.

NEED FOR BUSINESS ETHICS

1. Today a business manager is expected to serve as a trustee of various social groups. As a trustee he must observe the ethical values of the society.
2. When an organisation fails to behave in accordance with the social expectations, it may lose its image and market share.
3. Management develops a friendly and healthy environment in the business and subordinates contribute efficiently to organisational goals considering individual goals subordinate to organisational goals.
4. Customer's needs are served by supplying them right products at the right time, place and time. This is possible if the business enterprise engage in ethical practice.
5. A business executive must take into consideration the moral and social considerations because these are the real motivating factors.
6. Businessmen should consider the interest of the business unit. Unethical practices of a businessman will lead to closure of business unit. The closure of a business unit not only create problems to business but also to employees and the society in general.
7. A business could not be run in such a manner as is detrimental to the interest of society or business itself. So it is argued that there should be some business ethics for the growth of a business.
8. The prime objective of any business is to earn profit. At the same time, no business is allowed to earn profit without following business ethics. If business ethics are properly followed by a business, automatically that particular business unit earns a good name among the public.
9. Business ethics are necessary to improve the confidence of the customer, employees, etc. If confidence is infused, they will popularize the excellent consumer services of the business unit.
10. Ethical business activities improve company's image and give edge over competitors. This promotes sales and profits.

GUIDELINES FOR ETHICAL BEHAVIOUR

The following guidelines are prescribed by James O' Toole:

1. **Obey the law:** Obeying legal practices of the country is conforming to ethical values.
2. **Tell the truth:** Disclosing fair accounting results to concerned parties and telling the truth is also an ethical behaviour of managers.
3. **Respect for people:** Ethics requires managers to respect people who contact them.
4. **The golden rule:** The golden business principle is that "Treat others as you would want to be treated." This always results in ethical behaviour.
5. **Above all, do no harm:** Even if law does not prohibit use of chemicals in producing certain products, managers should avoid them if they are environmental pollutants.
6. **Practice participation:** Managers should not decide on their own what is good or bad for the stakeholders. They should assess their needs, analyse them in the light of business needs, and integrate the two needs by allowing the stakeholders to participate in the decision-making processes.

7. **Act when managers have responsibility:** Actions which have to be taken by managers only, must be responsibly taken by them for the benefit of the organisation and the stakeholders.

BENEFITS OF BUSINESS ETHICS

Benefits provided to different sections of society are as follows:

1. **Customers:** Malpractices like hoarding and black-marketing are minimised by adhering to formal code of business ethics, customers get good products at the right time, right place and right price.
2. **Employees:** Employees get fair wages, job security, better working conditions, etc. They can force the business enterprise to implement formal code of ethics.
3. **Management:** Management develops a friendly and healthy environment in the business and subordinates contribute efficiently to organisational goals considering individual goals subordinate to organisational goals.
4. **Industry:** The formal code of ethics provides healthy competition and protection of each other's interests through fair trade practices.
5. **Society:** Business being a product of society satisfies the needs of society. Social acceptance justifies the existence of a business.

CASE STUDY - 1

GE'S CONTRIBUTIONS TO MANAGEMENT

In 1878. Thomas Edison founded General Electric (GE) as a private stock company. He used the company as a way to raise funds for his research into electric light. By 1879, he had created the first incandescent light. In that same year, GE developed the first machine capable of turning mechanical energy into enough electric energy to power a neighbourhood of electric lights. Beginning with those innovations, GE became a company known for the quality of both its ideas and its implementation skills. Over the last 128 years, GE has produced innovative yet practical technologies, including the first electric-powered X-ray machine and television. The company was instrumental in developing a wide range of machines, from radios to locomotives, home appliances to radar systems. Medicine, manufacturing, and defense benefited from GE's inventions, as did households.

Yet these astonishing inventions are matched by GE's inventiveness in another arena—management. From its earliest days, GE has been a leader in developing new management techniques and practices. Many of these have been duplicated by other firms, but rarely does a firm surpass GE's skill in implementaion or beat it to a new development.

GE's first management innovation was a corporate research and development lab, established in 1900. By the 1930s, the company was the first to offer pension and profit sharing plans. These were used to establish cooperative relations with labour, excluding unions from the relationship. The company centralized decision making throughout its national operations in the 1950s, producing the unique "Blue Books" that governed managers' every move.

Strategic management was pioneered at GE in the 1960s and proved so popular that today the field is often the capstone course of an undergraduate degree in business. During this time, the company lent its name to the GE Business Screen, a technique developed jointly with consulting firm McKinsey. The Screen helped to identify the optimal portfolio of business units that can be held by a corporation. By the 1980s and 1990s, the company was building an effective global culture while being the first to offer programs such as Six Sigma quality initiatives and Work Out, a reengineering effort that simplified work and empowered employees.

There are other contributions from GE, in addition to its product and management innovations. They are able to change course frequently, abandoning whole programs. "Most people inside GE learn from the past but have a healthy disrespect for history", says CEO Jeff Immelt. "They have an ability to live in the moment and not be burdened by the past."

GE has also worked hard to develop leaders. One of its most controversial policies calls for the company to fire the lowest-performing 10 per cent of workers each year. While some have called this policy inhumane, the remaining employees represent the best, and they are motivated to exceed their strategic targets. Yet its training programs have produced many prominent alumni. CEOs who once were part of GE include Kevin Sharer of Amgen, Chris Kearney of SPX, Steven Bennet of Intuit, Larry Bossidy of Honeywell, and Larry Johnston of Albertson's.

GE doesn't have the fastest growth, most market value, highest profits, or largest size. Yet it's consistently ranked as one of the best firms. GE is the most admired firm in the world, according to 2006 surveys of business managers conducted by *Fortune, Barron's,* and the *Financial Times* of London. The firm has won that honor for 6 of the last 10 years. GE is the only one of the original Dow Jones Industrial Average 12, the dozen firms that made up the first DJIA in 1896, to remain on the list. The others have been acquired or gone out of business.

GE's important contributions to management are widely acknowledged. Many have been copied or used by other organisations. Dell Computer, for example, sends about 15 leaders through GE training programs each year. Larry Johnston, head of Albertson's, admires the firm's human resources skills the most. He says, "No one has better people. No one else's bench strength comes even close. It's that obsession with people that requires all GE leaders to spend a huge amount of time on human resources processes .... When you have the very best people, you don't have to worry as much about execution, because they make it happen." Others agree, "GE is the best school of management in the world bar none," is high praise from Dr. Clay Christensen, a management professor at Harvard Business School. The GE school has been teaching and leading businesses for over a century and will likely continue for the next 100 years.

QUESTIONS

1. Do the various management developments at GE over the last century seem to follow the same pattern as the development of management theory, described in your text ? Explain your answer.
2. Which of GE's management innovations seem to draw on classical management perspective ? Which seem to draw on a behavioural management perspective ? Explain.
3. How does the contingency perspective explain the management changes that GE has made over the years ?

REVIEW QUESTIONS

1. Explain the need for business ethics ?
2. Briefly explain the principles of business ethics.
3. Why should the business pursue ethics ?
4. Account for the growing concern for social responsibility of business.
5. Describe social responsibilities of business towards owners, employees and customers.
6. Explain the case for and against social responsibility of business.
7. Discuss the concept of social audit.
8. Explain in brief the scope of social responsibility of business.
9. Explain the meaning, nature and scope of social responsibility.
10. What is management ethics ? Explain the various factors that govern management ethics.

5

CHAPTER

Coordination

- Introduction
- Meaning
- Definitions
- Nature of Coordination
- Coordination and Cooperation
- Coordination Vs Cooperation
- Coordination Vs Control
- Coordination-Essence of Management
- Need for Coordination
- Principles of Coordination
- Problems in Coordination
- Steps to achieve Coordination
- Types of Coordination
- Vertical Vs Horizontal Coordination
- Techniques of Coordination
- Case Study - 1
- Review Questions.

INTRODUCTION

A modern business organisation is based on principles like division of work, departmentation, centralisation, decentralisation, delegation of authority, etc.

Different departments, divisions, branches and sections function to achieve the common objectives of the organization. In all these places, different persons work in different capacities. Under this complex structure and multidimensional system of an organisation, there is a vital need for maximum cooperation with minimum conflict, confusion and contradiction. Coordination is an important process of blending together all such functions. It is also considered the essence of management, as every managerial task is in practice an exercise in coordination.

Once the activities of the organisation are broken into smaller units which are re-grouped into departments, it becomes necessary for managers to coordinate the activities of these departments by communicating the organisational goals to each department, setting departmental goals and linking the performance of each department with that of others so that all the departments collectively contribute towards the organisation goals. Coordination is that, "the process of linking the activities of various departments of the organisation."

Mere application of the principle of specialisation does not enable an organisation to attain the desired results. With jobs specialised and divided among units, coordination becomes necessary. Coordination is the management inter dependence in work situations. It is the orderly– synchronisation or fitting together interdependent efforts of individuals, in order to attain a common goal. For instance, in a hospital, the activities of doctors, nurses, attendants, technicians must be properly synchronised if the patient is to receive good care.

MEANING

The term coordination may be defined as the process of bringing about unity and harmony in the functioning of all departments or divisions involved in organisation. Thus coordination is conscious and rational managerial function of pulling together various components of organised activity and weaving them into a unified and integrated whole for achieving pre-determined goals. Coordination is the process of integrating objectivities and activities of separate work units or functional departments in order to realise organisational goals. The process of coordination is inevitable and imperative, a group efforts as common goals can be achieved only by integrating, unifying and coordinating efforts made by various members.

DEFINITIONS

"Coordination deals with the task of blending efforts in order to ensure the successful attainment of an objective. It is accomplished by means of planning, organising, actuating and controlling." — G.R. Terry

"Coordination is balancing and keeping the teams together by ensuring a suitable allocation of working activities to the various members and seeing that these are performed with due harmony among the members themselves." — E.F.L. Breach

"Coordination is the efforts to ensure the smooth interplay of the functions and forces of all the different components and parts or organisation to the end that its purpose will be realised with a minimum of function and maximum of collaborativc effectiveness." — Ordway Tead

"It seems more accurate to regard coordination as the essence of managership for achievement of harmony of individual efforts towards the accomplishment of group goals as the purpose of management. Each of the managerial functions is an exercise in coordination." — Koontz and O' Donnell

"Coordination is the process whereby an executive develops in an orderly pattern an integrated, orderly, and synchronized pattern of group effort among his subordinates and tries to attain unity of effort in the pursuit of any common goal." — Mc Farland

NATURE OF COORDINATION

Coordination has the following features:

1. Continuous Process

Managers in every organization must perform this activity of coordination in the beginning, in the process and at the end regularly for all types of organizational activities. As it is a continuous process, it accomplishes unity of objective.

2. Group Effort

Coordination involves all such efforts which are involved in the harmonious blending of the different parts of an organization. Such an orderly arrangement should result in minimizing of conflict, confusion and friction and maximising collective effectiveness. Coordination helps in proper timing, balancing and integrating the different activities of an organization.

3. Dynamic Process

Coordination integrates and synthesises the efforts of people of all departments at all levels towards achievement of common organisational goals. It provides a positive and dynamic element to the entire organization and smoothens the process of administration.

4. Managerial Responsibility

Coordination is the responsibility of every manager at every level for every operative functions. All managers continuously coordinate the efforts of people working in their respective departments.

5. Unity of Action

Every individual and department has his own perspective or way of achieving the organisational goals. Coordination ensure unity of action amongst individual and departmental activities.

6. Unity of Objectives

The very purpose of coordination is to accomplish the objectives of the organisation. So, all the efforts of different groups should be directed towards the accomplishment of the common objectives.

7. Essence of Management

Coordination is not a separate function of management. It is required for every managerial function. Managers coordinate the human and non-human resources while carrying out all the managerial functions of planning, organising, staffing, directing and controlling. Coordination is, thus, called the "essence of management".

8. Deliberate Effort

Coordination is not spontaneous effort of managers. Managers make deliberate efforts to coordinate their inter-departmental activities. No manager can evade or avoid this responsibility.

COORDINATION AND COOPERATION

Cooperation refers to the collective efforts of people who associate voluntarily to achieve specified objectives. It indicates merely the willingness of individuals to help each other. It is the result of a voluntary attitude of a group of people. Coordination is much more inclusive, requiring more than the desire and willingness to cooperate the participants. It involves a deliberate and conscious effort to bring together the activities of various individuals in order to provide unity of action. It requires concurrence of purpose, harmony of effort and concerted action.

COORDINATION Vs COOPERATION

The main points of difference between coordination and cooperation are given below:

1. Coordination is a deliberate effort by the management for the achievement of certain goals. Cooperation denotes the collective efforts by the people working on the organisation voluntarily to accomplish a particular purpose.
2. Coordination is broader in scope than cooperation. It includes both cooperation and deliberate efforts to maintain unity of action and purpose.
3. Coordination of all interdependent activities is utmost necessary. But cooperation does not arise out of any limitations of organisation structure.
4. Effective coordination cannot be achieved without the actual cooperation of the groups members. Coordination without cooperation and cooperation without coordination are fatal to the enterprise. As a matter of fact, cooperation without coordination has no fruit and coordination without cooperation has no root. Therefore, every manager should try to achieve both simultaneously.
5. The basic objective of coordination is the synchronisation of efforts of individuals in a work group so that no effort goes in waste.

The basic objective of cooperation is to protect the interest of members of a cooperative group specially from the threats presented by conflicting groups.

COORDINATION Vs CONTROL

Control is one of the elements of the management process. Coordination is the essence of management itself and is an all-inclusive function. Similar to other managerial functions, control is an exercise in coordination. Both coordination and control are required in every organisation. Control is needed to maintain order and consistency in the behaviour of people and events. Coordination required to unify the differentiated activities and to integrate the diverse goals, interests and roles.

The points of distinction between the two are given below:

1. The focus of control is on regulation whereas coordination focuses on harmony.
2. Control is mainly a unitary function involving the regulation of activities in individual units to create a match between planned and actual results.

   On the other hand, coordination is a system function concerned with unification of two or more diverse or differentiated activities across functional units.
3. Control faces resistance and even hostility because it is associated with coercion and restriction. On the other hand, coordination is associated with positive and constructive efforts.

COORDINATION - ESSENCE OF MANAGEMENT

Coordination harmonise all the activities of a business in order to facilitate its successful functioning. Coordination is inherent in all managerial functions. Each of the managerial function is an exercise in coordination. According to George Terry, "It is erroneous to believe that coordination is fundamental function of management. Coordination is accomplished by means of planning, organising, actuating and controlling." Failure to perform any of the above functions efficiently shall be reflected in poor coordination. Management integrate objectives of the organisation with the objectives and activities of departments through coordination, in order to harmonise departmental goals with organisational goals. Coordination, thus, helps to coordinate the work of different departments and within each department, it integrates the functions of management. *Coordination is, therefore, rightly called the essence of management.* It helps each managerial function and each departmental activity contribute to overall organisational goals. This relationship between managerial functions and coordination is as under:

1. Coordination while Planning

A manager can create coordination through planning by integrating the plans of different departments. When plans are prepared with the mutual consultation and participation of all people involved in the plans, efforts of various managers are synchronised.

2. Coordination while Organising

While assigning duties and delegating authority among subordinates, the thought of coordination must be upper-most in the mind of a manager. If the activities are divided haphazardly without coordination, some activities may not be assigned to individuals and some may be assigned to more than one individual.

3. Coordination while Staffing

The jobs having been created, managers ensure that individuals are placed on different jobs according to their skills and capabilities. This ensures placing the right person at the right job in order to achieve coordination amongst their work activities. Management must bear coordination in mind while performing recruitment, selection, training, promotion and appraisal functions.

4. Coordination while Directing

Efficient direction is an important means of coordination. Continuous flow of communication creates mutual cooperation and coordination. When a manager directs his subordinates through motivation, leadership and communication, he coordinates the various organisational activities.

5. Coordination while Controlling

Frequent evaluation of performance is helpful in synchronising efforts of the subordinates. Corrective action brings about harmony between plan and performance. The very nature of the controlling function is designed to bring about coordination.

Thus it will be fair to consider coordination as essence of management as every function of management is an exercise in coordination and not as separate function of management.

NEED FOR COORDINATION

When a number of people are working to carry out a task, coordination is the only method of synchronisation. It is an important method by which a manager can avoid potential sources of conflict among members. The factors which contribute to the increasing complexity of coordination may be briefly listed below:

1. Economy and Efficiency

Coordination makes it possible to achieve economy and efficiency in operations. The economy is achieved through avoiding duplication of efforts and efficiency by proper correlation of activities.

2. Specialisation

Specialisation leads to concentration on very narrow areas of job activity. Individuals tend to overlook perspective of the job. This requires coordination to direct all the activities towards a common goal.

3. Good personnel relations

Coordination is achieved through systematic efforts. Good coordination gives job satisfaction to the employees which keeps their morale high. Moreover, there are good human relations because the authority-responsibility relationships are clear.

4. Complex Nature of Organisation

Modern business enterprises being large and complex in nature, involve greater degree of specialisation and division of labour and employ a large number of individuals. This requires coordination as a means of synchronising the efforts of individual members towards the accomplishment of organisational goals.

5. Dynamic Activities

Coordination helps in integrating activities which constantly change according to changes in the environment.

6. Team Work

The skills and efforts of various employees are to be integrated to achieve the objectives of the organisation. In the absence of coordination, the group efforts may be diversed and fail to achieve the objectives. Coordination eliminates the duplication of work which leads to economic and efficient management.

7. Unity in Diversity

Effective coordination is the essence of management. There are large number of employees and each has different ideas, views or opinions, activities and background in a large organisation. There is a diversified activity in a big business organisation where these activities will be inefficient in the absence of coordination. Therefore, coordination is essential.

8. Human Relations

Coordination helps to improve team spirit and morale of employees. In a well-coordinated organisation, organisational goals and personal goals of people are reconciled. Thus employees derive a sense of security and job satisfaction.

9. Key to other Functions

The importance of coordination largely lies in the fact that it is the key to other functions of management such as planning, organising, control, etc. Coordination makes planning more purposeful, organisation more well knit and control more regulative.

10. Retention of Good Personnel

If job satisfaction is present, executives will tend to remain longer with the company. They feel that they have a place in the organisation. They cannot afford to remain long under the confusing condition of poor coordination.

PRINCIPLES OF COORDINATION

Principles refer to fundamental truths on which an action is based. Mary Parker Follet has pointed out important essentials and principles which may be considered as a base for effective coordination. In order to achieve coordination, managers follow the following principles of coordination.

1. Direct Contact

Direct or personal contact between managers and subordinates can achieve better coordination than indirect or impersonal contact. This relationship can communicate with each other, can exchange their views and can develop mutual understanding among themselves regarding various problems and matters.

2. Continuity

Coordination should be a continuous process starting with planning and running through the managerial processes. It is something which must go on at all the time. It should be viewed as a never-ending process and every manager should strive for it constantly.

3. Reciprocity

This principle states that all factors in a given situation are interdependent and interrelated. For example, in a group, every person influences all others and is in turn influenced by others.

When people appreciate the reciprocity of relations, they avoid unilateral action and coordination becomes easier.

4. Dynamism

Principle of dynamism states that coordination does not work on the basis of rigid and fixed basis but a dynamic basis. Dynamism is required because changes occur in external factors which necessitate changes in the organisation and its processes including coordination.

5. Early Beginning

Coordination can be achieved more easily in the early stages of planning and policy-making. It becomes difficult to secure coordination at the execution stage. Therefore, coordination should start at the stage of planning.

6. Unity of Command

Unity of command means one boss for one subordinate. It will be difficult to achieve coordination if one individual has to report to more than one boss. Unity of command, thus, helps in coordinating the activities of individuals and departments.

7. Effective Communication

Effective communication is the key to proper coordination. The channels of communication used in the enterprise should be reliable so that they are able to create proper understanding in the mind of the receiver. Personal contacts should be encouraged as it is the most effective means of communication for achieving coordination.

8. Authority and Responsibility

There is a line of authority in every enterprise which indicates as to who is accountable to whom. This line of authority and responsibility should be clearly defined to achieve coordination. Clear-cut authority relationships help in reducing conflicts among different positions, particularly line and staff which is essential for sound coordination.

9. Well-defined Work Procedures

Well defined work procedures facilitate procedural coordination. When the work procedures are well defined and adhered properly, this will help to achieve coordination easily. Well established and designed work procedures are more important in those activities which have impact on other activities in the organisation which will enable them to achieve coordination.

10. Organisation Structure

Well designed and simplified organisation structure of business facilitates effective coordination. It has been suggested that design of organisation structure should be based on the principle of coordination.

PROBLEMS IN COORDINATION

The following are the difficulties for coordination:

1. Strategy and Objectives

An organisation can achieve and attain coordination with the help of well planned and designed corporate objectives and strategy of business. If the organisation do not have well developed corporate strategy and objectives which may lead to problem of coordination in business functions.

2. Inadequate Administrative Personnel

If the administrative talents are not professional and not having adequate knowledge, then they may not have the efficiency in coordinating various activities of business.

3. Increase in Size

Need for coordination arises as soon as the operations become multiple and complex. In a large organisation, a large number of individuals are employed. Personal contact is not possible and formal methods of coordination become essential.

4. Lack of Skill

Even in certain situations, where work flows smoothly, coordination becomes a problem if managers do not have the knowledge, skill and competence to coordinate.

5. Uncertainties about Future

Changes in environmental factors can make coordination difficult. Internal uncertainties like strikes, lock-outs, etc. make coordination difficult.

6. Different approach towards the same problem

If different departments look at the same problem in different ways, there will be problem of coordinating their activities. For instance, A company wants to increase its profits. There, the approaches by production department, sales department or finance department go for different techniques, for the same purpose. So, it is difficult to coordinate the conflicting opinions.

7. Personal Revalries

Personality clashes are quite common in modern organisations. Members from rival groups try to settle personal scores in organisational activities. Such revalry is disastrous to team work.

8. Different Outlook

Every individual in the organisation has his own way of working and approach towards problems. Capacity, talent and speed of people differ widely. It becomes imperative to reconcile differences in approach, timing and effort to secure unity of action.

STEPS TO ACHIEVE COORDINATION

The following steps should be taken for achieving effective coordination:

1. Clearly defined goals;
2. Well defined authority;
3. Effective Communication;
4. Cooperation;
5. Sound Planning;
6. Simplified Organisation;
7. Effective Leadership;
8. Precise Policies;
9. Chain of Command;
10. Indoctrination.

TYPES OF COORDINATION

Coordination may be divided on different bases, viz. scope and flow. On the basis of scope or coverage, coordination can be internal or external while on the basis of flow, coordination can be classified into vertical and horizontal. Coordination may also be procedural and substantive.

1. Internal Coordination

Coordination between the activities of departments and people working within the organisation is known as internal coordination. Internal coordination exists between:

(*a*) Different groups of employees of the same section or department;

(*b*) Managers and workers at different levels.

(*c*) Board of Directors and departmental managers;

(*d*) Different departments, branches, etc.

2. External Coordination

External coordination refers to coordination between an organisation and its external environment comprising Government, community, customers, investors suppliers, etc.

VERTICAL AND HORIZONTAL COORDINATION

Vertical coordination is what exists within a department where the departmental head is called upon to coordinate the activities of all those placed below him. On the other hand, horizontal coordination takes place sideways. It exists between different departments such as production, sales, purchasing, finance, etc.

Difference between Vertical and Horizontal

Vertical coordination is secured through delegation of authority and with the help of directing and controlling. There is no doubt that the power or delegated authority will carry great weight but vertical coordination cannot be achieved by the mere weight authority itself. This should rather come about as a by-product of the superiors efficient and expert performance of his managerial functions.

The term 'horizontal coordination' is used when coordination has to be achieved between departments on the same level in the managerial hierarchy. Thus, when coordination is brought about between production department, sales department, personnel department, etc., it is said to be horizontal coordination.

TECHNIQUES OF COORDINATION

The following are the important techniques of coordination which are widely used by modern management:

1. Rules and procedures of an organisation must provide an effective way of achieving coordination.
2. Remember, "Cooperation is a way of achieving coordination."
3. The management must ensure that all plans add up to the unified programme.
4. Communication of information is necessary both for making adjustments in plans and preparing programmes for future.
5. Group meetings are effective for achieving a high quality of coordination.
6. "Ideal coordination is voluntary coordination."
7. When one knows his position, the position of his boss and subordinates, in the organisation, it facilitates coordination.
8. Well defined plans and goals help to achieve coordination.
9. Free flow of information facilitate coordination.
10. Committees are to be formed to solve specific organisational problems.
11. Clear leadership communication among members facilitate effective coordination.
12. A coordination cell may be created along with a special coordinator.
13. Standing plans may be used for solving the routine and repetitive problems.
14. The need for coordination gets reduced if a unit is independent.
15. Coordination among interdependent units can be secured by putting them under one boss.

CASE STUDY - 1

Radiant Industries Ltd.

The workers of Radiant Industries Ltd. were not satisfied with their job conditions as a result of which their morale went down. To overcome this problem, the managing director reorganised the company and allowed the workers to take decisions and undertake activities which were earlier decided by managers, like deciding about pay structure of their fellow workers, making job assignments, deciding about promotions, transfers, etc. Workers were divided into work teams and each team member took decisions regarding production schedules, quality control, maintenance, etc. This reduced the need for managers and the span of management, thus, rose.

These changes reduced operating costs and rate of labour turnover and absenteeism. Workers' morale went up and they enjoyed their work and work place. After some time, problems began to crop up. Managers started feeling that their authority was being challenged and their importance reduced. Competition amongst work teams also increased. Workers and team leaders found it difficult to set standards of performance and financial incentives for their co-workers. This resulted in problem of coordination. The MD thought of redesigning the system and increasing the number of management levels by reducing the span of management.

QUESTIONS

1. Analyse the case.
2. What were the problems of coordination in the company ?
3. What steps do you suggest for improving coordination ?

REVIEW QUESTIONS

1. "Coordination is the essence of management". Discuss
2. How do you achieve effective coordination in an organisation ? Mention the steps.
3. Define coordination and explain the difference between coordination and cooperation.
4. Describe the need for coordination.
5. Explain the importance of coordination in modern management. Discuss the techniques of coordination.
6. "Coordination and communication are the sine-qua-non of management". Comment.
7. Discuss the need and importance of coordination. Why is it considered the essence of management ?
8. State the principles of coordination. Explain the steps to achieve effective coordination in an organisation.
9. Differentiate between cooperation and coordination.
10. Outline the principles and essentials of coordination.
11. Explain the techniques of coordination.
12. Narrate the problems of coordination.

Nature and Process of Planning

6
CHAPTER

INTRODUCTION

Primary function of a manager is planning. To get things done by others every manager has to plan. Planning is a basic requirement and important input of management process. Planning is traditionally considered to be a major function of management. Simply put, planning is identifying where you want to go, why you want to go there, how you will get there, what you need in order to get there and how you will know if you are there or not.

Planning is the essence of the management process and has been attracting the attention of management thinkers. Today, it is considered as a strategic area of management, especially in the context of the rapidly changing environment and globalisation of business operations. It precedes all managerial function and is closely related to controlling. It is required for all organisations - business and non-business and for every level of business organisation. It is done for all sizes of organisations: small , medium and large. Every individual and business firm plans the line of actions to be followed in future. Action follows planning and there is nothing to do unless the objectives and the ways of achieving them are decided. Planning is in fact a prerequisite to effective management.

MEANING

Planning is a managerial function that deals with framing organisational objectives and devising ways to achieve them. Managers plan business activities at all levels: top, middle and low, though more planning is required at top levels than lower levels. Planning is the management function of anticipating the future and the conscious determination of a future course of action to achieve the desired results. A plan is a blueprint of the course of action to be followed in future. Planning involves forecasting because in order to plan the future course of action, it is essential to anticipate the future. While planning, a manager prepares a map of the future, sets the goals to be achieved or the results and decides the activities required to accomplish those results.

DEFINITIONS OF PLANNING

Planning is a mental exercise that requires imagination, foresight and sound judgement. It is thinking before doing. Planning involves forecasting, laying down objectives of the firm, thinking of different course of action and deciding one of those to achieve the goals. Planning, thus, involves decision-making, that is, deciding a course of action for framing and achieving objectives. Definitions of planning given by some famous management thinkers are given below:

"Planning is deciding in advance what is to be done. When a manager plans, he projects a course of action for the future, attempting to achieve a consistent, coordinated structure of operations aimed at the desired results." — Theo Haimann

"Planning is fundamentally a mental predisposition to do things in an orderly way, to think before and to act in the light of the fact rather than of guesses." — L.F. Urwick

"The plan of action is, at one and the same time the result envisaged, the line of action to be followed, the stages to go through and the methods to use." — Henri Fayol

"Planning is deciding in advance what to do, how to do it, where to do it and who is to do it. Planning bridges the gap from where we want to go. It makes it possible for things to occur while would not otherwise happen." — Koontz and O'Donnell

"Planning as the continuous process of making present entrepreneurial (risk taking) decisions systematically and with best possible knowledge of their futurity, organising systematically the efforts needed to carry out these decisions and measuring the results of these decisions against the expectations through organised, systematic feedback." — Peter F. Drucker.

FEATURES OF PLANNING

Planning is characterised by the following features:

1. Planning is a Primary Function

Planning is the first function of management. Planning provides the basis for efficient organising, staffing, directing and controlling. Planning is flexible and continuous process, because one never knows exactly what the future holds, plans generally do not work-out precisely as expected. Planning precedes the execution of all other functions. Without planning there is nothing to organise, no one to actuate and no need to control. Therefore planning is the most basic function.

2. Planning is Goal Oriented

Planning seeks to achieve certain objectives and all plans are linked with the goals of the organisation. Planning has no meaning unless it contributes in some positive way to the achievement of desired goals. Planning identifies the actions that would lead to the desired results quickly. Thus planning is purposeful and goal oriented.

3. Planning is Future Oriented

No plan can be prepared without the knowledge of future events. Planning is an attempt to see through the uncertain future. The planning process calls for visualising the future with the help of analysis of past performance, and evaluation of present position. Futurism has become an integral part of planning. They anticipate future and incorporate changes in their activities to achieve organisational goals effectively.

4. Planning is Pervasive

Planning is a pervasive function. It is done for all organisations - business and non-business, profitable and non-profitable, small and big. In a business organisation, it is done at each level: top, middle and low. Managers at the top prepare long-term plans for the company as a whole, middle level managers formulate departmental and functional plans for medium term and at the lowest level, managers prepare operating and short-term plans.

5. Planning is an Intellectual Process

Planning is a mental process involving imagination, foresight and sound judgement. It is not guesswork or wishful thinking. It requires a mental disposition of thinking before doing and acting in the light of facts, rather than guesses. Managers should have judgement, intuition, foresightedness, imagination, etc. to make good plans. Thus, planning cannot be done in dark. It is an intellectual process.

6. Planning is a Continuous Process

Planning is a flexible and continuous process, because one never knows exactly what the future holds, plans generally do not work out precisely as expected. As is often said in this connection: *It is a bad plan that admits of no modification.* Planning involves a choice among alternative course of action. Actually, decision making is at the core of planning.

7. Planning Involves Choice

Planning involves decision making. Choosing goals out of multiple goals, deciding about ways to achieve them out of a number of alternatives, deciding about sources from where funds will be raised, etc. are some of the choices that managers have to make. Planning continuously involves decision-making. In fact, the process of decision-making starts much before the process of planning. There is no need for planning if there is only one way of doing something. Plans are decisions made after evaluation of alternative courses of action.

8. Feedback

Planning is closely related to control. It specifies future actions and control ensures those actions are carried out. Planning frames organisational goals and control ensures those goals are achieved. Controlling function provides constant feedback to managers about the efficiency of plans. Deviations in actual performance against planned performance helps managers in reviewing or abandoning plans to make fresh plans.

IMPORTANCE OF PLANNING

Planning is important because it enables the organisation to survive and grow in the dynamic and changing environment. It is important because of the following reasons:

1. Minimises Risks and Uncertainty

Business enterprises operate in an uncertain environment. Planning enables these enterprises to predict future events and prepare to face the unexpected events with the help of planning. Managers can identify potential dangers and take steps to over-come them. By providing a more rational, fact-based procedure for making decisions, planning allows managers and organisation to minimise risk and uncertainty.

2. Making Objectives Clear

The first element of planning is setting the goals and objectives for the organisation as a whole and all its components. This gives a sense of direction to the working of the organisation. As efforts are directed towards desired and well defined objectives, haphazard approaches are minimised, efforts are co-oriented and duplications are avoided.

3. Focuses Attention on Organisation's Goals

Planning helps the manager to focus attention on the organisation's goals and activities. This makes it easier to apply and coordinate the resources of the organisation more economically. The whole organisation is forced to embrace identical goals and collaborate in achieving them.

4. Guides Decision Making

Planning helps the organisation to keep on the right path. Employees understand how their action relate to organisational goals. Planning avoids aimless and ad-hoc action. It also avoids the need for snap decisions based in impulse and intuition.

5. Improving Efficiency of Operations

Planning facilitates optimum utilisation of available resources. It makes possible for things to occur which would not otherwise happen. It improves the competitive strength of an organisation by helping it to discover and exploit opportunities. As a rational solution to problems, planning results in the use of most efficient methods of work.

6. Facilitates Control

In planning, the manager sets goals and develops plans to accomplish these goals. These goals and plans then become standards or benchmarks against which performance can be measured. The function of control is to ensure that the activities conform to the plans. Thus, controls can be exercised only if there are plans.

7. Effective Coordination

Organisation is a structure of relationships where each person's authority and responsibility is clearly defined. Planning coordinates the functions performed by individual human beings and departments and unites them into a single goal - the organisation goal. It unifies inter-departmental activities so that all departments work according to plans.

8. Helps to Achieve Right Path

Planning is necessary for avoiding "hit or miss" actions or random decisions. Without planning, there will be confusion and chaos. Everyone in the enterprise is aware of what is to be done for achieving the goals of an enterprise, if plans are made in advance.

9. Moral Boost

If organisational plans succeed and goals are achieved, managers and employees feel satisfied and morally boost up to further concentrate on organisational activities. Successful planning, thus, promotes success of the organisation.

10. Proper Utilisation of Resources

Planning involves the development of one best way of doing things which is economical. Planning is the way to realise the business objectives in the cheapest and the best way. It paves the way for proper utilisation of company resources.

11. Provides sense of Direction

Planning saves an organisation from avoiding aimless activities. It directs human efforts into endeavours that contribute to the accomplishment of goals. "If you don't know where you are going, any road will get you there". Planning makes work more meaningful and activities more orderly. It bridges the gap between where we are and where we want to go. Without planning action is likely to become random activity, producing nothing but chaos.

STRENGTHS

1. It provides a coordinated effort by reducing risks.
2. Proper planning gives quick decisions.
3. It helps to implement future programmes.
4. Planning suggests new methodology.
5. It provides economies in operations.
6. It reduces wastage of resources.
7. It facilitates budgeting and budgetary controls.
8. It provides team spirit.
9. It facilitates smooth working.
10. It helps in proper control.
11. It enables an enterprise to be competent.
12. It eliminates possibility of mistakes.
13. It helps to discover alternative courses.
14. It enables adjustments to future changes.
15. Its main object is for better results.

LIMITATIONS

1. Planning is expensive.
2. It is time-consuming.
3. It delays in the process of decision-making.
4. It gives only approximate results.
5. It is based on assumptions.
6. It cannot predict the future accurately.
7. Planning is affected by external limitations.

8. Inaccuracy in planning invites wrong results.
9. Planning restricts individual freedom.
10. Longer the period of forecast, lesser will be the accuracy of planning.

PRINCIPLES OF PLANNING

The important principles of planning are illustrated below:

1. Principle of Primacy of Planning

Planning is considered as the first and the foremost function to be performed in the process of management. It is followed by other managerial functions like organising, staffing, directing and controlling.

2. Principle of Contribution to Objectives

Plans must be directed towards organisational objectives. that is, every plan and its components should help in the achievement of organisational objectives.

3. Principles of Planning premises

To develop consistent and coordinated plans, it is essential that planning be based upon carefully considered assumptions and predictions, known as planning premises.

4. Principle of Efficiency of Operation

Plans must be efficient in their contribution to objectives, that is, returns must exceed their costs.

5. Principle of Limiting Factor

While choosing from among alternatives, the planner should focus on those factor which are critical to the attainment of the desired goal. This will help in selecting the most favourable alternative.

6. Principle of Commitment

Planning should cover a period of time which can be forecasted. This principle is used for determining the length of the planning period, taking into account the future risk and fulfilment of commitments.

7. Principle of Revision

Every plan has to be executed, and in the process of execution, managers should check periodically the events and decisions, and if there is any necessity to redraw or readjust their plan to achieve the organisation objectives: they should make provision for such changes.

8. Principle of Flexibility

Every plan should be made in such a way that it adjusts and adapts itself to changed circumstances. There must be a high degree of flexibility in every good plan.

9. Principle of Navigational Change

Managers should review events and expectations on a regular basis and redraw the plan to maintain the course towards desired results. A navigational change can be brought about, if plans have an inbuilt flexibility.

10. Principle of Alternatives

In choosing from among alternatives, the best alternative will be that which contributes most efficiently and effectively to the accomplishment of a desired goal.

FEATURES OF A GOOD PLAN

The following *features* are essential for a *good plan;*

1. It should be clear, specific and logical.
2. It should be capable of being controlled.
3. It should be possible for implementation.
4. It should be reasonable.
5. It should be followed for considerable period of time.
6. It should be based on clearly defined objectives.
7. It must be simple and easily understandable.
8. It should be flexible to changing conditions.
9. It must be balanced in all respects and should be reasonably comprehensive.
10. It must provide standard for the evaluation of action.
11. It should be economical.
12. It should be practicable and unambiguous.
13. It should provide for proper analysis and classification of actions.
14. Different plans must be properly integrated and harmonised with one another.
15. It should be prepared with the consultation of concerned persons.

TYPES OF PLANNING

Planning is the function of management setting objectives and determining a course of action for achieving these objectives. Planning requires that managers be aware of environmental conditions facing their organisation and forecast future conditions. It also requires that managers be good decision-makers.

On the basis of time, planning may be of three types:

(*a*) Long Range Planning

(*b*) Medium Range Planning

(*c*) Short Range Planning

(*a*) Long Range Planning

It sets long-term goals of the enterprise and formulates specific plans for attaining these goals. It involves an attempt to anticipate, analyse and make decisions about basic problems which have significant effects beyond the present operating horizon of the enterprise.

(*b*) Medium Range Planning

It covers a period of over one year but less than five years. The length of period should not be taken to be rigid or inflexible. It may vary from one business to another depending upon the nature of business, risks and uncertainties, Government control, etc.

(*c*) Short Range Planning

Such planning covers a short period usually one year. It deals with specific activities to be undertaken to accomplish the objectives laid down under long-range planning. It relates to current functions and their sub-functions, for examples, work methods, employee-training, etc.

On the basis of scope, planning may be of three types:

(*a*) Corporate (organisation) Planning

(*b*) Operational (Tactical) Planning

(*c*) Departmental (Unit) Planning

(*a*) Corporate (organisation) Planning

Corporate planning or organisation planning is concerned with the organisation as a whole. It is usually for long term and is done by the top level of management. It is a process of determining overall objectives and discovering courses of actions for achieving them. It is broad and general in nature and scope. It lays down basic objectives, strategy, and policies to be pursued by managers for the whole organisation.

(*b*) Operational (Tactical) Planning

Operational planning involves conversion of corporate plans into detailed and specific ones, dealing with various activities. An individual activity generally does not take a long time. Operational plan is prepared for a short period, for less than a year and is known as *tactical or action plans* because it divides corporate, strategic and long-term planning into various sub-plans and programmes.

(*c*) Departmental (Unit) Planning

It involves development of specific plans for each department or a division so as to accomplish the divisional plans. The focus here is on day-to-day actions of work units and on meeting planned schedules and budgets.

THE PROBLEM - FINDING PROCESS

William Pounds has argued that the problem-finding process is often informal and intuitive. Four situations usually alert managers to possible problems.

1. **A deviation from past experience** means that a previous pattern of performance in the organisation has been broken. For instance, this year's sales are falling behind last year's; expenses have suddenly increased; employee turnover has risen. Events such as these are signals to the manager that a problem has developed.
2. **A deviation from a set plan** means the manager's projections or expectations are not being met. Profit levels are lower than anticipated; a department is exceeding its budget; a project is off schedule. Such events tell the manager that something must be done to get the plan back on course.
3. **Other people** often bring problems to the manager. Customers complain about late deliveries; higher-level managers set new performance standards for the manager's department; employees resign. Many decisions that managers make daily involve problems presented by others.
4. **The performance of competitors** can also create problem-solving situations. When other companies develop new processes or improvements in operating procedures, the manager may have to re-evaluate processes or procedures in his own organisation.

STEPS IN THE PROCESS OF PLANNING

There is no standard planning process. The steps generally involved in planning are as follows:

1. Analysing the Environment

The first step in planning process is the awareness of business opportunities and the need for taking action. Analysis of external environment will help to identify the opportunities and constraints for the enterprise. To be effective, planning must enable the organisation to adapt itself to the environmental changes, for example, market conditions, Government policies, technological developments, etc. Therefore, managers must carefully analyse and interpret the complex environmental forces. Managers have to understand external environment relating to competition, customers' requirements, wants, strengths, weaknesses, etc. Before venturing into new areas, the pros and cons of such projects should be evaluated. A beginning should be made only after going through a detailed analysis of the new opportunity.

2. Establishing Objectives

Plans are formulated to achieve certain objectives. Therefore, establishment of organisational objectives is an important step in planning. The organisational objectives should be established in the light of perceived opportunities and resources of the organisation. Need for planning arises either for solving a problem or for exploiting an opportunity that may arise in the future. Therefore, the problem to be solved or the opportunity to be utilised should be clearly defined.

3. Determining Planning Premises

Every plan has to be based on certain carefully considered assumptions and predictions, which are known as *planning premises.* A business organisation has to provide for various environmental factors. Planning premises supply important facts and information relating to the future, and because of that, they are very significant to the success of planning. Thus, it is forecast of those business conditions under which a plan is to operate, for example, population trends, production costs, Government policies, availability of materials, etc. Forecasts and trend analysis provide most of the information required in planning.

(NB) Classification of planning premises is explained, further, in detail, in this chapter.

4. Determining Alternative Courses of Action

After managers are clear of goals to be attained, they think of ways to achieve them. They should make alternative plans of action since there can be no best way of doing things. All possible alternatives to achieve the objectives should be considered by managers. In order to identify all possible alternatives, it is necessary to collect and analyse all relevant information. Information may be collected from primary or secondary sources. The data so collected will serve as the basis for development of an alternative course of action. The information used in discovering alternative must be upto date and reliable.

5. Evaluation of Alternative Courses of Action

Every alternative course of action has to be evaluated, and the relative importance of each one of them should be ascertained. Every alternative will have some strong and weak points, which are to be understood in the right perspective. The planner should study all the alternatives and then a final selection should be made. Best results will be achieved only when best way of doing a work is selected. Each course of action has costs and benefits. Managers should carry out a *cost-benefit* analysis and the plan which gives maximum return should be accepted by them.

6. Selection of a Course of Action

After analyzing and evaluating the available alternatives, the manager has to select the best course of action. In fact, it is the real point of decision-making. When the best course of action is determined, it should be finally selected by managers. Each plan should be supported by sub-plans, known as derivative plans.

7. Preparation of derivative Plans

There are sub-plans or departmental plans. The basic plan prepared for the whole enterprise cannot be effectively operated in the absence of such plans. Middle and lower level managers must draw up the appropriate plans, programmes and budgets for their sub-units. These are described as *derivative plans.* In developing these derivative plans, lower-level managers take steps similar to those taken by upper-level managers-selecting realistic goals, assessing their sub-units' particular strengths and weaknesses and analysing those parts of the environment that can affect them.

8. Sequence of Operation

Timing is an essential consideration in planning. After developing the plans and sub-plans, the starting and finishing times should be fixed for each plan. Scheduling is very useful not only in sales and production areas but in other functional areas also. It is better to associate all the managers in the planning process so that they develop a sense of participation in the management.

9. Considering the Strategy

Strategy has a significant contribution towards the execution of a plan. So, consideration of different strategies becomes an integral part of the planning process. A suitable strategy should be planned and followed for the successful implementation of the planned course.

10. Feedback

Feedback means response. When plans are selected and implemented, managers receive information about the success or failure of plans. If there are deviations in actual performance against planned performance, managers remove these deviations or make fresh plans. Planning is complete if its implementation is effective.

WHY PLANS FAIL ?

If managers know why plans fail, they can take steps to eliminate the factors that cause failure and thereby increase the probability that their plans will be successful. A study by K.A. Ringbakk determined that plans fail when:

1. Corporate planning is not integrated into the total management system.
2. There is a lack of understanding of the different steps of the planning process.
3. Managers at different levels in the organisation have not properly engaged in or contributed to planning activities.
4. Responsibility for planning is wrongly vested solely in the planning department.
5. Management expects that plans developed will be realized with little effort.
6. In starting formal planning, too much is attempted at once.
7. Management fails to operate by the plan.
8. Financial projections are confused with planning.
9. Inadequate inputs are used in planning.
10. Management fails to grasp the overall planning process.

PLANNING PREMISES

Planning is a fundamental managerial function. In simple words, planning is deciding in advance what is to be done, when, where, how and by whom it is to be done. Thus, a plan is a determined course of action. It is an attempt on the part of a manager to anticipate the future in order to achieve better results.

Plans are prepared for future. But future is uncertain. Therefore, management makes certain assumptions about the future. These assumptions should not be based upon hunch, intuition or guesswork. Rather these should be developed through scientific forecasting of future events. The assumptions about future derived from forecasting and used in planning are known as planning premises.

Types of Planning Premises

Different types of planning premises are:

(*a*) Internal and External premises;

(*b*) Controllable, Semi-controllable and Non-controllable premises;

(*c*) Tangible and Intangible premises.

(*i*) *Internal Premises:* Internal premises are those factors which exist within the firm, or which belong to the firm's own climate. Important internal premises include the resources, and abilities of the firm in the form of men, money and methods. They are definite, known and fully controllable factors: like sales forecasts, policies of the company, etc.

(*ii*) *External Premises:* External premises are derived from the external environment, like political, economic, social and technological forces, population trends, Government policy, national income, etc.

(*iii*) *Controllable Premises:* The factors which are entirely within the approach and control of management, are said to be controllable. Policies, programmes, rules, etc. are examples of such premises.

(*iv*) *Uncontrollable premises:* They are neither predictable nor controllable. Due to the impact of such factors, the management has to revise its plan and adjust them according to the current situations. Strikes, wars, new inventions, imposition of emergency, natural calamities, etc. are some uncontrollable premises.

(*v*) *Semi-controllable Premises:* They are those over which management has partial control. Worker's attitude and efficiency, firm's price policy, marketing programme, etc. are examples of such premises.

(*vi*) *Tangible Premises:* Tangible premises can be estimated in quantitative terms like, production units, cost per unit, etc.

(*vii*) *Intangible Premises:* Intangible premises can not be quantified, for example, goodwill of the firm, leadership qualities of the managers, employer-employee relationships, etc.

MAKING PLANNING EFFECTIVE

The following are some guidelines for making planning effective:

1. A sound system should be created for forecasting accurately the future events.
2. Planning should be kept flexible.
3. All plans must be realistic and practical.
4. It should be an interactive process.
5. Participation of all members of firm is necessary for effective planning.
6. All plans must be properly timed.
7. All plans must be based on cost-benefit analysis.
8. Objectives of plans must be clear.
9. Goals of firm must be properly communicated.
10. Planning include awareness and acceptance of changes.
11. Planning offsets future uncertainty.
12. Planning should avoid aimless activities.

OBSTACLES TO EFFECTIVE PLANNING

1. It becomes difficult to formulate good plans when reliable and timely information about the past and likely future events is not available.
2. Managers, who lack ability and knowledge, will not be able to make effective planning.
3. In times of sudden and unexpected emergencies, planning becomes difficult.
4. People develop patterns of thought that resist change.
5. Insufficient resources can limit the capacity of organisation to make sound plans.
6. If future events do not occur as planned, they will affect the plans.
7. Managers, who lack confidence to set definite and challenging goals, are generally poor planners.

CASE STUDY - 1

Radiant Industries

"Radiant Industries" manufactures electrical stamping. It supplies 50% of its output in domestic market and 50% in international market.

As on date, it is doing well in the domestic market, while it is unable to capture the international market successfully. Market research has identified the following reasons for this :–

1. Intense competition in the international market, as the product is not new there.
2. Quality is not upto the international standards.

However, the product is new to the domestic markets, thus, is readily acceptable here. The managing director (MD) of the company is worried about its international operations and thus, holds a meeting with Finance and Marketing managers (major departmental heads) to analyze the issue.

After extensive discussion, marketing manager came to the conclusion that the firm should continue working in the international markets, as he feels that the firm might face competition in the domestic market which may drive the firm out.

So, he wants to improve quality upto the international level and introduce product differentiation.

The finance manager, however is not very pleased with this opinion: as quality enhancement upto the international levels would require huge amount of capital investment: and the firm at present is not in a position to finance it. This would require some time; thus, the marketing manager's plan cannot be implemented immediately.

The MD knows that product differentiation and quality enhancement is a long-term procedure: but going with the opinion of marketing manager: he wants to continue its operations in the international markets.

The result was increasing losses for the company. The departmental managers then suggested the MD to reduce the sales targets in foreign markets and plan accordingly. The MD didn't listen. The company came close to bankruptcy.

QUESTIONS

1. Analyse the case.
2. What reasons do you account for company's failure ?
3. What would you have done in such a situation ?

REVIEW QUESTIONS

1. Explain the importance of planning. What are its limitations ?
2. "Planning is the essence of management". Elucidate.
3. Explain the various steps to be followed in planning.
4. Bring out the importance of planning.
5. What are the major limitations of planning ?
6. Explain the benefits of planning and enumerate the steps in the process of planning.
7. What are the different types of planning on the basis of time ? Explain each.
8. What are the planning premises ? Explain the classification of planning premises.
9. What is the nature and purpose of planning ?
10. "Planning is essentially forward looking." Explain.
11. Explain the advantages and limitations of planning.
12. Explain the importance of planning in business concerns. What are the essential of a good plan ?

CHAPTER 7

Methods and Types of Plans

- Introduction
- Types of Plan
    - Strategic Plans
    - Tactical Plans
    - Operational Plans
    - Single use Plans
        - Programmes
        - Budgets
        - Strategy
        - Projects
- Standing Plans
    - Objectives
    - Policies
    - Methods
    - Rules
    - Standards
    - Schedules
    - Procedures
- SWOT Analysis
- Long-term Plans
- Middle-term Plans
- Short-term Plans
- Production Plans
- Marketing Plans
- Financial Plans
- Case Study - 1
- Review Questions.

INTRODUCTION

Goals are the ends and plans are the means to achieve those ends. There is a difference between the terms, 'goals' and 'objectives'. Goals refer to non-measurable future ends. Goals are broader objectives which an organisation strives to achieve. The word 'purpose' is a broader term that applies to all organisations of similar type. For example, the purpose of all educational institutions is to provide quality education to society. Similarly business organisations are to provide quality goods to the society at the right time and price.

Mission is a specific term that explains why an organisation exists. The mission of educational institution may be to provide quality education to women only. And the mission of business organisation is to provide specific goods to society. A mission is, thus, more specific than purpose.

TYPES OF PLANS

Plans can be classified on the basis of (*a*) Organisational levels (plans for top level, middle level and lower level management) (*b*) use (single use and standing plans) (*c*) Time (Long-term, medium-term and short-term plans) and (*d*) functional areas (production marketing, financial), etc.

In an alternative way, plan can be classified as follows:

1. Classification on the basis of *levels in the organisation*

(*a*) Strategic plans (Top level Managers)

(*b*) Tactical Plans (Middle level Managers)

(*c*) Operational Plans (Lower level Managers)

2. Classification on the *basis of use*

(*a*) Single use Plans

(*i*) Programmes

(*ii*) Budgets

(*iii*) Strategies

(*iv*) Projects

(*b*) Standing Plans

(*i*) Objectives

(*ii*) Policies

(*iii*) Methods

(*iv*) Rules

(*v*) Standards

3. Classification on the *basis of time*

(*a*) Long-term plans

(*b*) Medium-term plans

(*c*) Short-term plans

4. Classification on the basis of *functional areas*

(*i*) Production plans

(*ii*) Marketing plans

(*iii*) Financial plans.

Plans classified, on the above basis, are discussed below:

1. Classification on the basis of Levels in the Organisation

(*a*) **Strategic Plan**

Strategic goals or plans are broadly defined as the targets or future end-results set by top management. Such goals typically address issues relating to the organisation as a whole and may sometimes be stated in fairly general terms. Strategic goals are sometimes called of official goals because they are formally stated by top management.

(*b*) **Tactical Plan**

Tactical goals or plans are targets or future end-results usually set by middle management for specific departments or units. Goals at this level spell out what must be done by various departments to achieve the results outlined in the strategic goals. Tactical goals tend to be stated in more measurable terms than is sometimes true of strategic goals.

(*c*) **Operational Plan**

Operational plans or goals are the means to support tactical plans. They are made to achieve operational goals of the enterprise. These plans are highly specific and determine what different sections of the organisation need to perform. While resources are allocated in strategic plans, their efficient use to achieve overall organisational goals is done by operational plans.

The above plans, when tabulated, appear as follows:

	Strategic Plans	***Tactical Plans***	***Operational Plans***
Scope	Relate to organisational goals	Relate to departmental goals	Relate to sub-units of department.
Period	More than 5 years.	1 to 5 years	Less than one year
Framed by	Top level manager	Middle level manager	Lower level manager
Focus	Strategic goals	Tactical goals	Operational goals

2. Classification on the basis of use

(*a*) **Single Use Plan**

Single use plans are made to serve a specific objective. They cease to exist once the objective is achieved. They are, thus, short lived plans and are made for non-recurring activities. For example, if a company wants to instal a machine, it has to plan its purchase: whether the company go for a new machine or second-hand machine or get it on lease etc. Thus, when the machine is purchased, the plan does not exist any more.

Different types of single use plans are *programmes, budgets, strategies* and *projects.*

(*i*) **Programmes**

A programme is a sequence of activities directed towards the achievement of certain objectives. A programme lays down the definite steps which will be taken to accomplish a given task. It also lays down the time to be taken to accomplish a given task. It also lays down the time to be taken for the completion of each step. A programme might include such general activities as purchasing new machines that will enable to increase output or hiring work force to operate new equipment or introduction of a new product in the market. Thus a programme is a complex set of objectives, policies, procedures, tasks, assignments, steps to be taken, resources to be employed and other elements necessary to carry out a given course of action.

Features of Programme

The following are the features of a programme.

(*i*) It is a single use plan. Once the goal of the programme is achieved, it will not be used again.

(*ii*) It outlines various steps in the form of small plans.

(*iii*) It is prepared for achieving the objects of a business enterprise.

(*iv*) It prescribes a fixed time table for each step.

(*v*) It should ensure co-ordinated planning efforts.

Steps in making a Programme

The following steps are involved in a programme.

(*i*) Identify the activities required for accomplishing the objectives.

(*ii*) These activities are divided into steps.

(*iii*) Each individual should be made liable for a specific activity.

(*iv*) The resource, e.g., materials, finance, etc., should then be determined for each step.

(*v*) Estimate the time needed for each step, *i.e.*, the starting time and competition time for each action is mentioned.

(*vi*) The last step is to fix up the definite dates for each part of the programme.

(*ii*) **Budgets**

A budget is a statement of expected results expressed in numerical terms for a definite period of time in the future. It is a plan expressed in quantitative terms. It is a statement of expected results always expressed in numerical terms. Hence it is called a numerical plan. It can be expressed in financial or in any other terms. A budget is an appraisal of expected expense projected against anticipated income for a certain future period. Like any other plan, the budget must have flexibility, objectivity and structural form. A budget is a single use plan.

According to George R. Terry, "Budget is an estimate of future needs arranged according to an orderly basis, covering some or all of the activities of an enterprise for definite period of time."

Objectives of a Budget

(*a*) It directs the attention of all concerned to the attainment of common goal.

(*b*) It leads to the disclosure of organisational weakness. The budgets are compared with actual performance and variances, if any, are investigated. This step helps in taking corrective and remedial measures.

(*c*) It aims at careful control over the performance and cost of every function.

(*d*) It contributes to coordinated efforts of all departments in order to achieve an integrated goal. Budgets grow from bottom and are controlled from top-level.

(*iii*) **Strategy**

The term *strategy* has been customarily used in respect of army organisations and games. But in view of growing competition and rapidly changing environment, it has become equally relevant for business organisations. Strategy may be defined as unified, comprehensive and integrated action plan designed to achieve specific objectives in the event of difficulty. It is concerned with the direction in which various resources of organisation will be mobilised and utilised for maximising the chance of accomplishing specific objectives in a disturbed state of affairs.

"Strategies are a general programme of action toward the attainment of comprehensive objectives".

"Strategy is a particular kind of policy. It is a policy which has been formulated by top management for the purpose of interpreting and sensing the meaning of other policies".

So strategy is concerned with the direction in which human and material resources will be applied in order to achieve the desired objectives. If plans are made without considering what our competitors are doing, it can be very harmful for the enterprise. A strategy is an action plan which must be implemented. The two important aspects of strategy are (*a*) formation of a plan (*b*) implementation of a plan.

Characteristics of Strategy

The following characteristics of strategy are evident:

(*i*) Strategy is a comprehensive and integrated action plan drawn for achieving objectives in changed situation which is specific and novel in nature.

(*ii*) Strategies are basically formulated not only on the basis of objectives to be pursued but on the basis of careful situational analysis of the organisation and its environment.

(*iii*) Strategy aims at deploying, mobilising and utilising limited resources for maximising chances of achieving objectives in the event of difficulties.

(*iv*) Strategies are formulated to handle changes arising out of environment. It ensures allocation of resources so as to exploit new opportunities, profitably.

(*v*) Strategy is flexible and dynamic in nature because it is formulated to cope with the changing business environment and maintain its survival, profitability, growth and development of the organisation.

(*vi*) Strategies are usually drawn for a long period of time but it has short-term implications also.

(*vii*) Strategies, to a large extent, are imposed externally by the government, trade unions, competitors, trade associations in the form of regulations, agreements, informal understandings and many other conditions.

"*Strategy is the complex plan for bringing the organisation from a given posture to a desired position in a future, period of time.*" — *D.I. Cleland*

"*Strategy refers to the determination of purpose (mission) and the long term objectives of the enterprise and the adoption of courses of action and allocation of resources necessary to achieve these aims.*" — *Harold Koontz*

Importance of Strategy

1. It provides a course of action to achieve a specific goal.
2. It is vital for long term survival and growth of the corporate system.
3. It provides direction to organisational activities.
4. It helps to achieve the objectives of the business.

(*iv*) **Projects**

"A project is a plan that coordinates a set of limited scope activities that do not need to be divided into several major projects in order to reach a major non-recurring goal". A project is part of the major programme plan with a distinct object achieved within the given time frame. Each project requires a plan layout and physical, financial and human resources for its successful completion and is, therefore, supported by budgets. Once the project is completed, the work force engaged in that project is disintegrated and the project plan ceases to exist. Each project plan is headed by a project manager who directs people to complete the project within the available financial and non-financial resources.

(*a*) **Standing Plans**

Standing plans are also known as repeated use plans since they are designed to be used over and over again. They are formulated to guide managerial decisions and action on recurring problems. Thus standing plans cover a variety of repetitive situations. Standing plans ensure quick decision and action whenever need arises. There is no need to repeat the reasoning and analysis required initially to design a standing plan whenever a similar situation arises. They tend to achieve consistency, uniformity and unity of efforts in meeting repetitive situations throughout the enterprise.

Benefits of Standing Plans

1. It provides a basis for quick action.
2. It facilitates fast decision-making.
3. It facilitates delegation.
4. There is a predetermined way to solve recurrent problems.

(*i*) Objectives

Objectives are goals or predetermined results towards which all organized efforts are directed. They are the end points. Objectives are multiple because an organisation wants to achieve several economic and social objectives simultaneously *e.g.*, profit making, market standing, executive development, social satisfaction, etc.

"*Objective is a term commonly used to indicate the end point of a management programme.*"
— Koontz & O' Donnell

"*Objectives are goals, aims or purposes that organisation wish to achieve over varying periods of time.*" — Dalton E. Mc Farland

Meaning of Objectives

According to Farland, "Objectives are the goals, aims or purposes that organisations wish to achieve over varying periods of time." Objectives are the expressions of what an organisation wants to achieve. Objectives are the ultimate targets and ends towards which an organisation and its members strive at all times. All functional activities and physical as well as human resources of the organisation is directed towards the achievement of common objectives.

Features of Objectives

The important features of objectives are:

1. Objectives may be specific or general.
2. Objectives are the most basic type of plans and all other plans are based upon objectives.
3. Objectives are plural as every organisation exists to achieve several rather than a single goal.
4. Objectives form a hierarchy, that is, they can be arranged in order of importance.
5. Objectives differ in time span, that is, some are long-term while others are of short-term.

Benefits of Objectives

The benefits of objectives are as under:

1. Clear definition of objectives encourages unified planning. The unifying effect arises when the plans are prepared by different departmental heads and are adjusted to a common objective.
2. Objectives provide motivation to people in the organisation. Objectives help in providing a sense of unity, harmony and accomplishment to co-operative efforts.
3. When the work is goal oriented, unproductive tasks can be avoided.
4. Objectives provide standards which aid in the control of human efforts in an organisation.
5. Objectives serve to identify the organisation and to link it to the groups upon which its existence depends.
6. Objectives act as a sound basis for developing administrative controls.
7. Objectives contribute to the management process. They influence the purpose of the organisation, policies, personnel, leadership as well as managerial control.

8. Objectives indicate the contribution to be made by each unit and thus it is the basis for decentralisation.

Hierarchy of Objectives

Objectives in the organisation are not singular. In many organisations, objectives are structured in hierarchy of importance. There are objectives within objectives. The hierarchy of objectives is a graded series in which organisational goals are supported by each succeeding managerial level down to the level of the individual. The objectives of each unit contribute to the objectives of the next higher unit. Usually, the hierarchy of objectives in an organisation is described through means ends chain. In the organisation, the relationship between the means and the ends in hierarchical goals established at one level require certain means for their accomplishment. These means then become the sub goals for the next level and more specific operational objectives are developed as we move down the hierarchy. In the goal hierarchy the objectives of each lower level become the means to the ends *i.e.,* objectives of the next higher level in the organisation.

Multiplicity of Objectives

Organisation pursue multifarious objectives. At every level in the hierarchy, goals are likely to be multiple. Every organisation has several objectives rather than one goal. In addition to the organisational objectives every stake holder in business has his own objectives. Objectives are required in every area of business where the survival and success of the business is important. According to **Peter Ducker,** to manage a business is to balance a variety of needs and goals, objectives are needed in every area where the performance and result directly and vitally contribute to the survival and growth of business. These areas are: market standing, innovation, productivity, profitability, management performance, physical and financial resources, worker's performance and attitude and public responsibility.

Multiplicity of objectives can be understood by the following example: The marketing division may have the objective of sale and distribution of products. This objective can be broken down into a group of objectives for the product, advertising research, promotion managers. The advertising manager's goal may include designing product messages carefully, create a favourable image of the product in the market, etc. Similar goals can be set for other marketing managers. As the enterprise has to meet internal as well as external challenges effectively, internal problems may however around profitability, survival, growth and so on. External problems may be posed by government, society, stockholder, customers, etc. In order to meet the conflicting demands from various internal and external groups, organisations generally pursue multiple objectives.

(*ii*) Policies

A policy is a general standing plan guiding the management in the conduct of enterprise management operations. The notion or idea of guidelines is common to both objectives and policies. Objectives describe what is wanted or what is to be achieved. Policy describes the major feature of how the accomplishment of objectives will be pursued. Both are equally necessary for effective action.

A policy is a general guide to thinking and action rather than a specific course of action. It defines the area or limits within decisions can be made to achieve organisational objectives. Policies are flexible and broad plans providing scope for judgement and interpretation on the part of subordinate managers. "Policies are general statement of understanding which guide or channel thinking in decision-making of subordinates." In the words of George R. Terry, "Policy is a verbal, written or implied overall guide, setting up boundaries that supply the general limits and direction in which managerial action will take place." A policy is a general guideline for decision-making.

"Policies include that body of understanding (members of the group), which makes the action of each member of the group in the given set of circumstances more predictable to other members."
— J.L. Massie

"Policies are general statements or understandings which guide or channel thinking in decision making of subordinates." — Koontz and O'Donnell.

Features of Sound Policy

1. The policy tries to contribute to the organisational goal.
2. Policy is formulated through the various steps in the decision-making process.
3. Policy can be interpreted from the behaviour of the top management.
4. Policy provides guidelines to the member of the organisation for choosing a particular course of action.
5. Policy making is the task of all managers, however, the higher a manager is in the organisation, the more important is his role in policy-making.
6. A sound policy must be flexible in its implementation.
7. A policy should be uniform in its application and it must be fair to all.

Importance of Sound Policy

1. Policies lead to a uniform pattern of action in respect of various matters relating to an organisation.
2. Policies speed up decision making since they provide a frame work within which the decisions can be taken.
3. Policies help both men and boss to work for better performance.
4. Policies help in securring effective coordination of efforts and activities in the organisation

Guidelines for Effective Policies

Policy formulation is based on the following principles:

1. It should relate to organisational objectives.
2. It should be easily understood, interpreted and implemented.
3. As far as possible, it should be in writing. Written policies are unambiguous and are available for ready reference.
4. It should be based on facts rather than personal judgement of managers.
5. It should be flexible to adapt to changing environment.
6. It should conform to organisation structure and value system.
7. It should be framed by managers in consultation with those who have to implement it.
8. It should be constantly reviewed and modified to keep in tune with organisational goals and needs.

(*iii*) Methods

A method is a prescribed way in which one step of a procedure is to be performed. The specified technique to be used in screening the applications or conducting a written test is a method, whereas the sequence of steps involved in the recruitment of personnel constitutes a procedure. The method that is selected for discharging a particular step under the existing conditions may become outdated in due course of time because of the discovery of better and more economical methods. The need for better and more economical methods of operation is great because of the pressure of competition in the markets for the products of the concern. Methods help in increasing the effectiveness and usefulness of the procedure. By improving the methods, reduced fatigue, better productivity and lower costs can be achieved. Methods can be improved in a number of ways. Manual methods of performing a task can be replaced by mechanical means, or the existing mechanised process may be improved or work simplified and unproductive efforts removed by conducting "motion study".

(*iv*) Rules

A rule is a guide to action. It is in the nature of a decision made by the management regarding what is to be done and what is not to be done in a given situation. A rule is more rigid. It may or may not be a part of a procedure. Rules will not have any scope for discretion, as they are specific and definite. The breach of rules usually carries a penalty. "*No credit facilities beyond 15 days*", "Smoking is strictly prohibited" are examples of rules.

(*v*) Standards

A standard is a measure of the level of achievement desired. For all future evaluation, it becomes a model. A standard helps in comparing accomplishments with the desired results. If there are major deviations from the plan, standards will help in ascertaining whether there are any deviations from the original plan. If there are any such deviations, they can be corrected.

(*vi*) Schedules

A schedule specifies time limits within which activities are to be completed. Scheduling is the process of establishing a time sequence for the work to be done. Schedules are essential for avoiding delays and for ensuring continuity of operations. A schedule lays down a time table fixing starting and finishing data for different activities.

(*vii*) Procedures

Procedures are clear-cut administrative specifications prescribing the chronological manner (or order) in which repetitive activity is initiated, carried forward and controlled. Thus, procedures are guides to action only. They tell how a particular activity is to be done. Hence, procedures are generally established for repetitive work so that some steps are followed each time that activity is performed. Examples are purchase procedure, procedure of raw materials issue from store, procedures of recruitment of workers, etc. In fact every repetitive activity procedures are established because routine jobs can be performed more efficiently if one best way of doing things has been established.

Distinction between Policies and Procedures

1. Policies are guides to decision-making while procedures are guides to action.
2. Policies leave some room for interpretation and discretion but in case of procedures there is no such thing. They are more rigid and specific.
3. Policies form part of the strategies of the organisation while procedures are operational and tactical tools.
4. Policies are the basic things. They form the basis for working out the procedures.
5. Generally, policies are formulated by the top management while procedures are laid down at somewhat lower level.

SWOT Analysis

SWOT is the abbreviation for STRENGTHS (S), WEAKNESS (W), OPPORTUNITIES (O) and THREATS (T).

Strengths: A strength is an inherent capability of an organisation which it can use to gain strategic advantage over its competitors, company image, wide distribution network, sound financial position, talented and dedicated work force, etc. are examples of strengths.

Weaknesses: A weakness is an inherent limitation or constraint of an organisation which creates strategic disadvantage to it in comparison with its competitors. Poor product quality, obsolete technology, high production costs, poor financial position, weak managements, etc. are examples of weaknesses.

Opportunities: An opportunity is a favourable condition in the organisation's environment which enable it to improve its competitive position. Economic liberalisation, privatisation of

Government undertakings, declining interest rates on bank loans, etc. are examples of opportunities for private sector firms.

Threats: A threat is an unfavourable trend in the organisation's environment which cause a risk or damage to its position.

3. Classification on the basis of time

There is no definite basis for classifying plans as long-term, medium-term and short-term. It depends on the nature of business, nature of product and adaptability of organisation to external environment.

1. **Long term plans:** These plans are normally prepared for a minimum period of 5 years. They relate to company's goals. Future being uncertain, these plans foresee environmental changes (by applying techniques of forecasting) and prepare the organisations to accept them when they occur. They relate to investment in fixed assets which generate returns over a long-period of time. They aim to achieve strategic goals of the organisation over a long time period.
2. **Medium-term plans:** These plans normally relate to a period of one to 5 years. They are the supporting plans that help to achieve long-term plans. Plans made to analyse the impact of advertisement campaign on expansion of business into new markets are medium-term plans. These plans usually relate to achievement of tactical goals.
3. **Short-term plans:** These plans are normally prepared for a period of one year, though in some cases, these may even relate to a period of less than one year. They look into immediate future of the company. Plans made to retain or promote sales, to train workers (so that labour turnover rate is reduced) are short-term plans. They relate to operational goals of the enterprise.

4. Classification on the basis of functional areas

"A functional plan describes the specific actions to be taken in the immediate future by people responsible for that particular functional area. It usually sets forth short-term objectives, the action to be taken to achieve those objectives, and a time frame for the accomplishment of each action."

1. **Production plans:** "Production plans consist of planning and overseeing the process of converting inputs into value - enhanced output". The areas of production plans are: production system, efficiency of operations, location of company facilities, design of company facilities, and day-to-day process planning.

   The plans set the targets of production. They are designed according to production policy of business organisations. Firms may follow a policy of producing throughout the year, piling inventories and selling them during peak season or a policy of producing only during the peak season of demand. In the latter case, they can diversify into other areas during slack season to keep their plant and machinery occupied.
2. **Marketing plans:** Marketing plans are designed by marketing managers. They "tell sales and marketing personnel who will sell what, where, to whom, in what quantity and how." They help to sell company's products and develop new products to increase their share of market; to plan for sale in cash or credit; if it decides to sell on credit, to determine the credit terms and credit policies for the sales department. Production plans and marketing plans aim to satisfy consumer needs and are, therefore, inter-dependent. The production department produces according to expected sale in the market and sales department sells what is produced.
3. **Financial plans:** Finance managers prepare financial plans for raising and utilising / allocating financial resources effectively. These plans meet the fixed and working capital requirements of the firm. They plan for financial cuts during recessionary economic

conditions and additional funds during boom. All departments need funds for their effective functioning. Production department needs raw material for smooth flow of production. Marketing department needs funds for advertising and sales promotion campaigns. Financial plans contribute to financial strength of the organisation through effective cost control techniques that reduce cost of its products.

CASE STUDY - 1

Anita Singh started an organisation 20 years ago when funding from Government and donor agencies was not common. She set up a programme for training and rehabilitating the physically disabled teenagers of her area in New Delhi. At that time, general society also did not make much donations for charitable purposes and, thus, her programme faced the problem of financial crunch. She managed her programme in a manner that she could raise money for running on its own. She approached the Ministry of Human Welfare and managed to get some donation. She also used her personal resources and raised personal loans. Along with two friends, thus, she set up the Help age Union to take care of the physically challenged teenagers.

She set up various work centres where the disabled were taught to work on assembly line operations like cotton, lamps, jute carpets, baskets, textile, wool, candles, tea, etc. Each person was placed on a specific operation and his output was passed at the next work station for further processing.

The goods produced were used for internal consumption and surplus was sold in the market for sustenance of the programme. The goods were produced, priced and sold according to market demand. People bought these goods because of their quality and not as charity.

Today, Anita's programme has grown to an enormous size. There are about 80 handicapped adult trainers who teach vocational skills to about 500 handicapped adults in the town. Financing is no more a problem. It is generating internal surplus and donations are also generously given by the organisations and society members. Her organisation is turning into a full-fledged Non-Government Organisation (NGO) working for a social cause.

QUESTION

1. Analyse the case in terms of its objectives and policies.
2. What was Anita's vision that helped her dream turn into reality ?
3. How would you have dealt with such a situation in the context of long-term planning ?

REVIEW QUESTIONS

1. What is policy ? State its importance in management. Explain the steps in the process of policy formulation ?
2. Distinguish between policy and procedure. Explain the advantages and limitations of procedures.
3. Explain the basis of classification of plans.
4. What are single use and standing plans ? State different kinds of single use and standing plans.
5. What are single use plans ? What are the different kinds of single use plans ?
6. How do programmes and strategies help in achieving the organisational objectives ?
7. Briefly explain the various type of plans.
8. Discuss the characteristics of objectives.
9. Explain the elements of planning.
10. Explain the meaning, types and limitation of policies.

Forecasting and Decision-Making

8
CHAPTER

- Introduction
- Meaning
- Definitions
- Features
- Forecasting Vs Planning
- Importance of Forecasting
- Process of Forecasting
- Limitations of Forecasting
- Advantages of Forecasting
- Effective Forecasting
- Forecasting Techniques
- DECISION-MAKING
- Introduction
- Meaning
- Definitions
- Characteristics
- Importance of Decision-Making
- Types of Managerial Decisions
- The process of Decision-Making
- Conditions of Decision-Making
- Problems that require Decision-Making
- Problems in Decision-Making
- Modern Techniques of Decision-Making
- Models of Decision-Making
- Quantitative Techniques of Decision-Making
- Case Study – I
- Review Questions.

INTRODUCTION

Forecasting is an essential part of the process of planning. It provides key information and pertinent facts relating to the future. Without forecasting planning is not possible. Forecasting is the technique of estimating the relevant future events and problems on the basis of past and present behaviour or happenings. The future cannot be guessed without knowing the events which have occurred in the past and are occurring presently. Thus, forecasting involves detailed analysis of the past and present events to get a clear-cut ideas about probable events in the future. Planning presupposes forecasting as the former is defined as deciding what is to be done in future.

MEANING

Forecasting is the process of predicting future conditions that influence and guide the activities, behaviour and performance of the organisation. It is a systematic attempt to probe the future by inference from known factors. According to Glueck, "Forecasting is the formal process of predicting future events that will significantly affect the functioning of the enterprise." Business forecasting refers to analysis of past and current events so as to obtain clues about future trends in the business environment.

DEFINITIONS

"Forecasting is a systematic attempt to probe the future by inference from known facts. The purpose is to provide management with information on which it came base planning decisions." — Louis A. Allen

"Business forecasting is the calculation of probable events, to provide against the future. It, therefore, involves a 'look ahead' in business and an idea of pre-determination of events and their financial implications as in the case of budgeting." — C.E. Sultan

"Forecasts are predictions or estimates of the change, if any in characteristic economic phenomena which may affect one's business plans." — Mc Farland

"Business forecasting refers to the statistical analysis of the past and current movements in the given time series so as to obtain clues about the future pattern of these movements." — Neter Wasserman

FEATURES

Forecasting techniques are made use of in all types of organisations - business or non-business. It provides a logical basis for determining in advance the nature of future business operations and managerial planning. In the words of Haimann, "the success of a business depends in a large measure upon the skill of management in forecasting."

On the basis of the above definitions of forecasting, the following features can be identified:

1. Forecasting is necessary for planning process. Planning is not possible without forecasting.
2. Forecasting considers all the factors which affect organisational functions.
3. The analysis of various factors may require the use of scientific, mathematical and statistical techniques.
4. Forecasting has become a specialised activity where in several techniques are available for predicting the future.
5. The quality of forecasts depends on the reliability of information.
6. Forecasts may be made for long-term or short-term. Long-term forecasts tend to be less accurate than short-term forecasts.
7. Forecasts are the estimates for the future trends.
8. These estimates for future are based on the analysis of past and present circumstances.

FORECASTING Vs PLANNING

Planning and forecasting both are concerned with future. However, there is some difference between the two and difference lies in the scope of the two process.

Forecasting	*Planning*
1. It is a tool of planning.	1. It is not a tool for forecasting.
2. It is a basis for planning.	2. Planning is the basis for future.
3. Few members are involved in the process.	3. Large number of persons are involved in the Process.
4. Forecasting is done by experts.	4. Planning can be done by anyone.
5. Forecasting is done at the middle and lower levels of management.	5. Planning is done at top-level management.

IMPORTANCE OF FORECASTING

Forecasting is an important part and parcel of modern business management. The success of a business depends largely upon the skill of management in forecasting and preparing for future events. Forecasting provides the following benefits:

1. Vital Role

Forecasting provides key information and facts relating to future. Most of the planning premises are merged in forecasting of one type or another. Planning without forecasting is impossible. Planning is the backbone of effective functioning of an organisation. Many organisations have failed because of lack of forecasting or faulty forecasting.

2. Coordination is Developed

People at different levels participate in the process of forecasting. Regular interactions between the members of the organisation facilitate cooperation and unity among them. Besides, forecasting helps in integrating various departmental plans into the corporate plan.

3. Progress in Business

Forecasting contributes in small measure to the overall success of business. By forecasting various internal and external factors, a business can plan to obtain maximum benefits from periods of expanding economy, and on the other hand to minimise any adverse effects when business activities slacken.

4. Basis for Control

Forecasting provides relevant information for exercising control. The managers can know their weaknesses in forecasting process and take suitable action to overcome these. Forecasting can disclose the areas where control is lacking. When such areas are identified steps can be taken to make control effective.

5. Executive Development

Forecasting requires executives to look ahead, think through the future and improve their mental faculties. Managers develop the habit of collecting, analysing and interpreting data instead of depending on guess work. According to Louis A. Allen, "A systematic attempt to probe the future by inference from known facts helps to integrate all management planning so that unified overall plans can be developed into which divisional and departmental plans can be meshed."

6. Accurate Decision

Forecasting brings exactness and accuracy in managerial decisions. It enables a manager to probe the future economic, social and political factors that might influence his decisions and his company. It improves the quality and validity of management decisions. It enables a company to take sound decisions with reference to production, sales and financing.

7. Vision of Future

Forecasting provides clues about the future happenings. With the help of this knowledge managers can save the organisation from the impact of trade cycles and other threats. Without business forecasting external forces may cause irreparable damage to the organisation and many opportunities might be lost. Forecasts provide a vision of the future.

PROCESS OF FORECASTING

Forecasting has been defined by Mc Farland, in these words, "Forecasts are predictions or estimates of the change. If any, in characteristics economic phenomina which may affect one's business plans." According to James Redfield, the following are the important elements of forecasting:

1. Understanding the Problems

The manager has to identify the actual problem about which the forecast is to be made. It may be regarding the technological conditions, location of site or mobilizing finance. A thorough investigation and analysis of various factors influencing the organisation is necessary. The past events should be analysed and compared with the present events. This will reveal the causes of various changes in the relevant factors.

2. Development of Foundation

It involves the collection of basic information relating to the product of company, market, competition and general environment of the industry and society. Study of these facts helps not only in analysing the present position but in making future estimates also.

3. Estimating Future Trend

After developing the ground-work, future estimates are made as regards to the sale and production of the company. The estimate of future sales is made with the help of sales executives. In sales forecasting, the trend values are determined on the basis of calculation and anticipation.

4. Comparing actual with estimated results

It is always better and safer to compare the actual results with the estimated results. If there is any major difference between the actual and the estimates, the reasons should be investigated.

5. Refining the Forecasts

Forecasting is not an exact science. It is simply an estimate, so the management should always review the forecasts periodically and future trend values should be revised according to the experience gained in the immediate past.

LIMITATIONS OF FORECASTING

Forecasts are only estimates of future conditions. Forecasts can never be hundred per cent complete and reliable. They give only estimates of future course of events. The following are some important limitations of forecasts:

1. Assumptions

All forecasts are based on certain assumptions which may not always be true. That is, the assumptions may not hold good in all cases. As a result forecasts may become unreliable. The business conditions are dynamic and ever-changing. They can never be forecasted accurately.

2. Not fully true

Forecasts merely indicate the trend of future events. They may not be fully true. Techniques of forecasting simply project the future trend. None can give guarantee that a particular trend will occur in future.

3. Expensive

Time and money are involved in the process of collection, analysis and interpretation of data for the purpose of forecasting. When forecasts are based on certain assumptions, we cannot expect hundred per cent accuracy.

ADVANTAGES OF FORECASTING

Forecasting is a key process in planning and it has the following advantages: (in brief)

1. Forecasting supplies vital facts and serious information.
2. It improves the creative abilities of managerial personnel.
3. It provides opportunities for team work and brings coordination.
4. It facilitates the workers to accept changes without any serious resistance.
5. It helps in minimising adverse effects and maximising opportunities.
6. It facilitates in the best utilisation of resources through proper direction.
7. It helps the management in achieving the objectives through proper control.

EFFECTIVE FORECASTING

Decision making and planning are based on forecasts. That is, forecasting provides information that facilitate decision-making and planning. Making plans, not based on forecasts, is more hazardous. Thus, forecasting is necessary. The following measures can help in increasing the effectiveness of forecasting:

1. Forecasting methods should be simple.
2. Forecasts should be based on facts and figures.
3. Length of forecasts should be shortened to improve their accuracy.
4. Several forecasting methods should be adopted to make predictions.
5. Longer the period of forecasts, lesser is their reliability.

FORECASTING TECHNIQUES

There are various techniques of forecasting. Every technique has certain special advantage. The degree of accuracy required and the cost-benefit of the forecasting should be considered before selecting any particular technique. These techniques may be either quantitative or qualitative. If the data are not readily available, these techniques can be used.

1. Quantitative Techniques

The various quantitative techniques involve the use of various statistical tools for predicting future trends. These include time series analysis, regression analysis, extrapolation, econometric models etc. A brief description of quantitative technique is given below:

(i) Time Series Analysis

In this method a historical series of data is decomposed into various components, viz., trend, seasonal variations, cyclical variations and random variations. After the original data are adjusted for seasonal and cyclical variations, a trend line can be fitted by using the method of least squares.

When the various components of a time series are separated, the trend for the variable under study can be known.

(ii) Extrapolation

Extrapolation is also based on time series because it relies on the behaviours of a series in the past and projects the same trend in future. This method does not isolate the effects of various factors influencing a problem under study but takes into account the totality of their effects and assume that the effect of these factors is of a constant and stable pattern and would continue as such in future. Since the projection of future is based on past, it is essential that the growth curve of a series is chosen after a very careful study of its past behaviour.

(iii) Regression Analysis

If two variables are functionally related, an understanding of one such variable will help in estimating the other. Such relationships between two variables are analysed through regression analysis. For example, if it is known that there is a correlation between advertising expenditure and sales volume, future sales can be estimated on the basis of changes in advertising expenditure.

(iv) Input-output Analysis

Under this method, a forecast of output is based on given input if relationship between input and output is known. Similarly input requirement can be known on the basis of final output with a given input-output relationship. It is because of this mechanism that the techniques is known as input-output analysis or end-use technique. This technique is based on the well established interrelationships between different sectors of the economy.

2. Qualitative Techniques

This group of techniques uses qualitative data and may or may not take the past into consideration. Such type of techniques are used when data are scarce, for instance, when a product is first introduced into a market. The qualitative forecasting techniques are described below:

(i) Delphi Method

This is a simple method of selecting a panel of experts to which questionnaries are given to obtain accurate and complete information. The speciality of this method is that the information obtained from one questionnaire, so that ultimately all the experts will have comprehensive information through such a series of questionnaires.

(ii) Market Research Method

Personal interviews, sending questionnaires, etc. are the methods to conduct market research. When a new product has to be released and sales forecasts have to be made, this method is more useful.

(iii) Historial Analogy

Here forecast is based on some analogous conditions elsewhere in the past. According to Rostow, an economy passes through certain stages in its development. Therefore, the economic situation of a country can be forecasted by making comparison with another country which has already gone through that stage.

(iv) Panel Consensus

This method is based on the assumption that several experts can arrive at a better forecast than one person. There is no secrecy and communication is encouraged. The information from one panel of experts may be presented openly in a group discussion to arrive at a consensus forecast.

DECISION-MAKING

INTRODUCTION

Decision-making is an essential part of modern management. A manager's life is filled with a constant series of decisions - Where to invest profits, what to do about an employee who is always late, where should the firm's new warehouse be built, what subject will have top priority at the departmental meeting, and so on. Hundreds of decisions are made by the manager, consciously and subconsciously every day. Minor decisions are taken almost subconsciously and major decisions however, are taken very carefully and consciously.

The success of a business depends upon the quality of the decisions it makes at each customer contact. Such decisions must reflect the business strategy, the interests of the customer, his value and risk to the business. In addition, because of growing customer expectations and increasing competition, businesses are under pressure to provide personalised customer service within mass market cost levels.

A decision is a choice made between two or more available alternatives. Decision-making is the process of choosing the best alternative for reaching objectives. We all face decision situations every day. A decision situation may involve simply choosing whether to spend the day studying, swimming or walking. It does not matter which alternative is chosen, only that a choice is made.

Managers make decisions affecting the organisation daily and communicate those decisions to other organisation members. Not all managerial decisions are of equal significance to the organisation. Some affect a large number of organisation members, cost a great deal of money to carry out or have a long-term effect on the organisation. Such significant decisions can have a major impact, not only on the management system itself, but on the career of the manager who makes them. Other decisions are fairly insignificant, affecting only a small number of organisation members costing little to carry out, and producing only a short-term effect on the organisation.

MEANING OF DECISION-MAKING

Decision-making means selecting a course of action out of alternative courses to solve a problem. Unless there is a problem, there is no decision-making. Decision-making and problem-solving are inter-related. It is the process through which managers identify organisational problems and solve them. The essence of management is making decisions. Managers are constantly required to evaluate alternatives and make decisions regarding a wide range of matters. Just as there are different managerial styles, there are different decision-making styles. Decision-making involves uncertainty and risk, and decision makers have varying degrees of risk aversion. Decision-making also involves qualitative and quantitative analysis, and some decision-makers prefer one form of analysis over the other. Managerial decision-making is the process through which managers in an organisation arrive at a suitable alternative solution to a given problem.

DEFINITIONS OF DECISION-MAKING

A few important definitions are given below:

1. "Whatever manager does, he does through decision-making" — Peter Drucker

2. "Decision-making is a conscious and human process involving both individual and social phenomenon based upon factual and value premises which concludes with a choice of one behavioural activity among one or more alternatives with the intention of moving towards some desired state of affairs." — Shull, Delberg and Cumming

3. "Decision-making is a process of identifying and choosing alternative courses of action in a manner appropriate to the demand of the situation. The act of choosing implies that alternative courses of action must be weighted and weeded out". — Kreitner

4. "Decision-making is the process through which managers identify organisational problems and attempt to resolve them." — Bartol and Martin

5. "A decision is an act of choice wherein an executive forms a conclusion about what must be done in a given situation. A decision represents a course of behaviour chosen from a number of possible alternatives. It is quite obvious that decision-making envisages two or more alternatives from which a final choice can be made." — Dalton E. Mc Farland

CHARACTERISTICS OF DECISION-MAKING

The basic characteristics of decision-making are enumerated below:

(*i*) **A Process of selection:** A decision is basically a process of choice-making. It chooses the best alternative from various alternative courses of action. If there is one alternative only, no decision-making is required.

(*ii*) **An intellectual abilities:** The process of decision-making is basically a human and intellectual activity. It is a mental exercise which considers and evaluates all the alternatives for realising certain objectives.

(*iii*) **Result oriented decision:** Decision-making is a propulsive activity because it is directed towards the achievements of goals and objectives.

(*iv*) **Evaluation of alternatives:** It involves all actions like defining the problem and probing and analysing the various alternatives which take place before a final choice is made.

(*v*) **Proper judgement:** Decision-making is a human and social process implying interference of individual as well as social factors. An intelligent manager will always take into account social and human implications of a decision.

Miscellaneous

(*vi*) Decisions are made to solve organisational problems and exploit environmental opportunities. Both problems and opportunities, thus, need decision-making.

(*vii*) It is a pervasive process. Decisions are made in business and non-business organisations. In business organisations, they are made at all levels.

(*viii*) Decisions are made at all levels in the organisation: though nature and importance of decisions vary at different levels. However, overall organisational effectiveness is determined by the quality of decisions made at all the levels.

(*ix*) It is an intellectual process. Managers use judgement, knowledge and creativity to develop solutions to the problems.

(*x*) It involves judgement and discretion of the decision-maker. It is not entirely a rational process because decisions are bound to be affected and coloured by personal likes, dislikes and whims of the manager.

IMPORTANCE OF DECISION-MAKING

The importance of decision-making cannot be over emphasized. Accordingly to Melvin T. Copland, "Administration essentially is a decision-making process and authority is responsible for making decisions and for ascertaining that the decisions made are carried out. In business, whether the enterprise be large or small, changes in conditions occur, shifts in personnel take place, unforeseen contingencies arise. Moreover, just to get wheels started and to keep them turning, decisions must be made."

Decision-making is the first step in management planning. It is a mental exercise. Several management authors, notable among them being Herbert Simon, Mc Farland, George R. Terry, etc. consider management and decision-making as one and the same. Decision-making is undoubtedly the heart and core executive activity in the business. As such we can safely conclude that decision-making is the primary task of the manager and really the essence of management.

At the heart of planning is decision making - the selection of a suitable course of action. It is an important function of management. Management without decisions is like a man without back-bone. Nothing can be performed without taking decisions. Every aspect of management functions, such as planning, organisation, motivation of control is determined by decisions, the result of which is the performance in the organisation. The days of "hit or miss" methods in management and over, and has been replaced by new concepts and scientific techniques. Decision-making is therefore, vital to all management activities. It helps in setting definite objectives, preparing plans of action, determining organisational structuring, motivating personnel and introducing innovations.

Decision-making is inherent in all managerial functions and embraces all areas of business. Management of an organisation has to take a series of decisions. A business executive is by profession a decision-maker. Decision-making is a pervasive function of management. Therefore, management is essentially a decision-making process and managers are called decision-makers. Managerial job is perpetually a decision-making challenge. In the words of Drucker," Whatever a manager does he does through decision-making." The quality of decisions determines the success or failure of management.

TYPES OF MANAGERIAL DECISIONS

The managerial decisions can be classified under the following categories:

1. Organisational and Personal Decisions

Organisational decisions are those decisions which the managers take under certain conditions relating to organisation. They take decisions independently or sometimes delegate to other colleagues. The decisions are based on the organisational environment.

Personal decisions are to be taken by the managers on their own. Others need not be consulted. For a manager, there is a lot of freedom and independence to take the decision.

2. Routine and Basic Decisions

Routine or tactical decisions are made repetitively following certain established rules, procedures and policies. They neither require collection of new data nor conferring with people. Thus they can be taken without much deliberation. They may be complicated but are always one dimensional. They do not require any special effort by the manager. Such decisions arc generally taken by the managers at the middle and lower management level.

Basic or strategic decisions, on the other hand, are more important and so they are taken generally by the top management and middle management. The higher the level of a manager, the more strategic decisions he is required to take. The strategic decision relate to policy matters and so require a thorough fact finding analysis of the possible alternatives. Finding the correct problem in such decisions assumes great importance. The managers are more serious about such decisions as they influence the decision making at the lower levels.

Strategic Decisions Vs. Tactical Decision

Strategic (Basic) Decision	*Tactical (Routine) Decision*
1. Top management take such decisions.	1. Lower level management takes decision.
2. Such decision has long-term implications.	2. Such decision has short-term implications.
3. Decisions are made on the problems which are important.	3. Decisions are concerned with routine and repetitive problems.

4. More management judgement and experience are needed for these type of decisions.	4. Established rules and procedures are needed. Special efforts are not needed.

3. Programmed and Non-programmed Decisions

Professor Herbert Simon has classified all managerial decisions as programmed and non-programmed decisions. Professor Simon has utilised computer terminology in classifying decisions. The programmed decisions are the routine and repetitive decisions for which the organiation has developed specific processes. Thus, they involve no extraordinary judgement, analysis and authority. They are basically devised so that the problem may not be treated as a unique case each time it arises.

On the other hand, the non-programmed decisions are the one-short, ill-structured, novel policy decisions, that are handled by general problem-solving processes. Thus, they are of extraordinary nature and require a thorough study of the problem. They are basically non-repetitive in nature and may be called strategic decisions.

Programmed Decision Vs. Non-programmed Decisions

Programmed Decision	***Non-programmed Decision***
1. Little judgement is required.	1. Need considereable judgement.
2. Deal with routine and repetitive problems.	2. Deal with non-repetitive problems.
3. Usually made at lower levels of management.	3. Generally made at top management.
4. Decisions are made by pre-determined procedures and rules.	4. Each problem is unique and needs a creative solution.
5. Decisions are made for problems - simple or complex.	5. Decisions are made for complex problems.

4. Policy and Operative Decisions

Policy decisions determine the basic policies of the organisation and are taken at top level management. The policies are decided at the top become the basis for operative decisions. No decision can go beyond the policy framework of the organisation. These are important in nature and have long term impact.

Operative decisions, on the other hand, are less important and related with day-today operations of the business. These decisions are taken in the light of policies decided by the management. Middle and lower management take these decisions since these involve actual execution and supervision. Whether to allow bonus to employees or not is a policy decision. Once it is decided to pay bonus then making calculation of payments to be made to different employees is an operative decision.

5. Individual and Group Decisions

This classification is based on the number of persons involved in decision-making. If the decision is taken by one person it is known as individual decision. In small firms only the owner takes all important decisions. Even in big concerns too, one person may be allowed to take decision about a particular matter. Generally, individual decisions are programmed one and are less important.

Group decisions are taken by a group of persons. The decision of board of directors or committees come under this category. These are generally important decisions and relate to policy matters. The decisions are taken after a thorough discussion among persons who are assigned this work. The problem of delay in taking group decisions may create difficulties but otherwise these are well discussed decisions.

THE PROCESS OF DECISION-MAKING

There is no standardised procedure for making-decisions. However the typical steps involved in decision-making procedure are given below:

1. Setting objectives
2. Identify the problem
3. Diagnosis the problem
4. Establish objectives
5. Collection of relevant information
6. Developing Alternative solutions
7. Evaluate Alternative
8. Make Final Choice
9. Implement the Alternative
10. Feedback

1. Setting Objectives

The first step in decision-making is to know one's objectives. An objective is an expected outcome of future actions. Therefore, before deciding upon the future course of efforts, it is necessary to know in advance what we are trying to achieve. Objectives are the criteria by which final outcome is to be measured. Decisions have to be taken to achieve a particular objective or goal of the organisation. The manager has to understand first the specific objective of taking the decisions before diagnosing a problem. Unless the problem is well defined, the decision, instead of solving the problem, may complicate it. For example, if a business is losing market share, it is only a symptom. The real problem may be inappropriate product, unsuitable price policy, faulty distribution or lack of sales promotion. Therefore, clear understanding of the problem is necessary.

The need for decision-making arises when there is a problem. The problems that are least important in the order of priority, should for sometime, be left unnoticed. After sometime, most of the trivial problems get solved on their own and if not, the matter should be brought to the notice of managers for problem-solving. It is not necessary that managers take decisions only when the problems arise. They must also find the problems. They should search for areas where threats or opportunities can arise in future and decide how to prevent threats from occurring and exploit the opportunities when they occur.

Process of Decision-Making

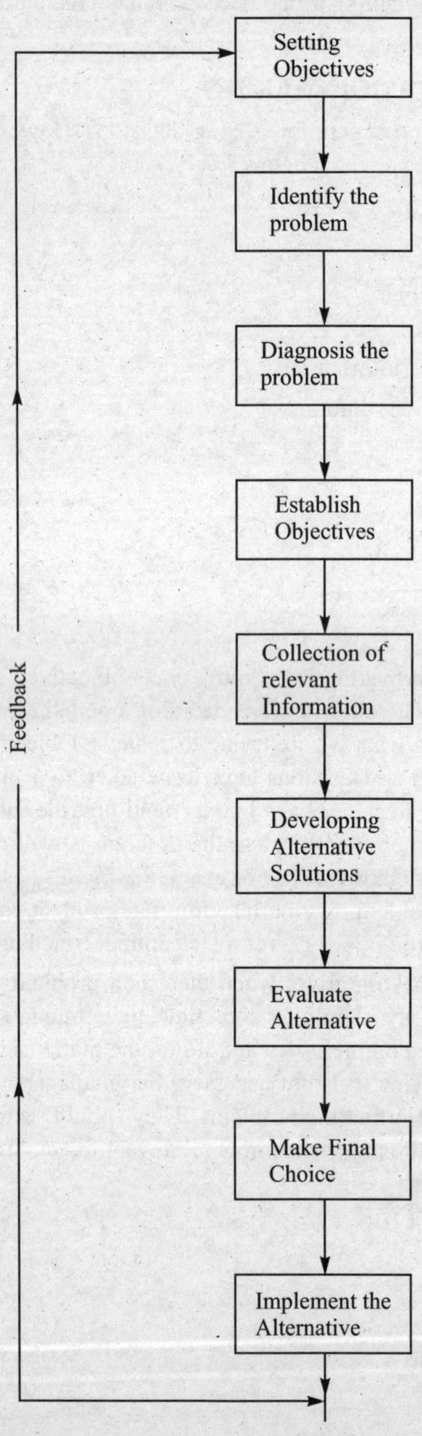

2. Identify the Problem

It involves defining and recognising the problem in a clear-cut manner. A clear understanding of the real problem is the most important task in the process of decision-making as the right answer can be found only for a right question. Problem is any deviation from a set of expectations. Managers scan the internal and external environment to see if the organisational operations conform to environmental standards. If not, it signals a problem. If a company's sales target is 10,000 units per month but actual sales are 6,000 units, managers sense problem of the company. The problem is identified with the marketing department. Managers use their judgement, imagination and experience to identify the problem and wrong identification leads to wrong decisions.

3. Diagnosis the Problem

Managers find cause of the problem by collecting facts and information that have resulted in the problem. Diagnosis helps to define the problem, its causes, degree of severity and origin so that remedial action can be taken. Managers get to the core of the problem and isolate the problem in a separate category of operations called the problem-solving area. Just like a doctor diagnosing a disease before prescribing a drug, a manager has to diagnose the real problem in the situation.

The quality of decision will depend upon the quality of information used. Therefore, collection of accurate and appropriate data is very important in decision-making. Data may be collected from external and internal sources. Sometimes, all the required information might not be available. In such a case, the manager has to judge the risk involved in the decision. If the problem is diagnosed, the half of it is solved.

4. Establish Objectives

The problem should be thoroughly analysed to find out adequate background information and data relating to the situation. The problem should be divided into many sub-problems and each element of the problem must be investigated thoroughly and systematically. There can be a number of factors involved with any problem, some of which are pertinent and others are remote. These pertinent factors should be discussed in depth.

Every problem should be correctly diagnosed. A manager should remember that the symptoms of a problem that he observes may sometimes mislead him. They may lead him to suspect one part of the system or operation when, in fact, the defect may lie hidden in another part which is perhaps less visible.

Objective is the end result that managers achieve through the decision-making process. Establishing objectives means deciding to solve the problem. The resolution forms the objective of decision-making. If the reason for low sales is poor salesmanship, managers form the objective of improving the skills of salesmen to promote sales.

5. Collection of Relevant Information

In order to generate alternatives to solve the problem, managers collect information from the internal and external environment. Information provides inputs for generating solutions. Information can be quantitative or qualitative. It should be reliable, adequate and timely so that right action can be taken at the right time.

6. Developing Alternative Solutions

Alternative means developing two or more ways of solving the problem. After analysing a problem, with the help of relevant information, the decision-maker should formulate several alternative solutions for the problem. There is hardly any problem in the world wherein alternatives cannot be developed. The development of alternative solutions for the problem is imperative. It is a right decision to be made. All the alternatives are weighed against each other with respect to their strengths and weaknesses. They are useful if they help to achieve the objective. Alternatives are evaluated in terms of acceptable criteria to analyse their impact on the problem.

7. Evaluate Alternatives

After developing various alternatives, the next step should be to judge and evaluate them through some decision criteria. As a result of these criteria one would like to see the ideal outcome of any action taken. The management has to evaluate the impact and implementation of all the alternatives. The tangible and intangible factors in implementing the decision must be studied. Sometimes, the qualitative and quantitative aspect also to be considered in evaluating a decision.

8. Make Final Choice

After evaluation of various alternatives, the next step is the selection of the best solution. It requires an ability to draw distinction between seen and unseen forces, between tangible and intangible forces, and between facts and guess. In attempting to select from alternatives, several basic approaches of decision-making are open to the manager. Among these are experimentation technique research and analysis techniques. Various organisational plans, policies, rules and other human factors are given due weightage.

A wrong choice would negate all efforts made in the previous steps. Optimal choice requires judgement as to the outcomes of consequences of alternatives. This judgement may be influenced by the intuition and personal value system of the decision-maker. The selected solution must be acceptable to those who must implement it and who are affected by it. In choosing from among alternatives, a manager must recognise clearly the factors which are limiting or critical to the attainment of the desired goals. But in making a final selection, the manager will invariably be guided by his past experience.

9. Implement the Alternative

After taking the final decision the next problem is to put decision into effect. This step involves gaining acceptance of the decision by those directly influenced by it and developing control to see whether the decision is being carried out properly. The means of communication of decisions, the motivation of employees and coordination of their efforts are other phases of implementation of decisions. In order to make the decision acceptable, a manager must explain what the decision involves, what is expected of the people and what benefits will occur to them. Subordinates become more committed to the decision if they are consulted while making decision. A manager should allow his subordinates to participate in the decision-making process by inviting suggestions from them regarding alternatives courses of action.

10. Feedback and Control

The implementation process should be monitored to know its acceptability amongst organisational members. The alternative should be regularly monitored, through progress reports, to see whether the objective for which it was selected is achieved or not. If there is any deviation, the same should be analysed to identify the causes. Wherever necessary, the decision should be modified. In spite of their best efforts and analysis, managers cannot make infallible decisions. So, the management should receive continuous information and evaluate them regarding the effect of his implemented decision.

Sometimes, a manager, in spite of his best efforts, may not make correct decision due to such limiting factors as non-availability of complete data, limited capacity of the manager himself and so on. As a safeguard against incorrect decision, the manager, while converting the decision into effective action, should institute a system of follow-up so that he can modify or alter his decision at the earliest opportunity.

CONDITIONS OF DECISION-MAKING

In order to make correct decisions the decision-maker must know the conditions under which decisions are to be made and implemented. Decisions should be made in the light of the decision situation prevailing in the environment. On the basis of the amount of information available and the degree of confidence in such information for predicting the future, three types of decision situations can be identified: (*a*) Risk Condition, (*b*) Complete Certainty and (*c*) Complete Uncertainty.

(*a*) Risk Condition

Most of the organisational decisions are made under the conditions of risk. In such a condition, information available is incomplete. Results or outcomes are not totally known but will probably fall within a certain range of outcomes. In other words, the probability of each possible outcome is known. The decision-maker has to select the alternative which will give him the largest expected value. Risk conditions frequently exist in deciding the level of inventories of a particular item to be kept for sale. Various techniques have been developed to make decisions under the conditions of risk.

(*b*) Complete Certainty

When the decision maker knows with reasonable certainty what the alternatives are, and what conditions are associated with each alternative, a state of certainty exists. Under this condition, managers have complete knowledge about a decision, so all they have to do is list outcomes for alternatives and then choose the outcomes with the highest pay off for the organisation. Few organisational decisions are made under conditions of true certainty.

In the environment of certainty, decision-makers have complete and reliable information about future. Information is reliable, correct and not too expensive. Results of each alternative can be predicted and therefore, managers can choose the best course of action. But such a situation does not in reality. In fact, managers make decisions on those aspects of environment about which information is available. They ignore the rest and call it a situation of certainty.

(*c*) Complete Uncertainty

It is a situation where no information is available about future. Whatever information is available, it is not reliable. Decision alternatives are totally unpredictable. Outcomes of decisions cannot be predicted. Decisions are based on manager's intuition and judgement. Some of the uncertain elements in the environment are economic, political, technological and natural changes. These changes cannot be predicted and accounted for in the decision-making processes.

PROBLEMS THAT REQUIRE DECISION-MAKING

Andre Theoret and others explain three types of problems that require decision-making:

(*a*) Crisis

It is a situation which requires immediate attention of managers and decisions to solve the problems. For example, if workers go on strike, management cannot sit back to think and take action. The problems need to be immediately resolved.

(*b*) Non-crisis

These problems do not require immediate attention but can be resolved over a period of time. Most of the decisions that managers make relate to situations or problems that are non-crisis in nature. An employee who is regularly late for work represents a non-crisis problem to be solved by managers. "A non-crisis problem is an issue that requires resolution but does not simultaneously have the importance and immediatly characteristic of a crisis."

(c) Opportunity

An opportunity problem is a situation that offers strong potential for significant organisational gain if appropriate actions are taken. Opportunities typically involve new ideas and non-directions and, therefore, are vehicles for innovation.

The situations of crisis and non-crisis reflect difficulties or problems for the organisation that need to be solved while opportunities offer ideas which improve organisational efficiency. Managers are in constant touch with the happenings around and take action immediately when opportunities are offered by the environmental forces to gain edge over competitors. Opportunities offer new ideas and directions to organisation's operations. They provide profits to the organisation if timely decisions are made by managers.

PROBLEMS IN DECISION MAKING

Some common difficulties faced in making decisions and implementing them are as follows:

1. Lack of Information

Lack of timely and adequate information is a common obstacle to sound decision-making. In some cases, the decision-maker is not sure of what type of data to collect from which sources. He even fails to differentiate clearly between relevant and irrelevant information.

2. Confusion with Symptoms

Very often it is found that people try to cure the symptoms rather than causes. In order to make sound decisions it is essential to isolate the root cause of the problem. Because 'causes' are different from 'symptoms'.

3. Ineffective Communication

Another important problem in decision-making is the ineffective communication of a decision. This makes implementation difficult. The manager should, therefore, take care to communicate all decisions to the employees in clear, precise and simple language.

4. Failure to Evaluate correctly

Choice of the best course of action requires accurate appraisal of the possible outcomes of different courses of action. It is also necessary to consider the constraints of the decision-making environment.

5. Incorrect timing

In decision-making, the problem is not merely of taking a correct decision. It is also of selecting an appropriate time for taking the decision. If the decision is correct but the time is inopportune, it will not serve any purpose. For example, if the manager wants to decide about introducing a new product in the market, he should take the decision at a correct time. Otherwise, he may lose the market to this competitors.

6. Indecisiveness

In certain cases managers cannot come to a conclusion easily because of fear of its outcome. Such managers are problem creaters rather than problem solvers. They make delay in taking decisions. Indeciveness results in loss of business opportunity.

7. Lack of follow-up of a decision

Making a decision is not the process but really a beginning. Proper implementation and effective follow-up of the decision are very essential for success in decision-making. But in many cases, it is not followed.

MODERN TECHNIQUES OF DECISION MAKING

A wide range of techniques are available to enrich the decision-making process. Traditionally, intuition, past experience and trial and error have been used to make decisions. Several scientific techniques have been developed to help the decision-maker. Decision-making has become a complex problem. A number of techniques, extending from guessing to mathematical analysis, are used for decision making process. The selection of an appropriate technique depends upon the judgement of decision-maker. The modern quantitative and scientific techniques of decision-making having greater application for solving complex, unique and novel problems. To make non-programmed decisions, the manager does not totally rely on his personal abilities like judgement, skill and creativity but uses these abilities through scientific methods. They use for solving complex problems like inventory control, plant capacity, complex problems like inventory control, plant capacity, product-mix, sales forecasting, production planning, budgeting etc. Some of the techniques are explained below:

1. Break-even Technique

It helps managers to determine that level of output at which total costs and total revenues are the same. Break even point is the point at which total revenue is equal to total cost. It is the point of no profit and no loss. Break even point analysis involves analysis of inter-relationships among costs, sales volumes and profits. Therefore, it is also known as cost-volume-profit analysis. The analysis is helpful in determining the volume of sales at which total cost is fully covered and beyond which profit will be earned.

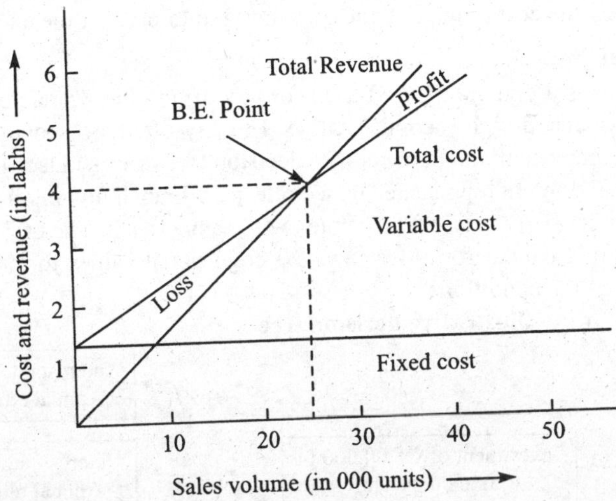

2. Inventory Models

Firms carry enough inventory with them so that they do not run out of stock. Though this ensures regular supply of goods to customers, they incur costs to carry the inventory like handling costs, storage costs, insurance costs, etc. These are known as carrying costs. In order to reduce these cost, firms keep minimum inventory in store and order fresh inventory when they need. This will reduce the carrying cost of inventory but the ordering cost will go up.

3. Linear Programming

This technique is used to determine the best use of limited resources for achieving given objectives. This method is based on the assumption that there exists a linear relationship between variables and that the limits of variations could be ascertained. Linear programme can be used for solving problems in areas like production, transportation, etc.

4. Simulation

Simulation is a systematic trial and error procedure for solving complex problems. In business there are many problems which are so complex and dynamic that they cannot be solved with the help of mathematical analysis. Under these circumstances simulating techniques are used. It is a technique to simulate the probable outcomes before taking action. A simulation need not be necessarily mathematical. But if in a problem, there are a large number of variables and constraints, the use of mathematics and computers becomes imperative. Inventory control and development of a new product line are some examples of areas where simulation technique works well.

5. Probability Theory

It is also an important statistical device which is used by OR experts. It is based upon the inference from experience that certain things are likely to happen in accordance with a predictable pattern. Probability is the number of times an outcome shall appear when an experiment is repeated. What is the probability that sales will increase if expenditure on advertisement is increased is answered through probability theory. These decisions are based on past experience and some amount of quantifiable data.

6. Queuing Theory

This technique describes the features of queuing situations where service is provided to people or units waiting in a queue. When people or materials wait in queue, because of insufficient facilities, it involves cost in terms of loss of time and unutilised labour. Queuing theory aims at smooth flow of men and material so that waiting time is reduced. This involves additional cost also. Thus, a balance is maintained between the cost of queues and cost incurred to prevent the queues.

7. Decision Tree

The decision tree is a graphic method used for identifying the available alternatives and the risk and outcome associated with each alternative. The pay-offs corresponding to each event are calculated. The four important components of a decision tree are: (*a*) Decision point represented by a square, (*b*) A chance point represented by a circle, (*c*) a branch flowing from the chance points and represented by a line, (*d*) A pay-off associated with each branch. The basic data is summarised in a pay -off matrix in a tabular form. It shows the conditional values for each alternative under both positive and negative conditions.

Look at the following illustrative decision tree

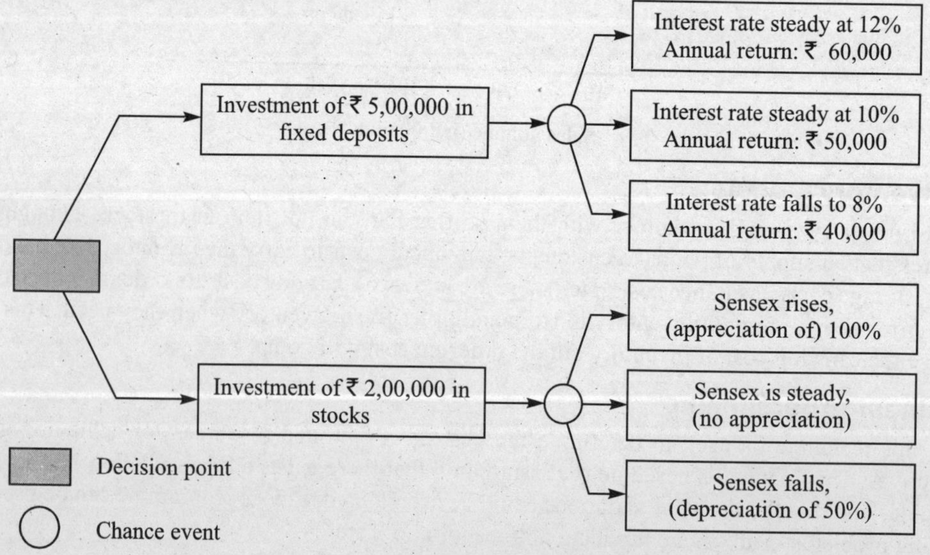

8. Game theory

Game theory is also a useful tool of OR, specially useful in the solution of business problems involving competitive situations. It provides a basis for determining under certain specific conditions, the strategy that will result in maximum gain (or minimum loss) no matter what the competitors do. This theory is based on these assumptions that at least two people are involved and one person wins exactly what the other loses.

9. Net Work Techniques

Network techniques of project evaluation and review technique (PERT) and critical path method (CPM) are used for planning, monitoring and implementing time-bound projects. These techniques help managers in deciding the logical sequence in which various activities will be performed. By applying these techniques, large and complex projects can be executed within the stipulated time and cost.

10. Brainstorming

Under this technique a small group of persons are stimulated to creative thinking. Maximum group participation and minimum criticism are employed to reduce inhibiting forces for generating ideas. A problem is posed and ideas are invited. Later these ideas are critically examined and the best ideas are selected. No evaluation of ideas is done during discussion to encourage free wheeling. Such free association and unrestricted thinking generates some novel ideas from which unique solution can be found.

11. Delphi Technique

The Delphi Technique is a group decision-making process that can be used by decision-making groups when the individual members are in different physical locations. The techniques was developed at the Rand Corporation. The individual in the Delphi "group" are usually selected because of the specific knowledge or expertise of the problem they possess. In the Delphi technique, each group member is asked independently to provide ideas, input, and/or alternative solutions to the decision problem in successive stages. These inputs may be provided in a variety of ways, such as e-mail, fax, or online in a discussion room or electronic bulletin board. After each stage in the process, other group members ask questions and alternatives are ranked or rated in some fashion. After an indefinite number of rounds, the group eventually arrives at a consensus decision on the best course of action.

12. Operations Research

Operations Research involves scientific analysis of decision problems. It facilitates decision-making by supplying quantitative information to the decision-maker. It provides scientific and objective basis so as to reduce intuition and subjectivity in solving organisational problems. Operations Research involves the construction and testing of model. Several techniques of operations research have been developed, for examples, probability theory, games theory, network analysis, queuing theory, etc. for analysis of problems. Operations Research has been widely used in managerial decision-making for inventory control, plant layout, quality control, allocation of resources, etc. But this technique can be applied only when all the elements of a problem can be quantified.

13. Synectics

This technique was introduced by William J. Gordon and was, therefore, originally called the Gordon technique. Subsequently it came to be known as Synectics. In this technique, the leader of the group reveals the problem to the members of the group so that they do not jump to conclusions in the first instance. Through gradual and continuous interaction, the group members arrive at the best solution to the problem.

MODELS OF DECISION-MAKING

Models represent the behaviour and perception of decision-makers in the decision-making environment. These are two models that guide decision-making behaviour of managers. They are 1. Rational or Normative Model and 2. Non-rational or Administrative model.

1. Rational or Normative Model

This model assumes that decision-maker is an economic man as defined in the classical theory of management. He is guided by economic motives and self interest. He aims to maximise profits and ignores behavioural or social aspects in making decisions.

What is a rational decision ? A decision is rational if appropriate means are chosen to reach desired ends.

Rational decision-making is a process of problem-solving in a scientific, systematic, objective and reasoned manner. It implies an ability and willingness to positively respond to reasons, to be logical, to coherently relate means with ends and to visualise the totality of the decision-making environment both immediate and long range. Rational decision making also implies knowledge of the facts so that problems are properly discovered and defined, objectives are specifically spelt out, alternative courses of action are developed and then final choice is made.

This model is based on the following assumptions:

1. Managers have clearly defined goals.
2. They must know what they want to achieve.
3. They must have ability to analyse and evaluate alternatives in the light of desired goals.
4. They must choose the alternative that best satisfies the goals.
5. They can collect reliable and complete information from the environment to achieve the objectives.
6. They can analyse all alternatives and rank them in the order of merits.

2. Non-rational or Administrative Model

Non-rational models are descriptive in nature. They do not describe what is best but describe what is most practical in the given circumstances. Managers cannot collect, analyse and process perfect and complete information and, therefore, cannot make optimum decisions. Absolute rationality is rate. It is seldom achieved. Based on whatever information decision-makers can gather and process, they arrive at the best decisions in the given circumstances. They are good enough and do not put undue pressure on manager's time and resources. They are easy to understand and implement. These decisions are not optimum decisions. They are satisfying decisions. This principle - Principle of Bounded Rationality - was introduced by Herbert Simon.

The decision maker is not an economic man but an administrative man who combines rationality with emotions, sentiments and non-economic values held by his team members. He follows a flexible approach to decision-making which changes according to situations. Manager's make feasible decisions which are less rational rather than rational decision which are less feasible.

"Bounded rationality refers to the limitations of thought, time and information that restrict a manager's view of problems and situations." — Pearce and Robinson

"Managers try to make the most logical decisions given the limitations of information and their imperfect ability to assimilate and analyse that information." — Herbert Simon

QUANTITATIVE TECHNIQUES OF DECISION-MAKING

The increasing complexity of organisational problems requires that improved methods of decision-making be discovered and utilised. Accordingly, various quantitative techniques have been developed to help in managerial decision-making, Operations Research (OR) is one of them. Operations Research has proved itself to be an invaluable tool in the hands of managers for decision-making, particularly with regard to planning and controlling function of management.

There are almost as many definitions of OR as there are writers on the subject. There is considerable divergence of opinion among authors regarding the meaning of this term. Some experts regard it as only a technique of applying mathematics and common sense to business problems. Others take it as application of scientific methods to the problem of decision-making. Some authors suggest it as application of quantitative techniques to the business problems. Perhaps the most acceptable definition of OR is that "It is the application of scientific methods, of the study of alternatives in a problem situation, with view to providing an quantitative basis for arriving at an optimum solution in terms of the goals.

OR is not a self-sufficient tool of decision-making. It does not provide a decision. It simply helps in analysing the problem and developing alternatives. It develops quantitative data to help the manager in making decisions. The following are the main characteristics of OR.

1. It examines a problem as a whole and not in parts,
2. A 'Model' is the logical representation of a problem.
3. This analysis is conducted by a team of trained experts.
4. The whole analysis is conducted by a team of trained experts.
5. OR approach assumes that there are alternative courses of action from which choices can be made.
6. It aims at the selection of best and most economical alternative.

Thus it is seen that OR does not provide a solution. It helps the executives in analysis of the problem and development of alternative solutions. It is very suitable technique for the analyses of those complex problems which can be measured in quantitative terms.

CASE STUDY - 1

S.K. Seth had barely reached his cabin. When he was informed that he's expected at the meeting of the faculty and administration. He was already late when he reached the meeting room and found everyone else in a deep discussion. Sitting next to Prof. John, his long time associate, he thought, "If only these meeting were not happening, I would have finished my article." He has just come back from the two week training programme, conducted by his department for a corporate house.

The dean said, "The next important issue is consideration of one feasibility report prepared by Prof. John, assistant dean, for launching a new programme, a variant of our MBA in Sri Lanka". Seth was surprised and he could not help asking what the issue was all about. Prof. John, handed over a thick report to him and said, "Professor Seth, perhaps you have not had time to read the whole presentation we had made to this Sri Lankan University, its summarised here".

Seth replied, "Yes, I was out of town". Prof. John smiled and said, "The report was circulated day before yesterday, so that the faculty was put in the picture before the final decision. Anyway, the decision is almost made".

The dean further said, "Prof. John, will now present a summary of his excellent report, I am sure that it is a golden opportunity for our institute to spread our wings internationally". Seth thought of the pending development issues of their MBA in their own campus. He wondered why the board never got time to settle these issues first, before going for new programmes in other countries. He thought of the issues related to his students, of recruiting a new research associate, new hostel and all other things at their campus which needed urgent attention of the management committee.

While John presented the summary, he went through the report and noticed a few issues. The college was offering identical courses in Sri Lanka and faculty from the college had to visit on periodic basis to their campus. He thought, "Why can't we get good faculty from that place and alter the course a bit to cater to their needs". But he kept silent and waited for the summary to end.

After taking 15-20 minutes, John ended on a note of inviting questions. Seth asked if the financial aspect to this proposal has been looked upon. The Dean answered, "Its in the report". Seth said, "I wonder how many people could actually read this entire report in two days". The dean answered, "Prof. Seth, Prof. John and I have spent a long time on this project covering and probing all issues, I think it is a good opportunity for us to showcase our talent and resources".

Seth still wasn't convinced. "What about our own internal issues which were pending for resources." The dean answered back, "Prof! we will meet next week again and address those issues, as of now, I don't see any valid objections coming up on our project. So before I move on, I confirm that our committee unanimously approves of this project. I would like to add here that our President is very happy with this project. He also appreciates the way we are taking decisions with shared vision and total commitment to our cause, *i.e.*, of spreading management education. While other colleges are battling over the issue of decision making we have made it work". The dean went further, "This is a great day for our institution, as we become a multinational institute. I hope its just a beginning before we make a significant mark on international scene". After the meeting, while coming back Seth said to John, "What a way to make important decisions. Most of the committee members don't have a clue about what has happened", John said slowly "Seth, what we teach need not necessarily be put in practice at work, just take it easy".

QUESTIONS

1. Analyse the case and outline the factors influencing this decision.
2. Decision making of this type does not happen in real workplace situations. Comment.
3. Shared decision making can be made more effective. Suggest how the situation can improve in the Institute of Management.

REVIEW QUESTIONS

1. "Decision-making is very important for management". Comment (*B.Com., Bangalore*)
2. Write a note on Bounded Rationality in decision-making. (*B.Com. Bharathiar*)
3. Explain the importance of forecasting. What are the limitations of forecasting ? (*B.Com., Madurai*)
4. "Decision-making is the primary task of management". Discuss the statement and explain the process of decision-making. (*B.Com., Madras*)
5. Explain the major techniques of forecasting. (*B.Com., MS University*)
6. Explain the process of decision-making ? (*B.Com., Kerala*)
7. Explain the merits and demerits of group decision-making. (*B.Com., Mysore*)
8. Discuss the different types of decision-making. (*B.Com., Delhi*)

9. What are the common difficulties in decision-making ? (*B.Com., Allahabad*)
10. Enumerate the types of decisions. (*B.Com., Madurai*)
11. What are the characteristics of forecasting ? (*B.Com., Bangalore*)
12. Discuss the steps in forecasting. (*B.Com., Banaras*)
13. Explain the various steps in the process of decision-making. Which one is most important and why ? (*B.Com., Jabalpur*)
14. Explain the quantitative techniques of decision-making. (*B.Com., Ujjain*)
15. What do you understand by rational decision-making ? (*B.Com., Bhopal*)

Management Information Systems

9

CHAPTER

- Introduction
- Meaning
- Reporting Needs of different Management Levels
- EDP
- MIS Emerges
- DSS
- Information and Data
- Importance of MIS
- Essentials Requisites of a good MIS
- Benefits of MIS
- Role of the CIO
- Implementing a Computer Based MIS
- Problems in Implementing a Computer-Based MIS
- Designing an MIS
- Guidelines for Making MIS Effective
- Case Study - 1
- Case Study - 2
- Review Questions.

INTRODUCTION

We can define MANAGEMENT INFORMATION SYSTEMS (MIS) as a formal method of making available to management the accurate and timely information necessary to facilitate the decision-making process and enable the organisation's planning, control and operational functions to be carried out effectively. The system provides information about the past, present and projected future and about relevant events inside and outside the organisation.

Information is the basis for decision-making in an organisation. The efficiency of management depends, to a larger extent, upon the availability of regular and relevant information to those who exercise the managerial function. A regular system of reporting is considered as a better guarantee of efficiency and operation than reliance on personal qualities. Thus it is essential that an effective and efficient reporting system is developed as part of accounting method. The main object of management reporting is to obtain the required information about the operating results of an organisation regularly in order to use them for future planning and control. The term 'report' normally refers to a formal communication which moves upward, *i.e.* by a lower level to a higher level of authority in response to orders received from higher level. A person, who is issued with instructions to do certain things, should report back what he has done in compliance thereof.

MEANING

The old techniques like intuition, rule of thumb, personal whim and prestige, etc. are now considered useless in the process of decision-taking. Modern management is constantly on thc look out for such quantitative and other information which can help in analysing the proposed alternative actions and choosing one as its decision. Thus, modern management functions are information-oriented more popularly known as 'Management by information'. And the system through which necessary information is communicated to the management is known as "Management Information System (MIS)." The management needs full information before taking any decision. Good decisions can minimise costs and optimise returns. Management Information System can be helpful to the management in undertaking management functions smoothly and effectively.

Management Information Systems (MIS) support an organisation's managers by providing daily reports, schedules, plans and budgets. Each manager's information activities vary according to his functional area, say, accounting or marketing, and management level. Whereas mid level managers focus mostly on internal activities and information, higher-level managers are also engaged on external activities. Middle managers, the largest MIS user group, need networked information to plan such upcoming activities as personnel training, materials movements cash flows, etc. They also need to know the current status of the jobs and projects being carried out in their department; What stage is it at now ? When will it be finished ? Is there an opening so we can start the next job ? Many of a firm's MIS · Cash Flow, Sales, production scheduling, shipping - are indispensable in helping managers to find answers to such questions.

REPORTING NEEDS OF DIFFERENT MANAGEMENT LEVELS

Generally the reporting levels in the internal management fall in three categories:

(A) Top Management Level

(B) Middle Management Level

(C) Lower Management Level

A. Top Management Level

The top level management comprises of Board of Directors, General Manager, Assistant Managers, Finance Directors, Production Directors, Sales Directors, etc. The top management is primarily concerned with the policy formulations, planning and organisation. They are, therefore, interested in the overall efficiency or inefficiency of the business. Generally, the top management should receive the following reports at different intervals:

1. Periodic report about Profit & Loss Account and Balance Sheet.
2. Statement of Funds Flow and Cash Flow at regular interval.
3. Report of plant utilisation.
4. Report of cost of production.
5. Report on research and development activities.
6. Periodic report on sales, credit collection, selling and distribution expenses, etc.

B. Middle Management Level

This comprises the heads of various departments such as Sales Manager, Production manager, etc. The report for this level should show the efficiency and cost data relating to respective areas or departments. The departmental managers are primarily concerned with the execution of plans, administration of policies, directing operating supervisors, etc. The work of co-ordinating activities of different departments is also undertaken by middle management. They receive the following reports: weekly or fortnightly.

1. Reports on material price and usage variances
2. Reports on labour rate and efficiency variances
3. Report on idle time, wastage of materials, etc.
4. Reports on stock levels
5. Reports on sales, production, etc.
6. Reports on orders booked, orders executed and orders still to be executed.

C. Lower Management Level

The lower level management is assigned the work of executing various policies. They are in touch with the day-to-day performance of their section. They may need reports on daily or weekly basis. Supervisors, formen, section-chief, sectional incharge, etc. come under this level. Reports are almost in the form of scrap of paper having no proper format. Reports are detailed and specific, restricted only to the activity with which they are concerned; Examples of such reports are:

1. Reports of over-time
2. Material usage variances
3. Labour efficiency variances
4. Material spoilage report
5. Accident report, etc.

EDP

When computers were first introduced into organisations, they were used mainly to process data for a few organisational functions - usually accounting, billing, etc. This was true at colleges and universities, too. Because of the specialised skills required to operate the expensive, complex and sometime temperamental equipment, computers were located in ELECTRONIC DATA-PROCESSING (EDP) department. As the speed and ease of processing data grew, other data-processing and information management tasks were computerized. To cope with these new tasks, EDP departments developed standardized reports for the use of operating managers.

MIS EMERGES

The growth of EDP departments spurred managers to focus more on planning their organisations' information systems. These efforts led to the emergence of the concept of COMPUTER-BASED

INFORMATION SYSTEMS (CBIS), which became better known as computer-based MIS - or simply MIS. As the EDP departments' functions expanded beyond routine processing of masses of standardised data, they began to be called MIS departments.

DSS

A DECISION SUPPORT SYSTEM (DSS) is an interactive computer system that is easily accessible to, and operated by , people who are not computer specialists, who use the DSS to help them plan and make decisions. The use of DSSs is expanding, as recent advances in computer hardware and software allow managers and other designated employees to gain "on-line" or "real-time" access to the databases in MIS's. The widespread use of microcomputers has enabled managers to create their own databases and electronically manipulate information as needed rather than waiting for reports to be issued by the EDP/MIS department. While MIS reports are still necessary for monitoring ongoing operations, DSS permits less structured use of databases as special decision needs arise.

INFORMATION AND DATA

Data are facts that are not currently being used for decision-making purpose. Payroll records, data on account receivables, personnel data, etc. are typical data in a business enterprise. On the other hand, information is processed data which is directly used in the process of decision-making. For instance, a customer's invoice in itself is data but, when it is processed for use in sales analysis, it becomes information.

IMPORTANCE OF MIS

MIS contributes towards effective management in the following ways:

1. Risk bearing can be minimised by collecting timely information. When the collection and interpretation of information collected are perfect, an accurate forecast can be made easily.
2. Information technology refers to the resources used by an organisation to manage information that it needs to carry out its mission. IT may consist of computers, computer networks, fax machines and other pieces of hardware. In addition, IT involves software that facilitates the system's ability to manage information in a way that is useful for managers.
3. For information to be of real value to a manager, it must be ACCURATE INFORMATION. Accuracy means that the information must provide a valid and reliable reflection of reality. It quantifies relationship among variables which can be projected to forecast future trends.
4. MIS can be effectively used for measuring performance and making necessary changes in the organisational plans and procedures. It identifies and meets separate needs of all units in a decentralised set-up without duplication of efforts.
5. Information needs to be timely. Timeliness does not necessarily mean speediness; it means only that information needs to be available in time for appropriate managerial action. What constitutes timeliness is a function of the situation facing the manager. The MIS is a major tool, to be used by management in solving day-to-day problems and taking quick decisions.

ESSENTIAL REQUISITES OF A GOOD MIS

The main purpose of MIS is to gather coordinated, systematic and continuous flow of relevant information. MIS is an organised set of procedures and routine. In brief, the requirements for a MIS are:

1. MIS makes available only the required information and is less time-consuming in making decisions.
2. It is a system which excludes unwanted information, thus saving the time of decision-makers.

3. The operation and design of the system is handled by specialists, who gather information and deal with it to meet the desired objectives.
4. To the top executives, MIS provides fast and accurate information.
5. It facilitates in taking suitable and quick decisions promptly.
6. It is a unified system.
7. It adopts the principle of selectivity in information.
8. It is very economical.
9. It is conceived and used as a tool.
10. It is ongoing process. It operates continuously.

BENEFITS OF MIS

The various benefits that flow from MIS are listed below:

1. It helps in planning by making available correct information on the external environment and the internal company realities.
2. The information if free from any bias towards the pre-conceived conclusion will have more value than otherwise.
3. The information if free from any error, will have more value than otherwise.
4. The quality of decisions are decided to a great extent by the quality of MIS available to the decision-maker.
5. It facilitates the development of action programmes for achieving set goals.
6. It helps in controlling of activities.
7. It helps effective tapping of opportunities and effective defence against threats.

THE ROLE OF THE CHIEF INFORMATION OFFICER (CIO)

The chief information officer (CIO) is the "human link" between top management and the company's information system. As the architect of the firm's computerized information systems, the CIO is responsible for overseeing the preparation and dissemination of policies and procedures for new and existing systems. The CIO also acts as a change agent who is responsible for the introduction of such technologies as telecommunications, office automation, MISs, DSSs, expert systems, and related activities. Unlike traditional data processing managers, who focus on day-to-day operations, the CIO focuses on planning and developing creative and innovative ways to meet manager's growing information needs.

IMPLEMENTING A COMPUTER-BASED MIS

The use of computers to address many organizational concerns has grown rapidly. Managers should be aware of the technological problems of systems design and installation. They should also be aware of the "people concerns" that are important for most managers to understand, are difficult to address, and can inhibit successful implementation of a computerized information system.

PROBLEMS IN IMPLEMENTING A COMPUTER-BASED MIS

Resistance to a new MIS can be every manager's nightmare. G.W. Dickson and John K. Simmons note five major factors that determine whether and to what extent the implementation of a new MIS will be resisted.

1. *Does the MIS disrupt established departmental boundaries ?* The establishment of a new MIS can result in changes in several organisational units. For example, inventory and purchasing departments may be merged to make more efficient use of the MIS. Such disruptions may be resisted by department members, who may resent having to change the way they do things or the people with whom they work.

2. *Does the MIS disrupt the informal system ?* The informal communication network may be disrupted as a new MIS alters communication patterns. If organization members prefer some of the earlier, informal mechanisms for gathering and distributing information, they may resist the more formal channels set up for the new system. Development and Alumni Office managers often talk informally about the university's graduates. A new MIS cannot interfere with that valuable communication channel.

3. *Does the MIS challenge specific individual characteristics ?* People with many years of service with the organization have "learned the ropes" and know how to get things done in the existing system. They may resist change more tenaciously than newer people who have been with the organisation for a comparatively short period of time and do not have as large an investment in organisational know-how and relationships.

4. *Is the MIS supported by the organizational culture ?* If top management maintains open communication, deals with grievances, and, in general, establishes a culture with high trust throughout he organization, there is likely to be less resistance to the installation of a new MIS. However, if top managers are isolated for aloof from other organization members, or if the organizational culture supports inflexible behaviour, then effective implementation of the MIS is likely to be hindered. At many colleges and universities, departments have been relatively independent by tradition. In this kind of culture, top management support must be supplemented by broad-based support from organizational members.

5. *Do employees have a say in how the change is implemented ?* As we have seen repeatedly in earlier chapters, the manner in which changes are designed and implemented affects the amount of resistance those changes will encounter. In general, when managers and employees make change decisions together, there is a greater likelihood that the changes will be accepted.

DESIGNING AN MIS

The following steps are suggested in designing a computer-based MIS:

1. It is necessary to analyse the decisions for which information is required. The needs of every level and functional area must be considered. From this analysis and assessment the information system needed by the organisation can be defined.
2. An analysis of the current information system is made to determine alternative information system designs with specific performance requirements. These alternative are then evaluated against the organisation's objectives, and information needs. An initial MIS design is selected.
3. Once the conceptual plan is formulated, performance specification of the new MIS can be developed. At this stage the actual system for collecting, storing, transmitting and retrieving information is developed. Components, programming, flow-charting and data bases are designed.
4. The formal requirements for the system are determined. The logistics of space allocations, equipment additions and form designs are worked out and enacted. The organisation's data bases are entered into the system. After a series of final checks, the MIS is ready for implementation.

Once the system is implemented, deficiencies may arise and the system may have to be adapted to the changing needs and environment of the organisation.

GUIDELINES FOR MAKING MIS EFFECTIVE

The following steps will help in making an MIS successful:

1. The design and implementation must be user-oriented: otherwise MIS is a waste. That is, user needs must be given priority.

2. There must be cooperation between the operating members and system designers.
3. The aim of MIS must be communicated to all members of the design team as well as users.
4. Proper education, training and orientation of MIS staff are essential.
5. Managers must understand how the MIS operates.
6. Installation of a new system must be on a cost-benefit basis: that is, because cost overruns are less likely to occur.
7. The new method must be clearly explained to staff.
8. It is necessary to pre-test the system before installation.
9. The system should be critically reviewed from time to time. Suitable steps should be taken to remove the deficiencies and to keep the system up-to-date.
10. In order to ensure security, the equipment must be placed in safe and supervised areas and by constructing password and read only files.

CASE STUDY - 1

Issues Management

Many corporations feel that their strategic and marketing planning groups focus too narrowly on forecasting of products and services provided by the company and thus fail to spot important trends in the business conditions. If such trends are detected early enough the corporate management can be alerted as to the consequences of the trend and can select an appropriate strategy to mitigate its impact on the corporation revenues. For example, the business and economic planners failed to predict the Arab oil embargo or the environmental revolution.

To supplement the business and marketing planning activities, top management executives set up trend-spotting departments. The mission of these departments is to deal with the upcoming issues. The issues manager considers the immediate future and the next one to five years, and is charged not only with identifying issues but also setting forth specific ways the company right deal with them. Essentially, the issues managers were assigned tasks previously done somewhat haphazardly by top executives. By tracking trends and issues early in their cycle, the top management could eliminate unpleasant surprises.

Today, about 70 corporations have issues managers. These include large oil companies, banking and insurance concerns and retailers. There are several examples that demonstrate the usefulness of this new kind of executive. When President Reagan cut the federal budgets, the issues managers at Atlantic Richfield Oil Company saw trouble ahead. They predicted that these budget cuts would prompt one state after another to try to compensate for lost federal money by taxing business. Atlantic Richfield with operations in 28 states felt that it may become a prime target. To deal with this situation, Atlantic Richfield mobilized corporate resources to defeat many bills aimed specifically at oil companies.

Atlantic Richfield has five clusters of issues: resources, environment, corporate and planning, manufacturing processes, and trade association participation. The group monitors hundreds of publications, opinion polls, and think-tank research reports. The information on any topic is available to top executives on one day's notice.

At Monsanto Company, an issues manager organizes a task force of middle managers and other employees to do the work and the results are sent to top executives.

Most issues tend to follow an eight-year cycle. For the first five years or so, nascent issues are emerging in local newspapers, are being enunciated by public-interest organizations and can be detected through public-opinion polling. It is easier to deal with issues at this stage as they are low-keyed and flexible. If it affects the corporate interests, companies can intervene and prevent the issue from reaching the legislative or active stage. In the fifth or sixth year, the national media get interested in an issue; then governmental action typically results in seventh or eighth year.

There are several examples where corporations anticipated issues and recommended actions that saved companies millions of dollars. With the advice of issues managers, S.C. Johnson & Sons, a privately held maker of floor waxes and other chemicals, removed fluorocarbons from its aerosol sprays three years before federal legislation forced others in industry to do so. Sears Roebuck & Co. spotted flammable nightware controversy early and got non-flammable goods into its stores well before governmental action required this.

QUESTIONS

1. Do you feel that issues managers are needed to spot trends and suggest early strategies to prevent later, adverse impacts ?
2. Is there a possibility that an early intervention to mitigate the impact of an issue would encourage corporations from discharging their social responsibility ?
3. How should the issues management department be organized to supplement corporate and market planning groups ?

COMMENTS

Marketers must anticipate well in advance the impending problems or issues due to every changing environmental forces, particularly economic, social, political and legal forces, and on the basis of such contingent changes, formulate most desirable plans and strategies so that changes when they occur can be met successfully and possible losses can be reduced. Issues managers are experts in forecasting issues and offering best solutions to them.

CASE STUDY - 2

Revamping of An Old-Line Investment Banker

Dillon Read & Co.

Dillon Read & Co. has been one of the nation's pre-eminent investment banking houses, built by Clarence Dillon, a Wall Street leader for decades. Dillon Read for years relied heavily on its enviable list of blue-chip clients such as Union Oil of California, Grumman, R.J. Raynolds Industries. They did little to generate new business areas. The company imposed a stringent code of honour that went beyond federal regulations. Each business was scrutinized and anything below standard was rejected.

Changing World & Competition

Dillon Read relied on the traditional approach: which involved offering financial advice to big corporation and managing securities underwriting. On the other side, there was a new brand of money makers, aggressive risk-takers who were aiming for profits through plunges into the frantic corporate-takeover game. They created merger ideas and sold them to companies and by betting their own money on stocks of takeover candidates. They also invested in new ventures.

Rival firms changed rapidly, Morgan Stanley & Co. pushed through a typical diversification drive and grew to 2,200 employees from mere 264 in 1970. Soloman Brothers, which boasts unmatched abilities in institutional trading established itself as a top under-writer. So did Merrill Lynch & Co. which commands the largest retail distribution system for securities in the country. Giant outsiders such as Prudential Insurance, American Express, and Sears Roebuck bought securities firms.

At the same time, big companies were turning less loyal to their traditional investment bankers.

Dillon Read, as a result, lost some prominent clients, including Superior Oil, CPC International and the New York Power Authority.

During 1980's, the outlook was for even more turbulent and drastic changes. With markets more volatile, investment banks have become bigger and diversified. In addition, increasingly aggressive foreign institutions and the huge commercial banks were eager to enter the investment banking field.

Dillon Read's Response

Dillon Read faced an uphill battle to play the catch-up with competition. It was already hurt by exodus of employees who were disappointed at the corporate strategy. Dillon Read brought in John Birkelund to become the chief operating officer and to *spur diversification.* He began to build retail brokerage business which would give Dillon Read a capability to distribute new securities. Mr. Birkelund began pursuing profits in venture capital, arbitrage and money management in addition to traditional corporate finance. Mr. Birkelund proposed developing actively a secondary market (over-the-counter market) for debentures—the fast growing popular investment.

QUESTIONS

1. Did Dillon Read wait too long to change in response to the changing environment ?
2. What other actions should Dillon Read take to stop its slide and regain a position of preeminence ?
3. Should Dillon Read go against the trend of "Bigness" and find a market niche in venture capital and arbitrage business ?

COMMENTS

Usually we have very keen competition among the marketers. Under competition, 'innovate or perish' is the rule. Hence, marketers must develop innovations and introduce them successfully. Innovation alone can assure favourable conditions to meet the changing environment. Marketer can fight competition and maintain or develop market share only through innovative management

REVIEW QUESTIONS

1. Define management information system. *(B.Com., MS)*
2. Describe in brief the components of an MIS. *(B.Com., Bhopal)*
3. What are the information needs of top management ? *(B.Com., Utkal)*
4. State the essentials of a sound MIS. *(M.Com., Allahabad)*
5. Discuss the steps involved in designing an MIS.
   What problems occur in its installation ? *(M.Com., Chennai)*
6. Explain the guidelines for making an MIS effective. *(B.Com., Jabalpur)*

Organising Functions

10

CHAPTER

- Introduction
- Definitions
- Meaning of Organising
- Importance of an Organisation
- Process of Organising
- Formal and Informal Organisation
- Formal Organisation
- Informal Organisation
- Formal Vs Informal Organisation
- Principles of Organisation
- Factors Influencing Organisation Structure
- Case Study - 1
- Case Study - 2
- Review Questions.

INTRODUCTION

Organisation came into existence in the early stages of human evolution, when persons began to cooperate and combine together to achieve a common goal. A sound management is based on proper organisational structure which is concerned with determining responsibility as assigning of authority to different superiors and establishing proper inter-relationship among them for achieving the desired objectives.

An organisation, by its most basic definition, is an assembly of people working together to achieve common objectives through a division of labour. People form organisations because individuals have limited abilities. An organisation provides a means of using individual strengths within a group to achieve more than it can be accomplished by the aggregate efforts of group members working individually. Business organisations are formed to earn profit by delivering goods or services to consumers.

In common parlance, 'organisation' refers to 'institution'. An educational institution, private agency, Government department or a business firm are organisations. In the context of management, it refers to formal arrangement of work among members of the institution with clear identification of authority and responsibility so that organisational goals are achieved optimally. If duties of each member and their relationship with peers, superiors and subordinates are well defined, the planning process will be effective.

It is essential for every institution to have sound principles of organisation to succeed in achieving its goals. The organisation should clearly define the tasks and duties of each member and relationship amongst them so that all members co-ordinate their activities to achieve the overall goals. The term 'organisation' as it is viewed today has emerged over a period of time from the traditional task-oriented to the modern people-oriented concept.

DEFINITIONS

Viewed as a group concept, different authors have defined 'organisation' as follows:

According to Oliver Sheldon, "Organisation is the process of combining the work which individuals or groups have to perform with facilities necessary for its execution that the duties so performed provide the best channels for efficient, systematic, positive and coordinated application of available effort."

Louis A. Allen defines organisation as "the process of identifying and grouping the work to be performed, defining and delegating responsibility and authority, and establishing relationships for the purpose of enabling people to work most effectively together in accomplishing objectives."

According to *Alvin Brown,* "Organisation defines the part which each member of an enterprise is expected to perform and the relations between such members, to the end that their concerted endeavour shall be most effective for the purpose of the enterprise".

According to Koontz and O'Donnell, "Organising involves, the establishment of an internal structure of roles, by identifying and listing the activities required to achieve the purpose of an enterprise, the grouping of these activities, the assignment of such group of activities to manager, the delegation of authority to carry out and provision for coordination of authority relationship horizontally and vertically in the organisation structure."

Pearce and *Robinson* define organising as a "process of defining the essential relationships among people, tasks and activities in such a way that all the organisation's resources are integrated and coordinated to accomplish its objectives efficiently and effectively".

MEANING OF ORAGNISING

Organising is a process of integrating, co-ordinating and mobilising the activities of members of a group for seeking common goals. It implies establishment of working relationships which is done by assigning activities and delegating authority. Oliver Sheldon says, "As a process of combining the work which individuals or a group have to perform with the facilities necessary for its execution, that the duties so performed provides the best channel for the efficient, systematic, positive and coordinated application of available efforts". A sound management is based on proper organisational structure which is concerned with *determining responsibility* as *assigning of authority* to different superiors and establishing proper interrelationship among them for achieving the desired objectives. It has been rightly pointed out that an organisation is not an end in itself; it is a means towards an end, i.e. the accomplishment of firm's goals.

The above definitions highlight the concept of organisation in two different senses. 1. Organisation Structure and (2) Organising Process.

1. Organisation as Structure

Organising is a set of relationships that defines vertical and horizontal relationship amongst people who are assigned various tasks and duties. The organisational task is divided into units, people in each unit (departments) are assigned specific tasks and their relationship is defined in such a way that maximises organisational welfare and individual goals. The relationship amongst people is both vertical and horizontal. As vertical relationships, the authority-responsibility structure of people at different levels in the same department is defined and as horizontal relationships, the authority-responsibility structure of people working in different departments at same levels is defined.

Organisation structure specifies division of work activities and shows how different functions or activities are linked; to some extent it also shows the level of specialisation of work activities. It also indicates the organisation's hierarchy and authority structure, and shows its reporting relationships. — *Robet H. Miles*

2. Organisation as Process

Organising defines relationships amongst people in such a way that organisational goals are achieved efficiently. It involves (*i*) identification of work, (*ii*) grouping of work into smaller groups, (*iii*) assigning work to each individual at every level in every department, (*iv*) defining its authority and responsibility, and (*v*) establishing relationships amongst people to make them work towards the organisational goal in an integrated and coordinated manner.

IMPORTANCE OF AN ORGANISATION

The importance of a sound organisation for any enterprise can hardly be over-emphasized. An organisation is definitely the backbone of management through which operations of an enterprise are run. It sets the relationship between people, work and resources to get productive results. Without good organisation, a one-man enterprise cannot successfully grow beyond the limits of the owner's strength and ability. As a matter of fact, a good organisation can contribute greatly to the continuity and success of an enterprise. Organisations is the framework through which managers operate. Sound organisation is the backbone of effective management due to the following reasons:

1. It Facilitates Administration

A sound organisation is the first requisite of effective management. It enables the top management to delegate responsibility to lower levels for routine functions. It can avoid confusion and delays as well as duplication of work and over-lapping of efforts. If the organisation is ill-defined, the management becomes difficult and ineffective.

2. It Promotes Growth of an Enterprise

Sound organisation helps in the growth and expansion of the enterprise by facilitating its efficient management. Sound organisation helps in keeping the various activities under control and increase the capacity of the enterprise to undertake more activities. It contributes to the growth, expansion and diversification of the enterprise. All such programmes can be successful to the extent the organisation structure permits.

3. It facilitates Coordination

Organisation is an important means of bringing coordination among the various departments of the enterprise. It creates clear cut relationship between the departments and helps in laying down balanced emphasis on various activities. It also provides for the channels of communication for the coordination of the activities of different departments.

4. Optimum use of Technology

It is the age of technological developments. Therefore, organisations not having well-developed technology will not be able to compete in the market. Well organised structures enable the organisations to optimally use and update their technology to remain competitive in the market.

5. It Stimulates Creativity

A sound organisation enables the top management to improve the ways of doing things by delegating routine affairs to people down the scalar chain. Creativity creates a sense of achievement in the manager in a well-organised structure that provides moral boost for further creative thinking.

6. Ensures Optimum use of Human Resources

Sound organisation ensures that every individual is placed on the job for which he is best suited. Such matching of job helps in better use of human talent. It also provides the benefits of specialisation which results in economy of operations and reduction in cost. A good organisation motivates the employees to contribute their best to the goals of the enterprise.

7. Executive Development

The pattern of an organisation structure has strong influence on the development of executives. Managers at different levels are continuously trained, developed and tested for assuming greater responsibilities and meeting new challenges of managerial positions. It also recognises merit for distribution of rewards and promotion.

8. It ensures Cooperation

A sound organisation disposes of conflict between individuals and the enterprise. It gives proper recognition to the contribution of each individual, values their cooperation, hence gaining their sincerity and loyalty. This improves interpersonal relationships of people working in the organisation.

9. It facilitates Communication

Communication is the essence of organisation. Efficiency of the organisation depends upon how well the organisational members communicate with each other. A well designed system of communication is facilitated through effective organising efforts of top executives.

10. It facilitates Control

Organisation provides sound direction to people's activities and ensures that they work according to plans. This facilitates control and achievement of organisational goals. Division of activities into various departments, facilitate to increase the organisational output.

PROCESS OF ORGANISING

The steps involved in the process of organisation are as follows: (in brief)

(*a*) Determine and formulate objectives, strategies, plans and policies.

(*b*) Determine the activities involved to accomplish the objectives.

(*c*) Grouping of similar activities into tasks, sections and departments.

(*d*) Define responsibility and accountability for every person.

(*e*) Delegate the required authority to perform the task.

(*f*) Integration of activities through authority relationships and communicate networks.

(*g*) Provide adequate physical facilities to perform the tasks effectively.

FORMAL AND INFORMAL ORGANISATION

On the basis of relationship, an organisation may be divided into two broad categories: (*i*) Formal and (*ii*) Informal. Both types of relationship are necessary for any group action just as two blades are essential to make a pair of scissors workable.

FORMAL ORGANISATION

A formal organisation refers to the structure of well defined jobs, each bearing a definite measure of authority, responsibility and accountability. The structure is consciously designed to enable the people of an organisation to work together for accomplishing common objectives. Thus a formal organisation is created through the coordination of efforts of various individuals. Every members is responsible for the performance of a specified task assigned to him on the basis of authority responsibility relationship in an organisation.

Characteristics of Formal Organisation

They are as follows:

1. It is developed through delegation of authority.
2. It is created by the top management.
3. It has written rules and procedures.
4. It focuses more on jobs than people.
5. It is based on specialition and division of work.
6. Work is officially delegated from top level to lower levels.
7. Division of work amongst people increases organisational output.
8. The organisation does not take into consideration emotional aspect.
9. Organisational charts are usually drawn.

Benefits of formal Organisation

A formal organisation offers the following benefits:

1. It clearly defines the objectives of the organisation.
2. There is an effective system of communication.
3. It avoids overlapping of activities between two persons or departments. That is, two persons are not assigned the same job.
4. It results in maximum utilisation of organisational resource.
5. The rate of labour turnover and absenteeism remains low.
6. Promotional avenues are clearly defined.

Limitations of Formal Organisation

1. There is loss of initiative and innovative abilities of employees due to strict adherence to rules.
2. In a formally designed organisation structure, employee's social needs remain unsatisfied as they are related to each other through a formal chain of command.

INFORMAL ORGANISATION

Informal organisation refers to the relationship between people in an organisation based on personal attitudes, emotion, prejudices, likes and dislikes, etc. These relations are not developed according to procedures and regulations laid down in the formal organisation. Generally large formal groups give rise to small informal groups. These groups are not pre-planned but they develop automatically within an organisation.

Informal organisations have always existed with formal organisations. They arise because of inevitable social and personal needs of individuals which cannot be satisfied by the principles of formal organisations. They represent non-planned, unofficial, social interactions amongst people working in formal structure. They arise out of common interests of people. These organisations are not governed by formal set of principles but nevertheless, are an important and integral part of formal organisations. While working in a formal organisation, people of different departments at different levels interact with each other, discuss their common interests - cultural, social, etc., and form groups to promote their goals. These goals are known as group goals and informal organisation is an important means to satisfy these goals.

Characteristics of Informal Organisation

The salient features of informal organisation are listed below:

1. The structure is not planned by top managers.
2. The basic purpose of information organisation is fulfilment of social and personal needs of people. Their social needs of friendship, love and support are strengthened by informal organisations.
3. Informal organisation does not have any formal structure. There are no superiors and subordinates in informal organisation. People contact each other in all forms - vertical, horizontal and diagonal.
4. It is based on common taste, language, religion, culture, etc.
5. It has no fixed rules and regulations that govern functions of the organisation. Rules are framed and changed by people according to their convenience.
6. The membership of information organisation is voluntary.
7. It is formed at the will of the people and dissolves at their will. It does not operate for a fixed period. Dissolution of informal organisation also does not follow any legal procedure.

Benefits of Informal Organisation

People form informal groups due to the following reasons:

1. Informal organisation satisfies the natural desire of people to associate with each other. It is created by members to achieve their personal goals.
2. It helps top managers to achieve their formal goals efficiently. They are relieved of the botheration of inspiring workers to work.
3. It provides a good training ground for development of leadership and personality.
4. People of informal organisation help managers, who is unable to take official decisions, by providing them help and support.
5. Communication travels much faster in informal organisations than formal organisations. People discuss their work and non-work related problems with each other and find solutions without the support of superiors.
6. If managers of formal organisation develop and maintain cordial relations with managers of informal organisation, it promotes an environment of understanding. This help to achieve formal goals of the organisation efficiently.

7. People of different departments discuss their work-related problems and solve them on their own without waiting for instructions of superiors of their departments.
8. People get a chance to exploit their creativity and work according to their judgement and skills without waiting for superior's instructions.
9. Informal organisation checks wrong acts of managers. Managers cannot frame goals, policies and plans not acceptable to members of information organisations. They cannot use discretion to frame goals.
10. Managers can get quick feedback on their official decisions from members through informal channel of communication.

Limitations of Informal Organisation

The information organisation suffers from the following limitations:

1. It reduce the influence of managerial authority.
2. The members of the group make their own norms and standards of performance which are followed by all group members, whether or not, they like them.
3. If attitude of leaders is negative, that is, he wants his personal interests to be satisfied at the cost of group interests: this attitude is harmful for all in the organisation.
4. Rumour is grapevine information that is communicated without secure standards of evidence being present. False information spreads in informal organisation at a very high speed.
5. Informal groups become over protective about their group goals and values. They oppose any change in their way of working.
6. If group goals are different from organisational goals, members generally pursue group goals, even if they are against the interests of formal organisational goals. This attitude is against the interest of the company and its members.

Difference between Formal and Informal Organisations

The above discussion on formal and informal organisations highlights the following points of differences between the two :

Formal Vs Informal Organisations

Nature	*Formal Organisation*	*Informal Organisation*
1. Power	1. It is attached to position.	1. It is attached to person.
2. Chain of Command	2. The chain is respected and authority is delegated by the top management.	2. Authority comes from personal knowledge and skills of group leaders and is given by the group itself.
3. Goals	3. Organisational goals are considered important.	3. Individual goals may clash with organisational goals.
4. Flexibility	4. Not flexible	4. Highly flexible.
5. Formation	5. They are deliberately created by managers.	5. They are created by members to achieve their personal goal.
6. Purpose	6. They are formed to achieve formal organisational goals.	6. Their objective is to achieve social satisfaction.
7. Flow of authority	7. Authority vests with managers. It flows from top to bottom.	7. Authority vests with the elected leaders.

8. Behaviour of members	8. Behaviour of members is governed by norms and standards framed by managers.	8. Behaviour of members is governed by norms and standards framed by group members.
9. Governance	9. Its working is governed by rules and regulations.	9. There are no fixed rules.
10. Winding up	10. It winds up according to legal procedures.	10. It winds up at the will of members.

PRINCIPLES OF ORGANISATION

Organisation is not an end in itself, but a means of achieving good business performance and business results. Therefore, it must be designed properly to make possible the attainment of desired objectives. The following principles or guidelines are helpful in designing a good organisation.

1. Principles of objectives

The objective of the organisation should be clearly defined and fully understood by all personnel. Objectives should be laid down not only for the organisation as a whole but for each department and (organisational) objectives. Objectives provide the organisation with a sense of purpose and direction.

2. Principle of specialisation

When every individual in the organisation concentrates on the performance of a single task, he can work with greater economy and efficiency. Therefore, as far as possible, each individual should be given a single function or activity to perform. The function or task entrusted to an individual should be appropriate to his qualification, skills and aptitude.

3. Principle of span of control

There is a limit to the number of subordinates which a superior can effectively supervise. The limit is known as the span of control or span of supervision. The span of every manager must be proper to facilitate effective control and better performance. The span of control determines the numbers of levels in the organisation and thereby influence the effectiveness of communication. The span of control should be determined in accordance with the nature and type of work, competence of the executives, quality of subordinates, etc. Generally, the span of control at higher levels of management is smaller as compared to the span at lower levels.

4. Principle of scalar chain

A scalar chain or chain of command refers to the unbroken line of authority from the top level to the bottom of an organisation. The scalar chain should be clearly defined so that every subordinate knows who is his superior and to whom policy matters beyond his own authority should be referred to for decisions. The line of authority is the route followed by all communications from the ultimate authority to the lowest ranks. The chain of command should be as short as possible.

5. Principle of exception

This principle implies that only those matters should be referred to higher levels of management which are of an exceptional nature or which can not be handled effectively at lower levels. The top management should be concerned only with important matters and routine problems should be divided by subordinate executives. This will relieve the top management of procedural delays and develop a sense of responsibility and initiative among lower level managers. The exception principle makes delegation of authority really effective.

6. Principle of unity of command

According to this principle, an employee should receive orders and instructions from one superior only. If a subordinate is answerable to more than one superior, his loyalty will be divided and there will be confusion and conflict in the organisation. Therefore, subordination should be avoided unless it is absolutely essential.

7. Principle of authority and responsibility

Authority and responsibility are co-extensive and two sides of the same coin. Therefore, they should go together. Whenever a person is made responsible for something, requisite authority should be given to him and whereever authority is delegated, a person must be held responsible for it. But responsibility is absolute or individual and a person can not escape his responsibility by delegating authority. Authority without corresponding responsibility result in misuse of authority while responsibility in the absence of adequate authority leads to frustration and ineffective performance.

8. Principle of co-ordination

Coordination is essential to bring unity of action in the organisation. Centralisation of control of an organisation can be achieved through interlocking all units of the organisation. To secure coordination, working relationship should be established. Each worker should be known by the organisational structure, his designation in it and the relationship of his work with other departments as well as his executive.

9. Principle of definition

The duties, authority and responsibility of every individual must be clearly and precisely defined. No individual should have a doubt as to what he has to do and for whom. The relations between various jobs and individuals should be defined in writing so that everybody knows what is expected of him and what are the limits of his authority. This will help to avoid confusion and overlapping of effort.

10. Principle of delegation

Authority delegated to an individual should be adequate to enable him to accomplish the results expected of him. Authority should be delegated to the lowest possible level consistent with necessary control so that decision is made as near the scene of action as possible.

11. Principle of efficiency

The efficiency of one organisation is judged by its capacity to achieve the predetermined objectives at the minimum cost. The organisation structure should ensure optimum utilization of all resources. It should help to satisfy the personnel and contribute to social welfare. The work should be completed with minimum members, in less time, with minimum resources and within the right time.

12. Principle of simplicity

The organisation structure should be simple so that the personnel can understand assignment of duties and authority relationships. A simple and clear structure allows the employees to work efficiently and effectively.

13. Principle of flexibility

The organisation structure should be so designed as to be adjustable to the changing conditions and requirements of the enterprise. It should be amenable to change if it is to remain efficient under a changing situation.

14. Principle of continuity

Organising is a continuing process and an organisation structure should be reviewed and revised regularly to keep it up to date and workable. The structure should ensure continuous growth and expansion of the business.

15. Principle to balance

Different departments and activities of the organisation should be given a proper weightage in proportion to their contribution to the overall objectives. An appropriate mix of centralisation and decentralisation should be created; over emphasis and under emphasis of all types should be avoided.

Work of all departments should be balanced in order to avoid conflict or overlapping of functions; with the object of ensuring smooth and efficient working of functions.

These principles lay down the essentials of a good organisation but they should not be treated as hard as fast rules. Rather, they are guides in designing an effective organisation structure. In exceptional situations, it may become necessary and desirable to modify some of these principles.

FACTORS INFLUENCING ORGANISATION STRUCTURE

While designing the internal organisation structure, management may consider the following factors:

1. Objectives and Goals

An organisation structure should be designed in such a way that it facilitates the achievement of organisational goals in the most efficient and economical manner. The goals of an organisation determine its tasks and activities. An organisation is a goal-oriented system.

2. Technology

Technology is an important variable in the design of organisation structure. It refers to the way in which work is done, that is, equipment and technical skills used and the type of work-flow in the transformation process. The type and nature of technology being used in an organisation has a definite impact on its structure.

3. Environment

An organisation is an open system which continuously interacts with its external environment in which it functions. Therefore, forces in the external environment must be carefully analysed while designing organisation structure. Researches have shown that different types of environments require different types of organisational structures for effectiveness.

4. People

Organisation structure defines work, groups it into departments and appoints people to run those departments. People at different jobs must possess the skill, knowledge and efficiency to accomplish the related tasks. Where people working in the organisation are skilled, experienced and motivated to satisfy their higher order needs, organic structure is more appropriate. If people are unskilled and inexperienced, mechanistic or classical form of organisation structure is more suitable.

5. Size

Size of the organisation is another factor affecting organisational design. As an organisation grows in size, there is a tendency to greater specialisation. The number of sub-units increases and more levels are created in the hierarchy. Impersonal rules and procedures increase formalisation and the organisation becomes more and more structured.

6. Strategy

Strategy is a contingent plan designed to achieve the objectives. It involves decisions as to what industry the organisation will enter, how will it compete and where. Studies revealed that the companies shifted their organisational design from a simple centralised pattern to a more elaborate divisionalised pattern following changes in population, technological innovations expanding product lines etc. Thus, changes in corporate strategy lead to changes in organisation structure.

7. Task

The task of an organisation is another major determinant of its structure. It is determined by the organisation's original charter and the role which the organisation decides to play in the society at large. The task of business is production and marketing of economic goods and services of Government, the fulfillment of such social needs as security and welfare: of a university, research and teaching: of a temple, administering to religious needs: and so on.

8. Culture

Another factor shaping the underlying structure of an organisation is culture. Culture sets the bounds on what may or may not be done, on what is desirable and what is not. Firms in North America tend to be more decentralised than firms in, say, Germany.

9. Span of Control

We have seen above that there is a very close relationship between the span of control and the shape of organisation structure. Small spans give rise to tall structures and big spans to flat structures.

10. Employee Characteristics

By "Characteristics" we mean their abilities, skills and experience as well as their needs and personality characteristics. If an organisation is generally composed of employees who are highly skilled and motivated, have strong needs for independence and self-realisation, a behavioural structure would be more appropriate than a classical one. On the other hand, if the organisation is generally composed of unskilled and poorly motivated employees, a classical structure may be more appropriate than a behavioural one.

CASE STUDY - 1

Hari Mohan has a position on the corporate planning staff of a large company in a high technology industry. Although he has spent most of his time on long-range, strategic planning for the company, he has been appointed to a task force to reorganise the company. The president and the board of directors are concerned that they are losing their competitive position in the industry because of an outdated organisation structure. Being a planning expert, Hari Mohan convinced the task force that they should proceed by first determining exactly what type of structure they have now, then determining what type of environment the company faces, now and in the future, and then designing the organisation structured accordingly. In the first phase, they discovered that the organisation is currently structured along classic bureaucratic lines. In the second phase, they found that they are competing in a highly dynamic, rapidly growing and uncertain environment, that requires a great deal of flexibility and response to change.

QUESTIONS

1. What type or types of organisation design do you feel this task force should recommend in the third and final phase of the approach to their assignment ?
2. Explain how the systems and the contingency theories of organisation can each contribute to the analysis of this case.

3. Do you think Hari Mohan was correct in his suggestion of how the task force should proceed ? What types of problems might develop as by-products of the recommendation you made in Question 1 ?

CASE STUDY - 2

Ice Cool Private Limited was an ice cream manufacturing company employing about 100 persons including persons at various levels of management. Because of increasing business, the company needed to strengthen its accounting procedure particularly through computerization. For this purpose, the company decided to hire a new manager designated as assistant manager. The company invited applications through press advertisement. After receiving the applications, it appointed a selection committee consisting of members of top management including business manager Rakesh Mohan. The committee interviewed several candidates and finally selected Bishwash as new Assistant Business Manager. Bishwash was neat, well dressed and quite articulate.

Bishwash joined the company immediately and started working very hard. He used to put extra efforts and even worked during holidays as he did not have any family responsibility. He gained the reputation of being a dedicated and competent employee, his strong point being his knowledge of accounting and computer system. He was reporting to Rakesh Mohan, the business manager who was quite impressed with his working.

At that time, the company had no computer system, and its accounting procedures were in need of considerable improvement. Anil Kumar' the managing director of the company, directed Rakesh Mohan to get the needful done. Since most of accounting work related to sales, no separate accounting department existed and the work was performed under the direction of business manager. Bishwash was mainly appointed to strengthen the accounting aspects of the business. He was asked to prepare a project report so that necessary changes could be made. In order to get the first hand information about the problem, Bishwash began meeting regularly with Anil Kumar without the knowledge of Rakesh Mohan. There was no attempt to have secret meeting: Anil Kumar would just call Bishwash in for a report without bothering to tell Rakesh Mohan. The management team, whose members were with the company for a quite long period had formed a tight-knit group and appeared satisfied with the company. They all worked together and the company prospered inspite of fierce competition.

The meetings between Anil Kumar and Bishwash continued and Rakesh Mohan was gradually losing contact with the project and its progress. In fact, Bishwash was almost reporting directly to the managing director though he was placed under business manager and retained his title of assistant business manager, rakesh Mohan was now visibly upset over the development and was also concerned about Bishwash's spreading share of influence. He started feeling let down in the company.

QUESTIONS

1. What is the nature of problem in this case ?
2. Could Rakesh Mohan have prevented Bishwash's assumption of power ? If so, how specifically, could it have been done ?
3. Suggest the course of actin now available to Anil Kumar, Rakesh Mohan and Bishwash ?

REVIEW QUESTIONS

1. Bring out the important characteristics of an ideal form of an organisation. (*B.Com., Bhopal*)
2. Explain the importance of organisation. (*B.Com., Jabalpur*)
3. What are the essential features of a good organisation structure ? (*B.Com., MS*)
4. Explain the principles of formal organisation. (*M.Com., MS*)
5. What are the principles of sound organisation structure ? (*M.Com., Chennai*)
6. Distinguish between formal and informal organisations. (*B.Com., Madurai*)
7. What is meant by organisation ? Describe the features of a sound organisation. (*B.Com., Bharathidasan*)

Departmentation and Organisation Structure

- Introduction
- Meaning
- Importance
- Definitions
- Types of Departmentation
    - Functional Departmentation
    - Product Departmentation
    - Territorial Departmentation
    - Departmentation by Customers
    - Departmentation by Process
    - Departmentation by Combined Base
    - Departmentation by Time
- Choice of Method of Departmentation
- Types of organisational Structure
    - Line organisation
    - Functional Organisation
    - Line and Staff Organisation
    - Line Vs Functional Organisation
    - Line and Line and Staff Organisation
    - Committee Organisation
- Misuses of the Committee Organisation
- Suggestions for making Committee Effective
    - Project Organisation
    - Matrix Organisation
    - Network Organisation
- What type of Organisation to Choose ?
- Case Study - 1
- Case Study - 2
- Review Questions.

DEPARTMENTATION

INTRODUCTION

Departmentation is an element of the organising process. It is a means of dividing the large and complex organisation into smaller and flexible administrative units. It involves horizontal differentiation of activities in an enterprise. A department is a distinct area, unit or sub-system of organisation over which a manager has authority for performance of specified activities. It is also known as division, branch, regiment, etc.

MEANING

Departmentation process is an essential part of organising process. The formal structure of organisation is created through the process of departmentation. Simply speaking it is a process of grouping of various activities into well defined divisions or departments. Such departments or divisions operate under the control of a manager known as departmental head. He has adequate authority over the activities and he is ultimately responsible for the smooth functioning of the department.

By conducting the process of departmentation, the activity structure of an organisation is prepared. The activities so grouped up are placed horizontally and around these groups, authority structure is also created. The process of grouping related work activities into manageable units is departmentation. The purpose of departmentation is to contribute to more effective and efficient use of organisational resources.

IMPORTANCE

Departmentation plays very important role in the entire process of organising. It is only with the help of this process, the structure of organisation is designed. Departmentation is required due to the following reasons:

1. Specialisation

Departmentation enables an enterprise to take advantage of specialisation. When every department looks after one major function of business, division of work becomes possible.

2. Fixation of Responsibility

Since similar activities are grouped in one department headed by departmental managers, it becomes easy for top managers to fix responsibility of respective managers for achieving the desired results. If planned performance is not achieved, the department responsible becomes answerable.

3. Smooth Functioning

Departmentation ensures clear cut division and grouping of various activities. It is interesting to observe that the various departments created through departmentation operate independently but in a related manner to contribute in smooth functioning of the whole organisation.

4. Facilitates coordination

Coordination is achieved through departmentation because the members of each department works on related jobs and tasks, follow same departmental rules and reports to the same departmental head.

5. Encourages expansion and Growth

When organisation grows, the large number of activities have to be performed for achieving its goal. It requires proper grouping of these activities and creating departments for handling them. So, the growth and expansion of organisational activities is possible through departmentation process.

6. Easy Appraisal

Appraisal of managerial performance becomes easier when specific tasks are assigned to departmental personnel. The sources of information, the skills and competence required for total managerial decision can be located.

7. Effective Control

Managers cannot control organisational activities if all the activities have to be collectively supervised. Departmentation facilitates control by each departmental manager over the activities of his department only.

8. Leads to Specialisation

Departmentation process is also considered as a means of decentralisation. The creation of various departments and divisions which requires operational freedom in order to manage and administer business activities with the help of adequate authority.

9. Management Development

Departmentation facilitates communication, coordination and control. It simplifies the training and development of executives by providing them opportunity to take independent decisions and to exercise initiative.

10. Flexibility

In large organisations, one person cannot look after all the managerial functions for all the departments. He cannot adjust his organisation to its internal and external environment. Such an organisation would become and inflexible organisation. Creating departments and departmental heads makes an organisation flexible and adaptive to environment.

DEFINITIONS

According to Koontz and O'Donnell, "A department is a distinct area, division or branch of an enterprise over which a manager has authority for the performance of specified activities."

In the words of Louis Allen, "Divisionalisation is a means of dividing the large and monolithic functional organisation into smaller flexible administrative units."

The form of organisation structure depends upon the basis of departmentation. With growing size of organisations, departments are created for activities of similar nature. Creating departments and sub-dividing the work of departments into smaller units creates organisation structure.

TYPES OF DEPARTMENTATION

There are several patterns or methods of departmentation, each of which is suitable for a particular situation. The following patterns may be used for grouping activities into departments:

1. Functional Departmentation
2. Product Departmentation
3. Territorial (Geographic) Departmentation
4. Departmentation by Customers
5. Departmentation by Process (or Equipment)
6. Departmentation by Combined Base
7. Departmentation by Time

1. Functional Departmentation

Under functional departmentation each major function of the enterprise grouped into a separate department. The major or organic functions are those which are essential for the survival of the organisation. In a manufacturing enterprise production, marketing and finance are the basic functions.

These primary functional departments can further be divided into secondary departments. For example: the marketing department may be divided into sales, marketing research and advertising, etc. Thus, the process of functional differentiation may take place through successive levels in the hierarchy. The process can continue as long as there exists a sound basis for further differentiation. Functional departmentation is the most widely used basis for grouping activities. It exists almost in every organisation at some level.

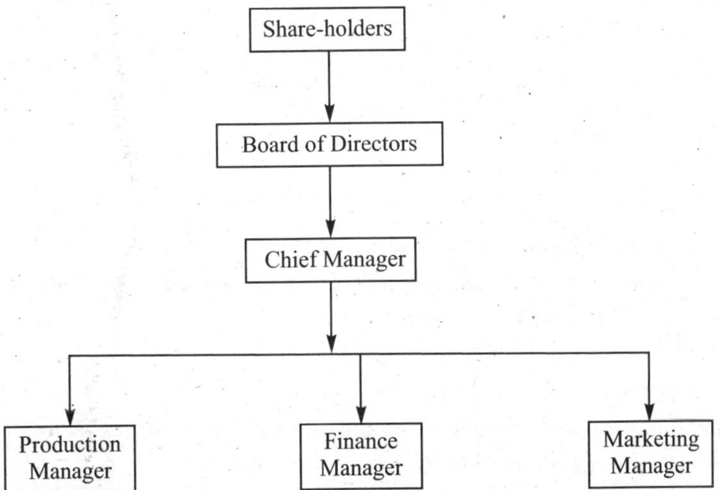

Functional Departmentation

Advantages: (Functional Departmentation)

1. It suits well the small enterprises for creating major departments.
2. It promotes specialization.
3. It economises operations and makes possible the adoption of logical and comprehensible structure.
4. It facilitates inter-departmental coordination.
5. It suits well for those organisation which have single product line.

Limitation: (Functional Departmentation)

1. It may lead to excessive centralisation.
2. Decision making process is delayed.
3. Poor inter-departmental coordination.
4. It is rather difficult to set up accountability and profit centres within functional departments, so the performance is not accurate.
5. It hinders human development in all the areas.

2. Product Departmentation

Certain companies produce different varieties of products and it is advantageous to boost the sales on the basis of product or product groups. A separate product manager is appointed for each product. He attends to the production and marketing of his products. When the market is competitive, the product type organisation with the product manager can concentrate its attention on the performance of a particular product or brand. Sales promotion, advertising, marketing research, etc., remain as the centralised activity for the product group.

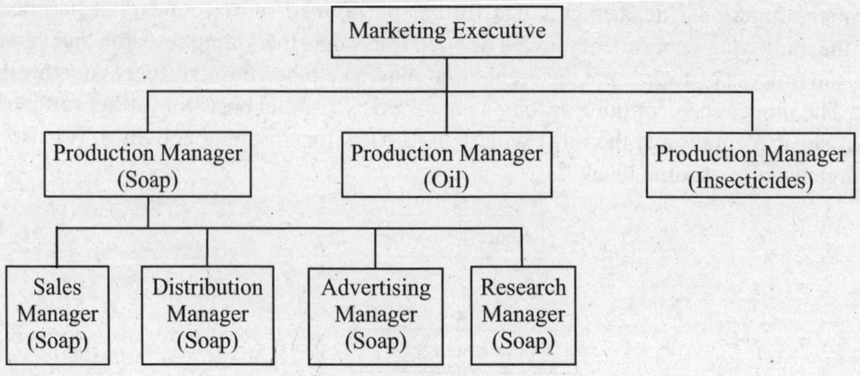

Product Departmentation

Advantages: (Product Departmentation)

1. The performance of individual products can be easily assessed to distinguish between profitable and non-profitable products.
2. Marketing strategy becomes more pragmatic.
3. It facilitates decentralisation.
4. Full attention is given to product lines and thus further expansion is possible.

Limitations: (Product Departmentation)

1. It increases management cost.
2. There may be under-utilisation of plant capacity when the demand for a particular product is not adequate.

3. Territorial (Geographic) Departmentation

The structure is based on territorial or regional basis. When business activities are expanded, the various parts of the market area are divided into territories. The whole world into continents, continent into regions, region into zones, zone into districts, etc. This type of organisation gives importance to the consumer's needs and desire, especially in pharmaceutical companies.

In this way, the market is fragmented into different sales territories like national market into regions, region into districts, district into areas as shown in the chart next.

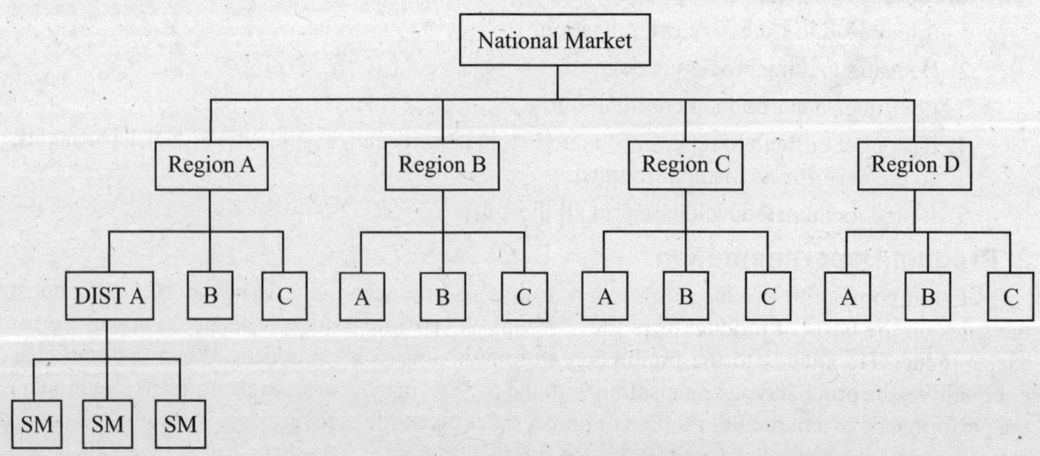

Territorial Departmentation

Salesmen are controlled by the respective district sales managers (DSM), DSM are controlled by their regional sales manager (RSM), RSM are controlled by the marketing executive.

This type of organisation, enjoys the knowledge of likes and dislikes of people in the particular areas. A firm can modify or alter the products, on the basis of the needs of the buyers who are represented by sales manager. The competitors can be counteracted soon.

Merits (Geographical Departmentation)

1. Geographical type of divisions allow a manager to pay special attention to the needs and problems of the local markets.
2. Geographic type of organisation provide opportunities for local talent to be utilised.
3. Geographic division helps managers to gain extensive knowledge of diverse activities.
4. This type of organisation improve an organisation's relationship with customers.

Demerits (Geographical Departmentation)

1. This type of organisation require more people to work.
2. There arise communication problems.
3. Cost of operations are high.
4. Top managers at HO find it difficult to control and supervise the activities in different locations.

4. Departmentation by Customers

This type of departmentation is based on the different types of customers. The enterprises have adopted customer-oriented marketing and thus there arise two sets of organisation through which the needs of customers or market are met; *i.e.*, sub-division of markets on the basis of government and non-grovernment customers, industrial individual customers, rich and poor customers and on the basis of sex, income, taste, age, etc. A firm may have different groups of customers, who have different needs and problems. Thus, each section can look into the needs of each group of consumers and facilitate their buying-wholesale section, etc.

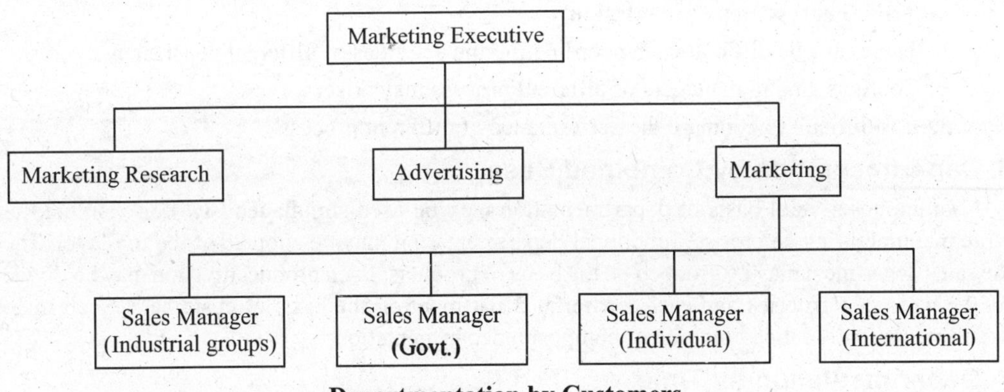

Departmentation by Customers

Merits (Departmentation by Customers)

1. This type of organisation can encourage consumers with clearly defined services.
2. The specialists can understand the needs of a particular segment of customers.
3. This type of organisation is useful to serve different type of customers.

Demerits (Departmentation by Customers)

1. Coordination between sales and other functions of marketing is difficult.
2. More man-power is required thus expenditure is high.

5. Departmentation by Process (Equipment)

This pattern of grouping activities is often used by manufacturing organisation having an assembly line production or production system which may consists of various processes to be conducted in a logical sequence. The output of a particular process becomes input for next succeeding process and same is repeated till the production of finished product. For example, in cotton textile manufacturing organisation entire production system is marked by various processes such as ginning, spinning, weaving, dyeing, colouring and finishing.

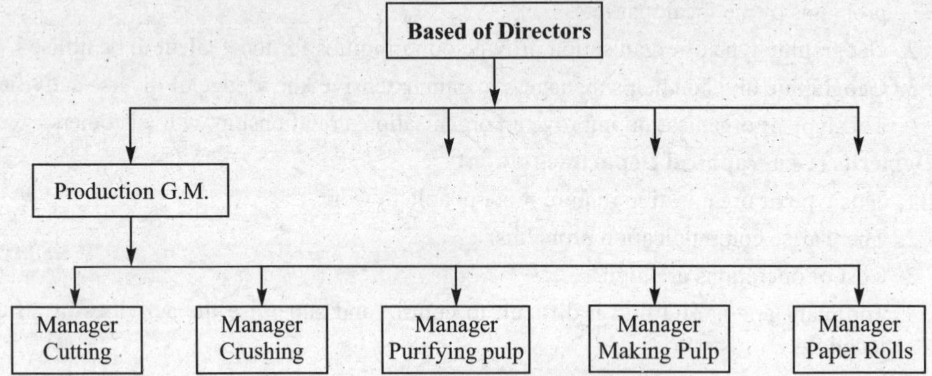

Process Departmentation

Merits (Process Departmentation)

1. It provides economy of operation.
2. The benefits of specilization are available.
3. Efficient maintenance of equipment is possible.
4. It simplifies supervision and plant layout.

Demerits (Process Departmentation)

1. There may be difficulties in coordinating the activities of different departments.
2. Conflicts among managers of different process may arise.
3. It is difficult to compare the performance of different process.

6. Departmentation by Combined Base

Sometimes several basis of departmentation may be used simultaneously. For example, in a large manufacturing enterprise, functional departmentation may be adopted at the top level. Then the sales department may be grouped on the basis of products. Each product division may be divided on the basis of territories and each territorial department on the basis of customers. Such mixed departmentation is called combine or composite departmentation.

7. Departmentation by Time

This method of departmentation is used in situations where work is done round the clock because: (*a*) the machine cannot be stopped before finishing the work; (*b*) the demand is high; (*c*) the services are essential in nature, etc. The activities are grouped on the basis of time of their performance. For example, a factory operating Twenty-four hours may have three departments, one each for morning, day and night shifts.

CHOICE OF METHOD OF DEPARTMENTATION

Management must be very careful in choosing the basis of departmentation because once a pattern is chosen it is very difficult and costly to switch over to another pattern. The process of departmentation is aimed at seeking sound and effective structure of organisation. It differentiates and integrates various activities and functions performed in the organisation for achieving objectives. It is obvious that if it is not conducted properly it may prove expensive, ineffective and wasteful exercise. Following factors are to be taken into consideration while deciding the bases for departmentation:

1. Specialisation

Departmentation should be such as to yield the advantages of specialisation which is the most widely recognised characteristics of modern enterprise. Specialisation helps to improve efficiency and economy of operations. However, over-specialisation should be avoided because it results into loss of motivation among the personnel.

2. Economy

The expense involved in creating separate departments for any activity is an important factor and should kept in mind. The costs involved in departmentation should always be less than the benefits. The pattern and number of departments should be so decided that maximum possible economy is achieved in the utilisation of physical facilities and personnel. The cost of additional facilities must be balanced against the benefits resulting from it.

3. Coordination

Managers have to coordinate the activities of various departments to ensure their optimum contribution to organisational goals. All activities are designed to achieve the organisational objectives. Coordination in the performance of different activities is necessary so that they contribute maximum towards the organisational goals.

4. Control

The departmentation should be such that it facilitates measurement of performance and timely corrective action. It should enable the management to hold people accountable for results. Effective control helps to achieve organisational goals, efficiently and economically.

5. Abilities of Workers

Departmentation should not only consider technical aspects of the job but also abilities of the workers who perform that job. Human values, cultures, belief and attitudes play important role in creating departments in the organisation.

6. Local Conditions

The management should take into consideration the local conditions also. They are the personalities of individuals, the nature of organisation, the pattern of informal relationships in the organisation, the attitude of management towards workers, the market to be served, etc.

7. Technology Employed

Technological factors are an important determinant of departmentation. The basis of departmentation should be ability to produce goods at minimum cost and contribute to organisational goals within the technological framework of the company.

8. Attention

The various activities should be given adequate attention so that each necessary activity is performed and there is no unnecessary duplication of activities. Proper weightage should be given to different functions depending upon their significance and the organisational needs.

9. Environment

Modern organisations operate in the dynamic environment where economic, social, political and technological factors are changing rapidly. The basis of departmentation should ensure that organisations can adapt to environmental changes.

TYPES OF ORGANISATION STRUCTURE

When there is one man, there is hardly any need for any organisation. When the enterprise expands, some pattern of organisation should be adopted. Generally, the following are the types of organisation.

(a) Line Organisation

This is the simplest and oldest form of organisation. It is also referred as the 'Military' or 'Traditional' or 'Scalar' or 'Hierarchical' form of organisation. An important feature of such types of organisation is the superior sub-ordinate relationship. In this type of organisation authority descends from the top to its bottom level through downward delegation of authority. Sub-ordinates become responsible to their immediate superiors. All decisions and orders are made by the top executives and handed down to sub-ordinates. This type of organisation is as that of military administration. The topmost management has full control over the entire enterprise.

Features of Line Organisation

1. There is no provision for staff experts.
2. Each subordinate is directly responsible to his superior for the work performance.
3. Every worker is responsible to one executive only.
4. The authority and responsibility of each position is specified.
5. The command is through a straight and unbroken line.
6. The line of authority are vertical flowing from the top to the bottom.

This form is suitable:

(*a*) If the business is comparatively small.

(*b*) If the labour management problems are easy to solve.

(*c*) If the processes are easily directed.

(*d*) If the work is of a routine nature.

Merits of Line Organisation

1. It is simple to work.
2. It is economical and effective.

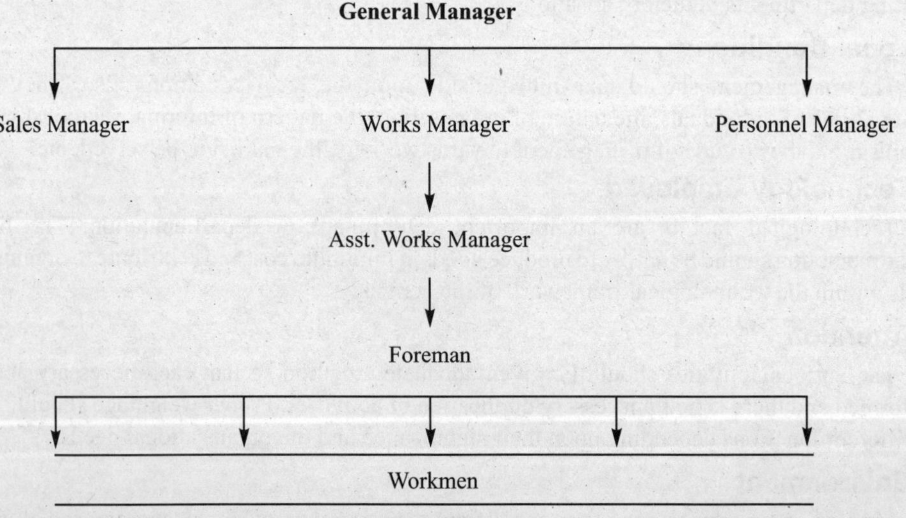

Line Organisation

3. It is easy to fix responsibility.
4. It facilitates quick decisions and prompt actions.
5. Quick communication is easy.
6. Discipline can easily be maintained.
7. 'Unity of Command' principle is followed.
8. The hierarchy in management helps in achieving effective coordination.

Demerits of Line Organisation

1. The organisation is rigid and inflexible.
2. It works on a dictatorial basis.
3. Departmental heads act in their own whims and desires; as such it is difficult to secure co-ordination of the activities of workers and department.
4. In big business it does not operate satisfactorily.
5. There is excessive work.
6. The emphasis is only on work related activities.
7. Specialised services by experts is not available.
8. There is scope of favourtism in the organisation.

There are two types of line organisation, that is, (*i*) Pure and (*ii*) Departmental.

(*i*) Pure Line Organisation

In pure line, similar activities are performed at a particular level. Every employee performs, more or less, the same job. The division of work is simply for the purpose of better control and direction.

(*ii*) Departmental Line Organisation

Under this form of organisation, the entire activities of the organisation are divided into various departments on the basis of some similarity headed by one departmental superintendent. Each department is self-contained unit in itself and is answerable only to the chief executive.

(b) Functional Organisation

The limitations of line organisation have been removed under this system. All types of work of the organisation are grouped and managed by the top executive. There are separate functional departments for major functions of the enterprise, for example personnel department, sales department, purchase department, finance department, etc. Each department does its function for the entire organisation. Sales department does its function for the whole organisation. Purchase department does its function for the whole enterprise. The functional organisation works through the line organisation. Functional organisation is based on expert knowledge and makes the greatest use of division of labour resulting in high efficiency and specialisation.

Features (Functional Organisation)

1. The whole task of the enterprise is divided into specialised functions.
2. Each function is performed by a specialist.
3. The specialist incharge of a functional department has the authority over all other employees for his function.
4. Specialists operate with considerable independence.

Merits of Functional Organisation

1. Greatest use of division of labour is possible.
2. The system is based on expert knowledge.

3. Functional efficiency of the worker can be maintained.
4. Mass production is made by standardisation and specialisation.
5. Separation of mental and manual functions is possible.
6. Methods and operations can be standardised.

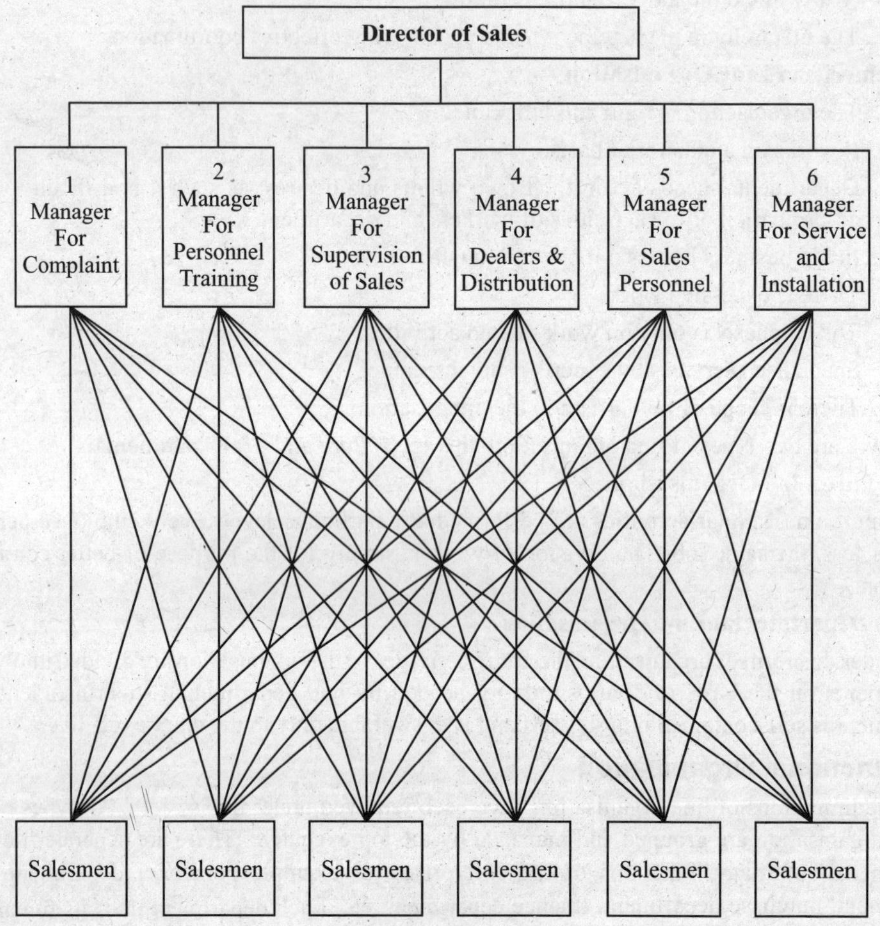

Functional Organisation

Demerits of Functional Organisation

1. Too many experts and bosses (high officials) create confusions in the minds of the worker.
2. It is difficult to fix responsibility on workers.
3. Discipline and morale of the workers are seriously affected, because of contradictory orders from different experts.
4. There are heavy overhead expenses.

(c) Line and Staff Organisation

In this type, the organisation is based on the line organisation and the functional experts advice the line officers as to the functions of the enterprise. The line officers are the executives and the staff officers are their advisors. Though the staff officers do not have the power to command the line officers, their advice is generally adhered to. The combination of line organisation with this expert staff forms the type of organisation-line and staff. The 'line' keep the discipline and the staff provides expert information. The line gets out the production and the staff carries on research, planning, fixing standard, etc. This type of organisation is suitable for large concerns. The line officers give orders, decisions, etc., to sub-ordinates in consultations or guidance with the staff officers. The underlying idea of this method is that specialised work is to be left to experts, who will give advice on specialised grounds investigation, research, etc. The staff officers have no executive positions in the concern and are the thinkers, while the line officers are the doers.

Features of Line and Staff Organisation

1. Line authority achieves the major organisational goal and staff authority assists the line authority in achieving these goals.
2. Staff has specialised knowledge in their fields and offer suggestions to line managers when they feel necesary to do so.
3. No formal relationship is established between line and the staff.

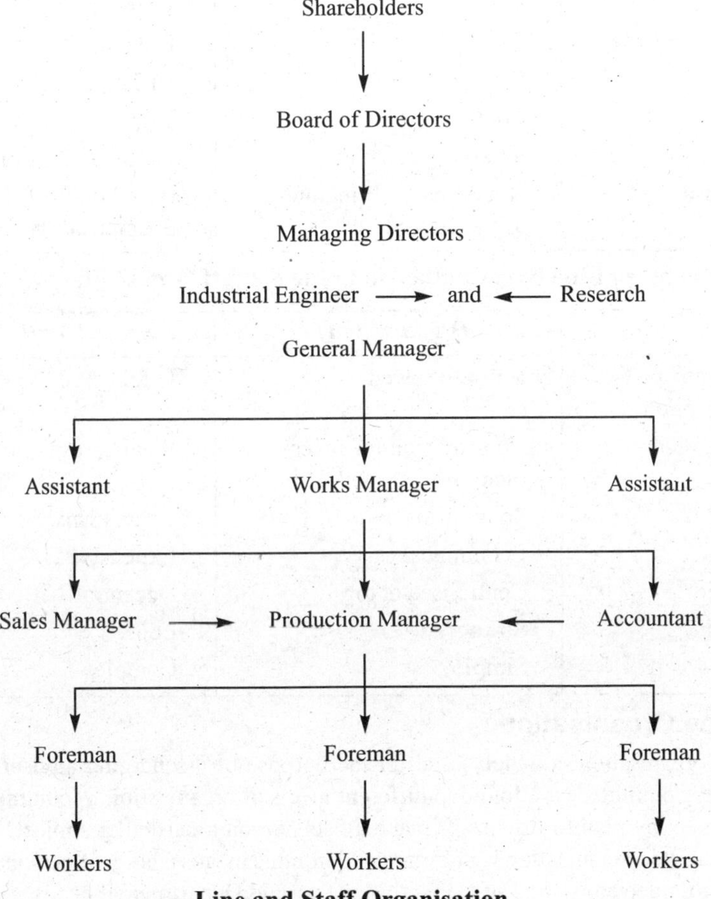

Line and Staff Organisation

Merits of Line and Staff Organisation

1. This type is based on specialisation.
2. It brings expert knowledge upon the whole concern.
3. Increased efficiency of operations may be possible.
4. Mass production is possible.

Demerits of Line and Staff Organisation

1. There arises confusion unless the duties and responsibilities are clearly / Indicated by charts and office manuals.
2. Advice and expert information are given to the workers through the line officers. It is possible that the workers may misunderstand or misinterpret.

Distinction between Line Organisation and Functional Organisation

Basis	*Line Organisation*	*Functional Organisation*
1. Discipline	High	Low
2. Cost	Economical	Expensive
3. Responsibility	Fixed	Divided
4. Authority	Centralised at top	Decentralised
5. Flexibility	Low	High
6. Decision-making	Quick	Delayed
7. Nature	Simple	Difficult
8. Stability	Low	High
9. Suitability	Small organisation	Large Organisation
10. Specialisation	Not based on Principles of Specialisation	Based on the Principles of Specialisation

Distinction between Line Organisation and Line & Staff Organisation

Basis	*Line Organisation*	*Line and Staff Organisation*
1. Principles of Specialisation	Is not followed	Is followed
2. Investigation	No provision for investigation	It encourages investigation
3. Suitability	Small firms	Large firms
4. Cost	Economical	Expensive
5. Authority	Centralised at top	Decentralised
6. Discipline	Strict	Loose
7. Nature	Simple	Complex

(d) Committee Organisation

Committee organisation is widely used for the purpose of discharging advisory functions of the management. Committees are found in different levels of organisation. A committee is a group of people who meet by plan to discuss or make a decision on a particular subject. Because of its advantages, committee organisation is preferred. Committee means a body of persons, for example, Management committee consisting of General Manager and Departmental heads.

According to Davis, "A committee is a group of individuals who meet for the purpose of effecting an integration of ideas concerning a solution for some problems."

According to Newman, "A committee consists of a group of persons specifically designate to perform some administrative act. It functions only as a group and requires the free intercharge of ideas among its members."

Committee have become an important instrument of management in modern organisations; they may be used for the following objectives:

1. To secure view-point and consultation of various persons in the organisations.
2. To give participation and representation to different groups or interests;
3. To co-ordinate the activities of different departments;
4. To review the performance of certain units;
5. To facilitate communication and co-operation among diverse groups.

Merits of committee organisation

1. It facilitates co-ordination of activity of various departments.
2. Pooled knowledge and judgement become available to the business thus its efficiency increases.
3. It is a good media of training and educating employees.
4. It helps to improve the motivation and morale of employees.
5. It promotes mutual understanding, team work and co-operation among employees.
6. Intelligent solutions can be secured for complex problems.
7. It is useful in coordinating plans and in their execution.
8. It is an effective instrument of communication.
9. It is a method of executive development.

Demerits of committee organisation

1. It is not only costly in terms of time it consumes, but also in terms of money involved.
2. Difficulty in reaching agreement results in indecision.
3. Compromise at the cost of efficiency is often affected.
4. Indecision may lead to a breakdown of group action.
5. Committee management is slower in reaching decisions than a one-man rule.

MISUSES OF THE COMMITTEE ORGANISATION

The committee organisations are generally found only in big business enterprise. Some examples of misuse of the committee organisation may be as under:

1. Decisions by Compromise

Decisions by compromise is a very common misuse of the powers of officers of the committee. It is interesting to note that some decisions are against the interests of firm.

2. Expensive

The members of the committee make many unnecessary expenses in the name of the organisation.

3. Injustice with minority

All the decisions of the committee are taken by the rule of majority. The decisions of committee are imposed upon minority.

4. Domination of few persons

Practically the committee is dominated by a few persons who can speak loudly and fluently. Such members influence the decisions of committee in undesirable manner.

5. More problems but limited time

The members waste their time on meaningless and fruitless discussions. There are many problems to be solved but time is limited. It becomes difficult to determine the responsibility of an individual member.

SUGGESTIONS FOR MAKING COMMITTEE EFFECTIVE

Committee Organisation may be made effective by following the guidelines, in brief:

1. The objective for forming a committee must be clearly specified.
2. Members of the committee must be rationally nominated.
3. The agenda for discussion should be sent to members in advance.
4. The Chairman of the committee should be effective in directing group-thinking towards committee objectives.
5. The meetings of the committee should be well planned.
6. The authority of the committee should be well defined.
7. The scope of the committee must be clearly defined and properly communicated.
8. The members must be capable enough to understand, analyse and decide the problems.
9. It is essential that the rights and duties of all members of committee must be clearly defined.
10. There should be periodic review of the functioning of a committee.

(e) Project Organisation

The project structure consists of a number of horizontal organisational units to complete projects of long duration. Each project is vitally important to the organisation. A team of specialists from different areas is created for each project. The size of the project team varies from one project to another. The activities of a project team are coordinated by the project manager who has the authority to obtain advice and assistance of experts both inside and outside the organisation. A bridge, dam or fly-over are constructed as project organisations. Once the objective is framed, work force is gathered and authority-responsibility structure is created by giving the project manager authority to exercise control over the activities of group members.

A project team is a temporary set up. Once the project is complete the team is disbanded and the functioning specialists are assigned some other projects. According to Hodgetts who defined a project organsiation as "the gathering of the best available talent to accomplish a specific and complex undertaking within time, cost and/or quality parameters, following by the disbanding of the team upon completion of the undertaking."

Benefits (Project Organisation)

1. It provides concentrated attention to the project.
2. It permits timely completion of the project.
3. The project manager lays responsibility of his group members and facilitates feedback and control.
4. It allows maximum use of specialised knowledge and skills.
5. It provides greater flexibility in handling specialised project.

Limitations (Project Organisation)

1. Organisational uncertainties may lead to inter-departmental conflict.
2. Project managers of small project organisations do not have formal authority over their group members.

(f) Matrix Organisation

Matrix organisation is also known as grid or project organisation. Matrix organisation is created by merging the two or more complementary organisations, say, purchase section and sales section. A team may be set up within the existing organisation, to conduct a study of a particular product or design or to complete a specific assignment in time. A project manager has a project team consisting of people from several functional sections. For instance, a project team is formed to market the television, and for this people will be drawn from different functional departments, say, production, research, marketing, engineering, etc. These specialists are drawn from respective departments, borrowed to perform their part in the project work. When the project work is complete, they go back to their respective departments. This type of organisation is needed when a special type of urgent assignment of jobs or complicated job or a new product etc., is introduced. Generally, such organisation may be temporary.

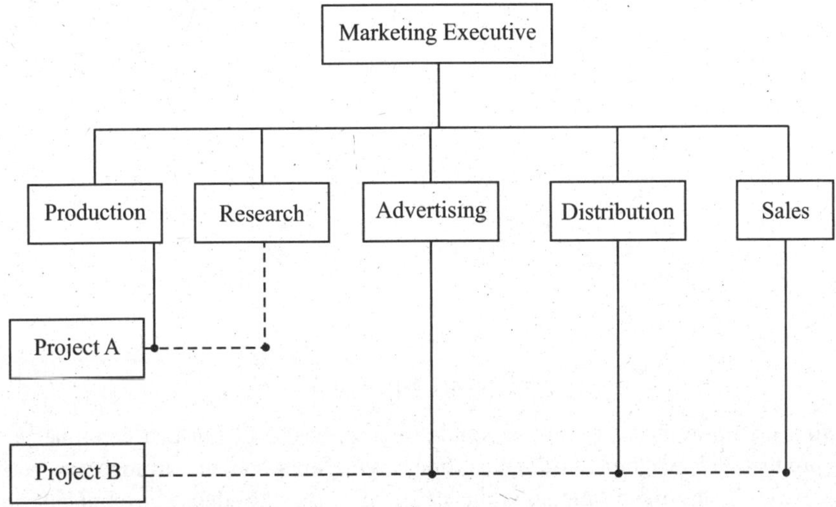

Merits (Matrix Organisation)

1. Specialised product knowledge is acquired.
2. It is economical to draw experts from various sections.
3. Expansion, improvements, diversification, etc., are the result.
4. The chances of success of the project are higher.
5. It allows effective use of resources.

Demerits (Matrix Organisation)

1. Administrative costs are high.
2. Workers under this type have to report to two bosses.
3. There arise conflicts between functional managers and project managers.

(g) Network Organisation

The network organisation is a collection of independent, mostly single-function firms that collaborate to produce a goods or service. As depicted in chart, the network organisation describes not one organisation but the web of relationships among many firms. Network organisations are flexible arrangements among designers, suppliers, producers, distributors and customers where each firm is able to pursue its own distinctive competence, yet work effectively with other members of the network. Often members of the net work communicate electronically and share information to be able to respond quickly to customer demands. In effect, the normal boundary of the organisation becomes blurred or porous, as managers within the organisation interact closely with network members outside it. The network as a whole, then, can display the technical specialization of the functional structure, the market responsiveness of the product structure, and the balance and flexibility of the matrix.

A very flexible version of the network organisation is the DYNAMIC NETWORK - also called the MODULAR OR VIRTUAL Corporation. It is composed of temporary arrangements among members that can be assembled and reassembled to meet a changing competitive one environment. The members of the network are held together by contracts that stipulate results expected (market mechanisms) rather than by hierarchy and authority. Pooly performing firms can be removed and replaced.

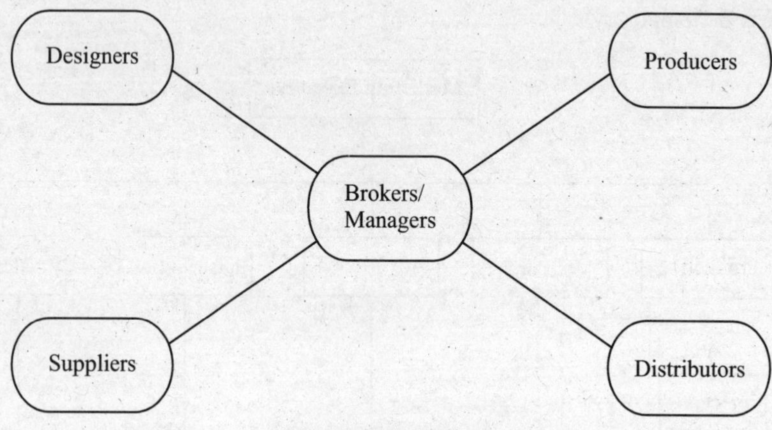

A Network Organisation

Network organisation is "a multinational structural arrangement that combines elements of function, product and geographic designs, while relying on a network arrangement to link world wide subsidiaries." This organisational format helps MNCs to take advantage of global economies of scale along with catering to local customer demands. This structure links subsidiaries of a company that are spread world wide. Some subsidiaries specialise in manufacturing while others in sales. All of them are, however, linked with headquarters. Some are closely controlled by headquarters while others are more autonomous. The structure is, thus, a combination of geographic, functional and product elements.

WHAT TYPE OF ORGANISATION TO CHOOSE ?

Choosing the right type of organisation for an enterprise is a difficult job. There are various factors to be considered in deciding whether any one of the above types of organisation or a variation of the same or an admixture of the two types will suit the particular requirements of the enterprise. Some of the important factors to be considered are briefly discussed below.

1. **Nature and Size of Business:** The size of the business is the most important factor. If a business is small, there are few management problems, a simple type of organisation (Line Organisation) would be suitable. But in a large business, which has a number of departments or sections and whose activities are various and many, the complexities of management problems call for a more complex type of organisation, *viz.,* a functional or a line and staff organisation.
2. **Continuity of Business:** The type of organisation suitable for an enterprise with steady flow of business throughout the year will be different from the type found suitable for an enterprise where flow of business fluctuates from season to season. The former will naturally require more permanent and complex type of organisation than the latter.
3. **Geographical Locations:** The grographical location of the various divisions or units of the enterprise is also an important factor in choosing the type of organisation. If the units, for example, factory, sales division, marketing division, etc., are located in the same premises or in close proximity to one another, a comprehensive but more complex type

of organisation will be suitable. But if the units are located in separate buildings situated kilometers apart, separate organisations based on line and staff type may be more suitable.

4. **Staff Strength and Degree of Mechanisation:** The degree of supervision needed and the placement of different functions at different levels will depend on the ratio of unskilled to supervisory staff. Again the degree of mechanisation (ratio of machines to operatives) is also an important factor. Both these factors will have to be taken into consideration in choosing the type of organisation.
5. **Period of Establishment:** An old established business is in a better position to evolve and develop its own kind of organisation over the course of years than a newly established business. A greater effort is required to set up even a simple type of organisation in a newly established business.

CASE STUDY - 1

Major Tools Ltd.

Robert, one of the field sales managers of Major Tools Ltd., had been promoted to his first headquarters assignment as an assistant product manager for a group of products with which he was relatively unfamiliar. Shortly after he had taken over this new assignment, one of the company's vice-presidents, Smith, called for a meeting of product managers and other staff to plan marketing strategies. Robert's superior (the product manager) was unablc to attend, so the director of marketing, Reynolds, invited Robert to the meeting to help and orient him to his new job.

Because of the large gathering, Reynolds was rather brief in introducing Robert to Smith. After the meeting began, Smith—a crusty veteran with a reputation for bluntness—began asking a series of probing questions, which most of the product managers were unable to answer in detail. Suddenly, he turned to Robert and questioned him quite closely about his group of products. Somewhat confused, Robert confessed that he really did not know the answers.

It was immediately apparent to Reynolds that Smith had forgotten or had failed to understand that Robert was new to the job and was attending the meeting more for his own orientation than to contribute to it. He was about to offer a discreet explanation when Smith, visibly annoyed with what he took to be Robert's lack of preparation, snapped, "Gentlemen, you have just seen an example of sloppy staff work, and there is no excuse for it."

Reynolds had to make a quick decision. He would interrupt Smith and point out that the he had judged Robert unfairly, but that might embrace both his superior and his subordinate. Alternatively, he could wait until after the meeting and offer an explanation in private. As Smith quickly became engrossed in another conversation, Reynolds followed the second approach. Glancing at Robert, Reynolds noted that his expression was one of mixed anger and dismay. After catching his eye, Reynolds winked at Robert as a discreet reassurance that he understood and that the damage could be repaired. After an hour, Smith, evidently dissatisfied with what he termed the "inadequate planning" of the marketing department in general, abruptly declared the meeting over. As he did so, he turned to Reynolds and asked him to remain behind for a moment. To Reynold's surprise, Smith immediately raised the question of Robert himself. In fact, it turned out to have been his main reason for asking Reynolds to remain behind. "Look" he said, "I want you to tell me frankly, do you think I was too rough with that kid ?" Relieved, Reynolds said, "Yes, you were. I was going to speak to you about it."

Smith explained to Reynolds that Robert was new to his job had not registered in his mind adequately when they had been introduced, and that it was only some time after his own outburst that the nagging thought began to occur to him that what he had done was inappropriate and unfair. "How well do you know him ?" he asked. "Do you think I hurt him ?"

For a moment Reynolds took the measure of his superior. Then he replied evenly, "I do not know him very well yet, but, yes, I think you hurt him."

"Damn, that is unforgivable," said Smith. He then telephoned his secretary to call Robert and ask him to report to his office immediately. A few moments later, Robert returned, looking preplexed and uneasy. As he entered, Smith came out from behind his desk and met him in the middle of the office. Standing face to face with Robert, who was 20 years and four organization levels his junior, he said, "Look, I have done something stupid and I want to apologize. I had no right to treat you like that. I should have remembered that you were new to your job, but I did not. "I am Sorry."

Robert was somewhat flustered. He muttered his thanks for the apology. "As long as you are here, young man," Smith continued, "I want to make a few things clear to you in the presence of your boss's boss. Your job is to make sure that people like myself do not make stupid decisions. Obviously, we think you are qualified for your job or we would not have brought you in here. But it takes time to learn any job. Three months from now I will expect you to know the answers to any questions about products." "Until then," he said, "thrusting out his hand for the younger man to shake, "you have my complete confidence. And thank you for letting me correct a mistake."

QUESTIONS

1. What do you think was the effect on Robert and the other managers of Smith's outburst at the meeting ?
2. Was Smith right to apologize to 'Robert or should he have left well enough alone ?
3. What do you think the apology meant to Robert ?
4. What would it be like to have Smith as a superior ? As a subordinate ?
5. How does Smith define Robert's responsibilities as an assistant product manager ? How does he define his own role as a top manager ?
6. What is the most important aspect of the relations between management levels in this company ?

CASE STUDY - 2

Electric Manufacturing Corporation

Roy, the president and founder of Electric Manufacturing Corporation (EMCORP), is wondering how he can follow the advice of his doctor, who had told him to take it easy after last year's coronary attack. EMCORP manufactures a full line of fractional horsepower electric motors sold to both original equipment manufactures and distributors throughout the country. At present, the company employs approximately 1,000 people.

Roy, an engineer, has maintained tight control over all major functions throughout the years, **and though each of the heads of the engineering, manufacturing, sales, finance and personne** departments has the title of Vice President, they come to Roy for approval before making any change in procedure. Usually, each of these executives sees Roy several times a day. The personnel director once suggested a weekly meeting, but Roy voted the idea as too time consuming. Now, worried about his health as well as the problems of the company, Roy is beginning to feel the need for some relief from the constant pressure.

The manufacturing department shows a picture of rising costs, consistent failure to meet delivery schedules, and an increasing number of quality complaints. John, Vice President Manufacturing, admits to poor performance, but says that the cost figures from accounting are pure history and of no use since they do not reach manufacturing until the fifteenth of the month following the month in which the work is completed. He states that his failure to meet delivery schedules is due almost entirely to the fact that the sales department makes unrealistic promises, and does not bother to check manufacturing schedules. John attributes most of the quality problems to the incessant flow of engineering changes that come without warning and with no time to work out the production problems present in all new products. Roy admits to himself that he had asked Symth, Vice President Engineering, to put all the approved changes into production immediately.

The Vice President and general manager of sales, Rita, recognizes that she has no knowledge of the manufacturing schedules and realizes that she, too is being criticized by Roy for many broken promises in regard to delivery dates. However, Rita's chief complaint at the present time is the result of having sold a large order of Standard Motors to a distributor having a supply of replacement parts in stock, and then discovering that engineering had changed specifications: a change that made all replacement parts in the field obsolete. Another irritant for Rita is the tightening of credit requirements instituted by the finance department without prior consultation with the sales department. Again, Roy admits to himself that it is the same engineering change which caused so much trouble in manufacturing that is causing trouble for the sales department and making obsolete the existing stock of replacement parts. He also realizes that at his request, due to an unusually short cash position, the finance department tightened up on credit requirement.

QUESTIONS

1. Define the major problem of EMCORP's management.
2. Will the formation of a committee be of any value in this situation ? If a committee is needed, assign a title to the committee and indicate, who should be the members of the committee ?
3. Is there a need for an outside member on the committee ?
4. Will an ad hoc committee be of any value ?
5. In the event that Roy decides to retire, will the presence of a committee make it easier or more difficult for Roy's successor ? Discuss.

REVIEW QUESTIONS

1. What do you meant by organisation structure ? Describe the factors affecting the organisation structure. *(B.Com., Delhi)*
2. Discuss the departmentation by functions. Explain its merits and demerits. *(B.Com., Jabalpur)*
3. Explain the basis of departmentation giving advantages and disadvantages. *(M.Com., Kerala)*
4. What do you understand by matrix organisation ? *(M.Com., MS)*
5. What is a departmentation by product-wise ? What are merits and demerits ? *(M.Com., Bangalore)*
6. What is departmentation ? Why are departments created ? *(B.Com., Andhra)*
7. What is line organisation structure ? Discuss its features, merits and demerits. *(M.Com., Mysore)*
8. What is matrix organisation ? Under what circumstances it is most useful ? Differentiate it with project organisation. *(B.Com., Calicut)*
9. Explain the merits and demerits of committee work. How can committees be made more effective ? *(M.Com., Madurai)*

10. Compare functional and line and staff organisation with their relative merits and demerits. *(M.Com., MS)*
11. How committee organisation should made more effective ? *(B.Com., Chennai)*
12. What is project organisation ? What are the advantages and disadvantages ? *(BA, Kerala)*
13. Explain the need and importance of departmentation. *(B.Com., Madras)*
14. Why is process departmentation necessary ? *(B.Com., MS)*
15. What factors affect the choice of a suitable form of departmentation ? *(B.Com., Calicut)*

Authority and Responsibility

12
CHAPTER

- Introduction
- Meaning of Authority
- Features of Authority
- Sources of Authority
- Power
- Sources of Power
- Authority Vs Power
- Influence
- Types of Authority
- Line Vs Staff Authority
- Line and Staff Conflict
- Reducing Conflicts between line and Staff
- Limitations of Authority
- Authority Vs Responsibility
- Responsibility
- Accountability
- Case Study - 1
- Review Questions.

AUTHORITY

INTRODUCTION

Underlying the task of management is the concept of organisational authority. Authority is essential to be able to discharge various managerial functions. It is the formal right of the superior to command and compel his subordinates to perform a certain act. Henry Fayol defines authority as "the right to give orders and power to exact obedience".

Koontz and O'Donnell define authority as "the power to command others, to act or not to act in a manner deemed by the possessor of the authority to further enterprise or departmental purpose". Authority may be official or personal. OFFICIAL AUTHORITY refers to authority of a superior which he possesses because of his official position and placement in the organisational structure. Subordinates should accept the official authority of the superior because of the propriety and legality of the rules involved. PERSONAL AUTHORITY, on the other hand, is the authority which a person enjoys because of his popularity, good public relations, excellent charismatic personality, etc.

MEANING

Simon defined authority as "Authority may be defined as the power to make decisions which guide the actions of another. It is a relationship between two individuals, one superior, the other subordinate. The superior frames and transmits decisions with the expectation that these will be accepted by the subordinate. The subordinate executes such decisions and his conduct is determined by them."

Authority is the right to carry out the assigned tasts (responsibilities). To carry out the assigned responsibility, subordinates need to issue directions, spend resources, make decisions, command people, etc. Authority must be delegated to them to do all this and effectively carry out the responsibility (assigned task). In simple terms, authority is the right of a person to give instructions to subordinates.

Authority, according to Koontz and Weihrich, it is "the right in a position (and, through it, the right of the person occupying the position) to exercise discretion in making decisions affecting others."

Pearce and Robinson define authority as "the organisation's legitimised power that is linked to each position within the organisation. It typically involves the right to command, to perform, to make decisions and to expend resources".

Thus, authority is the power enjoyed by a person to influence his subordinates, to direct them to work. It is derived by virtue of the position he holds in the organisation.

FEATURES OF AUTHORITY

The main features of authority are as follows:

1. It is the right of a person to issue orders and instructions to subordinates.
2. It is used to achieve organisational objectives.
3. Authority given to a person is legal and legitimate.
4. It is the legitimate right of an individual.
5. It can be delegated by a manager to his subordinates, but power cannot be delegated.
6. It is related to position that a persons holds in the organisation.
7. Authority is the right to influence others while power is the capacity to influence others.
8. It is the right to command and control others.
9. Authority is a relationship between two persons - one supervisor and the other subordinate.
10. Authority is exercised by making decisions and seeing that they are carried out.

SOURCES OF AUTHORITY

There are three different schools of thought about the sources of authority. These sources are known as theories of authority. They are as follows:

1. Formal Authority Theory
2. Acceptance Authority Theory
3. Competence Authority Theory

1. Formal Authority Theory

In this theory, authority flows from top to bottom through various levels of hierarchy. The ultimate authority in a joint stock company lies with the share-holders. Share holders entrust the management of the company to the Board of Directors and delegate to it most of their authority. The Board of Directors delegates authority to the chief executive and chief executive in turn to the departmental managers and so on. Every manager or executive possesses authority because of his organisation position and this authority is known as FORMAL AUTHORITY. Authority conferred by law is also regarded as formal authority. The formal authority theory further states that the superiors have the right to delegate their authority. Thus, formal authority always flows from top to bottom. Every manager in the organisation has only that much authority which has been delegated to him by his superior. Such authority may be called traditional and legitimate. It is legal and rational.

2. Acceptance Authority Theory

It is also known as bottom-up authority. It is based on the promise that authority does not flow from top to bottom but flows from bottom to top. It implies that superiors can exercise authority only if it is accepted by the subordinates. The flow of authority takes the form of request by top managers. If this request is accepted by subordinates, managers exercise the authority, and if subordinates do not accept it, no authority is exercised by managers. In other words, it is the authority which an individual gets when others accept or obey his orders and instructions. The subordinates accept the authority which an individual gets when others accept or obey his orders and instructions. The subordinates accept the authority if the advantages to be derived by its acceptance exceed the disadvantages resulting from its refusal.

The positive and negative consequences determine the acceptability of an order. Some orders may be fully acceptable, others partially acceptable and still others fully unacceptable. Barnard suggests that a subordinate will accept an order if he understands it well, if he believes it is consistent with the organisational objectives and compatible with his personal interests and if he is able both mentally and physically to comply with it.

3. Competence Authority Theory

This authority is derived by a person by virtue of his competence, skill and knowledge and not position. People from all departments at all levels approach the person who has competence authority disregarding the official chain of command. According to Urwisk, FORMAL AUTHORITY is conferred by organisation, TECHNICAL AUTHORITY is implicit in special knowledge or skill whereas PERSONAL AUTHORITY is conferred by superiority or popularity. Thus a person may get his order accepted not because he is having any formal authority, but because of his personal qualities. For example, if a person possesses expert knowledge in a particular subject, people will go to him for guidance in that matter even though he has got no formal authority.

POWER

Power refers to the ability or capacity to influence the behaviour or attitudes of other individuals. Power is an important means to enforce obedience to the rules, regulations and decisions of the organisation. Power may be derived on personal or institutional basis. Authority is derived from position, whereas power may be derived from many sources like technical competence, seniority, etc. A manager's power may be measured in terms of his ability to: (*a*) give rewards; (*b*) punish individuals; and (*c*) withdraw rewards.

Thus, reward, coercion, dominating personality, expertise, etc. are the main sources of power. Authority may be described as an institutionalised power since it is formally given by the organisation.

Power refers to the capacity of one person to influence the behaviour of another. It is defined as the ability to get an individual of another. It is defined as the ability to get an individual or group to do something. While authority is the right of a person to give directions to subordinates, power is the ability to do so. Power does not depend upon a person's position in the organisation. It is derived from a person's control over various resources of the organisation. For any organisation to effectively achieve its objectives, formal authority should be supplemented by informal system of power. Power is the ability to exert influence. A person can exert influence over others if he has knowledge or skills superior to those possessed by others. When a person has right to change the behaviour of subordinates, he exercises authority over them but if he is able to do so, he has power over them.

Power, like authority, is a means of exercising influence on the behaviour of people. But POWER IS STRONGER THAN INFLUENCE. Influence is a psychological force while power is a personal force that enables a person to change the behaviour of others. Influence also differs from authority. Authority is one means to exert influence.

SOURCES OF POWER

The various sources from where they derive power are as follows:

1. Legitimate Power

Legitimate power is the basis of classical theory of authority. It derived from formal position in the organisation hierarchy is legitimate power. Managers have power to issue directions to subordinates.

2. Reward Power

Rewards are more often used as forces that reinforce the positive behaviour of subordinates rather than forces that get them to comply with superior's orders. The rewards may be in the form of promotions, recognition or financial benefits.

3. Coercive Power

Compliance by subordinate is demanded through punishments. The punishment can be in the form of deducting salary or withholding promotions. It is the fear of being punished that makes subordinates obey their superiors.

4. Expert Power

Powers of expertise and referrent powers are earned by acquiring certain skills which make others to seek advise and help. The competence theory of authority derives its base from expert power. If purchase manager has specialised skills in marketing/sales, he will have expert power to influence the people of marketing/sales department.

5. Referent Power

Leaders or experienced workers influence people because of their personality or experience. Workers may approach the union leaders or the experienced workers to get their problems solved.

Distinction Between Authority and Power

Basis	*Authority*	*Power*
1. Formal	1. It serves as a basis of formal organisation.	1. It serves as a basis of informal organisation.
2. Delegation	2. It can be delegated to a subordinate by his superior.	2. It cannot be delegated. A manager, who is an able decision-maker, cannot hand over his ability to his assistant.
3. Position	3. It is related to position that a person holds in the organisational hierarchy. It is institutional in nature.	3. It is related to the person: his qualities, experience, etc. enables him to influence the behaviour of others. It is personal in nature.
4. Organisation chart	4. It can be depicted on the organisation chart.	4. It cannot be depicted on the organisation chart.
5. Parity	5. Parity between authority and responsibility is maintained in the organisation.	5. There is no parity between power and responsibility. A person with minimum responsibility can have maximum power.

INFLUENCE

Advice, suggestions, information, persuation and power are other means of exercising influence. Influence is the outcome whereas authority and power are the means to create this outcome. Influence is an all-inclusive concept that covers both authority and power. It includes all means by which the behaviour is modified, for example, authority, power, etc.

TYPES OF AUTHORITY

There are three types of authority:

1. Line Authority

In line authority, a supervisor exercises direct demand over a subordinate. Line authority is represented by the standard chain of command that starts with the board of directors and extends down through the various levels in the hierarchy to the point where the basic activities of the organisation are carried out. Managers exercise line authority by virtue of their position in the hierarchy. It is the right to issue orders, instructions and decisions to be implemented by people down the hierarchy. This authority is exercised to achieve the organisational goals. Though ultimate authority rests with the top managers, it is delegated to middle and lower level managers, thus, forming a formal chain of command or scalar chain.

2. Staff Authority

The nature of staff authority is merely advisory. A staff officer has the "authority of ideas" only. The information which a staff officer furnishes or the plans he recommends flow upward to his line superior who decides whether they are to be transformed into action. Staff authority involves giving advice and service to line managers on the basis of their specialised knowledge and skills. Staff specialists reduce the burden of line executives. Staff personnel have right to direct or command subordinates within their own departments. But with respect to line personnel they play an advisory or auxiliary role of recommending and assisting. In the words of Henry Fayol, "Staff is an adjunct, reinforment and a sort of extension of the manager's personality."

Distinction Between Line and Staff Authority (in brief)

Line Authority	*Staff Authority*
1. Doing function	1. Thinking function
2. Possessed by generalists	2. Possessed by specialists
3. Flows downward from a superior to subordinates	3. May flow in any direction
4. Right to decide and to command	4. Right to advice, assistance and information
5. Exercise controls	5. Exercise investigation and reports
6. Makes operating decisions	6. Provides ideas for decisions

LINE AND STAFF CONFLICT

The line and staff departments of an organisation are generally found to be at loggerheads with each other.

The line departments complain that:

1. The staff officers have only theoretical knowledge but not practical knowledge.
2. They get the credit when the goals are achieved but are not responsible for the failures.
3. The staff fail to give sound advice.
4. The staff officers unnecessarily increase the paper work of the line officers.
5. Since the staff officers are not responsible for the results they suggest unfruitful ideas.
6. Frequently, the staff officers go beyond their sphere of activity and assume that they nave line officers authority.
7. Much of the advice given by the staff officers is impractical.

The staff departments complain that:

1. The line officers completely neglect the advice given by the staff officers.
2. The line officers hesitate to accept new ideas.
3. The line officers do not follow the advice of staff officers properly.
4. Some line officer's simply reject the advice without considering its validity.
5. The line officers do not exploit the full services of the staff officers.
6. Line people distrust, non-cooperate and even sabotage staff plans.
7. Line people are generally ignorant and bull-headed. They resist new ideas.

REDUCING CONFLICTS BETWEEN LINE AND STAFF

The following suggestions are made in order to reduce the conflicts between Line Officers and Staff Officers:

1. The line and staff should understand their proper positions and functions in the organsiation.
2. The staff should render complete advice on the problems concerned; they should present realistic recommendations and solutions based on full consideration of all the pertinent facts.
3. A separate staff member should be appointed to bring about cooperation between the line officers and staff officers.
4. Only qualified persons should be selected and placed as staff officers.
5. A special previlege may be given to the line officers to reject or accept the advice given by the staff people.

6. Some line officers may resist the change, then it is the duty of staff officers to encourage the line officers to participate in the proposed scheme of change.

3. Functional Authority

According to Koontz and O'Donnell, "Functional authority is the right which an individual or department has delegated to it over specialised processes, practices, policies or other matters relating to activities undertaken by personnel in departments other than its own." Functional authority generally relates to laying down systems and procedures. For instance, the personnel manager may lay down the grievance procedure to be followed in all departments.

LIMITATIONS OF AUTHORITY

Acceptance of authority is not demanded by superiors, rather it is commanded from subordinates. It is evident that managers exercise authority within the limited area of discretion. Various factors limiting this scope of authority are:

(*a*) **Capacity:** It subordinates cannot do the work due to their physical and mental limitations, managers cannot issue directions to that effect.

(*b*) **Organisational Goals:** Directions issued by managers against the organisational goals will not be carried out by subordinates.

(*c*) **Legal Restrictions:** Every organisation is bound by a legal framework of rules and procedures. Any directive issued against the rule shall not be complied with.

(*d*) **Social Factors:** People collectively work in the organisation and form groups on the basis of their social values and cultures. Orders issued against these values have limited acceptance.

(*e*) **Personal Limitations:** Something that a manager cannot do himself, he should not expect from his subordinates also.

Difference between Authority and Responsibility

Authority and responsibility are closely interrelated but they differ from each other with respect to the following:

Points	*Authority*	*Responsibility*
1. Origin	1. It is attached to a particular positions and it is impersonalised.	1. Responsibility is attached to a particular person and it is personalised.
2. Concept	2. Right to issue directions.	2. Obligation to perform the assigned task.
3. Delegation	3. It is delegated from superior to subordinates.	3. The superior continues to remain answerable to his superior.
4. Nature of flow	4. It flows from top to bottom.	4. It flows from bottom to top.

RESPONSIBILITY

The term 'responsibility' means the work or duties assigned to a person by virtue of his position in the organisation. The person carrying the responsibility for the performance of a given task has also the authority to perform it. For example, if a project manager is responsible for the constructions of a bridge, he has also the authority to command his subordinates, procure the needed materials, procure personnel and seek assistance from functional departments for the completion of the project. Responsibility should be distinguished from accountability which is the obligation of an individual to render an account of the fulfilment of his responsibility to the superior to whom he reports.

Responsibility refers to the obligation to perform the given task to the best of one's ability. According to Koontz and O'Donnell, responsibility is "the obligation of a subordinate, to whom a duty has been assigned to perform duty". It is "the obligation to carry out duties and achieve goals related to a position. "The responsibility ends when the person has accomplished the assigned task. If a person is held responsible for the assigned task, he will committed to perform it successfully. Responsibility, therefore, must be fixed. It develops the skill, competence, initiative and ability of a person to his fullest.

The following are the concept of responsibility:

1. Responsibility cannot be delegated or transferred.
2. It always flows upwards.
3. It is the obligation to perform the assigned task.
4. It must commensurate with authority.

ACCOUNTABILITY

It refers to the obligation of the individual to report formally to his superior for the proper discharge of his responsibilities. It is accountability of the subordinate to render an account of his activities to his superior. The person who accepts responsibility is accountable for the performance of assigned duties. "*To be accountable is to be answerable for one's conduct in respect to obligation fulfilled or unfulfilled.*" Accountability is the obligation of an individual to keep his superior informed of his use of authority and accomplishment of assigned duties.

Louis A. Allen defines accountability as "the obligation to carry out responsibility and exercise authority in terms of performance standards established." It is "the requirement to provide satisfactory reasons for significant deviations from duties or expected results". It is "the obligation to account for and report upon, the discharge of responsibility or use of authority."

Accountability cannot be delegated. They cannot be held liable for the tasks not assigned to subordiantes. While authority flows downwards, from top managers to workers, accountability flows upwards, where each level is accountable to his superior who delegates him the authority.

CASE STUDY - 1

Conflict of Responsibilities

Problems are inevitable in day-to-day operations of any plant, if you have a look at technica aspects of it. You will realise that most of the problems occur due to the sheer size of the plant and workers. In one shift we have one thousand workers and engineers, at any given time and along with them, there is other staff such as administration and support staff. There are several production lines operating at top speed according to the production targets fixed by the PPC Manager.

Can you imagine the kind of pressure we have on, us, whenever we are performing and the kind of problems which keep coming our ways. If we don't give the required output it means that we are not performing and nobody will listen to the reasons. Even if one machine will be stopped, it increases the load on other machines and operators. It will also mean that workers of that machine will sit idle for all the time, it has stopped. Then who is answerable for the questions raised by plant manager Grover. He is not going to come to you and ask for explanations. He will give me a good piece of mind tomorrow morning. Now please, will you let me do my work or shall I go and discuss this matter with him on phone at this time. It is 10 o'clock: in the night and he will be really annoyed, if I call him now. The shift engineer Ajay Suri was getting impatient with every passing minute. Even as he stopped talking for a moment he was visibly upset.

The safety incharge, Gurpreet Singh, was listening to him and then he spoke very slowly. "Ajay,

I understand what all you are telling me. I am not new to these situations and quite used to handling such crisis. I am purposely not interrupting your schedule or trying to create problems for you. It is just that as you are interested in completing your work, I am also concerned about my work. As the safety incharge at plant right now. I am responsible for maintaining the norms and see that no damage is done to any of the equipment or property because of mishandling or lack of precautions.

This conversation is taking place during night shift at Plant number 2 of Pioneer Industries Limited, an electrical goods manufacturer. The conversation is a result of an incident which has happened about half an hour ago at the production line of a product. For last one week, it has been raining heavily and it has caused several Interruptions with power supply of the plant. The production lines are run on large generators whenever power supply is cut. In the evening around 8 p.m. again the shift supervisor installed the generator of their unit when the lights were off. The generator set is placed in a small tin roofed structure and the genset maintenance operator noticed that the roof is leaking and the water drops are creating sparks. He told this to the electric supervisor, Dinesh.

Dinesh at once called Gurpreet who decided to switch off the generator. He also called a few labourers to do the repair of the roof immediately. With all production halted, Ajay, the shift engineer came to the site, he took a view of the whole situation and decided that the generator can be used without much of a risk, he ordered Dinesh to start the generator and said, "Half an hour is already wasted, we will have electricity in another hour, till then this can work safely. Let these people do the work on the roof, its not a big problem". Dinesh called Gurpreet who told that as per his norms, the generator can't be started as it may cause damage to machine and fire might spread by these sparks.

In the end, Gurpreet simple locked the genset room and went away. Electricity was resumed within one hour and work continued but Ajay was very angry.

Next morning, Grupreet reached the plant and was immediately called by PPC manager. He found Ajay, works manager and his own boss Lt. Col. Singh sitting in the room. He explained the situation to his boss and also said that he would make sure that genset room gets concrete roof very soon, so that this kind of incidents don't happen again. Ajay was, however upset that shift wasted a lot of time.

The issue, however, did not die here. Next week Lt. Col. Singh called Gurpreet and showed him an analysis sent by the production engineer stating the loss due to stoppage of genset. Singh then went to have a word with works manager. Arora explained the circumstances in which Gurpreet stopped the genset, soon after, the production engineer and Ajay met Arora and showed him the report.

They also met Singh and discussed the matter. Singh was by now a little frustrated by all this and he said, "I don't know why you can't understand this simple thing that what Gurpreet has done is his job, his prime concern was safety. As the incharge he has the authority to decide what is in the best interest of the plant. My department is not responsible for production but for adhering to the norms of industrial safety only. I have been hearing all this for some time and now I don't want to discuss this issue any more. What do you want me to do, shall I compensate for your losses or punish my key person for carrying out his duty." This was followed by a heated argument between Gurpreet and production engineers, Rahul and Ajay.

The two engineers went to works manager and told him what all Singh had said and also told him about their argument. Later in the day, Singh met him and asked him, "Arora, I don't understand why are they so upset, It's not the first incident of this type, in last seven years, I have seen that every time we insist on going according to norms, somebody from production creates big issue out of a small incident and keeps making a noise about it." In the evening PPC manager came to Arora and said, "These people don't know our problems. We are also technical people and understand a little about plant. Every time they keep bringing their procedures and norms and insist that we are at fault. If they are so particular about norms then how come we have so many fire accidents happening all the time. They should look at their work first before preaching my men about norms."

The works manager has by now, got tired of serving as a referee, he just maintained his silence and wondered what he can do to prevent these incidents. After the manager left, Arora kept thinking about how to solve this problem as he felt that he could no more bear these endless stories and attacks.

Then he decided to tackle the issue directly as he felt that he cannot escape from it. He decided that next time any of these people raise this issue he will simply call all those who are concerned together and tell them to discuss the problem there directly. It will be awkward and tense but at least they will learn to deal with each other. Instead of bringing all these troubles to him. And once they discuss all these issues he may try to bring a resolution to tackle these kinds of problems.

QUESTIONS

1. What are the methods of resolving conflict in groups ? Is it appropriate for Arora to use a direct method ?
2. What are the mental blocks that work against resolving conflicts ?
3. What's the root cause of conflict in this case ? How can you avoid such an event from happening again ?

REVIEW QUESTIONS

1. "Authority should go with responsibility." Comment. *(B.Com., Madurai)*
2. State the relationship between authority and responsibility. *(B.Com., MS)*
3. Explain various types of authority. *(B.Com., Madras)*
4. Distinction between line authority and staff authority. *(B.Com., Ujjain)*
5. Explain various sources of authority. *(B.Com., Jabalpur)*
6. Discuss the limits of authority. *(B.Com., Kerala)*
7. Discuss the concept of responsibility. *(B.Com., Mysore)*
8. Explain the concept of Accountability. *(B.Com., Bangalore)*
9. Power and authority are not one and the same thing. Comment. *(B.Com., Andhra)*
10. What is power ? State the different sources of power. *(B.Com., Banaras)*
11. Explain in brief the relationship between authority and responsibility. *(B.Com., Bombay)*
12. State the different types of authority exercise by managers. *(B.Com., Chennai)*

Delegation and Decentralisation

- Introduction
- Meaning of Delegation
- What should be delegated ?
- Definitions of Delegation
- Features of Delegation
- Importance of Delegation
- Advantages of Delegation
- Process of Delegation
- Principles of Delegation
- Guidelines for Effective Delegation
- Types of Delegation
- Weaknesses of Delegation
- Need for Delegation
- Centralisation and Decentralisation
    - Decentralisation of Authority
    - Reasons for Decentralisation
    - Advantages of Decentralisation
    - Limitations of Decentralisation
    - Delegation Vs Decentralisation
- Factors determining Decentralisation
- Centralisation of Authority
    - Advantages of Centralisation
    - Disadvantages of Centralisation
- Span of Control
- Factors Determining the Span of Control
- Types of Span of Supervision
- Case Study - 1
- Review Questions.

DELEGATION

INTRODUCTION

Performance of a function or service by an individual is called duty or the activities that an individual is required to perform are a duty on him. He is answerable for the work he had done. Authority is a right of power required to perform a job on the basis of duty assigned to one. An authorised person is empowered to do the assigned job and take a decision. Power means an ability to do things or get things done by others. Delegation means assigning work to others and giving them authority to do it.

The Board of Directors or the partners or the sole trader possesses all the power or authority to run the firm concerned. If the top management goes for doing the works of the concern, it becomes difficult for it to conduct the business, because of lack of time. Therefore, the work is divided and entrusted to persons who are appointed to look after it. When persons have been appointed to do a particular job, it can be said that a duty has been assigned to them. The assignment of duty is not complete unless authority has also been given to them. Therefore, assignment of duty is followed by authority. When the authority is passed on to the employees, there is a transfer of power to the sub-ordinates; *i.e.*, delegation of powers. Delegation of required authority to the sub-ordinates is necessary to discharge their assigned duty. Delegation of authority is made on the basis of duty one does. When one is delegated the authority, it means permission is given to do the duties. To be short it can be defined that authority is power to command others to do an act in a manner desired. When authority is conferred on a person, he knows the responsibility. If authority is not delegated, the assigned duty will not be done by the entrusted person, because he has no authority. It may also happen that sometimes he assumes authority and does the job. In both the cases the position becomes bad. Therefore, responsibility must always be followed by corresponding authority or power.

The difference between authority and responsibility is that they move in opposite directions. Authority always moves from the top downward, whereas responsibility moves upward. Authority is derived from supervisors, to whom the employee is responsible for the proper performance of his work. An executive working in a particular position cannot transfer to his sub-ordinates greater power than he himself possesses. One can transfer what one possesses. Sometimes, the sub-ordinates may not be willing to accept the orders from the supervisors., and then the delegation of authority has no meaning.

MEANING

If all organisational activities, strategic and routine, could be managed by one person, the need for formal organisation structure with different functional departments. Staffed with people of different functional departments, staffed with people of different calibre, carrying out different activities would not arise. Since it is not possible, because of physical and mental limitations, for any person to perform all activities with respect to all functional areas, it becomes essential that he gives part of his work load to subordinates along with authority to carry out the assigned task. Delegation and decentralization are very important tasks in modern management, "Delegate and get the things done" is the essence of modern management. "Delegate and things will be done" is also another principle of management.

According to Louis A. Allen, "Delegation is the dynamics of management". It is the process a manager follows in dividing the work assigned to him and entrusting work to his subordinates, so that they perform it as he would do it himself. Delegation refers to the entrustment of responsibility and authority to another and the creation of accountability for performance. It also refers to conferring authority to another, usually a subordinate.

A manager in an enterprise cannot himself do all the tasks necessary for the accomplishment of group goals. His capacity to do work and to take decisions are limited. He, therefore, assigns some part of his work to his subordinates and also give them necessary authority to make decisions within the area of their assigned duties. This downward pushing of authority to make decisions is known as delegation of authority. According to L.A. Allen, "If the manager requires his subordinate to perform the work, he must entrust him with part of the rights and powers which he otherwise would have to exercise himself to get that work done." By delegating authority the manager does not surrender his authority.

WHAT SHOULD BE DELEGATED ?

According to Louis A. Allen, "A manager cannot effectively delegate responsibility and authority for initiating and making final decisions for planning, organising, coordinating, motivating and controlling the activities and positions that report to him". Preparing various types of plans: single use or multiple use, strategic plans, policies, procedures rules, etc. cannot be delegated to subordinates. These are the activities of supreme importance for the organisation and managers cannot delegate them to subordinates.

The kind of people to be recruited, selected, trained, placed on different jobs, the kind of leadership style to be adopted, the measures of reward or coercion used as motivational factors are the important business decisions that cannot be delegated to subordinates. With reference to overall plans and objectives of the organisation, the important managerial functions of planning, organising, staffing, directing and controlling are looked after by managers themselves and routine activities with respect to each functional area of production, finance personnel and marketing should be delegated to subordinates. Once decided, the routine matters of accepting applications, returning excess money and issuing share certificates, etc. can be delegated to lower level managers.

DEFINITIONS

According to *Allen*, "Delegation is the dynamics of management, it is the process a manager follows in dividing the work assigned to him so that he performs that part which only, he, because of his unique organisational placement, can perform effectively and so that he can get others to help him with what remains."

According to *G.R. Terry,* "to delegate means to grant or confer, and delegation means conferring authority from one executive or organisational unit to another in order to accomplish particular assignment".

"Delegation means the passing on to others of a share in the essential elements of the management process a share, that is to say, in the judgement / decision for determining specific objectives, plans and targets for directing given operations, and in the command/control of the activities of the persons performing those operations." — *Brech.*

"Delegation is the process where an individual or group transfer to some other individual organs the duty of carrying out some particular action and, at the same time, taking some particular decision." — *Mills and Standingfbord.*

If concern is a medium or large one, it becomes difficult for the office manager to do the works of the organisation. When he feels the lack of time to do a particular job within a specified time, he entrusts the work to his sub-ordinates. Now the sub-ordinates have the delegation of authority in doing the entrusted work. If the office manager divides the works among his sub-ordinates, he gets time to look after his managerial functions, which are more important to him.

In business concerns, the source of authority originates from the top of the firm; and the authority part by part, is delegated to the following persons-directors, secretary, managers, etc. and further from these persons delegation of authority is transmitted to various sub-ordinates.

Delegation of authority shares the managerial work and operating work between a manager and his-subordinates. At the top of concern the scope of authority is wider and as it passes to the subordinates, the scope of authority becomes narrower.

FEATURES OF DELEGATION

The above definitions reveal the following features of delegation of authority:

1. Delegation of power can be exercised by higher authority only.
2. Delegation may be "downward, upward and lateral".
3. Delegation does not mean the transfer of final authority.
4. Delegation does not involve any kind of surrender of power.
5. 'Delegated power' can be revoked at any time.
6. A person can delegate authority only when he himself has the authority.
7. Delegation does not imply reduction in the authority of the superior.
8. Delegation never means abdication of responsibility.
9. Delegation implies the inhabitation of the delegation of power in the delegated authority.

IMPORTANCE OF DELEGATION

The importance of delegation are as follows, in brief:

1. Managers and supervisors at all levels can lessen their burden by delegating authorities to subordinates.
2. Ability of subordinates increases as they are given more responsibility.
3. Delegation of authority reduces the work-load. Hence work is done very quickly and efficiently.
4. Delegation is the means by which a manager can get results through others.
5. Delegation provides a feeling of status and importance to subordinates.
6. Delegation helps to improve the quality of personnel at lower levels.

ADVANTAGES OF DELEGATION

The main advantages of delegation are as follows:

1. Reduction of Workload

Managers and supervisors at all levels can lessen their burden by delegating authority to subordinates. It enables them to assign the routine matters to subordinates. Managers can concentrate on important policy matters.

2. Tool of Training

Delegation of authority and responsibility allows subordinates to increase their ability. By delegating routine jobs and more challenging projects, subordinates can expand their skills and knowledge.

3. Specialisation

Through delegation, an executive can assign jobs to his subordinates according to their abilities and experience. Thus the benefits of division of work is obtained.

4. Job Satisfaction

Delegation provides job satisfaction to subordinates and motivates them to perform better when they achieve the delegated standards of performance.

5. Motivation

Delegation provides a feeling of status and importance to subordinates. Their independence and job satisfaction increases due to the authority they enjoy. Thus delegation promotes a sense of initiative and responsibility among employees. Delegation increases interaction of managers with their subordinates and promotes healthy relationships among them.

6. Faster Decisions

When authority is delegated, lower level employees can take decisions quickly without approaching executives. Subordinates have the authority to do a job assigned to them without going to the supervisors every time, when they face a problem.

7. Development of Business

Delegation of authority prepares executives for the future. This enables the organisation to face future challenges effectively. The business can afford to implement growth plans as managerial talent is available.

The delegation of authority may be done in the following manner.

1. The duty of a sub-ordinate should be defined clearly by the supervisor (duty list) and must be understood by the former.
2. Secondly, necessary authority may also be conferred upon him corresponding to the duty list, so that he knows his accountability and responsibility to the superiors.
3. Thirdly, though a manager may delegate certain authority on his sub-ordinates to perform certain acts, still he is responsible to his superiors *i.e.,* the manager cannot delegate his responsibility, but work can be assigned to his sub-ordinates. Therefore, in the initial stages, counter check by the assigning officer prevents unpleasant results.

The delegation of authority means fixing up of responsibility on the sub-ordinates by the superiors. Sub-ordinates cannot disown the responsibility. If a sub-ordinate neglects the responsibility after the delegation of authority, he is doing so at the cost of his job. The assigning officer has the authority to remove him from service.

The three components of delegation are Responsibility, Authority and Accountability. Each component depends on the others. They are equally important, interrelated and interdependent, and the three are inseparable features of process of delegation.

Responsibility

The work or duty of the sub-ordinates in the organisation is called responsibility. Responsibility is expressed in terms of functions, when a person is asked to control the working of a machine. Responsibility is expressed in terms of objectives, when a person is to produce a particular piece of product.

A manager assigns a certain function, work or duty to his sub-ordinate for performance. This is termed as assignment or responsibility.

Allen states, "Responsibility is the work assigned to a position. Responsibility refers to the mental and physical activities which must be performed to carry out a task or duty."

Donnell states, "Responsibility may be defined as the obligation of a sub-ordinate, to whom duty has been assigned to perform the duty."

Davis states, "Responsibility is the obligation of an individual to perform assigned duties to the best of his ability under the direction of his executive leader."

Authority

It means the powers and rights entrusted to a person to supervise the performance of work delegated. A manager grants authority *i.e.,* rights and powers to be exercised by the sub-ordinate.

It is the right to perform certain assigned work or duties. The supervisor should delegate sufficient authority to do the assigned work.

Mooney stated, "Co-ordination is the all inclusive principle of organisation and finds its foundation in authority, the supreme co-ordinating power."

According to *Simon,* "Authority may be defined as the power to make decisions which guide the actions of another. It is a relationship between two individuals, one superior and the other sub-ordinate. The superior frames and transmits the decisions with the expectation that these will be accepted by the sub-ordinate. The sub-ordinate executes such decisions and his conduct is determined by them."

According to *George R Terry,* "Authority is the official and legal right to command action by others and to enforce compliance. Compliance is obtained in a number of ways through persuation, sanctions, requests, coercion, constraint or force."

Accountability

It is an obligation to account for and report upon the discharge of responsibility, or use of authority. Accountability is the liability created for the use of authority. It is the answerability for performance of the assigned duties. Authority flows downwards whereas accountability flows upwards.

PROCESS OF DELEGATION

Delegation process involves the following steps:

1. Assignment of Work

The supervisor asks his subordinate to perform a particular task in a given period of time. It is the description of role assigned to the subordinate. Duties in terms of functions or tasks to be performed constitute the basis of delegation process.

2. Grant of Authority

The granting of authority is the second element of the delegation. The delegator grants authority to the subordinate so that the assigned task is accomplished. The delegation of work without authority is meaningless. The subordinate can only accomplish the work when he has authority required for completing that task. Authority is derived from responsibility.

3. Creating of Accountability

Accountability is the obligation to a subordinate to perform the duties assigned to him. The delegation creates an obligation on the subordinate to accomplish the task assigned to him by the superior. When a work is assigned and authority is delegated then the accountability is the by-product of this process. The authority is transferred so that a particular work is completed as desired. This means that delegator has to ensure the completion of assigned work. Authority flows downward whereas accountability flows upward.

Authority is delegated, responsibility is assumed and accountability is imposed. Responsibility is derived from authority and accountability is derived from responsibility. Authority is the medium for creating responsibility and for imposing accountability.

PRINCIPLES OF DELEGATION

Delegation of authority cannot be effective unless certain principles are followed in practice. While delegating authority, a manager may observe the following principles:

1. Functional Definition

Before delegating authority, the duties of the subordinates should be defined in clear and precise terms. Every subordinate must fully understand the nature and significance of his job, its relationship with other jobs and the limits of his authority.

2. Delegate by Results expected

Managers should first determine the objective of delegation, that is, what they want their subordinates to do and then delegate the tasks along with authority to them. This process involves first formulating a plan and then getting things done through the people in the organisation.

3. Parity between Authority and Responsibility

Authority without responsibility and responsibility without authority have no meaning. Authority and responsibility should be co-extensive. There should be no disparity between the authority granted to a subordinate and the responsibility imposed on him.

4. Unity of Command

There is one of the common principles of organisation advocated by Henry Fayol which stresses that subordinates should have only one boss to whom he should be accountable, to avoid confusion and friction.

5. Absoluteness of Responsibility

Responsibility cannot be delegated. No manager can avoid his responsibility by delegating his authority to sub-ordinates. Similarly, the subordinates remain accountable to their superior for the performance of assigned duties.

6. Well-defined Limits of Authority

Managers cannot delegate what they are themselves not authorised to do. For instance, if a manager does not have authority to raise funds from the open market without permission of top managers, he cannot delegate this task to his subordinates.

7. Maintain Adequate Communication

There should be free and continuous flow of information between the superior and the subordinates with a view to furnish the subordinate with relevant information to help him to make decisions and also to interpret properly the authority delegated to him.

8. Establish a Climate of Confidence

The subordinate to whom authority delegated must generally feel free from fear and have a feeling of confidence that delegation will not result in punishment but is an opportunity for his own self-development and growth.

GUIDELINES FOR EFFECTIVE DELEGATION

Barriers to delegation can be over come through the following measures:

1. Define the objectives in clear terms.
2. Adhere to the principles of delegation.
3. Select proper persons for delegation.
4. Motivate subordinates through various incentives.
5. Develop confidence in subordinates.
6. Assign authority proportionate to task.
7. Train the subordinates properly.
8. Determine the tasks to be delegated.
9. Create a climate of mutual trust and goodwill.

10. An effective system of communication should be developed.
11. Let there be no overlaps or slips in delegation.
12. Establish a good work climate free from fear.
13. Delegate sufficient authority to perform the job.
14. Provide all possible assistance.
15. Establish proper control and conduct regular reviews.
16. Evaluate the final results.

TYPES OF DELEGATION

The following are the types of delegation:

1. General and Specific Delegations

General Delegation: The subordinate is granted authority to perform all the functions in his department. However, the subordinate exercises this authority under the overall guidance and control of the supervisor.

Specific Delegation: A person is given authority regarding specific function. For instance, a sales-man may be given authority to collect payments from debtors.

2. Formal and Informal Delegations

Formal Delegation: When authority is delegated as per the organisation structure, it is called formal delegation. Such delegation is effective because it leaves no option to the subordinate but to obey the commands of the superior.

Informal Delegation: Informal delegation takes place when an individual or a group agrees to work under the direction of an informal leader. Need for informal delegation arises due to procedural delays and red tape.

3. Written and Oral Delegations

Delegation made by written orders and instructions is known as written delegation. Unwritten or oral delegation is based on custom and conventions.

4. Downward and Sideward Delegations

Downward delegation occurs when a superior assigns duties and grants authority to his subordinate. This is the most common type of delegation.

Sideward delegation takes place when a subordinate assigns some of his duties and authority to another subordinate of the same rank.

WEAKNESSES OF DELEGATION

(Obtacles of Delegation)

In spite of the advantages, many managers are found unwilling to delegate authority and many subordinates are found unwilling to accept it. The reasons for this unwillingness may be grouped into three categories:

(*i*) Superior (Delegator)
(*ii*) Subordinate
(*iii*) Organisation

1. On the part of Supervisor (Delegator)

A superior may not delegate authority because of the following reasons:

(*a*) "I can do it better myself" fallacy obstructs delegation of authority.

(*b*) Lack of ability of the manager to plan correctly and issue suitable directions.

(*c*) A manager may be afraid of their subordinates outshining them and proving more efficient.

(*d*) Some managers hesitate to delegate authority to their subordinates because they doubt their ability.

(*e*) Lack of confidence in the capacity and ability of the subordinates obstructs to delegate authority.

(*f*) Where the manager does not set up adequate controls, he may hesitate to delegate the authority.

(*g*) Some managers may not delegate authority because of their lure for authority. They desire that subordinates should come frequently and to dominate the whole show.

(*h*) When a manager is incompetent, his working methods and procedures are likely to be faulty. He keeps all the authorities to himself. They do not delegate authority. He is afraid of losing his importance, when delegation is made.

2. On the part of Subordinates

Subordinates may be reluctant to accept authority because of the following reasons:

(*a*) Lack of self-confidence.

(*b*) Desire to play safe by depending on the boss for all decisions.

(*c*) Fear of committing mistakes and being criticised by the boss.

(*d*) Lack of incentives

(*e*) Over-burdened with work.

3. On the part of the Organisation

Delegation may be hampered due to weaknesses in the organisation structure. A few such weaknesses are given below:

1. Inadequate planning
2. Defective organisation structure
3. Lack of unity of command
4. Absence of effective control techniques
5. Non-availability of competent managers.
6. Unclear authority relationships.

NEED FOR DELEGATION

Delegation is essential in modern management practice to accomplish effective results. It has become important because of the following reasons:

1. Limitations of one's ability and time

However capable an individual might be, he has limited energy and time. Therefore, delegation of authority alongwith workload are assinged at different workers.

2. Technological Needs

Modern organisations need the services of different specialists and technicians. One man cannot be expert in different fields of activities. Thus delegation becomes essential.

3. Tendency to diversify and decentralise Organisation

A modern large-scale business has a tendency to diversify and decentralize its activities. Delegation of authority to the branch managers can make diversified and decentralised branches function effectively.

4. Employees Motivation

More and more interest and enthusiasm can be introduced through delegation to the workers, so that they can feel that they are also participating in the decision-making.

5. Managerial development

Delegation, by providing sufficient opportunity for the workers to take decisions and to accept more and more responsibility, can create new generation managers.

6. Management by exception

Modern managers manage by exception. Delegation will relieve the botheration of managers in attending routine decisions, which others can attend to efficiently.

CENTRALISATION AND DECENTRALISATION

Centralisation and decentralisation help to coordinate organisational activities. While delegation refers to assigning responsibility and authority to people from one level in the organisational hierarchy to the other, centralisation and decentralisation refer to the extent to which authority and responsibility are passed to people at lower levels. If authority to make decisions is retained at top levels, the organisation is said to be centralised; if the decision-making authority is distributed widely throughout the organisation and lower level managers have the authority to use financial and non-financial resources, the organisation is said to be decentralised.

Decentralisation of Authority

According to *Allen,* "Decentralisation means the systematic effort to delegate to the lowest levels all authority except that which can only be exercised at the central points". Everything that goes to increase the importance of the sub-ordinates role is decentralisation. In a large and complex organisation, management cannot centrally control for everything.

Decentralisation of office means each department of the concern possesses its own office. There is no central office. Each department has supervisors, clerks, typists, etc. There is a delegation of authority to the lower levels. Thus the authority to take decision is delegated to the managers, Purchase Managers, Sales Managers, Works Managers, etc. The Managers are responsible to their superiors.

Reasons for Decentralisation

The reasons for the decentralisation of authority in an organisation are:

1. Larger size of an enterprise needs decentralisation. It is difficult for the top management to make all the decisions at a time.
2. Growth and diversification of activities leads to overburdened work. It is difficult to have an effective direction when the work is unwieldy.
3. The increase in competitive market calls for decenralisation.
4. Training of executives leads to decentralisation.
5. External and internal factors lead to decentralisation.

Advantages of Decentralisation

1. The chief executive of the firm will be free from the burden of overloaded problems arising in different departments. To make the top officials free, the adoption of decentralisation is needed. They, then, can attend to major problems.
2. Secrecy can be maintained, because all the papers of a department are kept by the department itself. In a centralised one, secrecy cannot be maintained.
3. Research can be facilitated to have more efficiency in production.

4. Co-ordination takes place from the low level which is preferred. In a centralised one, co-ordination takes place at the top level.
5. Since each department is assigned duties and is answerable, each department takes initiative so that better results are produced.
6. It avoids confusion and promotes speed in decision-making.
7. Lower level executives can introduce new ideas and techniques.
8. It is easy to achieve flexibility at all levels of management.
9. Achievement of better management employee relation is possible.
10. Efficient practice of management principles is possible.

Limitations of Decentralisation

1. Many competent executives are required to work because many departments may be there.
2. The operating cost is very high, because many persons are employed.
3. Co-ordination amongst the departments becomes a problem.
4. Chance of uniformity of action becomes less.
5. Top management may not be able to exercise effective control.

Distinction between Delegation and Decentralisation

Delegation	*Decentralisation*
1. Delegation is possible without decentralisation.	1. Decentralisation is not possible without delegation
2. It is vital and essential to the management process.	2. It is optional and it may or may not be practiced as a systematic policy.
3. It is the process of devolution of authority.	3. It is the end results.
4. It refers to the relationship between two individuals supervisor and immediate subordinate.	4. It refers to a relationship between top management and departments or divisions.
5. The delegator continues to exercise control over the activities of subordinates.	5. The top management exercise control only over strategic issues.
6. Lower level managers of each unit carry out the plans framed by their superiors.	6. Managers of each unit frame their own plans.
7. Power to control the delegated tasks vests with the delegator.	7. Power to control is delegated to lower level managers.

FACTORS DETERMINING DECENTRALISATION

While deciding the degree of decentralisation in a particular organisation, the following factors should be kept in view:

1. In large and complex organisations there is greater need for decentralisation.
2. When the production and sales of an enterprise are geographically scattered, there is great pressure for decentralisation of authority.
3. In a company having several diverse product lines, decentralisation is not only necessary but beneficial.
4. If it is expanded through amalgamation or absorption, it is likely to be more decentralised.

5. When the top executives believe in individual freedom, there will be a high degree of decentralisation.
6. Lack of trained executives will restrict decentralisation.
7. Basic functions like production and sales are more decentralised than staff functions, such as personnel, finance, etc.
8. In case communication system is effective, decentralisation should be advocated.
9. Environmental factors exercise significant influences on the degree of decenralisation.

CENTRALISATION OF AUTHORITY

According to *Allen,* "Centralisation is the systematic and consistent reservation of authority at central points within an organisation".

Centralisation of authority means all office works are carried on in a central place and managed by a single top official. It implies that decisions pertaining to office matters are taken at the top level. The other departments will have to do duties assigned to them. Centralisation may be physical and functional.

Centralisation increases the importance of the central authority in the organisation and reduces the importance of sub-ordinates.

Centralisation is desirable in the planning and control of the management. It is desirable in the determination of objectives of the organisation. It is desirable in legal and governmental relationship. It is desirable in diversification, modernisation, expansion or contraction of the business activities of the organisation.

Advantages of Centralisation

1. The office manager can distribute the work equally amongst the members of the staff. In decentralised method, some members of the staff have less work while some are overloaded. This unpleasant situation is avoided by equal distribution.
2. Under centralisation, duplication of work and expenditure are eliminated, *e.g.,* typewriter, duplicators, typists, stenos, etc. In centralisation, there will be one Section consisting of typewriters and typists-typist pool. Otherwise in decentralisation, every department has a typist and a typewriter. Therefore, there is less expenditure.
3. Better supervision is possible by a single man, because similar job is centralised; otherwise many supervisors have to be appointed.
4. Each worker will have to perform a particular type of work. He has to do it again and again. When he does a job over and again, naturally he gets speed in the job and becomes a specialist in the particular work.
5. Centralisation brings uniformity of action. Uniformity of action can be attained when a centralised authority manages the operating units.
6. There is no need to give overtime work to any department, as there are many clerks to handle the work without difficulty.
7. Quick decisions can be taken. Expert advice can be made available for managing the system.

Thus centralisation results in greater productivity, low cost, personal utilisation and greater administrative convenience.

Disadvantages of Centralisation

1. If one requires any information, he will have to approach the central office. If the central office is far, then there is a delay in getting the information.
2. The section-heads suffer from an inferiority complex for every information, the central office (supreme) is to be approached.

3. The staff working in the central office may feel proud, at the same time such feelings may wound the staff working in different sections.
4. Since the central office is overloaded, it is possible that mistakes or errors will creep in.
5. Too much concentration of authority or control over others may spoil the interest and initiative of the sub-ordinates.
6. Delays in accomplishing the work owing to the transmitting of the records from and to centralised units.

SPAN OF CONTROL

The term "span of control" is also known as "span of management", "Span of supervision", "Span of authority", "span of responsibility", etc.

Every person has a limited capacity for effective supervision and control other people. No one can control an infinite number of subordinates. If a person is asked to supervise many subordinates working under him, he cannot supervise them efficiently. The capacity and ability under him is limited on account of time at his disposal, knowledge, energy, and other capabilities: therefore the number of subordinates working under him must be manageable.

Span of management refers to the problem of "how many subordinates can be effectively managed by a manager". General Hamilton, who was the first person to introduce the concept "span of control" in his famous book—The Soul and Body of the Army, states that "the average human brain finds its effective scope in handling from three to six other brains. The nearer we approach the supreme head of the whole organisation, the more we ought to work towards groups of six."

In the words of Spriegal, "Span of control means the number of people reporting directly to an authority. The principle of span of control implies that no single executive should have more people looking to him for guidance and leadership than he reasonably be expected to serve."

Lyndall Urwirk, the famous British Consultant, in 1938 found that "No superior can supervise directly the work of more than five or at the most six subordinates whose work interlocks." If the number of subordinates is larger, then the superior may find it very difficult to supervise and coordinate their activities effectively.

FACTORS DETERMINING THE SPAN OF CONTROL

A superior cannot manage a large number of persons, but if the number of subordinates is too small, it is uneconomical. So, he has to determine the optimum span of management. It depends upon various factors. They are as follows:

1. Capacity and Ability of the Supervisor

The capacity and abilities such as leadership, administrative capabilities, ability to communicate, to judge, to listen, to guide and to inspire, physical vigour, etc. differ from person to person. A person having better abilities can manage effectively a large number of subordinates as compared to the one who has lesser capabilities.

2. Competence of Subordinates

If the subordinates are dynamic, competent, well trained and experienced, the manager can manage a large number of such subordinates. If there is perfect understanding and team spirit among the employees, he can manage more workers. If the manager has no confidence in the ability of his subordinates, the span will be narrower.

3. Nature of Work

The work involving routine, repetitive, unskilled and standardised operations will not call for much attention and time on the part of the supervisor. As such, the supervisors at the lower level of organisation can supervise the work of a large number of subordinates. On the other hand, at higher level of management, the work involves complex and variety of jobs and as such the number of subordinates that can be effectively managed should be limited to a lesser number.

4. Time Available

The capacity of a person to supervise and control a large number of persons is also limited on account of time available at his disposal to supervise them. At higher levels top managers have less time for supervision. They have to devote the major portion of their time in planning and organising. Therefore, span has to be narrow.

5. Degree of Decentralisation

When a manager does not delegate adequate authority to subordinates, they require frequent consultation and the manager has to take many decisions himself. As a result he can supervise few subordinates. If, on the other hand, a manager clearly delegates authority, subordiantes themselves will take many decisions and the manager can effectively supervise a large number of people.

6. Staff Assistance

An executive can supervise more subordinates when advice and assistance of staff specialists is available to him. Personal assistants can reduce the work load of a manager there by permitting him to handle a large number of subordinates.

7. Levels of Management

At higher levels of management, a lesser number of people can be managed: the lower the level of management, more workers can be managed. That is, the manager who personally makes more decisions is able to supervise fewer people than a manager who only has to provide occasional coaching and encouragement. At the supervisory level, work involved is of routine nature and, therefore, span tends to be wider.

8. Quality of Planning

If plans and policies are clear and easily understandable the task of supervision becomes easier and the span of management can be wider. Effective planning helps to reduce frequent calls on the superior for explanation, instructions and guidance and thereby saves time available to and of the supervisor enabling to have a wider span. In effective plans, on the other hand, impose limits on the span of management.

9. Communication Techniques

The span of supervision is also influenced by the effectiveness of the communication system in the organisation. Faulty communication puts a heavy burden on manager's time and reduces the span of control. On the other hand, if the system of communication is effective, larger number of managerial levels will be preferred as the information can be transmitted easily. Further, a wide span is possible if a manager can communicate effectively.

10. Control Techniques

Sophisticated information and control systems and objective standards reduce the need for close supervision. Use of objective standards helps to wide the span of control. The use of objective standards enable a supervisor management by exception by providing quick information of deviations or variances. Control through personal supervision favours narrow span while control through objective standards and reports favours wide span.

TYPE OF SPAN OF SUPERVISION

There are two types of span of supervision: 1. Wider span of supervision and 2. Narrow span of supervision.

1. Wider span of supervision

Wider span of supervision also known as flat organisation implies few levels of supervision. In this type of span, the supervisor controls and guides the activities of subordinates directly under his control. Wider span of supervision is favoured where workers are competent and trained, the control mechanism through standards is followed and the total number of workers is not very large. It reduces the cost of supervision.

2. Narrow Span of Supervision

Narrow span of supervision implies tall or verticle organisation. Under this type of supervision, there are many levels and more supervisors are required to perform the job of guidance and control for different activities. It increases the efficiency and supervision but the cost of supervision is very high as compared to wider span of supervisor.

CASE STUDY - 1

Introducing New Systems

The Super Steels Ltd. specialises in making steel moulded furniture. The MD, Mr. Sukhdev Singh, formed the company in 1980s with a working capital of ₹ 5 lakhs and 10 people and started with commercial pieces of furniture. Gradually, the business grew and work force was also expanded. Their main recruits are diploma holders in technical trades such as assembling, etc. The staff work in teams of six people to assemble inspect and approve as piece of furniture and teams were assigned for different products. The whole of production area is partitioned for separate teams. The teams consist of a team leader, two experienced workers and rest workers either fresh or on rotation. Teams are further organised in groups and each group has leaders of team as quality team. They take charge of production, output and quality of all teams as one group, discuss and improve upon themselves. All the groups are answerable to the production manager. Around twelve months ago, Mr. Singh in consultation with his old friend decided to diversify into home furniture and developed a massive restructuring. He decided to call an industry expert to advice on the process, who after study, recommended a flow-line production process for all their products. Mr. Singh accepted the plan and arranged for starting out the commercial operations.

To avoid a loss of production the new manufacturing layout was introduced during the summer closing down of their factory. The workers while, going on leave were informed that some changes would take place and they should be ready for it.

Under the flow-line process, the manufacturing of furniture piece has to be broken into 6 elements each element to be given to a worker, who sits in line alongside a track. The finished piece of furniture is then to be carried out to the inspection department and then to the quality department. After approval it is to be sent to stores. The track contains ten teams of six workers per track.

Once the workers returned this new process was explained to them. They were provided basic training on new systems and were given targets for individual performance.

After two months, Mr. Singh realised that the absenteeism at factory increased by 20 per cent and five of their workers left the job. Since the introduction of new system though the output level rose. It is still below their estimated level. The amount of time spent by their Production and Operation manager on dealing with production and workers's problems rose considerably

Not only that due to inadequacy and lack of knowledge among workers their wastage rose to almost 20 per cent.

QUESTIONS

1. Discuss the major problems faced by the organisation.
2. How could the changes in the organisation have been made more successful ?
3. What are the major pitfalls in implementing this change in any organisation ?

REVIEW QUESTIONS

1. What is delegation of authority ? How to secure better delegation ? *B.Com., Madurai)*
2. What is meant by decentralisation of authority ? What are its advantages and disadvantages ? *(B.Com., Calicut)*
3. What are the differences between delegation of authority and decentralisation of authority. *(B.Com., Delhi)*
4. Discuss the relative merits and demerits of decentralisation of authority. *(M.Com., Bhopal)*
5. What are the obstacles to delegation ? What measures do you suggest for effective decentralisation ? *(B.Com., Banaras)*
6. Discuss the concept of responsibility. *(B.Com., Kerala)*
7. Discuss the merits and demerits of centralisation. *(M.Com., Bombay)*
8. What guidelines will you suggest for ensuring effective delegation of authority ? *(M.Com., Bangalore)*
9. State the various factors that affect decentralisation. *(B.Com., Mysore)*
10. "Decentralisation is nothing but an extension of delegation". *(M.Com., Allahabad)*

Organisation Chart and Manual

14

CHAPTER

- Introduction
- Meaning of Chart
- Definitions
- Features of Organisational Chart
- Contents of Organisational Chart
- Type of Organisational Chart
- Master and Supplementary Charts
    - Advantages of Charts
    - Disadvantages of Charts
- Principles of Organisation Chart
- Organisation Manual
- Introduction
- Meaning of Manual
- Contents of Manual
- Types of Organisational Manuals
- Purpose of Manuals
    - Advantages of Manuals
    - Disadvantages of Manuals
- Preparation of Manuals
- Making Manual Effective.
- Review Questions.

INTRODUCTION

It is essential for efficient management that all members of the organisation clearly understand their authority relationship. Organisation charts and manuals are useful means of providing information about organisational relationships. They are used as tools of management controls. They give full information on a particular organisation. An organisation chart shows graphically the managerial positions and inter relationship in an enterprise.

MEANING OF CHART

Organisation is made up of a group of persons working together towards the accomplishment of certain specified objectives. It has a structure of planned relationships among the group members. These relationships can be shown in an organisation chart.

It also shows the positions held by the different executives and their sub-ordinates in the departments and units, the relationship between their functions and the lines of authority and responsibility among them. It enables each executive and employee to understand what is his position in the organisation structure, what are his functions, to whom he is responsible for his work and who is responsible to him.

An organisational chart is a pictorial representation of company's structure and reporting relationships. This chart can provide a great deal of information and may help organisational members to understand the overall structure of the organisation and its strategy.

DEFINITIONS

"An organisational chart is a diagrammatical form, which shows important aspects of an organisation including the major functions and their respective relationships, the channels of supervision, and the relative authority of each employee who is in charge of each respective function." — *George Terry*

"An organisation chart portrays managerial positions and relationships in a company or a department unit." — *Henry Halbers*

"The organisation chart is a graphic means of showing organisation data. Organisation charts are snap shots: they show only the formal organisation and they take it for only a given moment of time." — *Allen*

"An organisation chart is a plan of working relationships. It shows who is to do the work that is to be done and who is to direct and supervise the efforts of those who are to do the work."

— *Leffingwell*

"An organisation chart is a diagram of the formal authority structure." — *Ernest Dale*

It is made clear that an organisation chart shows the different departments, divisions and units into which the activities of the organisation have been grouped.

FEATURES OF ORGANISATION CHART

The following are the features of an organisation chart:

1. It is a diagrammatical presentation.
2. It represents the formal organisation structure.
3. It reveals the main lines of authority in the organisation.
4. It illustrates internal functions of relationships.
5. It reveals various units and their relations with other units.
6. It indicates the channels of communication.
7. It reflects the intentions of management.

8. Organisational charts provide complete picture of the entire organisation in a simple and understandable manner.

CONTENTS OF ORGANISATION CHART

An organisation chart may contain a variety of information. But, generally speaking, it includes the following:

1. Structure of the organisation.
2. Flow of authority.
3. Spheres of responsibility.
4. Line and Staff relationship.
5. Names and status of personnel in different positions.
6. Number of personnel, proposed promotions or transfers, salary, etc. of staff.

An organisation chart should be as simple as possible and as soon as it becomes complicated, it may defeat the purposes for which it is created.

TYPES OF ORGANISATIONAL CHARTS

The Structure of organisation can graphically be presented in the following manner:

1. Vertical Chart

This is the most widely used form. It shows the organisation structure in the form of a pyramid, the lines of command proceeding from top to bottom in lines. The highest position or person is placed at the top and after that the next highest. This process goes on upto the lowest level.

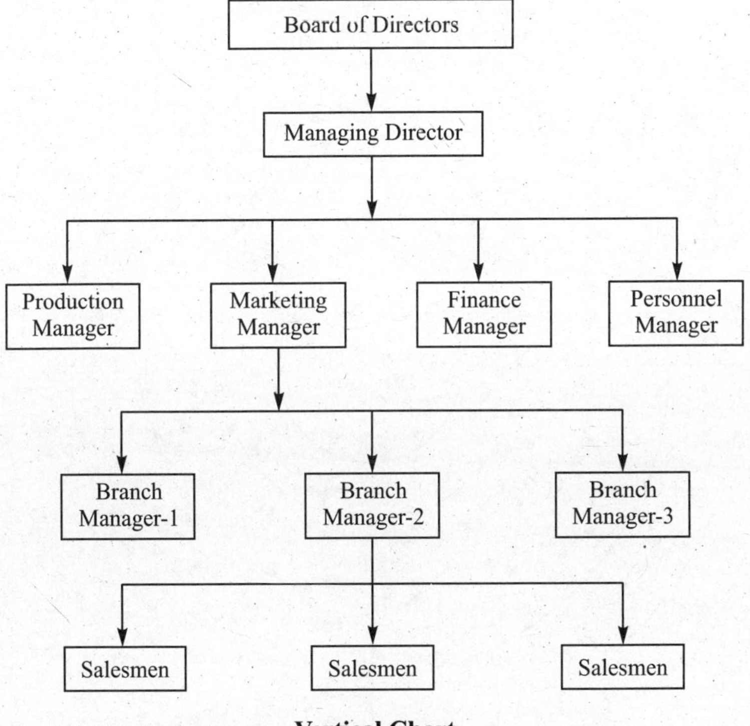

Vertical Chart

2. Horizontal Chart

In a horizontal chart the pyramid lies horizontally instead of standing vertically. The highest position is shown at the extreme left and the lowest position at the extreme right. In between each successive sub-ordinate position extends from left to right. Therefore, this chart is also called Left to Right chart.

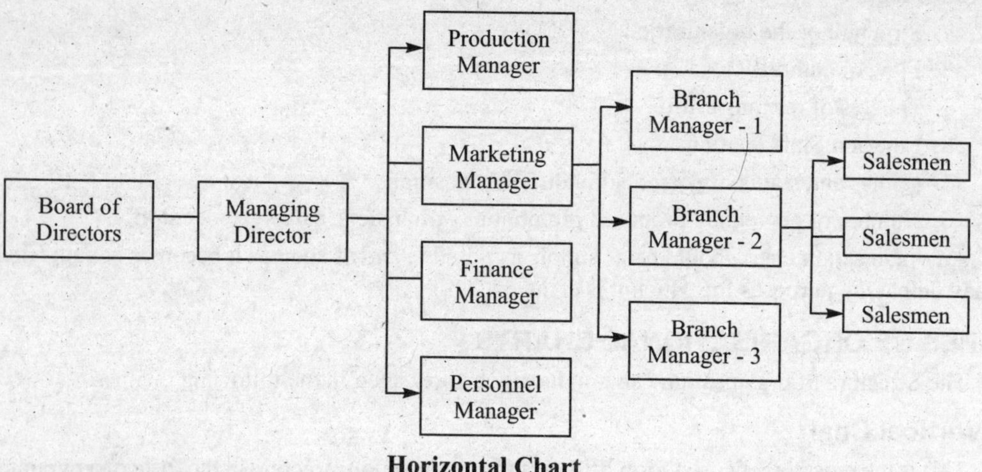

Horizontal Chart

3. Circular Chart

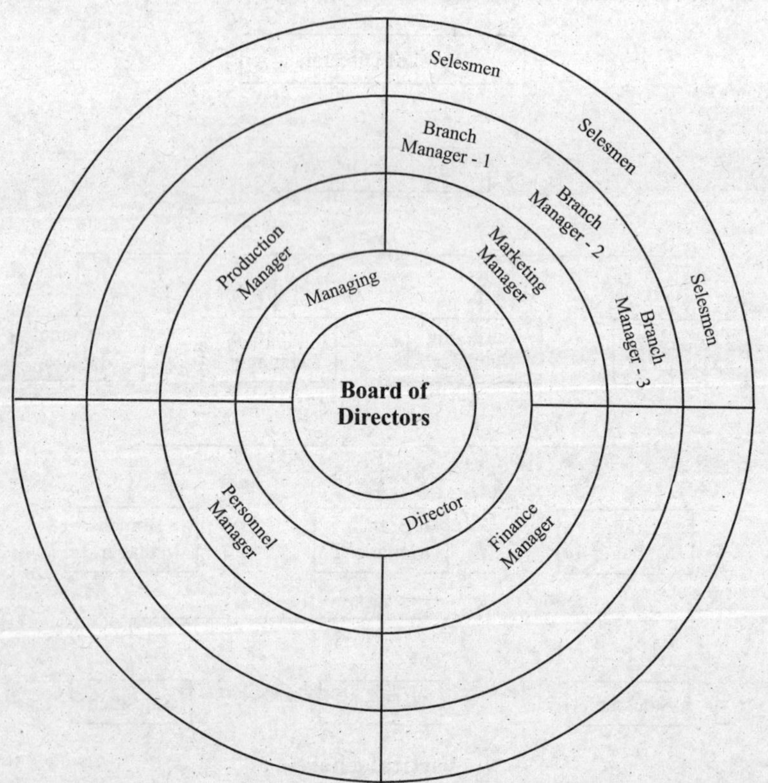

Circular Chart

In a circular chart, the highest position is shown in the centre and the lowest position at the outermost circle. Positions at successive echelons extend in all directions outward from the centre. Distance of a position from the centre indicates the degree of closeness to the top position. Positions of equal status lie at the same distance from the centre. This form is, however, rarely used.

MASTER AND SUPPLEMENTARY CHARTS

Organisation chart may also be classified into master and supplementary charts. A master chart shows the whole structure of the organisation and provides a clear picture of the entire structure.

A supplementary chart illustrates various units within a department and authority relationships among them.

Advantages of Organisation Chart

Organisational chart serves as a useful tool of management in the following manner.

1. It shows the whole organisation structure at a glance.
2. It defines the line of authority and responsibility.
3. It enables the management to locate defects.
4. It gives guidance to new employees.
5. It ensures a clear understanding of organisational objectives.
6. It provides guidance to outsiders.

Disadvantages of Organisation Chart

The following are the limitations of organisational chart.

1. It reveals only a partial picture of the organisation.
2. It shows only the formal relationship and not the informal relationship
3. Charts often lacks flexibility.
4. Most organisational chart are merely a 'snap-shot' of the existing organisation.
5. Poorly designed charts cause confusion and misunderstanding.
6. The relationship shown in the organisational chart does not prevail among the employees.

PRINCIPLES OF ORGANISATIONAL CHART

Organisational charts can be made more useful and effective by keeping in mind the following points:

1. The chart should have a clear title alongwith date and number.
2. The complete chart should be drawn and shown in a single sheet.
3. It should show clearly the lines of responsibility and authority so that there is no overlapping.
4. Colours may be used carefully to distinguish among various departments.
5. Positions of equal rank should be shown at the same level and the details should be well spaced and titles should be shown in boxes.
6. Staff relationships should be drawn by dotted lines and line authority should be shown in the form of solid lines.

ORGANISATION MANUAL

INTRODUCTION

An organisation manual is wider in scope and contents than the organisation chart. It describes the elements of the structure outlined in the chart. An organisation chart shows who has authority over whom. But it does not show the extent of authority or the duties each person in the organisation is expected to perform, except in so far as implied by job titles. So, large organisations prepare organisation manuals.

MEANING

The organisation manual contains the details of the work to be done in the organisation and other particulars of the concern. Generally, it will be helpful to the employees (especially new comers) to understand the work without any delay. The organisation manual contains all the details of the whole organisation work. If a new man is appointed to do a particular job, he has to know the details relating to the job to be performed. Therefore, it would be enough to give instructions which are necessary for his job. This can be copied from the manual and handed over to the person. This is enough. These written instruction as to the job to be performed can also be called as a Duty List. This is common in Government offices.

An organisation manual is an authoritative guide to the organisation. It is a source of information, a knowledge of which is essential for the performance of work. It may be in the form of a book or booklet and contains for the benefit of the staff, information on operating systems and procedures, methods and routines, executive decisions , standard practices, organisational policies and so on. If employees are supplied with copies of the manual, they do not have to approach their superiors again and again for necessary guidance, instructions and decisions; they do not therefore, cause any interruption of work, nor waste their own time and the time of the executives organisation manuals are used not only to fix responsibility for the performance of office jobs, but also to set up procedures for the performance of organisation jobs. Because instructions, rules and regulations are written down, each employee receiving a manual can be held responsible for them and for manner in which they are carried out.

CONTENTS OF ORGANISATION MANUAL

The following information is generally included in an organisation manual:

Introduction

1. Name of the organisation
2. Nature of the organisation
3. Objectives of the organisation
4. Location of the organisation
5. Purpose of the manual

Administration

1. Organisation structure
   – Major divisions and departments
2. Job descriptions
3. Organisation charts
4. Policies of the management
5. Rules and regulations

Procedures

1. Office procedures and practices
2. Specimen form to be used
3. Standard instructions
   — how to perform different jobs
4. Methods relating to accounting, budgeting etc.
5. Glossary of important terms.

TYPES OF ORGANISATION MANUALS

The main types of organisation manuals are given below:

1. Policy Manual

It contains a basic policies of the company. It describes the overall limitations within which managerial actions can take place. A policy manual lays down the decision, resolutions and pronouncements of the Board of Directors regarding the policies of the company. The main objective of policy manual is to inform all decision makers regarding their limits in the matter. This does not allow anyone to cross his limits and also provides guidelines.

2. Organisational Manual

The organisational manual contains the organisational structure, duties, rights and powers of the officials, the liabilities of each one and mutual relationships between the two of the officials, departments, etc. and their interrelationship.

3. Administrative Practice Manual

This manual consists of administrative structure, systems, procedures, methods of work of each department in the organisation. This also spells out the duties, rights and responsibilities of the departments concerned. This also gives the proforma records returns, etc. to be prepared from time to time.

4. Departmental Practice Manual

It contains detailed information about the organisation, policies and procedures of one department. Inter-departmental relationships are also shown with the help of charts and diagrams. Each department has its own manual.

5. Rules and Regulations Manual

This manual gives information about operating rules and employment regulations. It describes rules regarding hours of work, timings, leave, canteen, library, recreation, etc. It may also explain employee benefit plans like group-insurance, hospitalisation, housing, safety, etc. This type of manual helps the management to explain the personnel policies relating to employees. And this type of manual helps in eliminating misunderstanding and frictions between the management and employees.

PURPOSE OF MANUALS

Three purposes of manuals are: (*i*) to make instructions definite, (*ii*) to find answers in connection with procedures and (*iii*) to improve administrative controls. For the successful controlling of organisation, there must be complete and up-to-date manuals which inform the employees what they have to do, when and how. A manual contains general information, general office rules and regulations and many other essential clarifications.

Advantages of Manuals

Manual helps management in the following ways:

1. It is easy for the supervisor/manager to supervise the work.
2. Doubts, if any, can be referred to the manuals.
3. Changes can be made whenever necessary.
4. It includes delegations of authority along with assignment of job.
5. Expensive training is reduced.
6. The worker understands the job to be performed, because the method is also written in it.
7. Responsibility can be fixed on individuals.
8. Good manuals lead to reduction of office costs.
9. The employees can get necessary information at any time they want.
10. It permits quick decision at lower levels.

Disadvantages of Manual

The limitations of the organisation manuals are as under:

1. Organisation manuals are costly and time-consuming.
2. It is difficult to keep a manual up-to-date.
3. It may discourage team work because somebody may not like the recorded relationship.
4. A manual may be misinterpreted if it is not written clearly.
5. Sometimes the details given in the manuals are inadequate or incomplete or vague.

PREPARATION OF MANUALS

The task of preparing the manual is generally entrusted to a committee consisting of departmental heads. If the organisation plans to have a manual of a particular department, say, sales department, then the Sales Manager will be a member of the committee. And he who takes initiative of supervising the preparation as well as revision of the manual. Revision of manuals is as important as the preparation of the manuals, The committee will prepare the manual by following the steps:

1. An outline of subjects to be covered should be prepared. It will include history of the organisation, its products, objectives, office rules affecting office hours, holidays, etc. Suggestions, ideas, etc. as to the subjects to be collected in the manual should be invited from departmental heads, supervisors and employees, etc. of the enterprise.
2. The number and types of manual to be prepared and their contents will be determined. This will help in determining procedures being used in different departments to be standardised.
3. The committee will consult the important executives and employees from each department regarding the flow of work and the job analysis of each position. It will assemble the information and compile it for proper use in preparing the manual.
4. The committee will study the data to determine the overlapping of jobs and duplication of functions. The information and data included should be accurate and complete. The language should be simple. As far as possible short sentences and words should be used.
5. Lastly, the draft manual will be prepared and edited. It may be either in bound or loose leaf form depending upon the use to be made of the manual.

A limited number of copies of the draft manual should be prepared for key executives, supervisors, employees, union representatives. Criticisms and suggestions should be received from them and in the light of which the manual should be given final shape by the committee and send it to the top management for approval.

The work of revising the manuals becomes easier and less expensive if the manuals are prepared in the form of loose-leaf books, rather than bound books. If it is in loose-leaf form the pages requiring revision can be extracted from the book and substituted easily.

MAKING MANUAL EFFECTIVE

The following guidelines are helpful in making manuals more effective:

1. The manual should be prepared by experts.
2. The information to be included in manual should be properly classified in a logical order.
3. The manual should be kept up-to-date.
4. Periodic revision must be made whenever there is a change.
5. Manual must be freely available to all staff.
6. It should be in simple and flexible.
7. It is prepared as per the needs of the enterprise.

REVIEW QUESTIONS

1. What is an organisation chart ? What are its features ? *(M.Com., Jabalpur)*

2. What is an organisation manual ? What are its contents ? *(M.Com., Bhopal)*

3. Enumerate the types of manuals. *(B.Com., Kerala)*

4. Narrate the limitations of manuals. *(B.Com., Madras)*

5. State the guidelines for preparation of manuals. *(B.Com., MS)*

6. Discuss the types of organisational chart. *(B.Com., Madurai)*

7. Discuss the merits and demerits of organisation chart. *(B.Com., MS)*

Nature and Scope of Staffing

15

CHAPTER

- Introduction
- Meaning of Staffing
- Features of Staffing
- Importance of Staffing
- Need for Staffing
- Staffing Process
- Job Grading
- Job Description
- Job Analysis
- Job Specification
- Job Standardisation
- Job Classification
- Job Evaluation
- Manpower Planning
    - Recruitment
    - Selection
    - Placement
    - Orientation
    - Training and Development
    - Remuneration
    - Performance Evaluation
    - Promotion and Transfers
    - Separations
- Case Study - 1
- Review Questions.

INTRODUCTION

Most employers truly believe the fact that their staff is their greatest asset, and the right recruitment and induction processes are vital in ensuring that the new employee is groomed within the shortest time possible. The success of an organisation depends on having the right number of staff, with the right skills and abilities. Organisations may have a dedicated human resource function overseeing this process, or they may rest these responsibilities to line managers and supervisors. Many people may be involved, and all should be aware of the principles of good practice. Even in large organisations with a specialist personnel department, it is essential to involve others in the task of recruitment and induction.

Staffing is a very crucial function of management. For efficient functioning of the organisation, competent incumbents are needed and staffing is the function which provides human resource to the organisation. In the small organisation, this function is normally performed by the top executives, but in the complex organisations this function is entrusted to a separate department and staffing is considered as a distinct managerial function. While the ultimate decisions relating to staffing are taken by the top line executives, the personnel department functions are the advisory and in supporting capacity. Keeping in view the increasing importance of appointments and complex employee problems, it is in the interest of the organisations to establish a separate department of efficient performance of this function.

MEANING OF STAFFING

Management is the art of getting things done through people. The process of recruitment, selection, development, training, identifying, assessing, placing, evaluating and developing people can be called STAFFING. Haimann states that "staffing relates to the recruitment, selection, development, training, compensation of subordinate managers." In other words, staffing may be defined as the process of hiring and developing the required personnel to fill in various positions in the organisation. It involves estimating the number and type of personnel required, recruiting and developing them, and maintaining and improving their competence and performance.

According to Harold Koontz and O'Donnell, "the managerial function of staffing involves manning the organisational structure through proper and effective selection, appraisal and development of personnel to fill the roles designed into the structure." It involves determining the need for people at various organisational posts, appointing and retaining them at those posts by training and developing their abilities and skills.

FEATURES OF STAFFING

The above description reveals the following features of staffing:

1. Management Function

Staffing is an important management function that appoints people at different posts to run the organisation. Staffing is a universal function. It is the responsibility of every manager. In large organisations, there exists generally a personnel department. But this department only advises and helps the line managers in performing the staffing function.

2. Pervasive Function

People are the most important asset that convert inputs into outputs. People are appointed at all levels - top, middle and low and in all functional areas - production, finance etc. Staffing ensures that right persons are appointed at the right job so that organisation can efficiently achieve its objectives. In large organisations, there is generally a separate human resources department. The manager of human resources is responsible for the recruitment, selection, training and appraisal of his subordinates.

3. Continuous Functions

Staffing is a continuous managerial function. People keep leaving and joining the organisations. Departments and organisations grow and, therefore, need for people keeps arising. Hiring, training and compensating people (staffing) are, therefore, continuously performed by managers.

4. Concerned with human element

Functions of staffing, recruitment, selection, training and appraisal of subordinates of all departments are performed by managers at all levels as all departments need people to function. In performing these functions, managers seek assistance of the personnel department.

5. It deals with Active Resources

Staffing deals with the most important resource (people) that converts inactive resources, that is raw materials, into productive outputs. It deals with the live resource, that is, people without whom organisation's resources would remain as resources only. That means resources will not be converted into outputs.

IMPORTANCE OF STAFFING

Staffing function is important for the following reasons:

1. Human force is the most important and productive asset of the organisation which carries out the functions and productive activities of various departments.
2. Managerial staffing ensures that all positions in the organisations are occupied by right individuals who are competent and willing to discharge their responsibilities.
3. If staffing function is properly carried out, managers provide leadership facilities so that individuals can satisfy their personal goals alongwith organisational goals.
4. It helps in discovering and obtaining talented and competent personnel for various jobs.
5. It provides the continuous survival and growth of the business through the development of efficient and effective executives.
6. It helps to ensure optimum utilisation of the human resources by avoiding over manning. It prevents under utilisation of human resources and high labour costs.
7. Managerial training programmes assures availability of qualified and trained personnel. Managerial appraisal assures more specific management results. It helps a lot in solving the problems of salary, promotion, etc.
8. Well trained staff works according to plans and deviations in actual performance will be reduced. This helps managers in controlling various organisational functions.
9. Since staffing helps to place the right person, with the right knowledge, at the right place and the right time to perform the organisational activities, efficiency of the organisation increases.
10. In the modern era of globalisation, every enterprise faces touch competition from national and international competitors. A well-staffed organisation provides management sound policies and procedures for adapting to the environment and face competition.
11. In order to make use of the latest technology, the appointment of right type of persons is necessary. Right personnel can be procured, developed and maintained for new jobs only if the management performs its staffing effectively.
12. Efficient performance of the staffing function is essential to make the best use of personnel. For instance, if right type of people are selected and trained, management can obtain optimum results from the expenses incurred on recruitment, selection and training.

NEED FOR STAFFING

Staffing is an important function that provides man-power to the organisation. The increase in size of organisations, rapid advancements in technology and growing complexity of human behaviour has led to the increase in the significance of staffing. Efficient staffing provides the following benefits:

1. It helps in discovering talented and competent workers and developing them to move up the corporate ladder.
2. It helps to improve the quantity and quality of the output by putting the right man on the right job.
3. It helps to avoid a sudden disruption of an enterprise's production run by indicating shortages of personnel, if any, in advance.
4. It reduced the costs of personnel by avoiding wastage of human resources.
5. It facilitates the growth and diversification of business with the help of talented employees.
6. It provides information to management for the internal succession of managerial personnel in the event of an unanticipated turnover.
7. To increase loyalty and commitment of workers towards individual and organisational goals.
8. To make optimum use of human resource to achieve organisational objectives.
9. To make people to realise their potential at work and develop them for promotion to higher managerial posts.
10. To make record of achievement of people so that managers can make policies with respect to their transfers, promotions and demotions.
11. To define equitable and adequate remuneration for people by providing them monetary and non-monetary incentives. This promotes active contribution to organisational objectives.
12. To develop people's abilities to assume jobs of higher skill, competence and responsibility.

STAFFING PROCESS

The object of staffing is to obtaining the best available people for the organisation and to develop the skills and abilities of those people. Human Resource Management (HRM) is a staff function. The staffing process consists of several interrelated activities such as human resource planning, recruitment, training, etc. The elements of staffing or staffing process consists of the following basic activities:

1. Man Power Planning
2. Recruitment
3. Selection
4. Placement
5. Orientation (Socialization)
6. Training and Development
7. Remuneration
8. Performance Evaluation
9. Promotion, Transfer, etc.
10. Separation.

We will discuss all the above, one by one. In this chapter, we deal with Man Power Planning. The remaining topics, in detail, will be taken up in succeeding chapters.

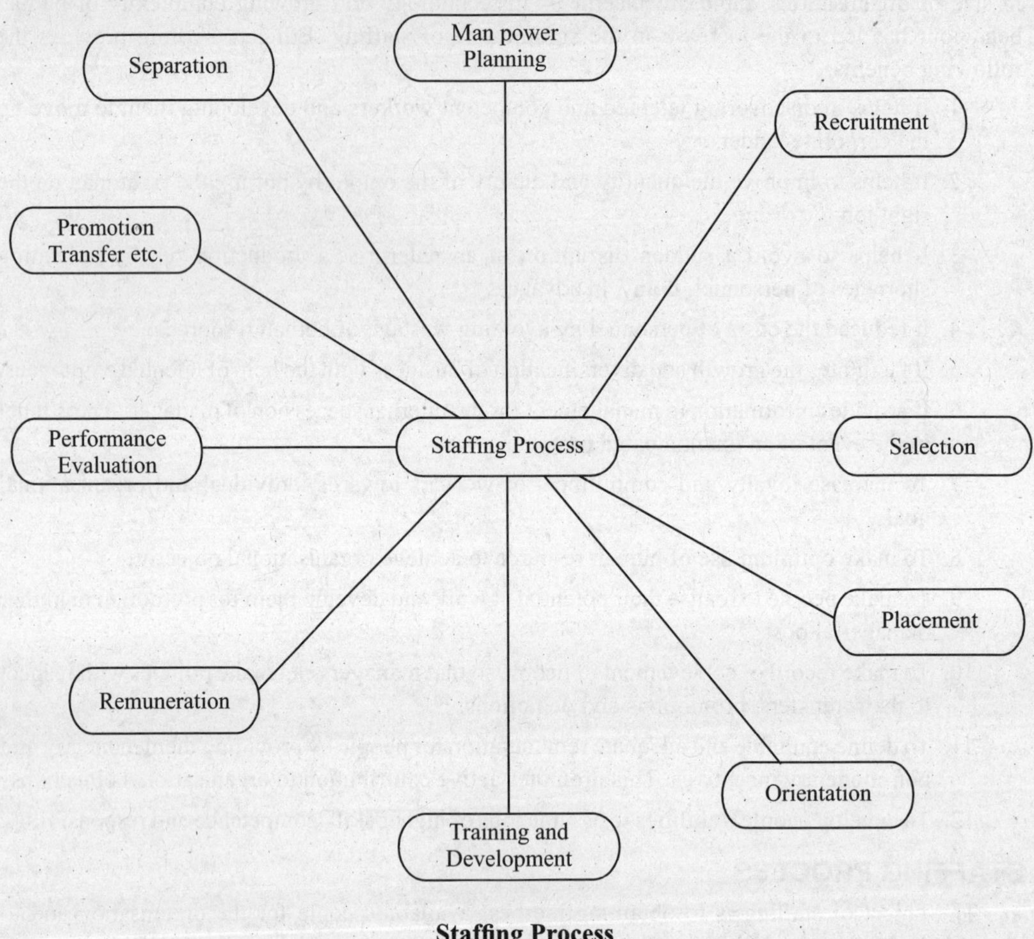

Staffing Process

1. Manpower Planning

Adwin B. Geisler states that "manpower planning is the process by which a firm ensures that it has the right number of people and right kind of people, at the right time, doing things for which they are economically most useful." So, manpower planning involves the determining of the manpower requirements for a period, which includes the acquisition, employment and development of human resources. It helps in the selection and development of personnel and also in effective control over labour costs by avoiding shortages and surpluses of manpower.

Human resource planning is designed to ensure that personnel needs will be constantly and appropriately met. It is accomplished through analysis of (*a*) internal factors, such as current and expected skill needs, vacancies, and departmental expansions and reductions, and (*b*) factors in the environment, such as the labour market. The use of computers to build and maintain information about all employees has enabled organisations to be much more efficient in their planning of human resources.

In the words of Beach, "Human Resources Planning is the process of determining and assuring that the organisation will have an adequate number of qualified personnel, available at the proper times, performing jobs which meet the needs of enterprise and which provide satisfaction for the individuals involved."

The basic elements of manpower planning may be considered, such as:

(*i*) Forecasting the future needs of manpower.

(*ii*) Developing the sound recruitment and selection procedure.

(*iii*) Proper utilisation of available manpower.

(*iv*) Controlling and reviewing the manpower costs. Shortages may occur due to the following reasons:

(*a*) Absenteeism: Temporarily shortage may occur due to absence of planned leaves (medical leave, etc.)

(*b*) Retirement, resignation, transfer or death may cause permanent shortages.

(*c*) Changes in technologies, new jobs, new skills, etc. may cause shortages.

Exists due to retirement can be planned but resignations and deaths cannot be anticipated. They have to be estimated. Past experience will give some indication about what may happen in future. Both, over-estimates and underestimates are costly, the former causing over-staffing and the latter causing shortages.

Recruitment of staff involves selection of the source from which staff is to be recruited, selecting the most suitable candidates through interviews, and various forms of tests and the actual appointment of the staff through letters of appointment, services agreement, etc. But before taking steps for the recruitment of staff, the manager must obtain accurate and detailed information regarding the contents of the jobs to enable him to determine what qualities and abilities to look for in the staff to be recruited. Thus, it is important to understand and meaning of the term "job" and other connected terms. Let us discuss these aspects.

JOB GRADING

The system of job-grading is followed both in selecting the workers and at the promotional stages. In dealing with the selection of workers it is necessary to measure the relative values of different jobs. All types of jobs are paid according to their relative difficulties and the basic purpose of job evaluation. Job evaluation is a system of which each job is rated and its relative worth determined as per the procedure laid down. When recruitment is done, the requirement of the job is thoroughly considered-educational qualifications, special training, experience, etc., laid down for the smooth functioning of the job. Arrangement of job-grading is done from the simplest job to the highest job or vice-versa: Thus jobs are graded in the ascending or decending order. This is done along with job description. Job description gives detailed information pertaining to a job.

According to *Denyer,* "Job grading consists of a scientific study of all jobs and then the placing of these jobs into broad categories called job grades. It is fundamentally a technique of determining the differences between jobs and rationalising the rates of pay in large organisations."

Job grading is the classification and analysis of each type of job being performed in an organisation. As a matter of fact, job grading can be made in various manners, such as, skilled, semi-skilled, and unskilled or Grade A, Grade B and Grade C or Grade I, Grade II and Grade III, etc.

Job grading is done after undertaking job analysis, job description and job specification for each job. It is done by studying the essential characteristics of each job. These characteristics are:

1. The experience required;
2. The skill needed;

3. The initiative required;
4. The level of responsibility entailed; and
5. The level of supervision needed for the job.

Advantages of Job Grading

1. Salary can be paid on the basis of graded job, which is proper and justifiable.
2. Able worker gets the chances of promotion. Ability rather than seniority is to be given consideration.
3. Improvement in the morale of the employees and good relationship between the management and the employees can be maintained.
4. The right man can be given the right job; right salary is paid and thus wage disputes are avoided.
5. It increases output and improves the morale of employees.
6. It reduces labour turnover.
7. It is a valuable guidance in work simplification.

The Institute of Office Management, London has suggested the following grading system for office work:

Grade A : Simple tasks allotted to be done under close supervision.

Grade B : Simple copying and making entries from original documents; tasks requiring the knowledge of a limited number of well-defined rules. Simple operations requiring manual dexterity. Measure of responsibility small, work mostly checked and closely supervised.

Grade C : Work of a routine character but where the responsibility is somewhat greater than grade B. Checking Grade B Work.

Grade D : Work calling for the exercise of some initiatives. Daily routine varying. Little supervision given.

Grade E : More important clerical work with a degree of control over the sequence of jobs or over the work of small groups of staff. Work demands special knowledge or involves individual responsibility without supervision.

Grade F : Supervisions of sections and responsibility for the efficient execution of a complete division of the work. Regular contact with the management and administration. Work demanding knowledge of a special character for example, legal, accounting, engineering, etc.

JOB DESCRIPTION

A job description is a written statement outlining the purpose and the Principal duties and responsibilities of a job. A specimen of job description is given below:

Post	:	Clerk (in mail department)
Age	:	18 to 25 years
Sex	:	Male or female
Qualifications	:	Matriculate, preferably graduate
Salary	:	₹ 3,000-50-5000 plus ₹ 1800 per month
Duties	:	Sorting out letters handling of mail opening machine, handling of the opened letter to the section-head, writing of addresses on the envelopes and minor clerical jobs

Responsibility	:	Punctuality in morning hours is essential. Honesty is required, (for cheques, drafts, etc., are received)
Personal	:	Pleasing habit, co-operative nature, accuracy, good appearance, etc.
Experience	:	Not necessary
Promotion	:	If the worker proves worthy, he may be taken in the accounts department on a higher scale.

In the words of *Bethel,* "the job description is a 'boiled down' statement of the job analysis and serves to identify the job for consideration by other job analysts." That is, it is an abstract of information gained from the job analysis report. It describes the work performed, the responsibilities involved, the skill or training required, the conditions under which the job is done, and the type of the personnel required for the job.

JOB

Otis and *Leukart* defined a job as "A group of position involving substantially the same duties, skills, knowledge and responsibilities." The job is impersonal. The position is personal. Each job or sub-division of a job must have an unambigous name or title to avoid confusion. A job is a collection of task, duties and responsibilities which as a whole is regarded as the regular assignment to individual employees.

JOB ANALYSIS

(JOB STUDY)

According to Harry L. Wylie, "Job analysis deals with anatomy of the job. This is the complete study of the job (or position) embodying every known and determinable factor including the duties and responsibilities involved in its performance; the conditions under which performance is carried on, the nature of the task; the qualifications required in the worker, and the conditions of employment, such as pay, hours, opportunities and privileges." Job analysis is the process of studying and collecting information relating to the operations and responsibilities of the specific job. Job analysis is based on job description, job specification and job classification. According to *Terry*, "Job analysis is the process of critically examining the components of a job, both separately and in relation to the whole, in order to determine all the operations and duties." Job analysis has two aspects - (*a*) Job-aspect-description of features of the work and (*b*) man - aspect - consisting of the detailed description of the necessary physical, mental and personal characteristics of the worker.

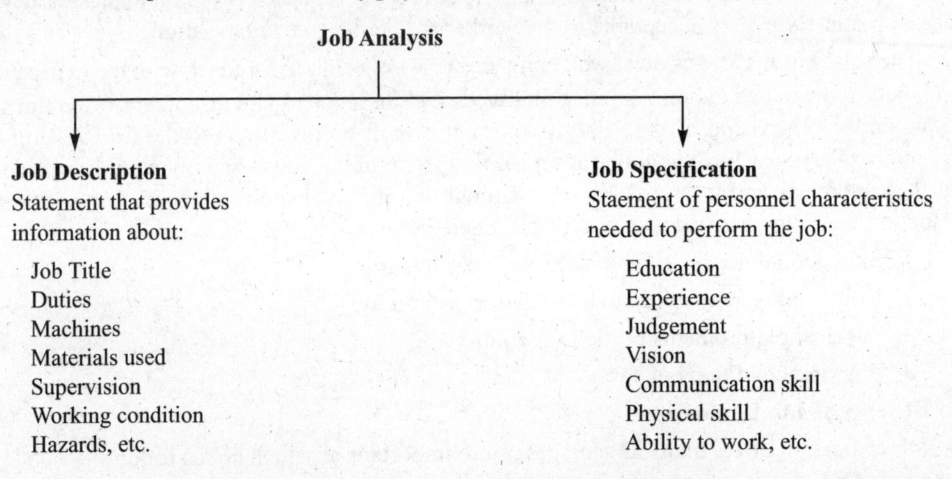

JOB SPECIFICATION

Job specification is a statement of the minimum acceptable human qualities necessary to perform a job properly. It is a product of job analysis and description. While job description describes the duties and responsibilities of a particular job, specification specifies the personnel qualities required for the performance of a job-formal education, experience, aptitude and attitude, etc. That is, a job description is a study of the job, while a specification is a study of the qualities required for the performance of a job.

JOB STANDARDISATION

Job standardisation includes the establishment of specifications for tools, equipment, working conditions and methods. These specifications are arrived at by scientific analysis. Standards of performance cannot be maintained unless conditions of work, systems and personnel are standardised.

JOB CLASSIFICATION

This branch of job study refers to comparative study of jobs. It embodies the comparison of individual jobs and the determination of identical duties and qualifications so as to achieve the objective of grouping similar jobs into classes so that identical and consistent titles may be assigned.

JOB EVALUATION

Job evaluation is the rating of each job or work according to a particular procedure in order to determine its relative worth. It is the system by which each job is rated in relation to other jobs of the firm. The purpose of job evaluation is that each job is paid according to the relative difficulties in performing it. One will not accept a job when he is not satisfied with the salary offered.

In the words of *Dale Yoder,* "Job evaluation is a practice, which seeks to provide a degree of objectivity in measuring the comparative value of jobs within an organisation and among similar organisations. It is essentially a job rating process, not unlike the rating of employees."

According to *B.H. Walley,* "Job evaluation is a systematic of the value of a range of jobs, so that ultimately wages or salary payment scale is produced for them."

According to *Brech,* "Job evaluation is the method of determining the relative worth of jobs on some scale, usually by an analysis of the contents of jobs under classified headings."

The basic purpose of job evaluation is to determine the relative worth of each job so that proper remuneration can be fixed for different categories of jobs. Proper job evaluation helps in devising a wage structure which is acceptable to the workers as well as the organisation.

The salary or the wages must well compensate a worker in accordance with the expected skill and labour to be expanded on his job. Employees feel dissatisfied and discontent when the salary is low, on the other hand, if the salary is too high it will be disastrous to the firm. Therefore, a systematic salary structure should be accepted for the common well-being of both the management and the employees and it is possible only through the job evaluation methods. For a proper job evaluation the following factors are to be considered:

1. Skill and labuor required to perform a particular job.
2. Effort and responsibility to be undertaken for a job.
3. Physical requirements needed for a job.
4. Working conditions of a job.

Benefits of Job Evaluation

Job evaluation offers many advantages, more important of which are as follows:

1. Proper and rational salary and wage structure can be formulated.
2. When job evaluation is practised, wage rates can be reviewed with ease.

3. Job evaluation helps in evolving uniform standards to be applied to all jobs in the organisation.
4. Settlement of grievances and disputes regarding individual wage rates is greatly facilitated.
5. Job evaluation helps in the maintenance of harmonious relations between employer and employee.
6. Job evaluation allows for simplification of wage administration because it brings about uniformity in wage rates.
7. Job evaluation helps in the elimination of personal prejudice in establishing rates by putting the rate structure on an objective basis.

2. Recruitment

Once the recruitment of manpower is known, the process of recruitment starts. It can be defined as the process of identifying the sources for prospective candidates and to stimulate them to apply for the jobs. That is, recruitment is the generating of applications or applicants for specific positions. According to Dalton E.Mc Farland, "It is the process of attracting potential employees to the company.

According to Flippo, "Recruitment is process of searching for prospective employees and stimulating them to apply for jobs in the organisation."

Dale S. Beach states that "Recruitment is the development and maintenance of adequate manpower resources. It involves the creation of a tool available upon whom the organisation can draw when it needs additional employees."

The object of recruitment is to attract potential employees with the necessary characteristics and in the proper quantity for the jobs available. It locates available and willing people to work in the enterprise. It precedes selection. The purpose of recruitment is to seek out or explore or evaluate, to induce and to obtain commitment from the prospective employees so as to fill up positions required for the successful operation of an enterprise. Recruitment provides an adequate pool of candidates to enable management to select suitable candidates for different jobs.

There are two sources of recruitment:

1. Internal Sources
2. External Sources

1. Internal Sources

Internal recruitment can be made from the following sources:

(*a*) *Notice Boards:* Job vacancies are put on the notice board so that candidates can see them and apply for the posts.

(*b*) *Transfer:* It involves the shifting of an employee from one job to another. At the time of transfer, it is ensured that the employee to be transferred to the new job is capable of performing it. In fact, transfer does not involve any drastic change in the responsibilities and status of the employee.

(*c*) *Promotion:* It leads to shifting an employee to a higher position depending upon their experience and qualifications. Promotion involves reassignment of duties to an employee to higher position with higher pay, benefits and enlarged responsibilities. According to Myers, "Promotion is an advancement of an employee to a better job - better in terms of greater responsibilities, greater skills, higher status and higher pay." Filling vacancies from within organisation has the following benefits:

(*i*) Employees are motivated to improve their performance.

(*ii*) Morale of the employees is increased.

(*iii*) Industrial peace prevails in the organisation.

(*iv*) It is economical.

2. **External Sources of Recruitment**

External recruitment can be made from the following sources:

(*a*) *Advertisement:* The post may be advertised in local or national newspapers which have enough circulation. Advertisement, can also be done in trade journals.

Sometimes blind type of advertisement is also done by giving box number, so as to keep the firm's name unknown to the applicants. This is done so, because recommendations can be avoided. The full information of the post must be given in the advertisement, so that the applicant may not have any doubt. Through advertisement the best candidate can be selected with advantage.

(*b*) *Colleges and Universities:* Generally, Universities maintain a register of employment bureaux in order to help the students. A firm that has vacancies can inform such bodies in order to get information of suitable candidates. One has to inform the bureaux along with the description of jobs. This is the easiest way of filling vacancies. But the drawback is that a good selection is not possible.

(*c*) *Employment Exchange:* Government has set up a department to provide the required staff to any concern. The employment exchange will be informed of all the description of the job, so that they can send proper candidates for the job: Usually it sends local persons. In such a case a proper selection is not possible. The merit is that the post can be filled in very soon, without any expenditure for advertisement. Moreover, when most of the candidates are from local area, travelling expenses need not be paid.

(*d*) *Professional Organisation:* Institute of Chartered Accountants, Institute of Cost and Works Accountants, Institute of Company Secretaries, etc., can be contacted in order to get trained and qualified candidates. They recommend the names of candidates along with full particulars to the needed firm. They always keep a register having such information. There is an advantage that a qualified accountant or secretary can be selected.

(*e*) *Media:* Television and Radio sometimes announce lists of candidates with specific qualifications. Companies can approach the media and recruit people of their requirements.

(*f*) *Factory Gate Recruitment:* A notice is placed on the notice board of the enterprise specifying the details of the jobs available. Job seekers assemble outside the premises of the organisation on the specified data and selection is done on the spot. This is known as recruitment at factory gate.

(*g*) *Trade Unions:* Trade Unions have a list of workers which can be used for recruiting labour with varying degrees of skilled.

(*h*) *Other Organisations:* Some organisations have competent, qualified and skilled employees who may be interested in leaving their jobs and joining other organisations which offer them better compensation packages.

(*i*) *Ex-employees, Job-seekers, Friends, etc.:* Job-seekers may sometimes apply directly. Old employee of the concern can also suggest names of candidates to be selected. The vacancy can also be informed to the friends, who may suggest candidates.

(*j*) *Circular Letters:* It is also seen that sometimes the management writes circular letters or places the information on the notice board of the firm, inviting applications. Through the workers of the firm, the news goes out and they bring candidates to personnel department.

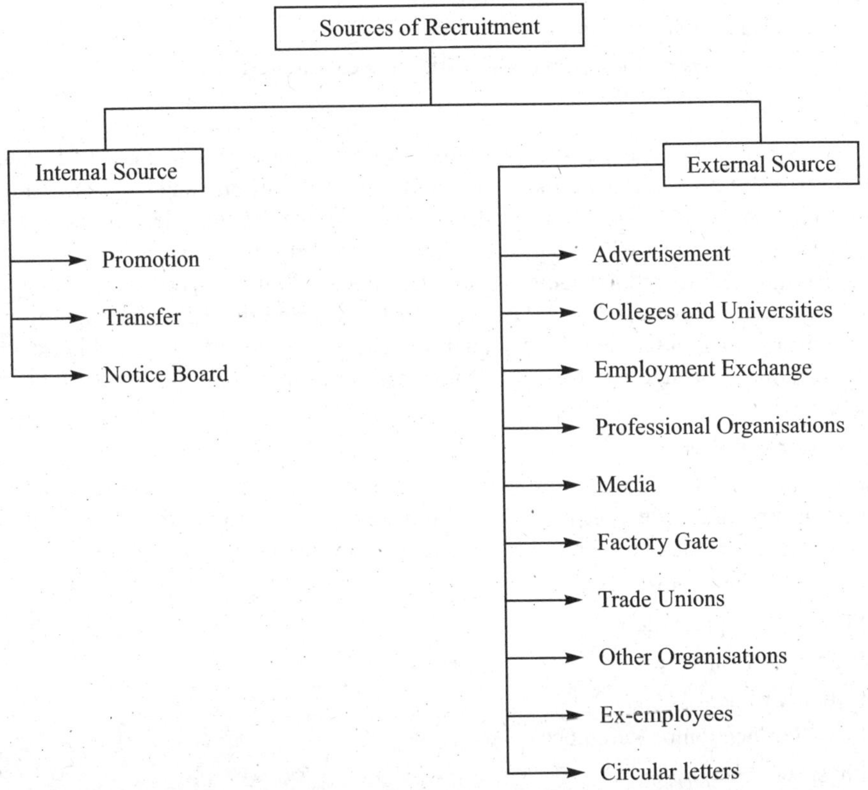

Advantages of Internal Recruitment Source

1. Continuity of service and stability.
2. Employees have a feeling of security.
3. Fosters Loyalty, integrity and honesty among the staff.
4. Familiarity with the organisation set-up.
5. Low grade workers are encouraged, to higher posts.
6. Cost of recruitment is negligible.

Limitations of Internal Recruitment Source

1. It reduces competitiveness among employees.
2. It ensures job security even to inefficient persons.
3. Transfers increase cost of training.
4. Transfers without competence reduce productivity.

Advantages of External Recruitment Source

1. It makes better qualified and skilled persons available.
2. It improves the competitive spirit.
3. It improves productivity because selection of the best candidates out of available candidates.
4. It eliminates the selection by recommendations.

Limitations of External Recruitment Source

1. The process of recruitment is a lengthy and time consuming.
2. The cost is generally high.

3. It creates dissatisfaction amongst existing staff.
4. Firms have to spend lot of time in orienting the candidates.

3. Selection

The selection process ideally involves mutual decision. The organization decides whether to make a job offer and how attractive the offer should be, and the job candidate decides whether the organisation and the job offer fit his needs and goals. In reality, the selection process is often more one-sided. In situations when the job market is extremely tight, several candidates will be applying for each position and managers at the organisation will use a series of screening devices to identify the most suitable candidate. On the other hand, when there is a shortage of qualified workers or when the candidate is a highly qualified executive or professional being courted by several organizations, managers at the organization will have to sweeten the offer and come to a quicker decision.

Selection Procedure

There can be no standard procedure to select different types of employees to be adopted by all concerns. In practice, selection procedure differs from job to job and from organisation to organisation. The main steps in selection procedure may be as follows:

1. Receipt of Application form
2. Scrutiny of Applications
3. Preliminary Interview
4. Conducting Tests
5. Cross verification of Reference
6. Physical Check-up
7. Formal Interview
8. Final Section
9. Job Offer
10. Placement

1. Receipt of Application Form

All candidates who apply for the job fill an application form. This form contains information about candidate's age, qualification, experience, skill, etc. This form provides a written record of the candidate's profile. It also indicates his desire to work at the post for which he was applied. It helps the interviewer to screen the candidate and ask them questions related to their professional profile.

2. Scrutiny of Application forms

In this form, the applicant gives relevant data such as his qualification, specialisation, experience, firm in which he has worked, etc. The application blanks are carefully scrutinised by the company with reference to the specifications prescribed for the jobs to decide the applicants who are to be called for interview.

3. Preliminary Interview

Those who are selected for interview on the basis of particulars furnished in the application, are called for initial interview by the company. This interview, according to Mandell, is the most important means of evaluating the poise or appearance of the candidate. It is also used for establishing a friendly relationship between the candidate and the company and for obtaining additional information or clarification on the information already on the application blank.

4. Conducting Tests

Psychologists and other experts have developed certain tests by which a candidate's particular traits or abilities, his likes and dislikes, his intelligence, manual dexterity, his capacity to learn and the benefit from training, his adaptability, etc. can be estimated. There are several types of tests that are used in selection procedure. Commonly used tests are:

(*a*) *Intelligence Tests* (Ability Tests): These tests are conducted to judge the mental capacity, sensory capacity (vision and hearing), mechanical and clerical abilities of the candidates. "Tests of verbal and numerical ability, with questions on vocabulary, similarities, opposites, arithmetical calculations, etc. are referred to as intelligence tests.

(*b*) *Aptitude Tests:* This test measures the applicant's capacity to learn the skill required for a job. It helps in finding out whether a candidate is suitable for a clerical or a mechanical job. His test helps in assessing before training as to how well the candidate will perform on a job after he is given the necessary training.

(*c*) *Personality Tests:* Personality reflects a person's emotional stability. personality tests judge personal traits of a person (their feelings, risk taking, etc) and test his ability to perform the job. Personality tests assume direct relationship between one or more of the personality factors and ability of a person to do certain jobs.

(*d*) *Performance Tests* (Achievement Tests): These tests are designed to measure the skills and abilities which a candidate already possesses. They indicate the level of knowledge acquired by the applicant. A sample of the individual's behaviour is taken as replica of the actual work situation. For example, a typing test may be given to measure speed and accuracy of a candidate for the post of typist.

(*e*) *Interest Tests:* The purpose of these tests is to measure a candidate's interest - likes and dislikes - in a particular kind of work. Such tests identify the areas in which the individual shows a special concern, fascination and involvement. These tests suggest what types of job may be satisfying to workers.

Advantages

The following are the benefits of a test:

1. These serve as a fair system of evaluation.
2. The test serve as standard of criterion for all candidates.
3. It helps to avoid personal bias.
4. They help in increasing accuracy in selection.
5. They enable employers to make most objective selection.
6. They can prove economical in the long run.
7. They help in reducing the employee turnover.
8. They are helpful in establishing standards of job performance.

Disadvantages

The following are limitations of test:

1. Tests do not consider the interest qualities or skills of a candidate.
2. Tests are not conclusive evidence of intelligence of a person as some may not perform well while being subjected to a test.
3. Test do not consider the socio-economic factors.
4. Dishonest persons may misuse tests to obtain misleading results.
5. Some candidates dislike the idea of being tested for fear of exposure.
6. Tests are not infallible.
7. If they are used by unqualified personnel, they can be defective.

5. Cross Verification of Reference

Applicants are usually required to provide two or three references. References can provide useful information about the character, history and reputation of the candidate. References can be made to the previous employers, the college authorities or the references mentioned in the application. If it is essential, the present employer of the candidate can also be contacted on phone.

6. Physical Check-up (Medical Examination)

Candidates found suitable after interview undergo a medical examination. This is done to ensure that the candidate is physically and mentally fit to perform the job for which he is selected. It also avoids selecting candidate suffering from any contagious diseases as they can spread the disease to other in the organisation and also claim medical benefits after joining the job.

7. Final Interview

After the manager receives positive response from cross references about candidate's suitability for the job, he holds interview with candidates. Interview is face-to-face interaction between manager and candidates where managers get to know the candidate's personality, knowledge, skills and competence on the job. They give complete picture about the organisation and job structure to the candidates.

Important types of interview are described below:

(A) *Structured or Patterned Interview*

This type of interview is also known as directed or guided interview. It is a straight-forward, face-to-face question-answer session. Under it, the interviewer uses a list of predetermined questions and records answers to those questions given by different candidates. The list of questions is prepared in advance on the basis of job specification. Such an interview facilitates comparison between different candidates. The approach is standardised as standard methods of recording observations and interpretation are used.

(B) *Unstructured or Depth Interview*

This is a non-directed interview wherein no specific questions are asked. There are minimum constraints on the applicants. The interviewee is allowed to talk freely about his achievements or aptitudes. The interviewer plays mainly a listening role. Such an interview allows the candidate to determine the tone and direction of the discussion by his answers. Being informal in nature, it puts the candidates at ease. It is highly flexible as the interviewer can adapt his approach to the prevailing situation.

Importance of Interview

1. It helps in knowing details about candidate's personality.
2. It is a method of direct contact between the employer and the candidate.
3. It helps interviewer and the interviewee know each other in detail.

Limitations of Interview

1. Interview is not always the perfect method of selection.
2. The candidate may give answers to please the interviewer but the answers do not truly reflect his personality. Thus a wrong candidate may be selected.
3. Job related skills cannot be determined through interviews.
4. Selection on the basis of biased interview is not correct.

Guidelines for An Effective Selection Interview

1. Prior to interview, review the applicant's details.
2. Find a quiet place free from interruptions.
3. Take notes during the interview.

4. Use a brief warm-up period.
5. Ask open-ended questions.
6. Follow an interview format.
7. Encourage the job candidate.
8. Dig for additional details.
9. Spend most of the interview time listening.
10. Provide the candidate pieces of information about the firm.

8. Final Selection

Candidates who have crossed all the hurdles in the selection procedure are recommended for appointment by the personnel department. The final approval is given by the line executives. After approval a job offer is made to the candidates. If a candidate accepts the offer, he is formally appointed by issuing an appointment letter or by entering into a service agreement with him. The appointment letter contains the terms and conditions of employment.

9. Job Offer

After the candidate accepts to join the job, manager offer him the appointment letter. The letter contains information about salary, working hours, leave benefits, retirement benefits, etc. The candidate is assumed to have accepted the offer according to organisation's rule. The job is initially offered on probation. If the candidate is found suitable during probation period, his job is made permanent after the probation period.

10. Placement

Selected candidates should be put on the job. In fact, it is the final step in the selection process. The candidate should be introduced to the organisational culture and environment. He should be made familiar with the policies, objectives rules and regulations of the organisation.

4. Placement

See above para.

5. Orientation (Induction)

After accepting the job offer, it is important that individual's expectations from the organisation and organisation's expectations from the individual match each other. When employees join an organisation, they want to know their superiors, co-workers, organisation structure, basis of departmentation, framework of authority-responsibility structure, etc. To enable the candidates to know about the organisation, induction programmes are conducted by managers.

The main objects of orientation are as follows:

1. Company history, products and operations.
2. Structure of the organisation.
3. Functions of various departments.
4. Company policies and regulations.
5. Recreational service available.
6. Opportunities for promotions, etc.

6. Training and Development

The employees may not be able to fully satisfy the job requirements. Their actual performance may be short of planned performance. The need, therefore, arises to increase the skills and competence of employees to improve their job performance. There are two ways: (*a*) Training and (*b*) Development.

(NB: For Details on Training and Development see Chapter 16)

7. Remuneration

Refer Chapter 16

8. Performance Evaluation

It measures actual performance of employees to see whether or not it is in accordance with standard performance. Performance appraisal means appraising the performance of employees on a continuous basis and providing them the feedback. It ranks employees in the order of merit and finds candidates suitable for promotion.

(NB for more details, see Chapter 17)

9. Promotions and Transfers

After employees are ranked according to their performance, they are transferred to higher, lower or different posts at the same level. That is, there are three forms of transfer - Promotions, Demotions, and Transfer at the same level.

(NB: For more details, see Chapter 17)

10. Separations

When employees are not able to cope up with the working environment in the organisation and training programmes are also ineffective to improve their working skills, it is in the interest of both the organisation and individuals that employees separate themselves from the enterprise.

Hints for Conducting Tests and Interviews

1. Plan a test programme.
2. Devise tests that may be easy to value.
3. Prepare a list of candidates to be tested.
4. Decide upon the knowledge required.
5. Test must consume normal time.
6. Fix the place of interview.
7. Inform the applicants.
8. Provide proper waiting place.
9. Fix the members of the interviewing board.
10. Decide how to make the final Selection.

Tips for Interviewers

1. Plan the interview (Job Specification)
2. Smile and provide a warm greetings.
3. Start the interview with non job questions.
4. Follow structured set of questions.
5. Watch candidate's nonverbal behaviour.
6. Avoid "yes or no" type questions.
7. Give enough time to answer.
8. Listen carefully the answers.
9. Encourage the candidate.
10. Conclude the interview by thanking.

CASE STUDY - 1

Major Tools Ltd.

Robert, one of the field sales managers of Major Tools Ltd., had been promoted to his first headquarters assignment as an assistant product manager for a group of products with which he was relatively unfamiliar. Shortly after he had taken over this new assignment, one of the company's vice-presidents, Smith, called for a meeting of product managers and other staff to plan marketing strategies. Robert's superior (the product manager) was unable to attend, so the director of marketing, Reynolds, invited Robert to the meeting to help and orient him to his new job.

Because of the large gathering, Reynolds was rather brief in introducing Robert to Smith. After the meeting began, Smith—a crusty veteran with a reputation for bluntness—began asking a series of probing questions, which most of the product managers were unable to answer in detail. Suddenly, he turned to Robert and questioned him quite closely about his group of products. Somewhat confused, Robert confessed that he really did not know the answers.

It was immediately apparent to Reynolds that Smith had forgotten or had failed to understand that Robert was new to the job and was attending the meeting more for his own orientation than to contribute to it. He was about to offer a discreet explanation when Smith, visibly annoyed with what he tool to be Robert's lack of preparation, snapped, "Gentlemen, you have just seen an example of sloppy staff work, and there is no excuse for it,"

Reynolds had to make a quick decision. He could interrupt Smith and point out that he had judged Robert unfairly, but that might embarrass both his superior and his subordinate. Alternatively, he could wait until after the meeting and offer an explanation in private. As Smith quickly became engrossed in another conversation, Reynolds followed the second approach. Glancing at Robert, Reynolds noted that his expression was one of mixed anger and dismay. After catching his eye, Reynolds winked at Robert as a discreet reassurance that he understood and that the damage could be repaired. After an hour, Smith, evidently dissatisfied with what he termed the "inadequate planning" of the marketing department in general, abruptly declared the meeting over. As he did so, he turned to Reynolds and asked him to remain behind for a moment. To Reynold's surprise, Smith immediately raised the question of Robert himself. In fact, it turned out to have been his main reason for asking Reynolds to remain behind. "Look," he said, "I want you to tell me frankly, do you think I was too rough with that kid?" Relieved, Reynolds said, "Yes, you were. I was going to speak to you about it."

Smith explained to Reynolds that Robert was new to his job had not registered in his mind adequately when they had been introduced, and that it was only some time after his own outburst that the nagging thought began to occur to him that what he had done was inappropriate and unfair. "How well do you know him ?" he asked. "Do you think I hurt him?"

For a moment Reynolds took the measure of his superior. Then he replied evenly, "I do not know him very well yet, but, yes, I think you hurt him."

"Damn, that is unforgivable," said Smith. He then telephoned his secretary to call Robert and ask him to report to his office immediately. A few moments later, Robert returned, looking perplexed and uneasy. As he entered, Smith came out from behind his desk and met him in the middle of the office. Standing face to face with Robert, who was 20 years and four organization levels his junior, he said, "Look, I have done something stupid and I want to apologize. I had no right to treat you like that. I should have remembered that you were new to your job, but I did not. I am sorry."

Robert was somewhat flustered. He muttered his thanks for the apology. "As long as you are here, young man," Smith continued, "I want to make a few things clear to you in the presence of your boss's boss. Your job is to make sure that people like myself do not make stupid decisions. Obviously, we think you are qualified for your job or we would not have brought you in here. But it takes time to learn any job. Three months from now I will expect you to know the answers to any questions about products." "Until then," he said, "thrusting out his hand for the younger man to shake, "you have my complete confidence. And thank you for letting me correct a mistake."

QUESTIONS

1. What do you think was the effect on Robert and the other managers of Smith's outburst at the meeting ?
2. Was Smith right to apologize to Robert or should he have left well enough alone ?
3. What do you think the apology meant to Robert ?
4. What would it be like to have Smith as a superior ? As a subordinate.
5. How does Smith define Robert's responsibilities as an assistant product manager ? How does he define his own role as a top manager ?
6. What is the most important aspect of the relations between management levels in this company ?

REVIEW QUESTIONS

1. Explain the meaning and feature of staffing. *(B.Com., MS)*
2. Explain the elements and process of HRP. *(M.Com., Delhi)*
3. What is job analysis ? What are its purpose ? *(M.Com., Bhopal)*
4. Explain orientation or induction ? *(M.Com., Mysore)*
5. Discuss the principle and types of tests. *(M.Com., Bombay)*
6. What is placement ?
7. Enumerate job descriptions. *(M.Com., Chennai)*
8. What is recruitment ? What are its sources? *(M.Com., Jabalpur)*
9. Discuss the process of selection. *(M.Com., Punjab)*
10. "Mind your men, men will mind all other things." Explain the statement with reference to importance of staffing. *(M.Com., MS)*
11. Explain the various sub-functions of staffing. *(B.Com., MS)*
12. Explain the term "manpower planning". Describe the steps involved in manpower planning. *(M.Com., Banaras)*

Training and Development

16
CHAPTER

- Introduction
- Meaning
- Need for Training
- Importance of Training
- Advantages of Training
- Methods of Training
  - On-the-Job Training Methods
  - Off-the-Job Training Methods
- On-the-Job Vs Off-the-Job Training
- Development
- Executive Development
- Features of Development
- Training Vs Development
- Methods of Management Development
- Types of Training
- A Good Training Programme
- Compensation
- Meaning
- Objectives of Paying Compensation
- Factors Affecting Wages
- Factors Affecting Executive Compensation
- Forms of Compensation
- A Good Compensation Plan
- Time Rate Vs Piece Rate Systems
- Methods of Wage Payments
- Types of Incentives
- Advantages of Non-Monetary Incentive Schemes
- Case Study - 1
- Review Questions

INTRODUCTION

After the selection of people for various jobs, the next function of management is to arrange for their training and development. This is because a person, however carefully selected is not moulded to specifications and rarely meets the demands of his jobs adequately. Formerly, it was thought that the training of personnel was unnecessary on the ground that the new employees would gradually pick up all the particulars of the job. But as the processes and techniques of production are becoming more and more complicated, it is being increasingly realised that the formal training is important not only for new candidates but also for existing employees. Training function, in fact, has become the corner stone of sound management.

MEANING

Training follows the recruitment of workers. A job may be simplest one, but guidance is necessary in order to have efficiency in the work. That is, in all types of posts, a little training is essential, to instruct as to how a particular job is performed. Even the most simple job like, despatch of letters, requires some training for its efficient performance. The basic purpose of training is to guide and direct the learning of employees so that they may perform their duties as efficiently as possible. A good training programme lays down the procedure by which people gain knowledge and skill for a definite purpose. According to Little Field, "Training is the process of increasing the skills and knowledge of personnel for the purpose of improving individual and organisational performance." It is the duty of the personnel department to suggest training programme for the new-comers. The skill and aptitude can be increased by training. Training is not only necessary for new entrants, but also for the old workers, whenever, new technological development has been brought into work because the old workers may not possess knowledge to work upon the new techniques. Therefore training programme is a must to achieve a given aim.

Training and development activities are highly required in any organisation to prepare the employees to work in the organisation as per the requirement. As these are playing a significant role in the organisational success, several companies have established separate training and development centres to provide training and development activities. The employees will become useful assets when proper training development activities are provided.

NEED FOR TRAINING

Need for training arises on account of the following reasons:

1. Lack of Trained Personnel

It is always not possible to recruit and select trained employees. Majority of the newly employed persons do not know how to perform their jobs. When workers with little or no training are selected, they require training for efficient performance on the job.

2. Prevention of Accidents

Training is needed to prevent industrial accidents. For this purpose safety consciousness must be created among workers so that they realise the significance of safe working. Moreover, they should be given instructions in the use of safety devices.

3. Faulty Methods

Some employees might have picked up defective ways of doing work which may result in wastage and inefficiency. Training is required to remove these defects and to teach them correct methods of behaviour patterns.

4. New Environment

It helps employees to settle quickly in the organisation. It helps them to know the company's structure, culture, rules, policies, etc. so that they can blend their personality with that of the company.

5. Rapid Technological Changes

It updates the knowledge and skills of employees. Today, technology is changing at a fast rate. Organisations are automating their systems to keep pace with changing technology. Training helps employees to learn new skills to work with new technology. Learning of computers, for instance, became necessary when computers replaced the typewriters.

Further, the following may also be noted:

6. It reduces the need for supervision to the minimum.

7. It improves knowledge and skills of persons.

8. It helps in promoting employees to higher posts.

9. It identifies the need of individuals to understand job's requirements.

10. It reduces the rate of labour turnover and absenteeism.

IMPORTANCE OF TRAINING

Training is important as it gives various benefits to employers and workers. It plays an important role in human resource development. The basic purpose of training is to development of skills and efficiency. The need for systematic training has increased because of rapid technological changes which creates new jobs and eliminate old ones. Training is important not only from the point of view of the organisation but also that of the employees. It is valuable to the employees because it will give them greater job security and an opportunity for advancement. A skill acquired through training is an asset for the organisation as well as to the employees.

The importance of training are discussed below:

1. High Motivation

Trained employees perform better than untrained ones. This brings them rewards, job satisfaction and motivation to work hard. Training is, thus, a non-financial incentives that brings financial gains to business organisations.

2. Less Supervision

Trained employees know their jobs. They maintain discipline and control on their activities. This reduces the need for supervision or control on their work. Less supervision means savings in time and money and better performance.

3. Organisation Growth

Training not only helps in growth of individuals, it also helps in growth of the organisation. Organisations whose employees are trained can anticipate and adapt to changes in the environment. Organisations can compete in the market and grow their operations.

4. Reduced Labour Turnover

As training provides job satisfaction and boosts employees' morale to work hard, employees feel satisfied with their jobs and improve their performance on the job. This reduces the rate of labour turnover and absenteeism.

5. Better Use of Resources

Well trained employees make better use of machines and materials. As a result the rate of spoilage or wastage of material is reduced. There is less breakage of machinery and tools. The maintenance cost is reduced and life of the machines is increased.

6. Uniformity of Procedures

In formal training, the best methods of performing the work can be standardised and taught to all workers. Standardisation of work procedures and practice help to improve the quality of performance.

7. High Morale

Training helps to improve the job satisfaction and morale of employees. As their productivity increases, there is an improvement in their earnings, job security and career prospects. By developing positive attitude, training makes employees more cooperative and loyal to the organisation.

8. Higher Productivity

Training increases the skill of employees in the performance of particular job. An increase in skill usually helps to increase in both quantity and quality of output. It helps them to increase their level of performance on their present job assignments.

9. Confidence

Training creates a feeling of confidence in the minds of workers. It gives safety and security to them at the workplace.

10. Preparation of Future Managers

When totally new skills are required by an organisation it has to face great difficulties in the selection process. Training can be used in spotting out promising men and in overcoming defects in the selection process.

11. Better Management

A manager can make use of training to manage in a better way. To him, training the employees can assist to improve his planning, organising, directing, etc.

12. Increased Safety

Training to workers help them to handle the machines safely. They also know the use of various safety devices in the factory. Thus, they are less prone to accidents. Training provides more remuneration and other monetary benefits to the workers. It does not eliminate the need for supervision, but it reduces the need for regular, supervision of the workers.

ADVANTAGES OF TRAINING

The main benefits of training are given below:

1. Training helps to improve the quantity and quality of work output.
2. Number and costs of accidents are reduced.
3. Standardisation of work procedures improve the quality of performance.
4. Systematic training results in improvement of the organisation.
5. It reduces the industrial accidents, damage to machinery, etc.
6. The cost of supervision is reduced to the minimum.
7. It facilitates delegation and decentralisation of authority.
8. It helps promotion of workers to higher posts.
9. It permits personal growth of employees.
10. It allows to improve organisational climate.

METHODS OF TRAINING

Methods of training can be classified into two categories:

1. On-the-Job Training Methods

This is the most effective method of training. In this case the training is provided by the immediate superior or the person supervising the employees. This training is considered to be the most effective and the oldest method of training the operating personnel. This method is suitable where work is not complex and number of workers are not too large. A brief narration of the different methods are explained below:

(a) Job Rotation

Under this method, the employees is transferred from one job to another as per a predetermined transfer policy. This technique of on the job training is adopted for broadening work experience of the trainees in various related positions because he is to work in different jobs by rotation. This exposes them to variety of tasks and enhances their knowledge to perform the jobs. It develops employees and increase their capabilities to perform different jobs. It promotes creativity, innovation and exchange of ideas amongst people working at different jobs.

(b) Apprenticeship

In apprenticeship training, the trainee is placed under the supervision of an experienced person who teaches him the necessary skills and observes his performance. The advantages of apprenticeship training to the trainees, are that they receive stipend while learning and acquire a valuable skill which commands a high wage in the labour market. The apprentice learns by observing his senior. Carpenters, plumbers, computer operators usually adopt this method of training.

(c) Internship

The object of this type of training is to bring about a balance between theoretical and practical knowledge. Under this method, students from a technical institution possessing only theoretical knowledge are sent to some business enterprise to gain practical work experience. Similarly, the employees of business enterprises are sent to technical institutions to gain the latest theoretical knowledge on the subject. For instance, engineering students are sent to big industrial enterprises for gaining practical work experience: medical students are sent to big hospitals to get practical knowledge.

(d) Brainstorming

People with different backgrounds work on a common problem. This enhances their ability to analyse and solve the problem by using their intellectual and conceptual skills.

(e) Delegation

Managers delegate part of their work load to subordinates along with authority. Subordinates are allowed to make decisions, increases their leadership and decision-making skills and the knowledge to manage these tasks alone.

2. Off-the-Job Training Methods

Training is given to workers outside the work place. Emphasis is more on learning than doing. Employees do not learn while working on-the-job but learn in conditions which are more or less similar to actual workplace. Training is provided by experts who arrange special training programmes at a place other than the workplace. Employees do not disturb the work schedule during the training period. They concentrate on training and pick the job skills faster when they actually perform their jobs.

(a) Class Room Training

Under this method, workers are required to attend classes for a fixed period. The classes are arranged with in the organisation or at some vocational institute. These classes are in the form of special courses designed to suit the requirements of the organisation. The classroom method involves lectures, conferences, group-discussion, demonstration, slides and films, etc.

(b) Vestibule Training

This method involves the creation of a separate training centre within the plant itself for the purpose of providing training to the new employees. An experience Instructor is put in-charge of this training. Machines and tools are also arranged in the training centre so as to create working conditions similar to those in the workshop. This method has several advantages. As the trainee remains free from the confusion and pressure of the work situation, he is able to concentrate on learning.

(c) Lectures

Most commonly used method of imparting training is the lecture method. Under this method a subject specialist is either invited from outside or from within the organisation to deliver lecture on specific subjects to increase the knowledge of participants. The specialist delivering lecture allows participants to share with him the specialised knowledge. This technique is considered more suitable for imparting the theoretical knowledge on principles, generalisations and concepts related to job performance to participants.

(d) Conferences and (e) Seminars

Often an executive is deputed to attend a conference, seminar or workshop to receive a quick orientation in various areas of management with which he might be unfamiliar. One advantage of this type of training is that all the participants coming from different organisations get an opportunity to pool their ideas and experience in attempting to solve mutual problems. The attitude is one of joint exploration. This encourages cross fertilisation of ideas.

(f) Case Study

A case similar to actual working conditions or organisational problems is prepared and presented to trainees. The trainer presents the facts of the case to trainees. Trainees analyse the case, use judgement and initiative and arrive at alternative solutions. Through a careful comparison of costs and benefits of each case, they arrive at the best solution to the problem. This method develops mental abilities of trainees to deal with actual organisational problems.

(g) Role Playing

Trainees are assigned different roles to play similar to those they have to perform at actual work places. They may, for instance, be made to act as managers, salesmen, etc. in classroom conditions to know the way they have to perform their roles actually.

(h) Sensitivity Training

Sensitivity or T-group training is an important technique of "laboratory training." The main objective of sensitivity training is the development of awareness and sensitivity to one's own behavioural pattern through interaction with others. The sensitivity training programme is absolutely unstructured. The main goals are: increased openness with others, increased understanding of any change in the attitude, group learning, increased awareness, etc.

DIFFERENCES

Differences between on-the-job and off-the-job training methods are given below:

on-the-job Training Method	*off-the-job Training Method*
1. It is less costly	1. It is costly.
2. Training is given at the workplace	2. It is provided outside the workplace.
3. It is provided by supervisors to subordinates	3. Training is given by experts.
4. It is always quick.	4. It is time consuming.
5. It disturbs work schedules.	5. It does not disturb work schedule.

DEVELOPMENT

While training improves skills of a person on the present job, development improves his skills on future jobs. It is the "long-term training designed to increase an employee's job effectiveness and to develop his ability related to assume greater job responsibilities." Training is, thus, related to the job that a person is performing. Development improves his ability to perform present and future jobs with greater competence and skill. "Training increases the skill while development shapes attitudes."

EXECUTIVES (MANAGEMENT) DEVELOPMENT

Executive development is staffing function of management. An enterprise must provide opportunities for the development of its present and potential managers. Executive development is a systematic and continuous process through which executives learn advanced knowledge and skills in managing. It is a planned and organised process of learning and growth designed to improve managerial behaviour and performance. Through executive development programmes, managers cultivate their mental abilities and inherent skill and they learn to manage more effectively. Management development involves training in improving knowledge, skills and attitudes of managers. It is the progress by which a manager is facilitated in learning how to manage. Management training programmes facilitate this learning process. Management development is designed to improve theoretical effectiveness of managers in their present positions and to prepare them for greater responsibility when they are promoted.

FEATURES OF DEVELOPMENT

The following are the main features of development, in brief:

1. Management development is mainly 'self development'. It depends on the executives themselves than on the efforts of the organisation.
2. It is an on-going process and never stops. According to Koontz and O'Donnell "Developing a manager is a progressive process in the same sense that educating a person is. Neither development nor education should be thought of as something that can ever be completed, for there are no known limits to the degree to which one may be developed or educated."
3. It prepares a person to assume jobs of higher skills and competence.
4. In the words of George R. Terry, "Management development should produce change in behaviour which is more in keeping with the organisation's goals than the previous behaviour."

DIFFERENCES BETWEEN TRAINING AND DEVELOPMENT

The following are the difference between training and development:

	Training	*Development*
1. Perspective	1. Short-run perspective	1. Long run perspective.
2. Purpose	2. To perform present job	2. To perform present and future jobs.
3. Level of person	3. It is given to non-managers.	3. It is given to Managers.
4. Scope	4. It increases skills to perform present jobs.	4. It increases skills to perform present and future jobs.
5. Aim	5. It retains a person on the job.	5. It promotes a person to responsible jobs.

METHODS OF MANAGEMENT DEVELOPMENT

Similar to the methods of training, management development programmes fall into two categories:

1. on-the-job Methods

(a) Coaching
(b) Job Rotation
(c) Training Positions
(d) Multiple Management, etc.

2. off-the-job Methods

(a) Classroom Coaching
(b) Sponsored Programmes
(c) Seminars
(d) Simulation
(e) Case Study
(f) Brainstorming, etc.

Some of the above methods, viz, coaching, rotation, seminars, simulation, case study, etc. have already been explained, under the heading, "methods of Training."

(a) Training Positions

The fresh appointees work under managers as trainees and assistants. Gradually, they develop managerial skills and become competent to take over higher managerial positions.

(b) Classroom Coaching

Classroom coaching develops various case studies and role playing methods to enhance managerial skills of managers. It introduces managers to new concepts, principles, theories and business situations and enhances their knowledge on management development areas.

(c) Sponsored Programmes

Various outside agencies and Universities conduct programmes for management development. Managers attend these courses rather than getting training within the organisation. Lectures and demonstrations form part of such development programmes.

TYPES OF TRAINING

Training is required for several purposes. All training programmes can be of anyone of the following types:

1. Orientation (Induction) Training

It is a training programme used to induct a new employee into the new social setting of his work. The new employee is introduced to his job situation, and to his co-workers. Every new employee needs to be made fully familiar with his job, his superiors, subordinates and with the rules and regulations of the organisation.

2. Job Training

In job training, workers are enabled to learn correct methods of handling machines and equipment, avoiding accidents, removing bottlenecks, minimum waste, etc. The object of job training is to increase the knowledge of workers about the jobs with which they are concerned so that their efficiency and skill of performance are improved.

3. Promotional Training

When the existing employees are promoted to superior positions in the organisation, they are required to shoulder new responsibilities. For this, training has to be given to them so that they may not experience any difficult to shoulder the responsibilities of the new position to which they have been promoted. Many concerns follow a policy of filling some of the vacancies at higher levels by promoting existing employees. This policy increases the morale of workers. They try to put up maximum efficiency so that they may be considered for promotion.

4. Refresher Training

At the time of initial appointment of employees, they are formally trained for their jobs. But with the passage of time, they may forget some of the methods which were taught to them or they may become outdated because of technological development and improved techniques of management and production. Hence refresher training is arranged for existing employees in order to provide them an opportunity to revive and also to improve their knowledge. Refresher training programmes are designed to avoid "personnel obsolescence."

5. Corrective Training

This training is designed to correct the mistakes and short comings in the behaviour and performance of employees.

The 'problem employees' are explained in privates their mistakes and need to reform their behaviour. For instance, smoking in a "No smoking area". The manager should handle the problem with treatment that corrects rather than punishes. Thus, remedial training should be imparted by people who have knowledge of human nature and industrial psychology.

A GOOD TRAINING PROGRAMME

Essentials of a good training programme consists of the following steps:

1. Identification of Training Needs

Identification of training needs requires organisational analysis, operational analysis and manpower analysis.

While discovering the training needs, the following takes are to be performed:

(i) Compare the actual performance against the standards.

(ii) Determine what kind of training is to be given to the employee to overcome difficulties in performing the given task.

(iii) List the duties and responsibilities or tasks of the job under consideration.

(iv) List the standards of work performance on the job.

(v) Determine the areas of the job where employee is struggling to perform effectively.

2. Who is to be Trained ?

The next important step in developing an effective training programme is to decide the employees who are to be trained. These include the supervisory staff, the newcomer, old employee, or all these.

3. Imparting Knowledge

The trainer should clearly tell, show, explain, illustrate and question in order to put over the new knowledge and operations concerning the job. The trainee should be told the sequence of performing a given task, and why each step in the performance of the job is necessary. The trainer should give the instructions to trainees clearly, unambiguously and completely. The trainer should ask questions to check whether the trainee understands what he taught and encourage the trainee to clear doubts, if any.

4. Actual Job Performance

To know the effectiveness of training, strategy is prepared by various means and all the trainees are tested. And asking the trainees to do the job to ascertain their performance.

5. Follow up

This step is undertaken to test the effectiveness of a training programme. A follow up is essential to find out whether the trainees have improved their performance or not. Providing feedback encourages the trainees to perform better because they will be able to identify the crucial areas where they are lacking; to know their weakspots and their strong points in performing the given task. After knowing the limitations it becomes very easy for the trainees to remove them and become successful on their jobs.

COMPENSATION

Employees work to earn money which is broadly termed as compensation. It is the reward they want from management in return for services rendered by them to the organisation. Compensation or paying employees for their work is an important responsibility of human resource managers. How much compensation a worker wants, depends upon his economic needs. However, from the point of view of organisation, a good compensation not only attracts talented employees but it also retains them in the organisation for long run.

With a good compensation plan, employees are happier in their work, cooperation and loyalty are more pronounced, productive output is up, and quality is better. In the absence of such plans, compensations are determined subjectively on the basis of haphazard and arbitrary decisions. This creates several inequities which are among the most dangerous sources of friction and low morale in an enterprise.

Employee compensation is a systematic approach to providing monetary value to employees in exchange for work performed. Employee compensation may achieve several purposes and mainly assisting in recruitment, job performance and job satisfaction.

MEANING OF COMPENSATION

"Compensation is a comprehensive term which includes wages, salaries, all other allowances and benefits." It involves remunerating people for services rendered by them and motivating them to reach a desired level of performance. Compensation may be paid in cash, kind or both. Paying compensation evolves a system of wages or salaries, their timely payment, job evaluation, individual pay determination, incentive plans, etc. The personnel manager should spend enough time to determine compensation in exchange for employees' services. An unbalanced compensation policy can lead to industrial disputes affecting industrial productivity and profits.

OBJECTIVES OF PAYING COMPENSATION

A good compensation policies have the following objectives

1. Attract Good Workers

In the competitive environment of today, managers have to pay high compensation to attract qualified personnel.

2. Retain Personnel

Compensation must not only attract workers, but it must also retain them.

3. Cost Control

Proper compensation policies help the company to maintain control over its cost.

4. Equity in Pay

Compensation must be commensurate with the qualification of employees on their jobs and with what similar workers are getting in competing jobs.

5. Easy to Understand

The wage system should not be complicated. It should be easily understood by employers and employees.

FACTORS AFFECTING WAGES

1. Demand and Supply of Labour

If there is a short supply of labour, the wages may be high, whereas if there is no dearth of labour, the wages tend to be low.

2. Labour Union

If the labourers are well organised into strong trade unions, their bargaining power would be high and they can demand higher rates of wages.

3. Cost of Living

The cost of living of workers has a strong influence on the rate of wages.

4. Competition

The degree of competition for the products of an industry is yet another factor which has influence on the wage rates.

5. Prevailing Wage Rates

Prevailing wages in a particular industry are also taken into account by the employers while deciding wage levels for their employees.

6. Ability to Pay

The wage leave, to large extent, is determined by the ability of the enterprise to pay its workers.

7. Job Requirements

Jobs requiring specialised knowledge or involving much mental or manual efforts are priced higher than those which are light or which do not need any specialised knowledge.

8. State Regulations

State Regulations is another factor influencing wage rates.

9. Court Judgements

In recent years, this factor has emerged as the most important factor in determining wages.

10. Philosophy of Management

Some progressive organisations in order to attract, motivate and hold employees, believe in paying them more than the established bench-marks.

FACTORS AFFECTING EXECUTIVE COMPENSATION

Following factors may govern the compensation paid to an executive in an organisation:

1. Job Complexity

The compensation to be paid to an executive depends upon (a) sales volume of the company, (b) number of States in which the company carriers its business operation, (c) the company's rate of growth, etc.

2. Employer's Ability to Pay

Companies with greater ability to pay can offer higher remuneration in order to compete for the scarce executive talent.

3. Employee's Qualification and Experience

At the top the job and the person become inseparable from each other so that the determination of an executive's salary becomes highly subjective in nature and does not lend itself to standardisation.

4. Statutory Limits

In India the Companies Act puts statutory limits on the amount of remuneration payable to different categories of managerial personnel of a public company or a private company.

5. Individual Incentives

They are not linked to one's regular pay, but to the achievement of meeting certain targets. These incentives are announced to increase individual performance quite significantly.

FORMS OF COMPENSATION

There are three forms of compensation are existing:

(a) Primary Compensation

(b) Supplementary Compensation

(c) Incentive Compensation

(a) Primary (Base) Compensation

Primary compensation is paid in the form of salary or wages. Salaries are paid to white collar workers and wages are paid to blue collar workers. Salaries and wages generally mean the same thing. Primary compensation is the basic pay for various categories of jobs. Primary compensation is always paid in cash.

While determining primary compensation, the following factors may be remembered:

(*i*) Job content

(*ii*) Power of Trade Unions

(*iii*) Remuneration paid by similar firms

(*iv*) Firm's ability to pay compensation

(*v*) Rules and Regulations of the Government

There should be equal pay for equal work. Workers with different skills, qualification, training and working conditions are paid according to their relative skills and abilities. Human resource manager should maintain equity to avoid disparity in compensation and conflict amongst managers and workers.

(b) Supplementary Compensation

Supplementary compensation is based on individual output or output of the group as a whole. This is additional compensation paid to motivate the workers. Employee profit sharing, production sharing plans, employees equity compensation, etc. determine supplementary compensation, which must be flexible in nature. They represent (*i*) Allowances, such as Dearness Allowance, House Rent Allowance, City Compensatory Allowance, etc. and (*ii*) Prerequisites such as, Rent free accommodation, interest free loans, medical facility, leave travel concession (LTC), etc.

(c) Incentive (Variable) Compensation

A good compensation plan attracts and retains employees. It provides incentives and motivates them to improve their performance. They can be monetary and non-monetary. Human resource manager may consider the following factors while designing the plans.

(*i*) Performance standards should be set.

(*ii*) Incentive schemes should be fixed for performance level.

(*iii*) The plan should be framed in consulation with unions leaders.

(*iv*) They should be flexible.

A GOOD COMPENSATION PLAN

A good compensation plan has the following features:

1. It should be simple and easy to understand.
2. There should be equal work for equal pay.
3. It should not be very costly in operation.
4. A guaranteed base rate should be included in any plan.
5. The plan should not be detrimental to the health and welfare of the employees.
6. All employees and supervisors must have full knowledge of the plan.
7. It should offer minimum wages to workers and incentives for good performance.
8. It should attract and retain people in the organisation.
9. It should motivate workers to contribute their best to organisational goals.
10. It should maintain balance and harmony amongst managers and workers.
11. It must be consistent with what competitors are paying to their workers.
12. It must be consistent with cost of living.
13. It should have scope for promotions and pay hikes.
14. It must be based on merit and job evaluation of workers.
15. It should satisfy all employees-lower as well as higher grade.
16. Standards once fixed may not be altered.

17. It must reduce labour turnover.
18. It must be fair to both - employer and employees.
19. The system, once introduced, should not be discontinued.
20. It must be based on merit and job evaluation of workers.

DIFFERENCE BETWEEN TIME RATE AND PIECE RATE SYSTEMS

Comparative merits and demerits of the Time Rate System as against the Piece Rate System are briefly summarised as follows:

Time Rate System	*Piece Rate System*
1. It is simple to calculate and easy to understand.	1. These rates have to be carefully fixed so as to avoid possible loss to the management.
2. This pertains to hours or work.	2. This pertains to output.
3. General supervision is needed.	3. Careful supervision is needed.
4. It does not promote efficiency.	4. It promotes efficiency in working.
5. Individual efficiency is looked upon.	5. Individual efficiency is measured and accounted for.
6. Cost reduction is not possible.	6. Cost reduction is possible.
7. Benefit of efficient worker goes to the employer.	7. Benefit of efficient workers is shared by the worker and the employer.
8. There arises more idle time.	8. There is no chance of idle time.
9. There is no distinction between efficient and inefficient workers.	9. It makes distinction between efficient and inefficient workers.
10. It is suitable where quality is important than quantity.	10. It is suitable where quantity is important than quality.
11. It ensures efficient handling of machines and tools.	11. It may result in inefficient handling of machines and tools.
12. It results in high cost of production.	12. It results in low cost of production.

METHODS OF WAGE PAYMENTS

Methods of wage payment broadly fall into two categories:

1. Time Rate System

This is the simplest, oldest and the most common method of wage payment. The system under which the payment is made to the workers according to the time for which they work is known as Time Wages System. Again under this system, payment is made on the basis of time, which may be an hour, day, week or a month, irrespective of the output. It means that a definite amount of payment is guaranteed for the specified time. The payment is calculated as follows:

Earnings = Hours worked × Rate per hour.

Suitability of Time Rate System

The method is suitable in the following cases:

1. Where the quality of work is more important than quantity of work, for example, watch making, precision work, tool-making, testing, etc.
2. Where it is difficult to measure the work accurately, as in the case of indirect workers, such as watchman, drivers, supervisors, cleaners, etc.

3. Where machine restricts the speed, the operator has no control, e.g., the flow of work is regulated by the speed of conveyor belt.
4. Where the operation or job is not repetitive.
5. Where earners or apprentices are working.
6. Where the work is to be done by experts, skilled workers, etc.
7. Where a worker does the work in his own interest.

Merits

1. It is simple to understand and easy to operate.
2. Each worker is assured of minimum wages.
3. Standard of the quality is maintained.
4. It is preferred by trade unions.
5. There is no discrimination among the workers.
6. It is benefitted by average and below average workers.

Demerits

1. Efficient and inefficient workers get the same wage, *i.e.*, efforts and rewards are not correlated.
2. Equality in wages to all, will depress the superior worker.
3. Labour cost cannot be estimated in advance.
4. Slow worker goes further slow, thus leading to overtime.
5. Constant supervision is needed to reduce idle time; thus labour cost increases.

2. Piece Rate System (Payment by result)

Here speed is the basis of payment, instead of time. This system is opposite to time wage system. According to this system, the volume of work done is the basis for payment of wages to workers. Efficiency is recognised in this system. The worker gets payment according to his speed, ability, efficiency, etc. A specific rate is fixed per unit of output, and the worker is paid accordingly, irrespective of the time taken by him.

This method is applicable where:

1. Quality of the work is not important.
2. Work is of a repetitive nature.
3. Job rate can easily be fixed.
4. There is a good demand.
5. Job is a standardised one.

Merits

1. The output is increased.
2. The system works as an incentive to workers.
3. Efforts and rewards are correlated.
4. Efforts and rewards can be made confidentially and accurately.
5. Supervision work is low.
6. Breakage of machine will reduce wages, hence machines are handled with care.
7. Idle time has no place.
8. The worker develops skill and zeal to work.
9. The rate of fixed overhead is reduced.

Demerits

1. Workers are always in a hurry, hence accidents may happen.
2. Quality of the products will be examined, as workers are interested in quantity; as a result overhead cost increases.
3. Inefficient workers will be thrown out.
4. High speed work is injurious to the health of the workers.
5. In order to maximise production, it is possible that machines are used recklessly.
6. Breakdown of machine or power failure may disappoint the workers.
7. When there is less demand, over-production may arise.
8. Fixation of a satisfactory piece rate is a difficult task.
9. It is possible that materials may be wasted or spoiled, as the workers are only anxious about speed.

TYPES OF INCENTIVES

Incentive may be financial or non-financial.

(a) Financial Incentive

Financial incentive is in terms of money and it provides higher emoluments for higher efforts or increased output. It includes money payments based on results in addition to wages and salaries. In this respect, piece rate system of wage payment provides greatest incentive to the workers as in this system remuneration is directly linked to their output. Similarly, there are many premium bonus systems, like Galsey premium system, Rowan premium bonus system, etc. under which basic time wage is guaranteed and a bonus is paid, for achieving a saving in time, in proportion to the time saved.

(b) Non-Financial Incentive

Under this system, incentives are provided in the form of better facilities, instead of paying cash. The object is to attract the employees and such benefits may be in several ways:

1. Favourable working conditions.
2. Free medical facilities to worker and his family
3. Rent free quarter
4. Free education to children
5. Welfare facilities
6. Subsidised canteen
7. Pension schemes
8. Protective clothing, liveries uniforms, etc.
9. Opportunity for advancement
10. Subsidised transport facilities.

ADVANTAGES OF NON-MONETARY INCENTIVE SCHEMES

Advantages to Organisation

(a) Reduce labour turnover

(b) Create a sense of loyalty and co-operation in them

(c) Enhance general goodwill of the company

(d) Reduce absenteeism

(e) The best labours are attracted.

Advantages to Workers

(a) **Increase in the wages of workers:** These systems increase the total wages of workers because workers get besides prescribed wages, the premium or bonus also. Different schemes have different premium amounts. An increase in total earnings improves their standard of living which eventually increases their efficiency.

(b) **Improvement in work capacity:** Every worker tries to work more and more and one who is unable to do his prescribed work, tries his best to reach the standard work level so that he may also get premium.

(c) **Improvement in standard of living:** This system increases the wages of the workers on one side while on the other hand, producer has to pay less for more work proportionately. This reduces the cost per unit. People get goods at cheap rates. Thus standard of living of workers, producers and buyers goes up.

Advantages to Producers

(a) **Minimum Supervision:** Workers work more themselves and do not waste time. Hence very less supervision is required.

(b) **Increase in Production:** When production increases, the cost of production decreases. Prices go down. Workers are happy. Buyers get goods at lower price. There will be more demand for goods. Sales are increased.

(c) **Good labour relations:** Workers and employers both have same interest. Both like saving in time and increase in output. Hence labour disputes come down automatically.

(d) **Improvement in Organisation:** Wages according to work and extra motivation improve the climate of organsation. Misuse of time and such other bad practices are hardly visible.

(e) **Standardisation:** All premium schemes are based on standardisation. By time and motion studies, jobs are standardised and on this basis evaluation of work, labour is done. Further, standardisation improves the method of production.

CASE STUDY - 1

The Southern Steel Company manufactures tin plated steel primarily for sale to canning companies. It employs 5,000 persons. The company applies modern scientific methods wherever possible.

The personnel department applied one such scientific method in the selection of management trainees. A battery of tests was used to determine the interest, emotional ability, general intelligence and personality of the candidates. The tests were supplied by an agency which has an excellent reputation in preparing and analysing tests. The company purchased the tests from the agency, gave them to the applicants and returned them to the agency for grading and analysis.

In addition to the tests, the personnel director analysed the application forms. The applicants with the highest grades on the tests, the personnel director analysed the application ratings were selected for interviews with the personnel director. After the interviews, selection was done.

By the end of the one year, the company has hired thirty applicants by this method. Upon evaluation of these trainees, the company was surprised to find that fourteen did not have the qualifications considered necessary for executive personnel. The total expenditure on these unqualified trainees amounted to approximately ₹ 1,15,000.

The personnel department then took steps to evaluate the testing and hiring procedure. It found that the tests had been used successfully by other steel companies. It found no fault in the tests or in their administration. The personnel director was undecided as to what to do. He referred the problem to the Executive Committee comprising of eight departmental heads. The head of the Industrial

Relations Department suggested that error was in the tests and that they should abandon them and set up another method for selecting management trainees.

QUESTIONS

1. What are the shortcomings in the company's hiring procedure ?
2. On the basis of the information given what action should be taken to solve the problem of selection ?

REVIEW QUESTIONS

1. What is training ? Explain the importance of worker training. *(M.Com., MS)*
2. Describe in brief the different methods of imparting training. *(B.Com., Mysore)*
3. What is meant by executive or management development ? *(B.Com., Bangalore)*
4. Define the term staffing. What functions are covered under staffing ? *(M.Com., Madras)*
5. What do you mean by training ? Why is it needed ? State its importance. *(M.Com., Madurai)*
6. What do you mean by development ? State the need for development. How is it different from training ? *(B.Com., Kerala)*
7. What are the methods of wage payment ? Explain the benefits and limitations of time rate and piece rate system of paying compensation. *(B.Com., Madras)*
8. Explain the features of a good compensation plan. *(B.Com., MS)*
9. Explain the various methods of training. *(M.Com., MS)*
10. Describe various factors affecting executive compensation. *(M.Com., Banaras)*
11. Discuss the advantages and disadvantages of incentives compensation. *(M.Com., Bangalore)*
12. Discuss the merits and demerits of time rate system of wage payment. How does it compare with the piece rate system ? *(M.Com., Mysore)*
13. What is orientation ?
14. Give the importance of training for employees. Discuss the different methods of training. *(B.Com., Calicut)*
15. Describe any two methods of on-the-job training. *(M.Com., MS)*

Performance Appraisal and Promotion

- Introduction
- Meaning
- Who can be the Appraiser ?
- Why use Performance Appraisal ?
- Handling Performance Appraiser
- Purposes of Appraisal
- Benefits of Appraisal
- Essential of good Appraisal System
- Methods of Performance Appraisal
- Appraisal by Results
- Advantages of Goal Setting Method
- Criticism of Goal Setting Method
- Promotion
- Advantages of Promotion
- Limitation of Promotion
- Bases for Promotion
- Termination
- Transfer
- Case Study - 1
- Review Questions.

INTRODUCTION

Performance appraisal is the process of determining and communicating to an employee how he is performing the job. Performance appraisal is also know as 'merit rating' or 'employee appraisal'. Some other terms which are less commonly employed to mean performance appraisal are the 'progress report, 'staff assessment, 'service rating,' personnel review, 'employee evaluation, or 'behavioural assessment'. The main objectives of an appraisal system are usually to review employees' performance and potential.

MEANING

Performance appraisal is a formal exercise in which organisation evaluates its employees, in terms of contribution made towards achieving organizational objectives. It evaluates their strengths and weaknesses in terms of attributes and behaviours for meeting the organisational objectives.

"Performance appraisal is the process of defining expectations for employees performance; measuring, evaluating and recording employee performance relative to those expectations; and providing feedback to the employee".

According to Yoder, "Performance appraisal consists of all formal procedures used in working organisations to evaluate personalities and contributions and potentials of group members".

Flippo has stated the concept of performance appraisal as follows: "Instead of rating an employee on characteristic such as dependability, initiative and the like, there is now a tendency towards establishing job goals and appraising the work done towards these goals."

According to Dale S. Beach, performance appraisal is "the systematic evaluation of the individual with respect to his performance on the job and his potential for development." Spriegal has defined it as, "the process of evaluating the employee's performance on the job in terms of requirements of the job."

Performance appraisals seek to evaluate employees performance at work primarily for the following sreasons:

(a) Identify his strong and weak points with a view to identifying specific development needs.

(b) Find out his potential for different kinds of functions and for growth.

(c) Determine his training requirements to strengthen potential or correct deficiency.

(d) To guide decisions on increments, transfers, promotions or other rewards.

Once employees are trained and settled into their jobs, one of management's next concerns is performance appraisal. PERFORMANCE APPRAISAL is a formal assessment of how well employees are doing their jobs. Employees' performance should be evaluated regularly for many reasons. One reason is that performance appraisal may be necessary for validating selection devices or assessing the impact of training programmes. A second reason is administrative — to aid in making decisions about pay raises, promotions, and training. Still another reason is to provide feedback to employees to help them to improve their present performance and plan future careers.

One of the most important responsibilities of a manager is performance appraisal, the assessment of an employee's job performance. When a right person is selected and is good at work, it can help employees to improve their performance, chances for promotion, etc. When a wrong person is selected, the performance is poor, it can cause resentment, reduce motivation, and even expose the organisation to legal action.

Performance appraisal has two basic purposes. *First*, appraisal serves an administrative purpose. It provides managers with the information they need to salary, promotion, and dismissal decisions; helps employees understand and accept the basis of those decisions; and if necessary, provides documentation that can justify those decisions in court. *Second*, and atleast as important, appraisal serves a developmental purpose. The information gathered in the appraisal can be used to identify and plan the additional training, learning, experience or other improvement employees require. In addition, the manager's feedback and coaching based on the appraisal help employees to improve their day to day performance and can help to prepare them for greater responsibilities in the future.

WHO CAN BE THE APPRAISER ?

It is possible for the appraisal to be done by one or a combination of the following:

1. The immediate manager,
2. Immediate supervisor,
3. A high-level manager,
4. Specialist (from personnel department)
5. The employee's peers,
6. The employee himself,
7. Employee's subordinates, etc.

WHY USE PERFORMANCE APPRAISALS ?

Douglas McGregor has suggested the following three reasons for using performance appraisals:

1. They provide systematic judgement to support salary increases, promotions, transfers, and sometimes, demotions or terminations.
2. They are a means of telling subordinates how they are doing and of suggesting needed changes in behaviour, attitudes, skills, or job knowledge; they let subordinates know where they stand with the boss.
3. They furnish a useful basis for the coaching and counselling of individuals by superiors.

HANDLING PERFORMANCE APPRAISALS

If performance appraisals are not handled well, their benefits to the organisation will be minimum. Several guidelines can assist management in increasing the appropriateness with which appraisals are conducted. The *first* guideline is that performance appraisals should stress both performance in the position the individual holds and the success with which the individual is attaining organisational objectives. Although conceptually separate, performance and objectives should be inseparable topics of discussion during performance appraisals. The *second* guidelines is that appraisals should emphasize how well the individual is doing the job, not the evaluator's impression of individual's work habits. In other words, the goal is an objective analysis of performance rather than a subjective evaluation of habits.

The *third* guideline is that the appraisal should be acceptable to both the evaluator and the subject — that is, both should agree that it has benefit for the organisation and the worker. The *Fourth*, and last, guideline is that performance appraisals should provide a base for improving individuals' productivity within the organisation by making them better equipped to produce.

PURPOSES OF APPRAISAL

Performance appraisal system involves setting performance standards and comparing actual performance with the standards. Comparison of actual performance against standards enables the managers to know whether or not employees have contributed towards corporate profits.

Appraisal of employees serves several useful purposes:

1. It can serve as a basis for job change or promotion and it helps to suitable placement.
2. It helps to identify employee's shortcomings so as to overcome them through guidance and training.

3. It serves as a feedback to the employee. An employee knows where he stands so that he can be motivated to develop himself.
4. It serves as an important incentive to all employees. Employees realise that not only they are being continuously observed but feel happy that they have not been forgotten.
5. Permanent appraisal serves as a means for evaluating the effectiveness of devices for the selection and classification of workers.
6. Permanent appraisal enables to pinpoint the faults in working pattern and habits of employees.
7. Regular appraisal seeks to standardise and regularise procedures.
8. Permanent performance appraisal records of employees help the management to give up sole reliance upon personal knowledge of supervisors who may be absent/shifted.
9. The manner and approach of evaluation is standardised so that ratings are easily comparable.
10. It is scientific evaluation of performance and quality designed to minimise human bias and prejudices. It is subject to impartial review and check.
11. Both the personal qualities and job performance of the employee are considered. The qualities to be rated include knowledge of work, ability to do the job, quantity and quality of output and personal traits like initiative, self-confidence, leadership, etc.
12. There must be right man for the right job. This is possible by an appraisal method. What will happen if the firm gets a wrong man ?

BENEFITS OF PERFORMANCE APPRAISAL

A sound system of performance appraisal provides the following benefits:

1. Appraisals can help to improve employees' job performance by identifying strengths and weaknesses, and determining how their strengths can be best utilised within the organisation and weaknesses to overcome. They can help to reveal problems which may be restricting employees' progress and causing inefficient work practices.
2. There must be right man for the right job. This is possible by an appraisal method. In the absence of performance appraisal system, wrong persons may be assigned with wrong jobs.
3. It becomes easy for managers to convince employees and give them feedback on inputs and outputs. The result of appraisal can be known to the employee. Thus, the employees can understand where they stand and can take proper steps to improve their performance.
4. Identification of competent workers provides information to decide for promotion of deserving employees and they are transferred as per information provided. Performance appraisal thus helps to formulate policy for promotion and transfers.
5. Performance appraisal serves as a scientific basis for judging the work of individual employees. Employees are evaluated in a systematic and objective way. The systematic performance appraisal helps to distinguish efficient and inefficient workers.
6. It helps in designing training programmes. The weakness of workers and their potential for development are revealed. It helps in spotting exceptional talent. The training and development programmes can be designed accordingly.
7. Performance appraisal enables the superiors to identify the reasons for poor and bad performance. This helps the superiors to guide and help their subordinates wherever they lack.
8. Compensation for achievement is the most powerful motivating force. One of the strong motivating factors is promotion. Such decisions need sufficient data and cases. This is possible because of appraisals.

ESSENTIALS OF GOOD APPRAISAL SYSTEM

Whatever the system is adopted, it must have the following features:

1. Objectives of appraisal system should be defined clearly.
2. The plan must be simple to operate and easy to understand.
3. The plan should be designed by keeping the objectives of the appraisal programme.
4. Suitable appraisal forms should be designed according to the nature of the job. The form must be suitable for organisation's existing operations.
5. The system must be data-based.
6. The raters should be carefully selected and trained. The raters must be familiar with the job and the person to be rated.
7. The plan should lay down the standards of performance in clear and precise terms. The standards must be known to all employees well in advance.
8. The plan should fit the structure and operations of the organisation.
9. The performance appraisal should be a continuous process.
10. The ratings should be discussed with the concerned workers. This facilitates the employee to know his strength and weakness. He can also know where he stands.
11. The system should provide for guidance and counselling of the employees.
12. There should be a systematic procedure for the redressal of grievances arising out of the performance appraisal. The appraisal plan should be valid and reliable. The system should be periodically evaluated to ensure that it meets its goal.
13. The system should define the responsibility of the appraiser and appraisee.
14. It must maintain a good balance between efforts and rewards.
15. The plan must be reliable and free from errors.

METHODS OF PERFORMANCE APPRAISAL

Several different methods have been evolved to evaluate the performance of employees in an organisation. Most of them represent an attempt to quantify the supervisor's observations and secure an objective measure of employees' performance. The major methods used in performance appraisal are outlined below:

1. Ranking Method

Under this method, the supervisor ranks or arranges his men in order of merit from the best to the poorest. Thus if there are five employees working under one supervisor, they may be rated as No. 1, No. 2 and so on upto No. 5 who will be the least meritorious of the lot in terms of performance. Though simple, the method cannot be conveniently used where the number of men is too large.

2. Paired Comparison Method

According to this method, the supervisor or evaluator has to compare each individual with all of the others in the group. The number of comparisons to be made will thus be $\frac{N(N-1)}{2}$. Assuming there are ten employees to be rated, the supervisor will have to make $\frac{10(10-1)}{2} = 45$ comparisons. The number of comparisons will further increase if each employee is to be rated on, say, five traits each. In that case, comparisons will total up to $45 \times 5 = 225$. Obviously the method is comber some, unless, of course, it is to be for over-all comparison of employees and the number of employees is reasonable.

3. Graphic Rating Scales

In this method, a graphic scale is established which measures different degrees of a quality or factor to be rated. Generally several degrees are used for each factor, ranging from highest to lowest. The rater can estimate the degree to which each quality or trait is present in an employee by observing his behaviour on the job. The factors rated include quality and quantity of work, dependability, initiative, etc. Various types of rating scales may be used, for example, reversed scales, discontinuous scales, etc. An example is given below:

Graphic Rating Scale

Name of worker ....

Designation ....

Work assigned ....

Qualities	*Excellent*	*Very good*	*Average*	*Poor*
1. Quantity of output				
2. Quality of output				
3. Knowledge of the job				
4. Judgement and initiative				
5. Dependability and Loyalty				
6. Capacity to get along with staff				

4. Forced Distribution Method

Under this method, the raters are forced to distribute the ratings into predetermined scales. Employees are rated on the basis of overall performance. The ratings must be distributed in such a way that a normal frequency distribution is created. In other words, the appraiser is asked to distribute the ratings as 10% in 'poor, '20%' 'below average', 40% 'average', 20% above average and 10% 'outstanding'. This method eliminates the subjective judgement or bias on the part of raters so that ratings do no cluster around a particular point in the rating scale. It is also easy to understand and administer.

5. Checklist Method

A checklist is a standard list of statements about the traits of employees which can be checked by the evaluator to show whether the employee being rated satisfies the trait contained in the statement or not. The supervisor or rater has simply to put a mark (say, (+) sign) before a statement if it applies to an individual and another (say, (–) sign) if it does not apply to him. A cross-section of a checklist show how this method is used.

6. Critical Incident Method

In this method, the rater is required to record one exceptional (critical) event and the behaviour of each employee during such events. Employees are rated on the basis of whether their behaviour was proper or not. For example, the behaviour of five workers to be rated during a "fire accident" might have been as follows:

Workers	Behaviour	Score
A	Informed his supervisor	3
B	Used fire fighting equipment	5
C	Rang up the brigade	4

D	Became anxious of loss	2
E	Ran away from the place	1

The scores are assigned according to the extent to which the behaviour was considered satisfactory. The method has the advantage that ratings are based on concrete evidence. The behaviour patterns indicate traits like judgement, loyalty, presence of mind, etc.

APPRAISAL BY RESULTS (GOAL SETTING APPROACH)

The goal setting approach of performance appraisal is also known as management by objectives or appraisal by results. Under this approach, an employee is appraised on the basis of his performance in the achievement of agreed goals or objectives. The essential feature of this approach is the mutual establishment towards the accomplishment of predetermined and specific objectives and goals. The result oriented approach to appraisal involves the following steps:

1. The superior and each of his subordinates jointly decide the subordinate's tasks and responsibilities.
2. The subordinate meets his superior and the final target to be achieved is decided through mutual consultation.
3. Through mutual consultation, check points for the evaluation of progress are established.
4. At the end of the specified period, the supervisor evaluates the subordinate's performance on the basis of mutually agreed criteria. Corrective measures, if necessary, and the mutually agreed targets are fixed for future.

ADVANTAGES OF GOAL SETTING METHOD

The advantages of the method are given below:

(1) Employees are appraised against objective standards fixed in advance with mutual agreement.

(2) The supervisor plays the role of helper and advisor rather than that of a critic and boss.

(3) The subordinates know their goals and the standards by which their performance will be measured. It is a more operational system.

(4) This is a problem solving rather than a tell and sell approach.

(5) The tension and hostility between management and workers are reduced.

CRITICISM

Appraisal by results is considerably superior to traditional approach. However, it suffers from the following weaknesses:

(1) It is not suitable for the blue collar workers.

(2) The goal setting approach is not easy to administer. It involves considerable time.

(3) Goal-setting approach emphasises result alone.

PROMOTION

The word promotion means shifting a worker to higher post with more responsibilities and higher salary. There is a change in the designation and in the status. Upgrading or promotion systems are used to reward the employees for their better service. Upgrading of salary, without the corresponding changes in the post means higher grade of salary for the existing work. The annual increment is not a promotion. Promotion must involve changes in the status. Promotion means filling higher posts with the junior workers instead of taking fresh hands. And of course, it is a good system to create a healthy atmosphere in the organisation, and this every worker does his best for the promotion.

The term promotion denotes the idea of advancement of an employee to a higher job with more emoluments and prestige, higher status and higher responsibility. If higher posts are filled up by promoting the existing employees, the morale of employees will be high, they will be loyal to the concern and they can put in their best.

A promotion takes place when an employee moves to a position higher than the one formerly occupied. Thus, there is an increase in pay apart from more responsibilities and status. When there is no increase in the employee's pay, as a result of promotion, it is called DRY promotion. Promotion may be of two types: (1) Horizontal promotion and (2) Vertical promotion.

Horizontal promotion is a minor promotion within the same classification of a job, such as from Lower Division Clerk to Upper Division Clerk or from second grade Foreman to first grade Foreman. **Vertical promotion** crosses the boundary of a job classification, for example, the promotion of a clerk to office Superintendent or Foreman to the post of Production Manager, etc.

ADVANTAGES OF PROMOTION

Promotion provides the following benefits:

1. Promotion serves as a powerful incentives for employees.
2. It is a tool for reward to better work performance.
3. It keeps the job satisfaction and morale of employees high.
4. It leads to reduction of labour turnover.
5. Employees remain loyal and dedicated to the organisation.
6. Promotion of people internally is easier than selecting from outside.
7. The costs of orientation and training them are low.

LIMITATIONS OF PROMOTION

The promotion policy of filling vacancies from within the organisation is not free from limitations:

(1) The persons promoted may not have required skills.
(2) The decision may involve favouritism.
(3) More talented outsiders may not be employed.
(4) Growth of enterprise is doubtful.

BASES OF PROMOTION

The following are the bases for promotion:

(1) Seniority
(2) Merit
(3) Combination of both.

1. Promotion on the Basis of Seniority

It is a widely recognised basis of promotion where a person is promoted on the basis of his length of service. Most of the Government organisations follow this basis of promotion though, however, it is a matter of dispute in business organisations between management and employees' union.

Advantages of promotion on seniority basis:

The system of promotion has the following benefits:

1. Promotion depends upon the length of services, which can easily be measured. There is no chance of favoritism.
2. Their morale is likely to be high and labour turnover will be minimised.

3. Trade unions prefer this system as it does not differentiate between efficient and inefficient employees.

2. Promotion on the Basis of Merit

It gives promotion on the basis of performance of employees. The best performing employee is promoted to the higher post. Competence of a person is, thus, the basis for promotion and ensures efficiency in the organisation as the person promoted can understand and perform the job of higher based on his potential. When merit is taken as a base for promotion, efficiency is ensured in the organisation.

Benefits of Promotion on the basis of Merit

The following are the advantages on promotion on the basis of merit:

1. The young and ambitious employees have incentive to improve their skills and efficiency.
2. Negative appraisal can be removed through further training.
3. The job satisfaction and motivation of employees are higher. Therefore, productivity and profitability are likely to improve.

Limitations on Promotion based on Merit

The following are the drawbacks of this system:

1. Trade Unions do not favour merit based promotion.
2. Ability criterion ignores the values of experience.
3. Biased judgement plays its role. Management may use merit as a cover to promote its own favourites.

A good Promotion Policy

A sound promotion policy may have the following features:

1. It must provide for a uniform distribution of promotional opportunities throughout the organisation.
2. The promotion policy should be explained to the staff.
3. The promotion policy should be flexible.
4. Employees should be given the right to appeal against promotion decisions.
5. Accurate and up-to-date records of seniority and performance of each employee should be maintained.
6. The basis of promotion and the relative weight to be given to merit and seniority should be specified as clearly as possible.
7. The promotion system should be "open" and not "Closed". So that all individuals within the firm have chances.
8. Employees may be given facilities to increase their knowledge and skills.
9. The lines of promotion should be clearly specified.
10. The employees are known with the qualifications and experience needed for promotion to a particular position.

TERMINATION

Despite our best efforts to manage the performance of our employee. We may find that we may have to terminate an employee. Termination of an employee takes place for criminal behaviour, such as theft of company's property or for violating the company's policies, such as sharing confidential information with its competitors. Most companies have detailed and written policies about the criteria for "cause terminations" and steps that a manager must follow towards such an employee, who meets these conditions. An employee can also be warned for *failing to perform.* Again, most companies have detailed policies about what must be done first before an employee can be warned for a poor performance. If the employee's performance does not improve sufficiently, within the time allowed, termination may take place.

TRANSFERS

Transfers serve a number of purposes. They are used to give people broader job experiences as part of their development and to fill vacancies as they occur. Transfers are also used to keep promotion ladders open and to keep individuals interested in work. For example, many middle managers reach a plateau simply because there is no room for all of them at the top. Such managers may be shifted to other positions to keep their job motivation and interest high. Finally, inadequately performing employees may be transferred to other jobs simply because a higher level manager is reluctant to demote them. Increasingly, however, some employees are refusing transfers because they do not want to move their families or jeopardize a spouse's career.

CASE STUDY - 1

1. Laxmi Savings is an investment company. Its employees are annually rated by means of a graphic scale. The qualities are responsibility, dependability, initiative, interest in work, potential leadership, and community activity. Resulting ratings are used to counsel employees, to influence promotions and salary adjustments, and as criteria for evaluating sources, methods of selection, and training.

   At this time, some trouble has arisen. Three of the company's employees have expressed their dissatisfaction with ratings they have received before the chief executive. The aggrieved employees have argued that their ratings do not accurately represent their qualifications or performance. They have insisted that "community activity" is not properly a part of their job, and that what they do off the job is none of the employer's business. They insist that salary increases be automatic.

   Prepare a memorandum outlining your position as a personnel manager for possible submission to the chief executive.

2. Basanti Lal accepted a new promotion with mixed feelings. He was proud of having his work recognised, but he had some doubts about how he would like the new work. His former job had involved regular contacts with salesmen—trouble-shooting, helping them with special customer problems, and so on. His new job in market research was essentially a research job. Working with industry marketing reports, and the like.

   Basanti Lal missed the routine of his old office and the men he had worked with. He had a private office now, but he felt he really did not have the educational background for the job. When he submitted his first report, the division head was nice enough—suggesting some changes that in fact meant that Basanti Lal had really used the wrong approach. His boss said not to worry, "We all have to learn a new job."

   (a) What should now be done to correct this situation ?

   (b) Could this situation have been avoided altogether ? How?

REVIEW QUESTIONS

1. What is appraisal by results ? (*B.Com., Delhi*)
2. Explain in brief the advantages of performance appraisal. (*M.Com., Kerala*)
3. What are the requirements of a good promotion policy ? (*M.Com., MS*)
4. Describe the various bases for promotion. (*B.Com., Chennai*)
5. What are the factors to be considered while giving promotion ? (*B.Com., Calicut*)
6. What do you mean by performance appraisal ? State its objectives. (*M.Com., Madurai*)
7. Why is performance evaluation of employees important ? What are the essentials of a good appraisal system ? (*M.Com., Mumbai*)
8. Explain the meaning and process of performance appraisal system. (*M.Com., Jabalpur*)
9. What are the methods of performance appraisal ? (*M.Com., Allahabad*)
10. State the benefits and features of an effective performance appraisal method. (*M.Com., Banaras*)
11. Explain the merits and demerits of performance appraisal ? (*M.Com., Bangalore*)
12. Differentiate job evaluation and performance appraisal. (*M.Com., Mysore*)

Direction and Supervision

18

CHAPTER

INTRODUCTION

Organisations are social systems, composed of roles, interactions and relationship among people occupying various positions in its structure. Success of an organization in accomplishing its goals significantly depends on the nature and patterns of cooperation among individuals, and formal and informal groups. As such, people, as individuals as well as group members, constitute the pillars of organized effort. It is they who provide an organization an enduring competitive edge over its competitors and determine its ability to survive and grow in a dynamic environment. Technological, product, or strategic superiority of an organization over its competitors provides it only a temporary gain as all these things lend themselves to adaptation by competitors. But employee motivation, capabilities and climate of human endeavour are the things which one organization cannot copy from another. The importance of human factor in the success of organized effort also arises from the fact that people are not subject to manipulation like machines, as they have their own free will, and respond to organizational environment in accordance with their attitudes, motives, feelings, apprehensions, aspirations, etc. No doubt, these are all influenced by organizational policies and practices but not determined and governed by it. Moreover, human assets of organization, unlike physical assets, continuously appreciate in value, as knowledge, abilities and skills and all grow with training and experience. The ability of an enterprise to optimize its efficiency and effectiveness, therefore, significantly depends on its ability to integrate its people with the organization. The process through which this integration is achieved is called *directing or actuating*. The processes through which this is sought to be accomplished are the processes of motivation, communication and leadership. These processes have been treated in detail in the next chapters.

MEANING

Planning and organising provide foundation to the organisation and direction initiates action by its workforce towards achievement of its goals. Having appointed the workforce, managers ensure that they work to achieve the organisational standards of performance and in the course of doing so, satisfy their personal wants and needs. They act as catalysts for achieving organisational and individual goals. They act as agents who influence the behaviour of employees to achieve the organisational goals and also to ensure that organisation's plans and policies satisfy the interests of workforce. Managers, thus, direct employees' behaviour towards organisational and individual or group goals.

Direction is essentially concerned with mobilising and synthesising human efforts to accomplish the goals of the organisation. A manager's most important job is to direct the efforts of employees. Direction is, in fact, the heart of management-in-action. It provides necessary guidance and inspiration to the employees to contribute their efforts to organisational goals. Directing is the process of integrating the people with the organisation so as to obtain their zealous cooperation for the achievement of goals of the organisation. It is the interpersonal aspect of management which deals with guiding, influencing and motivating the employees.

DEFINITIONS

Directing is "a managerial function that involves the responsibility of managers for communicating to others what their roles are in achieving the company plan".

—Pearce and Robinson.

It is "getting all the members of the group to want and to strive to achieve objectives of the enterprise and of the members because the members want to achieve these objective".

—Terry and Franklin.

According to Urwick and Breach, "Directing is the guidance, the inspiration the leadership of those men and women that constitutes the real core of the responsibility of management.".

Therefore, directing involves, issuing orders and instructions, overseeing of the subordinates and supervising the work being performed by them.

According to Koontz and O' Donnell, "Directing is a complex function that includes all those activities which are designed to encourage subordinates to work effectively and efficiently in both the short and long run."

ELEMENTS OF DIRECTION

The directing involves the following elements:

1. The manager issues orders and instructions to the subordinates to get the work done from them. Orders and instructions must be clear and complete.
2. The manager continuously provide guidance to subordinates to ensure that they do the assigned job, efficiently and effectively.
3. The manager should motivate the subordinates to work for the achievement of organisational goals.
4. Leadership is the quality of behaviour of a manager whereby he guides his subordinates in the desired direction.
5. The manager, by maintaining discipline, should try to achieve cooperation of the subordinates.

NATURE OF DIRECTION

Direction is the heart and soul of management. It is the direction which provides impetus to the whole managerial functions. Planning, organising and staffing are concerned only with the preparation for work performance and it is the direction which alone stimulates the organisation and its staff to execute the plans. Hence, it is also called management-in-action.

The following points highlights the nature of direction:

1. Important Function

Direction is an important function of management. Without direction, management functions may come to standstill. It is through direction that management initiates action in the organisation.

2. Continuous Process

It is a continuous process. It goes on. As long as work is in progress, the direction has to continue. The superior has to direct the activities of subordinates regularity. It is a process continually provide motivation to get the orders or instructions executed.

3. Pervasive

Managers at all levels and in all functional areas direct their subordinates. Top managers guide middle and lower level manager, who further direct supervisors and workers.

4. Creative Function

Direction makes things happen and converts plans into performance. It is the process around which all performance revolves. Without direction human factor in the organisation become inactive and consequently physical factors become useless.

5. Get things done by others

Directing is a sub-process of managing process. The planning, organising and staffing are followed by directing and controlling to get things done by others.

6. Initiating Function

It is an initiating function, because it implies giving orders and instructions for converting decisions into actions.

7. Action Oriented Process

Directing is a result or action oriented process. Through directing plans are converted into organised actions for achieving objectives.

8. Understanding the Group Behaviour

While working in the organisation, subordinates become part of the informal groups. The behaviour of a person is different as an individual and as members of the group. It is, therefore, essential that managers understand the importance and nature of group behaviour in order to direct effectively.

ADVANTAGES OF DIRECTION

Direction is the heart of administration as it is indispensable for work performance. Direction is needed to tell them what to do, how to do and when to do. Effective direction provides the following advantages.

1. Initiates Action

A good plan may have been prepared, a sound organisation may have been developed and a team of efficient workers may be employed. But without direction, planning, organising and staffing become ineffective.

2. Achieves Coordination

Directing aims at continuous supervision of employees' activities. It achieves coordination by ensuring that people work according to planned activities in a coordinated and integrated manner. Direction helps in coordination among various operations of the enterprise. The coordination is considered as a by-product of effective directing.

3. Facilitates Growth

Through direction, managers encourage and influence employees to contribute to the best of their capability for the achievement of organisational objectives. This facilitates organisational success and growth.

4. Facilitates Control

Coordination of employees' efforts brings actual performance in conformity with planned performance. The controlling function is, thus, facilitated through effective directing.

5. Means of Motivation

Employees are motivated to work willingly and efficiently, through the process of directing. The superior who directs the activities of subordinates inspires them to follow given orders and instruction whole-heartedly.

6. Development of Everyone

To produce desired results from all these functions – planning, organising, staffing, etc., the directing function is crucial. Through directing, other managerial functions are initiated and actuated. And without effective directing, managerial functions remain less effective. If managers and employees cooperate with each other and work in harmony, it promotes skills of the employees and develops managers to assume responsibilities of higher levels in the organisation.

7. Facilitates Changes

Changes can be introduced and managed effectively with the help of directing. Through directing the manager provides dynamic leadership and free and frank communication with subordinates as to convince them regarding the positive side of change. They may be taken into confidence and persuaded for accepting the change and giving their full cooperation for implementing it.

PRINCIPLES OF DIRECTION

Direction is one of the important functions of management. Direction is a complex function. It deals with people whose behaviour is unpredictable. Managers perform the complex function of direction through the following principles of direction:

1. Effective Communication

Communication is an important instrument of direction. A good system of communication between the manager and subordinates helps to improve mutual understanding. The manager must ensure that plans, policies, instructions, etc. are fully understood by the subordinates in the right direction.

2. Follow through

Direction is a continuous process. Mere issuing orders or instructions is not an end itself. Direction is necessary, so the management should watch whether the subordinates follow the orders and whether they face difficulties in carrying out the orders or instructions.

3. Unity of Command

A subordinate should get orders and instructions from one superior only, that is, all directions, orders and instructions should come from one boss. If one subordinate receives instructions from more than one superior, there will be confusions, conflicts, disorders and indisciplines in the organisation; and the subordinate may not be able to carryout the instructions of any of them.

4. Individual Contribution

Directions aim at getting maximum contribution from employees by exploiting their talent to the best. Subordinates can generally contribute more than their present performance and direction helps in enhancing their contribution.

5. Direct Supervision

Direction becomes more effective when there is a direct personal contact between a supervisor and his subordinates. Such direct contact improves the morale and commitment of employees. Therefore, wherever possible direct supervision should be used.

6. Effective Leadership

Managers as leaders, they should guide and counsel subordinates in their personal problems too. In this way, they can win the confidence and trust of their subordinates. When employees face problems in carrying out their tasks, managers provide them the necessary counselling and guidance. This makes direction effective as employees can approach their superiors for counselling whenever required.

7. Efficient Motivation

Cooperation of subordinates can be secured if they are ready to act for the organisation voluntarily. People will volunteer themselves for the accomplishment of goals if they are properly induced and motivated. Direction should be such that it inspires the employees to contribute fully towards the well being of the organisation.

8. Unity of Direction

An employee may get orders from one superior only. That is, he works under one head. For instance, all activities related to marketing must be headed by marketing manager and those related to personnel should be headed by the personnel manager. This avoids duplication of actions and instructions and results in optimum use of scarce resources.

9. Feedback Information

Direction does not end with issuing orders and instructions to the subordinates. Sometimes, suggestions given by the subordinates are necessary for the development of the management. So, a good procedure of the feedback system furnishes reliable ideas to the management.

10. Harmony of Objectives

Individuals have their own objectives. Organisation has its own objectives. The management should be in such a way that the individuals can integrate their objectives with the organisational objectives. That is, management should reconcile the personal goals of subordinates with the organisational goals.

ESSENTIALS OF A GOOD ORDER

According to Koontz and O'Donnell, "As a directional technique, an instruction is understood to be a charge (command) by a superior requiring a subordinate to act or refrain from acting in a given circumstance." Orders or instructions are always issued by a supervisor. A good order, to be effective tool of direction, must possess the following essentials:

1. An order should be clear and complete so that it is easily understood by subordinates.
2. It should be reasonable.
3. It should specify the time within which it should be carried out.
4. It should be in unambiguous words.
5. As far as possible it should be in writing.
6. It should be as brief as possible.
7. Proper tone in issuing the orders should be observed.
8. Suggestions of subordinates are to be considered.
9. It should be compatible with the objectives and policies of the organization.
10. It should also be compatible with employees' personal interest.
11. It should be constantly followed up.

SUPERVISION

INTRODUCTION

Supervision means overseeing or observing the work of subordinates with authority. It is an important part of directing function of every manager. It means observing the subordinates at work to see that they are working according to plans and policies of the organisation and keeping the time schedule and to help them in solving their working problems. Supervision involves actual translation of plans into action. They should provide day-to-day guidance and instructions to the operative employees. Managers at the top supervise the activities of middle level managers, who supervise the activities of lower level managers who finally supervise the conduct of non-managers, that is employees or workers of the organisation. The supervisor act as a link between managers and the work-force. Directions given by managers at the top reach the workers through supervisors. The workers grievances or complaints reach the higher levels through supervisors.

MEANING

Supervisor is a representative of management and a key figure from the point of view of employees. He is responsible for issuing orders and instructions, laying down work methods and procedures and initiating action. He is primarily responsible for the successful performance of work on the operating level. He is a man in the middle because he represents both management and workers. He has to keep the workers in good spirits. Motivation is one of his important functions.

Supervisors have to maintain the workers and machinery in good and efficient condition and secure efficient work from the workers. The first-line supervisor occupies a strategic position in the hierarchy of an organisation. The term SUPERVISOR is generally associated with managers at the lowest level who supervise the activities of the workers. He acts between two opposite forces — managers and workers. He tries to satisfy the needs and desire of managers and workers both. He is also known as first-line managers or as foreman, section-head, etc. The bottom-line management has got a basic responsibility of supervising the workers in their day-to-day performance. He should be in direct touch with the actual workers. A supervisor is basically line executive. He has to develop team spirit and performance standards.

WHO IS A SUPERVISOR ?

"A supervisor is a person who is primarily in-charge of a section and its employees, and is responsible for both the quantity and quality of production, for the efficient performance of the equipment, and for the employees in his charge and their efficiency, training and morale." He issues orders, instructions and guidance to the subordinates, directs their activities at work and reports to the manager or departmental heads on the performance of his section. Some people consider his role as that of a BEHAVIOURAL SPECIALIST, who analyse and interpret human behaviour to get the work done through them. Supervision is concerned with instruction, guidance and inspiration to workers towards better performance.

QUALITIES OF A SUPERVISOR

A supervisor to be effective in his job should possess the following attributes:

1. Technical Knowledge of the work

A supervisor must have technical competence. He must have good knowledge of machines, equipment, materials, tools, operational processes, plant-layout, location and ability to judge, power to convince, self confidence, creativity, maturity, etc.

2. Managerial Knowledge

The supervisor must have managerial vision to comprehend company policies and practices in their proper perspective. He should keep himself aware of changes in such policies and procedures.

3. Knowledge of Rules and Regulations

The knowledge of the policies, principles, plans, programmes, rules, regulations, and procedures of the entrie organisation, etc. are of significant to improve the effectiveness of a supervisor. It is desirable for a supervisor to possess a working knowledge of labour laws, Company Acts, Contract Acts, Compensation Act, etc.

4. Communication Skill

A supervisor has to issue instructions and orders continuously to his subordinates. Therefore, he must have perfect clarity in communication. He must have ability to tell, to listen and to understand the workers properly.

5. Human Relation Skill

A supervisor is expected to treat his subordinates as human beings. He requires the ability to judge the people correctly. He must have patience and emotional stability. He is mainly concerned with instructing, guiding and inspiring people to perform their job effectively and efficiently. He must motivate the workers and keep them in good spirits. Whenever necessary, he has to understand their individual problems and to provide good solutions for such problems. He must build up a team spirit and unit among workers.

6. Integrity

A supervisor should be a leader in the true sense of the term. As a leader, he will be able to guide the subordinates and promote harmonious relations among them. He must be honest and fair in dealing with subordinates, without favour and fear. He must recommend pay-increases, promotions transfer, etc. of the right subordinates.

7. Physical Vigour

He must be physically fit. He must have stamina and energy to undertake tight work schedules. He should not irritate or angry when dealing with workers. His health condition must cooperate to take prompt and accurate decisions. He should always be mentally alert. He should adopt a helping attitude towards his subordinates.

SUPERVISOR'S ROLE IN MANAGEMENT

A supervisor performs the following role in management:

1. To determine individual job assignment;
2. To give orders and instructions;
3. To ensure proper working conditions;
4. To instruct the working methods and procedures;
5. To inspire the workers for efficient performance;
6. To maintain discipline in the work place;
7. To communicate managerial decisions to workers;
8. To convey workers' suggestions to management;
9. To maintain team work;
10. To attend to grievances of subordinates;
11. To provide guidance to workers;
12. To take corrective action, if necessary;
13. To recommend promotion or pay increases for workers;
14. To treat subordinates as friends;
15. To encourage workers' participation in decision-making.

FUNCTIONS OF A SUPERVISOR

The main functions of a supervisor are a follows:

1. He is concerned with the planning of day-to-day operations at the place of work.
2. While communicating the intention of managers to subordinates, he performs all the managerial functions of planning, organising, staffing and controlling the activities of workers.
3. Supervisor is holding a middle position, between management and workers — two opposite forces. If intentions of both the parties are agreeable to each other, there is no problem. But in case the intentions of either party are not acceptable to the other party, the supervisor has to act wisely and intelligently to convince the two parties for an amicable agreement.
4. He motivates workers to work hard and to improve their productivity. For this, he may praise the workers and recommend to promote or to pay increases.
5. The supervisor listens to the grievances and complaints of his subordinates. He helps to solve these at the workplace and bring these grievances to the notice of management.
6. He explains how to use safety devices and lays down safety standards at the workplace. He evaluates the work performance of his subordinates in the light of predetermined standards.

REVIEW QUESTIONS

1. Explain the principles of directing.
2. Describe the human aspects of management.
3. Describe the basic principles of direction.
4. What is meant by supervision ?
5. "A supervisor is a man in the middle" Comment.
6. State the responsibilities of a supervisor.
7. Describe the essentials of effective supervision.
8. Distinguish between supervision and directing.
9. Describe the importance of direction as a managerial function.
10. What are the different functions performed by supervisor ?
11. What is the nature of direction ?
12. Narrate the need and significance of directing.

Motivation and Morale

19

CHAPTER

Motivation

- Introduction
- Meaning
- Definitions
- Importance
- Benefits
- Nature
- Principles
- Types of Incentives
- Positive and Negative
- Intrinsic Motivation
- Extrinsic Motivation
- Money as a Motivator
- Carrot and Stick Approach
- Theory of Motivation
    - Need Hierarchy Theory
    - Two Factor Theory
    - ERG Theory
    - Acquired Needs Theory
    - Expectancy Theory
    - Equity Theory
    - Goal Setting Theory
    - Reinforcement Theory
    - Theory X and Theory Y
    - Theory Z
- Job Design
- Job Specialisation
- Job Simplification
- Job Rotation
- Job Enlargement
- Job Enrichment

Morale

- Introduction
- Morale and Productivity
- Motivation and Morale
- Factors Determining Morale
- Morale Depressants
- Review Questions.

MOTIVATION

INTRODUCTION

The term motivation has been derived from the word motive. Motive is anything that initiates or sustains activity. It is an inner state that energies, activates or moves and that directs or channels behaviour towards goals. Motive is a psychological force within an individual that sets him in motion. Behind every human action there is a motive. According to Brech, "Motivation is general inspirational process which gets the members of the team to pull their weight effectively, to give their loyalty to the group, to carry out properly the tasks that they have accepted and generally to play an effective part in the job that the group has undertaken."

Motivation represents the force that moves people and causes them to act. Motivation is something that motivates a person into action and continues him in the course of action enthusiastically. It is a psychological technique which executes the plans and policies through the efforts of others. However good the resources of an organisation may be, these cannot automatically result in the realisation of the aims of the business enterprise. Merely recruitment of the staff and allocation of duties amongst them cannot by itself complete the management process. Ultimately the most decisive factor is the human factor. Best performance can be had from the staff only by creating in them the necessary urge or desire to do so. Creation of this urge or desire or inculcation of the urge to give better performance is called motivation. This means making the workers to take interest in the work. Manager can buy a man's time, he can buy a man's physical presence but the real difficulty is how to get his enthusiasm, initiative or loyalty to work. Motivation is able to generate in men the willingness to use their ability and perform the work.

MEANING

Motivation is an important function of every manager. It deals with actuating the people to work for the accomplishment of objectives of the organisation. Issuance of well conceived instructions and orders does not mean that they will be followed. A manager has to make appropriate use of motivation to induce the employees to follow them. Effective motivation succeeds in having an order accepted and also in gaining a determination to see that it is executed efficiently and effectively. In order to motivate the employees, the management has to understand their needs and satisfy them by providing financial and non-financial incentives. As management is the art of getting things done by workers, this art of getting work done will depend mainly on whether a worker has been motivated properly or not. That is, motivation creates a sense of responsibility and an interest in the work. It increases the desire to work. To motivate means to provide a motive, to impel people to action and to create incentives to work. Motivation is an energizer of human behaviour and is a special urge to move in a particular direction. With motivation, a person can be made to work willingly with zeal and enthusiasm.

Motivation is an important factor which encourages persons to give their best performance and help in reaching enterprise goals. A strong positive motivation will enable the increased output of employees but a negative motivation will reduce their performance. Motivation is an effective instrument in the hands of a manager for inspiring the work-force and creating a confidence in it. By motivating the work-force, management creates "will to work", which is necessary for the achievement of organisational goals. Motivation involves getting the members of the group to pull weight effectively, to give their loyalty to the group and to carry out properly the purpose of organisation. Motivation is always directed towards achievement of high levels of work. Thus motivate means "to provide with a motive, to impel or incite." Motive is an inner state that prompts or incites the individual to action. Motives are expressions of person's needs and hence they are personal and internal. Motives and needs are "ways" of behaviour. They start and maintain activity. Motives give direction to human behaviour because they are directed towards certain goals. Motives arouse and energise a person's activities.

DEFINITIONS

Let us see some important definitions of motivation:

"Motivation refers to the way in which urges, drives, desires, aspirations, striving or needs direct control or explain the behaviour of human beings" — McFarland

"Motivation is the process of attempting to influence others to do your will through the possibility of gain or reward." — Flippo

"Motivation is the act of stimulating someone or oneself to get the desired course of action"

— Julius

"Motivation refers to the complex of forces starting and keeping a person at work in an organisation. To put it generally, motivation starts and maintains an activity along a prescribed life. Motivation is something that moves the person to action and continues him in the course of action already initiated." — Dubin

"Motivation is a general term applying to the entire class of drives, desires, needs, wishes and similar forces. To say that managers motivate their subordinates is to say that they do those things which they hope will satisfy these drives and desires and induce the subordinates to act in a desired manner." — Weihrich and Koontz.

"Motivation is the process of being influenced to take action or accomplish a goal. In an organisation, people are motivated if they are willing to perform efficiently and effectively."

— Littlefield and Rachel.

IMPORTANCE OF MOTIVATION

Motivation is one of the most important factors determining organisational efficiency. The organisational facilities will go to waste in the absence of motivated employees to utilise these facilities effectively. A manager guides the employees in a desired manner in order to achieve organisational objectives. There is a need for motivation to create willingness in the minds of employees to do a job. The performance of human beings in the organisation is dependent on the ABILITY and MOTIVATION: that is,

Performance = Ability × Motivation

The relationship, between motivation and performance, can be expressed by the equation:

$$P = M \times A,$$

Where P stands for performance, M stands for motivation and A stands for ability. This can also be expressed in different way, symbolically:

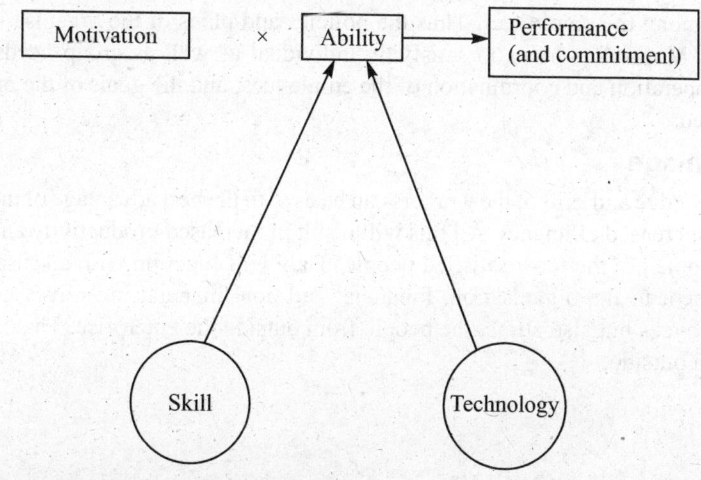

BENEFITS OF MOTIVATION

The importance of motivation lies in its following benefits:

1. Higher Efficiency

Motivated employees make higher contribution towards the realisation of organisational goals. One can be physically and mentally fit to work but he may not be willing to work. This is because there is a difference between CAPACITY TO WORK and WILLINGNESS TO WORK. Motivation bridges the gap between capacity to work and willingness to work.

2. Reduction of Labour Problems

Motivation leads to job satisfaction and high morale. The important contribution of motivation is that employees prefer to stay in the organisation. It reduces labour turnover, absenteeism, indiscipline, etc. because of increase in real wages by the motivational plans. Motivated employees have higher commitment and loyalty to the organisation.

3. Increase in Production

The employees give their best performance which helps in increasing the productivity of the organisation. The employees try to put efforts to produce more, thus increasing their efficiency and as a result of this, general production and productivity of the organisation increases. They work in the best interest of the organisation.

4. Best Utilisation of Resources

Motivation inspires employees to make best uses of different factors of production. The enterprise can make maximum use of its physical and financial resources. It helps in decreasing the wastages, accidents, complaints, etc.

5. Basic of Cooperation

Motivation helps in securing voluntary cooperation from workers. It creates the will to work, and confidence in the workforce. Motivation helps to satisfy the needs of workers; naturally there will be a sense of belongingness and total involvement on the part of the workers in the achievement of organisational goals. Motivation is a basis of cooperation to get the best results out of the efforts of the employees on the job. Efficiency and output are increased through cooperation. The cooperation could not be obtained without motivation. So, motivation is a basis of cooperation.

6. Job Satisfaction

When employees are properly motivated, they use their skill and knowledge upto their maximum ability to show better results to the management. This promotes the feeling of job satisfaction among the employees. Thus the policies and plans of the organisation are effectively implemented. Motivation helps in satisfying individual as well as group needs. It results in the voluntary cooperation and coordination of the employees; and the goals of the organisation can be easily achieved.

7. Better Image

The knowledge and skill of the workers can be used to the best advantage of the organisation and there will be increased efficiency. All this will result in increased productivity and quality of work. Motivated people are the most satisfied people. They will function with a sense of responsibility and commitment to the organisation. Financial and non-financial incentives not only retain the existing employees but also attract the people from outside the enterprise. That is, right people are attracted from outside.

8. Organisational Changes

The technological changes taking place in the world have brought about revolutionary changes on the production side. Generally employees resist these changes but with proper motivation, they accept these change thereby keeping the organisation in line with the other competing firms.

9. Better Industrial Relation

A properly motivated team will not have unnecessary friction with the management and fellow workers. This will help in maintaining a good industrial relations. A firm that offers good financial and non-financial incentives enjoy a very good reputation in the labour market. Its public image is improved. Therefore, it can easily attract competent persons for filling vacancies.

NATURE OF MOTIVATION

On the analysis of definitions of motivation, the following characteristics of motivation can be identified:

1. Motivation is a Continuous Process

Human needs are infinite. As soon as one need is satisfied new one arises. In the words of McGregor, "Man is a wanting animal, as soon as one of his needs is satisfied another appears in its place. This process is unending". Motivation is an unending process.

2. It is an Internal Force

Motivation is an internal feeling which generates within an individual. The degree of motivation cannot be measured in quantitative terms. It can only be observed through actions and performance of employees. Motivating factors are always unconscious but they are to be aroused by managerial action.

3. It is Complex

It is difficult to explain and predict the behaviour of workers. Motivation is a complex and difficult function. The needs are mental feeling which cannot be desired and measured accurately. Every person adopts a different approach to satisfy his needs and one particular need may cause different behaviour on the part of different people.

4. Motivations Change

Human needs are unlimited and go on changing continuously. People must at all times be provided with the stimulus to work because the satisfaction of one need gives rise to another need. Motivation of each individual change from time to time, even though he may continue to behave in the same way. For example, a temporary employee may produce more in the beginning to become permanent; when made permanent, he may continue to produce more, — this time to gain promotion and so on.

5. Goals are Motivators

Man works to achieve his individual goals. Whenever the goal is achieved, he will be no longer interested to work. So, the management should identify the goals of individuals and it can persuade them to work by directions.

6. The Whole Individual is Motivated

An individual is motivated fully and not partly because motivation is related to psychology. Besides, the basic needs of man determine motivation to a great extent. All these needs are interrelated and cannot be separated from each other.

7. A Psychological Concept

Motivation deals with the psychology of workers. An efficient worker will not perform the work desirably well unless he is properly motivated. So effective performance requires proper motivation. Proper motivation is possible only through proper analysis of the psychology of workers.

PRINCIPLES OF MOTIVATION

The main principles of motivation are as follows:

1. The principle of participation is one of the most important principle of motivation that people in the organisation should be induced to participate in decision-making process in matters concerning them.
2. The organisation must provide an opportunity to the workers to tell their grievances to their seniors. Two-way communication – upward and downward – will be more meaningful in motivating the workers.
3. All human motivation is basically selfish, that is, people do things for their reasons not ours.
4. Giving people authority to make their own decision gives them a vested interest in the result they accomplish, and they feel that they are a part of the organisation.
5. You cannot motivate other people because all motivation comes from within.
6. People will be motivated to work hard if they get continuing recognition for their efforts. Recognition tends to motivate the people to work. The management should follow the rule, "praise in public and criticism in private."
7. The job of the management is to guide the employees towards the attainment of goals. The managers should give suggestions instead of orders.
8. Everyone should be treated differently in a way that they all feel important for the organisation.

TYPES OF INCENTIVES

Incentives can broadly be classified into two categories: (A) Pecuniary Incentives and (B) Non-Pecuniary Incentives.

(A) Pecuniary (Financial) Incentives

Financial incentives is in terms of money and it provides higher emoluments for higher efforts or increased output. It includes money payments based on results in addition to wages and salaries. In this respect, piece rate system of wage payment provides greatest incentive to the workers as in this system, remuneration is directly linked to their output. Similarly, there are many premium bonus system, like Galsey Premium, Rowan Premium Bonus System, etc., under which basic time wages is guaranteed and a bonus is paid for achieving a saving in time, in proportion to the time saved.

(B) Non-financial Incentives

Non-financial incentives provide psychological and emotional satisfaction rather than financial rewards. Status, responsibility, recognition of work, job security, team spirit, competition, etc. are examples of non-financial incentives. These incentives are very important for the satisfaction of socio-psychological needs which cannot be satisfied by money alone.

Advantages of non-financial Incentives

1. Reduce labour turnover
2. Reduce absenteeism
3. Create a sense of loyalty and cooperation in them
4. Enhance general goodwill of the company.
5. The best labourers are attracted.

Advantages to Workers

1. Increase in the wages of workers;
2. Improvement in work capacity;
3. Improvement in standard of living.

POSITIVE AND NEGATIVE MOTIVATION

Motivation may be of two types: (1) Positive motivation and (2) Negative motivation.

1. Positive Motivation

In real sense, motivation means positive motivation. Positive motivation induces people to do work in the best possible manner and to improve their performance. According to Flippo, "Positive motivation is a process of attempting to influence others to do your will through the possibility of gain or reward." Praise, participation in decision-making process, pride and delegation of authority and responsibility are some of the methods of positive motivation. Positive motivation seeks to create a brighter, more cheerful and optimistic atmosphere in the enterprise.

2. Negative Motivation

Negative motivation aims at controlling the negative efforts of the work and seeks to create a sense of fear for the worker, which he has to suffer for lack of good performance. If the worker fails to complete the work, they may be threatened with demotion, dismissal, pay-cut, etc. The negative motivation gives maximum benefits in the short-run. In the long-run, there are no such benefits available to the organisation.

INTRINSIC MOTIVATION

Intrinsic motivation refers to motivation that comes from inside an individual rather than from any external or outside rewards, such as money or grades. The motivation comes from the pleasure one gets from the task itself or from the sense of satisfaction in completing or even working on a task.

EXTRINSIC MOTIVATION

Extrinsic motivation refers to motivation that comes from outside an individual. The motivating factors are external or outside, rewards such as money or grades. These rewards provide satisfaction and pleasure that the task itself may not provide. An extrinsically motivated person will work on a task even when they have little interest in it because of the anticipated satisfaction they will get from some reward.

MONEY AS A MOTIVATOR

Traditionally, money has been considered a very important motivator. This is because money is an essential instrument for satisfying primary or basic needs of food, clothing, shelter, etc. Money also has got a symbolic appeal. It often stands for prestige and power. Over a period of time, people form groups and group behaviour becomes more powerful than money in influencing their behaviour. Once the basic needs are satisfied, people are influenced by the desires of their co-workers, job enlargement, job security, growth opportunities, recognition and many other factors other than money. Money can only fulfil our needs but non-monetary incentives like recognition, praise and acceptance develop us to assume positions of higher importance. Non-monetary rewards shape the culture of the individual and the organisation.

THE CARROT AND STICK APPROACH

Use of rewards and penalties or incentives and disincentives to promote desired behaviour find their reference in the carrot and stick approach to motivation.

The 'carrot' refers to rewards. Rewards may be financial or non-financial. When workers perform well, managers recognise their activities and offer them rewards in the form of increase in pay, bonus, vacation or promotion to a higher grade. There can be many other forms in which employees can be rewarded.

Conversely, the 'stick' refers to penalties and punishments. The fear of loss of job, transfer to other office, demotion, cut in salary and other disincentives act as strong motivators that influence workers' behaviour in the desired direction. Though effective in use, this approach should not be used as it develops fear, resentment and agony amongst employees. Workers' behaviour, in such cases is not 'satisfying behaviour'.

THEORIES OF MOTIVATION

There is no shortage of motivation theories which try to provide explanations for the behaviour-outcome relationship. Motivation theories have played a dominant role in emerging field or organisational behaviour. Workers should be persuaded, inspired and motivated for contributing their best efforts in achieving the objectives of the organisation. To motivate workers effectively, mangers should prepare certain plans. There are various plans, strategies or theories of motivation. Some of the important theories of motivation are:

NEED OR CONTENT THEORIES

Need hierarchy Theory – Maslow
Two-factor Theory – Frederick Herzberg
ERG Theory – Clayton Alderfer
Acquired-Needs Theory – David C. McClelland

COGNITIVE THEORIES

Expectancy Theory – Victor H.Vroom, Porter & Lawler
Equity Theory – J.Stacy Adams
Goal Setting Theory – Locke and Latham

REINFORCEMENT THEORY – B.F. Skinner

BEHAVIOURAL THEORIES

Theory X and Theory Y – McGregor
Theory Z – Ouchi.

Some of the popular need theories are discussed below:

1. Need Hierarchy Theory: (Maslow)

The need hierarchy theory is formulated by Abraham Maslow. He advocates a hierarchy of needs present in all individuals. At a point of time, the individual's behaviour reflects his desire to satisfy the strongest need present in him. Once that need is satisfied, the next strongest need arises in him and he strikes to satisfy that need. Managers determine that need and adopt motivators to satisfy it. He developed a general theory of motivation, known as the Need hierarchy theory, which is as follows:

(a) Physiological needs

(b) Safety needs

(c) Social needs

(d) Ego needs

(e) Self-actualisation needs.

According to Maslow, first the lower level needs are to be satisfied, then the person tend to move higher in the hierarchy for satisfaction of his needs. Once one need is satisfied, another emerges and demands satisfaction.

(1) Physiological Needs. Physiological needs are the basic needs of the organism and are essential for survival. These are needs for food, thirst, exercise and shelter. In organised cooperation, these needs are satisfied through adequate compensation in terms of employee needs of this kind and through job security.

(2) Safety Needs. Safety needs are more important when a man is in a dependent relationship and fears arbitrary deprivation. Since people in the organisation stand in dependent relationships safety needs become important informal structure.

(3) Social Needs. As a Social element, it is the desire of human being to be accepted by others. Need for belonging is manifested in the form of social groups formed on informal basis.

(4) Ego Needs. These are needs relating to one's self esteem, such as self-respect, self-confidence and achievement. Ego needs relating to reputation may be satisfied through promotions and allotment of status symbols to deserving individuals in the organisation. Ego needs relating to self-esteem may be satisfied by assigning challenging and stimulating work the accomplishment of which will result in recognition.

(5) Self-Actualisation Needs. These are needs relating to personal growth and realisations of man's full potential. The need for self-actualisation is not strong in all subordinates. At the same time, organisations usually offer limited opportunities for satisfying self-actualisation needs.

1. Critical Evaluation of Maslow's Theory

The criticisms of the theory are as under:

1. There may be overlapping in hierarchy of human needs.
2. The need priority model may not apply at all times, in all places.
3. There can be people whose higher order needs are stronger than lower order needs, even though lower level needs are not fully satisfied.
4. The need hierarchy is different for people belonging to different cultures.

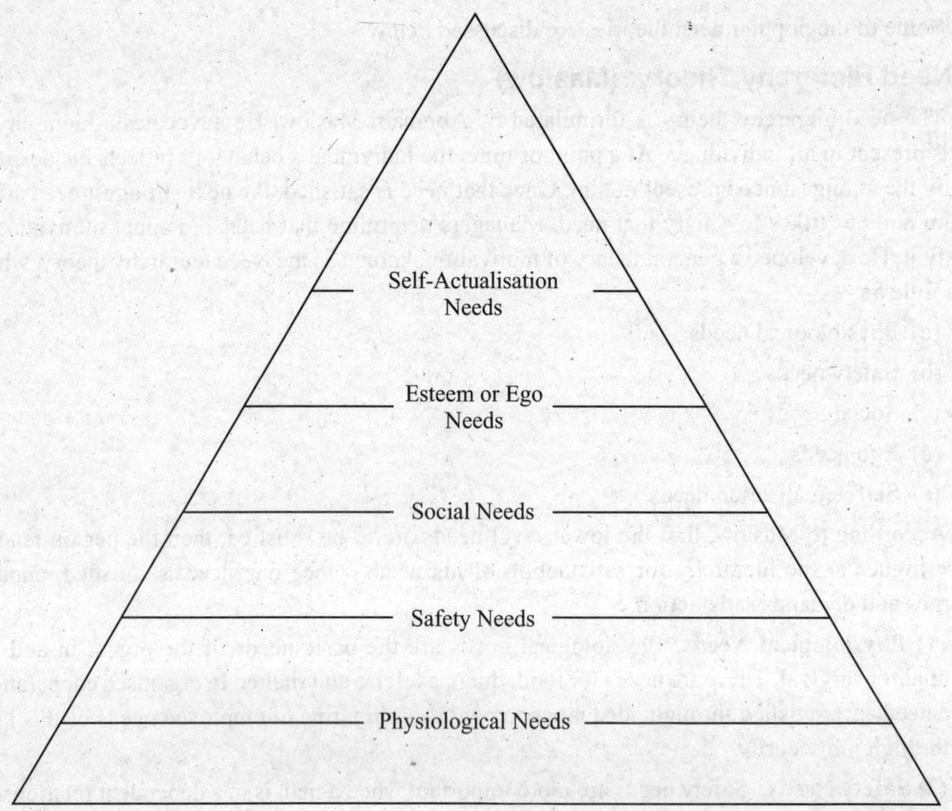

2. Two Factor Theory (Frederick Herzberg)

Frederick Herzberg and his associates conducted a research study based on the interviews of 200 engineers and accountants working in eleven different firms in USA. The findings of this study are that there are two sets of factors which affect satisfaction or dissatisfaction of employees. Some job conditions operate primarily to dissatisfy employees when they are absent but their presence does not motivate them in a strong way. These are called DISSATISFIERS OR HYGIENE FACTORS as they are required to support the mental health of the employees. They are also known as MAINTENANCE FACTORS as they are necessary to maintain a reasonable level of satisfaction among the employees.

Another set of job conditions operate primarily to build strong motivation and high job satisfaction but their absence does not create strong dissatisfaction among employees. They are called MOTIVATIONAL FACTORS OR SATISFIERS. It is because of the two fold classification that Herzberg theory is called two factor theory.

From this viewpoint, individuals may be of two kinds—motivation seekers and maintenance seekers. The motivation seekers are motivated primarily by the motivation factors while maintenance seekers are concerned mainly with hygiene factors.

Hygiene factors and motivating factors

Hygiene Factors (Maintenance)	*Motivational Factors*
1. Company policy and administration	1. Achievement
2. Technical Supervision	2. Recognition
3. Interpersonal relations with supervisor	3. Advancement
4. Interpersonal relations with subordinates	4. Work itself
5. Interpersonal relations with peers	5. Possibilities of growth
6. Salary	6. Responsibility
7. Job security	
8. Personal Life	
9. Working conditions	
10. Status	

Criticisms of Herzberg's Model

1. The conclusions of the theory are based on small sample which is not true representative of human nature.
2. The distinction between motivational maintenance factors are not rigid.
3. The theory oversimplifies the relationship between satisfaction and motivation.
4. It does not attach much importance to pay, status and interpersonal relationships which are held generally as important determinants of satisfaction.

3. Alderfer's ERG Theory

In a reaction to the famous HIERARCHY OF NEEDS by Maslow, Alderfer distinguishes three categories of human needs that influence worker's behaviour: existences relatedness and growth. These ERG theory categories are:

(a) **Existence Needs.** Physiological and safety needs (such as hunger, thirst and sex). The first two levels of Maslow.

(b) **Relatedness Needs.** Social and external esteem (involvement with family, friends, co-workers and employers). The third and fourth levels of Maslow.

(c) **Growth Needs.** Internal esteem and self-actualization (the desire to be creative, productive and to complete meaningful tasks). Maslow's fourth and fifth levels.

Alderfer, while formulating this theory talks of two principles:

(1) **Satisfaction - Progression Principle.** According to this principle, as one need is satisfied, even if in part, it leads to progression, that is, satisfaction of other needs. People can also satisfy two needs at a time. Social needs and growth needs may be present in a person at the same point of time.

(2) **Frustration - Regression Principle.** If people are not able to satisfy their growth needs, because of their inability or because of their superiors do not cooperate with them, they will feel frustrated and regress to satisfy their needs of the lower-order. Managers, therefore provide motivators (to satisfy their growth needs) to avoid frustration in people's attitude and regression down the need hierarchy. This will be of interest to both, individuals and the organisation.

4. Acquired Needs Theory (David C. McClelland)

Another theory about human needs, called McClelland's Acquired Needs Theory, focuses on the needs that people acquire through their life experiences. This theory, formulated by

David C. McClelland in the year 1960 emphasises three of the needs human beings develop in their life-times:

(1) Need for achievement (n Ach) – the desire to do something better or more efficiently than it has ever been done before.

(2) Need for power (n Power) – the desired to control, influence, or be responsible for others.

(3) Need for affiliation (n Aff) – the desire to maintain close, friendly, personal relationships.

The individual's early life experiences determine which of these needs will be highly developed and therefore dominate the personality.

McClelland's studies of these three acquired human needs have significant implications for management.

(A) Need for Achievement. McClelland claims that in some business people, need to achieve is so strong that it is more motivating than the quest for profits. To maximise their satisfaction, individuals with high achievement needs set goals for themselves that are challenging, yet achievable. Although such people are willing to assume risk, they assess it carefully because they do not want to fail. Therefore, they will avoid tasks that involve too much risk. People with a low need for achievement, on the other hand, generally avoid challenges, responsibilities and risk.

(B) Need for Power. People with a high need for power are greatly motivated to influence others and to assume responsibility for subordinates' behaviour. They are likely to seek advancement and to take on increasingly responsible work activities to earn that advancement. Power-oriented managers are comfortable in competitive situations and enjoy their decision-making role.

(C) Need for Affiliation. Managers with a high need for affiliation have a cooperative and team-centered managerial style. They prefer to influence subordinates to complete tasks through team efforts. The danger is that managers with a high need for affiliation can lose their effectiveness of their need for social approval and friendship interferes with their willingness to make managerial decisions.

5. Expectancy Theory (Victor H. Vroom)

Expectancy theory, developed by Vroom and others, explain why people choose one behaviour in preference to another. Motivation to engage in a given behaviour is determined by : (*i*) individual's perception or expectancy about outcomes or rewards likely to result from his given behaviour; and (*ii*) valence of attractiveness of that reward to the satisfaction of his needs. Thus motivation is the product of an individual's perception of what he is going to achieve if he follows a particular course of action, and whether what he achieves will satisfy his needs. Symbolically,

$$M = \text{Valence} \times \text{Expectancy}$$

where valence is the attractiveness of outcomes for need fulfillment and expectancy is the probability that a particular action will lead to desired outcome. This theory demonstrates that an individual will choose a behaviour only when he believe that there is high probability of getting the desired outcomes and that these outcomes are attractive enough to him in the sense of their ability to satisfy his needs. A person will not choose a behaviour pattern if expectancy of the desired outcomes is low or negative. Therefore, motivation to do something will depend on both valence and expectancy.

6. Equity Theory (J.Stacy Adams)

According to J. Stacy Adams, people compare the rewards of their performance with the rewards of their follow workers get for similar performance. Rewards are the outcomes of a person's performance and performance is the input of a person by virtue of his knowledge, skill, ability, education and competence. After comparing rewards in relation to his inputs with those of others, they judge the fairness of the rewards received.

The relationship between inputs and outcomes of one person and inputs and outcomes of another person is mathematically expressed as follows:

$$\text{Equity} = \frac{\text{Person's outcomes}}{\text{Person's inputs}} = \frac{\text{Other's outcomes}}{\text{Other's inputs}}$$

The impact of inequity on the person is as follows:

(*i*) Perceived inequity creates tension in the person.

(*ii*) The amount of tension is proportional to the magnitude of inequity.

(*iii*) The tension created in the person will motivate him to reduce it.

(*iv*) The strength of the motivation to reduce inequity is proportional to the perceived inequity.

The theory provides *useful guidance* to managers:

(*i*) It tells managers that equity motive is one of the important motives of employees.

(*ii*) Perceptions or feelings are as important in motivation as facts.

(*iii*) While determining a wage and salary structure in the organisation managers must pay attention to equity considerations.

Demerits

(*i*) The theory is somewhat narrow in its emphasis on visible rewards.

(*ii*) The theory is easily understood but its application is difficult.

7. Goal Setting Theory

Edwin A. Locke and Gary P. Lathman assert that setting of goals can also be a motivational factor affecting the human behaviour. If goals are attainable, measurable, challenging and within the reach of individuals, they will be motivated to work towards the attainment of these goals. When people feel committed to organisational goals, they are motivated to work hard to achieve those goals and also associate their hard work with returns and rewards.

8. Reinforcement Theory (B.F. Skinner)

Events that happen to people following their behaviour – the consequences of their performance – can reinforce their tendencies to continue or discontinue that behaviour. The consequences can be positive, neutral or negative and can vary from insignificant to overwhelming. The deliberate and appropriate application of them, however, provides a manager with potentially powerful set of motivational tools.

The two principal approaches that can be used to increase the probability of behaviour desired by the manager or organisation are positive or negative reinforcements.

(A) Positive Reinforcements. Positive reinforcements, often referred to as "rewards", are desirable consequences that increase the likelihood of behaviour being repeated in the future. In many instances, the use of positive reinforcements, such as a manager praising an employee for good performance, strengthens the likelyhood of that behaviour in future. Especially if the subordinate does not see such praise as routine.

(B) Negative Reinforcements. The removal of undersirable, or negative, consequences - that is, consequences a person performing an act does not want - can increase the likelyhood of that behaviour being repeated in the future. Removing undersirable consequences is referred to as NEGATIVE REINFORCEMENT, just as the addition of desirable consequences is called POSITIVE REINFORCEMENT. In both cases, they are reinforcing if they cause behaviour to be maintained or increased.

(C) Punishments. Punishments are unwanted consequences given following undesirable behaviour to decrease the likelyhood it will be repeated. In some organisations, punishments are seen as an effective way to prevent behaviour that is not wanted. However, many other organisations discourage punishments often because their use is seen as either inappropriate or ineffective. Also, punishments can have the inadvertent effect of increasing behaviour that isn't wanted.

(D) Extinction. Another way to decrease undersirable behaviours is to avoid providing any positive consequences as the result of that behaviour. This process is referred to as EXTINCTION. It is a well-demonstrated research finding, and a fact of everyday work life, that behaviours that do not lead to positive reinforcements tend not to be repeated, or atleast repeated as much. Managers can use the principle of extinction to their advantage by deliberately not reinforcing employees behaviour that they considerable undesirable.

9. Mc Gregor Theory X and Theory Y

The work of Mayo and his associates paved the way for the development of a popular classification scheme of acceptable and unacceptable managerial styles in management literature. Mc Gregor termed the classification as Theory X and theory Y. He developed two sets of assumptions about human behaviour which held managers in adopting motivators for them. One set of assumption is called Theory X and the other set of assumption Theory Y.

Theory X

Mc Gregor has described the first set of assumptions Theory X, the traditional theory. It represents a conventional approach to motivation and makes negative assumptions about people. Theory X is based in the following assumptions about human behaviour:

1. People in general have in inherent dislike for work and avoid it if they can.
2. They are basically lazy and like to work as little as possible.
3. Most people have lack of ambition.
4. They try to avoid responsibility for fear of failure.
5. They prefer to be led as they are incapable of directing their own behaviour
6. They are by nature resistant to change.
7. They are inherently self-centred and indifferent to Organisational Needs
8. They are gullible not very bright.
9. Workers' lower-order needs are stronger than higher-order needs

This is a pessimistic approach of human behaviour. It provides rigid control, close supervision, one way communication and autocratic style of leadership for motivating human beings. The theory defines management as the art of getting things done by following the carrot and stick approach.

Theory Y

Mc Gregor points out that theory X assumptions are not true representation of human nature and the approach based on such assumptions fails to satisfy the higher level needs of people. He has propounded Theory Y which he believes better represents human behaviour.

The theory Y is based on the following assumptions:

1. People are not by nature passive or resistant to organisational goals.
2. They want to assume responsibility.
3. They want that their organisation to succeed.
4. People are capable of directing their own behaviour.
5. They have need for achievement.
6. Workers are not lazy.
7. The average person learns, under proper conditions, not only to accept but to seek responsibility.
8. People are ambitious.
9. Motivation of work does not come from outside.
10. People are not resistant to change.

Theory Y, thus establishes cooperation between the man in authority and the man at work is achieving the objectives of the organisation. The fact of inter-dependence in human organisation is widely recognised. The theory is participative in the sense that supervisors consult their subordinates about proposed course of action before taking any decision. However, management still takes decision for organisation as a whole.

The points of difference between Theory X and Theory Y are given below:

Theory X	*Theory Y*
1. People do not take initiative to work.	1. People like to initiate work on their own
2. It holds a pessimistic view about human nature	2. It holds optimistic view about human nature
3. People prefer to be directed by managers to work.	3. People are self-directed to work.
4. Focus on lower level needs.	4. Focus on higher level needs.
5. Autocratic leadership.	5. Democratic leadership.
6. Financial incentives more effective.	6. Non-financial incentives more effective.
7. Lack of creativity and resist to change.	7. Creativity widely spread.
8. People are not committed to organisational goals.	8. They integrate personal goals with organisational goals.

10. Theory Z

This theory is propounded by William Ouchi. He made comparative analysis of Japanese and the US-based companies, analysed the way the Japanese and the US managers managed their companies and concluded that most of the successful companies operating in America had integrated the Japanese style of management with the American style of management. Theory Z is, thus, not an independent theory but a hybrid theory of management which incorporates the features of both Japanese and American managerial styles.

It is a new way of viewing the essential nature of man and the factors that motivate him. Theory Z has originated from the Japanese management philosophy. A notable feature of Japanese management is that managers seem to make better use of human capital. One reason why Japan has received utmost attention in the recent past by the organisation scientists is its success in many fronts. At the outset one can notice three apparent reasons for relative success of Japanese system view, their *technology, culture* and the *management system.* The most substantial explanation for the success of these organisations can therefore be in terms of their management system. Actually, their system is such that it integrates individual into the organisation to produce efficiency. Organisational scientists who are working on exploring the realities of the "industrial miracle" of Japanese concerns have been responsible for this new theory called Theory Z. William Ouchi and Alfred Jaeger have been credited with studying and exploring the differences in styles of management of American and Japanese companies.

Features of Theory Z

The distinguishing features of Theory Z are as follows:

1. Employment. Various incentives, financial and non-financial, should be promoted to retain employees in the organisation during sound and adverse conditions.

2. Control. It refers to the methods of control wielded – whether employees are controlled with formal, explicit standards or implict, informal standards. Control of employees through informal standards is advocated by the Japanese philosophy. The appraisal systems take into a number of factors apart from the current level of performance like personality traits, cooperation with co-workers, etc.

3. Decision-making. Since decisions are implemented by subordinates, they should participate in the decision-making processes. There should be free flow of information for consensus in decision-making and effective implementation of decisions.

4. Responsibility. Theory Z focuses on individual responsibility. Every individual should be responsible for his acts.

5. Concern. The focus is on holistic concern. Superiors and subordinates should develop mutual trust and confidence and work as a team towards the organisational goals. People are viewed as human beings, not as mere factors of production.

6. Promotion. The emphasis is on slow evaluation and promotion. Performance-bound promotions are preferred to time-bound promotions.

7. Careers. It focuses on developing the personnel or human resource through job enlargement and job enrichment. Managers should train them for growth and development.

JOB DESIGN

Meaning of Job Design

The organisational work is broken into different jobs and each job involves different activities. The specifications of different activities related to a job comprise the job design. Job design refers to specification of task activities associated with a particular job. It defines a job in terms of content, function and relationship. It is the determination of an individual's work-related responsibilities. Job design involves specifying the contents of a job, the work methods used in its performance and how the job relates to other jobs in an organisation.

JOB SPECIALISATION

Job specialisation is the degree which the overall task of the organisation is broken down and divided into smaller component parts. Job specialisation evolved from the concept of division of labour.

Benefits of Specialisation

1. Workers performing small, simple tasks will become very proficient at each task.
2. Transfer time between tasks decreases.
3. The more narrowly defined a job is, the easier it is to develop specialised equipment to assist with that job.
4. When an employee who performs a highly specialised job is absent, or resigns, the manager is able to train someone new at relatively low cost.

JOB SIMPLIFICATION

It is a way of designing the job where the job is broken into simple and narrow set of activities. It makes a job very simple to perform.

JOB ROTATION

Continuous handling of tasks related to simple jobs can make work monotonous and dull. Job rotation helps workers do away with the monotony by allowing them to work on different jobs which involve different skills and work activities. Job rotation is the practice of shifting employees from one job to another in a planned and systematic manner.

JOB ENLARGEMENT

Combining several routine jobs into one or enlarging the scope of a job by adding variety of tasks is called job enlargement. It removes the dullness of performing the same activity over and over again by giving the employees more tasks to perform on the same job. Workers perform a wider variety of tasks on the job which increases their job satisfaction.

JOB ENRICHMENT

Job enrichment is a concept pioneered by Herzberg when he asserted that enriching a job with more responsibility, autonomy, skills and decision-making power serves as a strong motivational force to increase employees' potential for growth and development. It is a more comprehensive approach than job enlargement. It not only increases the variety of tasks on a job but also the control that worker has over the job.

Benefits of Job Enrichment

1. It provides job satisfaction to employees.
2. It satisfies their growth needs.
3. It helps to reduce absenteeism and labour turnover.
4. It increases employees' internal motivation.
5. It helps to improve productivity and quality of work.

MORALE

INTRODUCTION

Morale is a mental condition or attitude of individuals and groups which determines their willingness to co-operate. It is the attitude that creates a feeling of enthusiasm and happiness during and after working hours. It is sometimes defined as moral condition of an individual as regards discipline and confidence in relation to his job. For some people, it includes the mental and emotional feeling of an individual regarding the tasks expected of him, for still others, morale may mean personal acceptance of group goals. In relation to job, morale may be defined as the extent to which an individual perceives satisfaction of his needs as they stem from his total job situation. A few definitions of the term 'morale' may be noted:

1. "Morale may be defined as the collective attitude of workers towards one another, towards their employer, the management or their work." —J.C. Denyer
2. "Morale has been defined as an attitude of mind which conditions how well or how badly duties are performed." —W.H. Walley
3. "Morale is the capacity of group of people to pull together persistently and consistently in pursuit of a common purpose." —Dr. Leighton
4. "Morale means the co-operative attitude or mental health of a number of people who related to each other on some basis." —Spreigel
5. "Morale represents the attitude of individuals and groups towards their work environment and towards their voluntary co-operation to the full extent of their ability in the best interest of the organisation." —Keith Davis
6. "Morale is mental condition or attitude of individuals and groups which determines their willingness to co-operate. Good morale is evidenced by employee enthusiasm, voluntary conform once with regulations and orders, and the willingness to co-operate with others in the accomplishment of organisation objectives. Poor morale is evidenced by surliness, case of insubordination, discouragement and dislike of job, company associates."

—Edwin P. Flippo

An analysis of the above definitions clearly indicate that morale is the enthusiasm and willingness or readiness with which the individual members of a group set out to accomplish the task given to him. Industrial morale has also be described as the "sense of feeling by an employee, of being accepted and belonging to a group, of employees through adherence to common goals and confidence in the desirability of these goals." Morale of an employee is a collection of attitude, feelings and sentiments towards his employer and also his willingness to strive for the attainment of goals of a particular group of organisation to which he belongs. High morale encourages effective work and low morale tends to poor work. High morale is associated with less industrial troubles and less complaint of disobedience, good feelings among the workers, fewer strikes and lock-out, etc. They are in reverse with the low morale workers.

Prof. Jucius observes, "Definitions of morale are many, a review of them all would show that they define it in terms of what it is, what it does, where it resides and whom it affects and what affects." Thus morale is composed as follow :

1. What it is? - An attitude of mind, an esprit de corps, a state of well (or unwell) being and an emotional force.
2. What it does? - Affects output, quality, costs, discipline, enthusiasm, co-operation and other aspects of success.
3. Where it resides? - In the minds, attitudes and emotions of individuals and groups.
4. Whom it affects? - Immediately employers and executives and ultimately the customer and the community.
5. What is affect? - Willingness to work and co-operate in the best interests of the enterprise.

Morale should be distinguished from motivation. The two concepts are inter-related but differ from each other. Morale is composite of attitudes and feelings whereas motivation is the process of inspiring people. Morale is a group phenomenon while motivation is basically an individual's willingness to work. Morale indicates predisposition towards all aspects of work but motivation is basically predisposition towards the job itself. Morale is a function of group relationships. On the other hand, motivation is a function of needs and incentives. Morale is concerned with the mobilisation of sentiments while motivation is concerned with energy mobilisation.

Morale is the indicator of the attitude of employees towards their jobs, superiors and the organisational environment. Employees with high morale like their jobs and co-operate fully with the management towards the achievement of organisational objectives. High morale is key to proper action by the employees. It keeps the office running smoothly by bringing efficiency and economy in office operations. Low morale refers to a reverse situation, that is, low morale might well lead to the following consequences:

1. Frustration of employees.
2. Excessive complaints and grievances.
3. Friction among the employees.
4. Low productivity.
5. Increased rate of absenteesim.
6. High labour turnover.
7. Waste of materials.
8. Unnecessary disputes over discipline.
9. Creation of resistance groups.
10. Failure to co-operate with management.

MORALE AND PRODUCTIVITY

It is generally assumed that morale is directly related to productivity of the employees. If the morale of the employees is high, it would automatically, lead to higher productivity and conversely if the morale is low, the productivity of the employees will be less. According to *Koontz and Donnell,* "There is evidence from the long experience of many managers that morale does materially influence productivity". The following suggestions may be followed in order to *improve morale* in the organisation:

1. Evolving of an effective system of two-way communication.
2. Keeping the employees informed about organisation policies and inviting their comments there on.
3. To provide suitable job incentives relating to job, security, working conditions, opportunity for promotion, benefits, social status, etc.
4. Making provision of welfare amenities like health, recreation, housing accommodation, medical facilities, etc.
5. Encouraging workers participation in management.
6. Analysing and removing the cause of workers' dissatisfaction in the organisation, if any.
7. Encouraging group activities by the employees, like sports, social get-togetherness, picnics, etc.
8. Providing an effective grievance settlement machinery within the organisation, to hear, employees' complaints and to take steps to remove them.

Distinction between Motivation and Morale

Motivation	*Morale*
1. A person may or may not be motivated to work towards the organisational goals.	1. There may be high or low morale but no situation represents absence of morale.
2. Motivators – positive or negative – both promote the performance of workers.	2. Only positive or high morale improves workers' performance.
3. High motivation leads to high morale.	3. High morale may not lead to high motivation
4. It reflects individual's attitude towards his job.	4. It reflects individual's attitude not only towards his job but also towards his organisation.

To Improve the Morale

1. To create good feelings among the workers and a healthy atmosphere in the firm, the management must promote a high morale in workers.
2. To create harmony among the workers, weekly staff conference may be conducted and everyone will be given a chance to express his feelings.
3. Proper placement is necessary. When a man is not interested to do a particular work, he will be allowed to do the job which he likes.
4. Workers will be allowed to meet his superiors whenever he needs.
5. Workers must be protected from accidents and diseases.
6. Promotion. transfer, demotion, etc.. must be dealt with properly.
7. Settling grievances, facilitating employee-management collaboration, contact with employees union ensuring the co-operation between the workers and the management etc., must be permissible.

Factors Determining Morale

Morale factors are those that affect or influence personnel interest of individuals in relation to their organisation. Any factor which tends to produce favourable attitudes among employees towards organisation and its management is a moral stimulant. On the other hand, any factor that tends to produce unfavourable attitude is a moral depressant.

Morale Stimulants: *Davis* outlines the following factors to be the most usual moral factors in any business organisation:

1. **Worthwhile Objectives** that are compatible with public interests as well as personnel interests of organisation.
2. **Good leadership** is based on a sound philosophy of managements.
3. **Homogeneity** of group characteristics and interests.
4. **Symbolism** and a degree of identity of organisation and personnel interest.
5. **Decentralization and delegation** of responsibility and authority.
6. **Good Techniques** used for handling men, including those for order giving and disciplinary action.
7. **Individual and group opportunities,** including financial and non-financial incentives.
8. A satisfactory physical **work environment.**
9. **Training, education and indoctrination.**
10. **Organisational confidence** based on equity as well as material success.

Morale Depressants

B.H. Walley lists out the following factors to be the *morale depressants:* (Low morale results in:)

1. **Salary**
   (a) Low salaries compared with other departments, other companies in the same area, or other companies in the same industry.
   (b) Disproportionate salaries for effort and responsibility.
2. **Promotion prospects**
   (a) Apparent lack of promotion prospects.
   (b) Promotion of 'wrong' people (favouritism).
3. **Supervisory problems**
   (a) Dislike of supervisors.
   (b) Absurd disciplinary actions for minor infringements of discipline by supervisor.
   (c) Lack of leadership and decision taking.
   (d) Supervisors who do not know their job.
4. **The job**
   (a) Muddle in handling work.
   (b) General lack of efficiency in the office.
   (c) Insufficient work to keep clerks busy.
   (d) Wrong kind of work-clerk either over or under qualified to handle the job.
5. **Working conditions**
   (a) Poor office environment.
   (b) Sub-standard office equipment desks, chairs, lighting, etc.
6. **Management and the worker**
   (a) Badly organised company, dual reporting.
   (b) Lack of knowledge of what is going on in the company.
   (c) Feeling is isolation: sense of being ignored.
7. **Personal factors**
   (a) Wrong size of working group.
   (b) Inability on the part of the clerk to fit into the team.
   (c) Personality factors which affect others in the office.

8. General

(a) Irritating and petty regulations.

(b) Badly introduced changes in the company.

REVIEW QUESTIONS

1. Explain Maslow's theory of need hierarchy. How does this theory help managers in motivating the employees ? (*M.Com., Bangalore*)
2. What is motivation ? What does Maslow's hierarchy of needs tell us about people's needs? (*B.Com., Banaras*)
3. Theory Z is a comprehensive philosophy of management". Comment. (*M.Com., Delhi*)
4. State the various theories of motivation. How do need theories differ from behavioural theories ? (*B.Com., Bhopal*)
5. What do you mean by job design ? What are the different approaches to job design ? (*B.Com., MS*)
6. What is morale? How is it different from motivation? What is morale affect productivity ? (*M.Com., Mysore*)
7. Discuss various methods to promote motivation. (*B.Com., Calicut*)
8. Discuss Herzberg's theory of motivation. (*B.Com., Kerala*)
9. Explain the meaning and importance of morale. (*B.Com., Burdwan*)
10. Compare Theory X and Theory Y of McGregor. (*B.Com., Madurai*)
11. What do you mean by incentives ? Specify non-financial incentives. (*B.Com., Bangalore*)
12. State the salient features of Theory X.

20
CHAPTER

Leadership

- Introduction
- Meaning
- Definitions
- Types of powers
- Nature of leadership
- Functions of a leader
- Importance of leadership
- Manager and a Leader
- Qualities of a leader
- Leadership style
- Theories of Leadership
- Review Questions

INTRODUCTION

Leadership is an abstract quality in a human being to induce others, that is, his followers, to do whatever they are directed to do with zeal and confidence. It is a quality or ability of an individual to persuade others to seek defined objectives enthusiastically. Every organisation, — family, group, society, business or any other organisation — needs a leader who leads the organisation to the best of his ability. The leader is a force of the organisation that designs, executes, coordinates and controls all the functions of an organisation, that is, planning, executing, organising, directing and controlling.

Leadership is an important element of directing process. To get things done by subordinates, the manager has to lead and guide their activities. Leadership is an influence process. By influencing the working behaviour of subordinates, the manager directs it towards the accomplishment of organisational objectives. Leadership is a universal phenomenon found in every group of people. The leader is a person who influences the attitudes and behaviour of others in group activity. A leader guides and directs other people towards the achievement of group objectives. Leadership is a social influence process. Leadership cannot exists without a leader and followers. Leadership elicits voluntary action on the part of followers. Finally, leadership results in followers' behaviour, that is purposeful and goal-directed in some sort of organised setting.

MEANING

Leadership is required in every organisation, the success or failure of an organisation to the great extent depends on the quality of leadership particularly on the part of top management. It is true that the manager can manage without having qualities of leadership but if he has leadership qualities, he can manage efficiently. Peter Drucker has rightly points out that "the managers or business leaders are the basic and scarce resource of any business enterprise and most of the failures of business establishment has been attributed to ineffective leadership." It is because by using leadership qualities, the manager develops vision about organisation and directs the activities of members in that direction.

Leader is an integral part of work and social life. In any situation, where a group of people want to accomplish a common goal, a leader is required. Leadership behaviour occurs in almost all formal and informal situations. Leadership behaviour occurs in business organisations where the leader influences people to work towards common goals. People have to be guided to contribute to organisational goals with zeal and confidence. Zeal is ardour, earnestness and intensity in the execution of work and confidence reflects experience and technical ability. The ability of individuals to influence the behaviour of others is known as leadership. Leaders exploit human potential and transform it into output.

A leader is one who guides and directs other people. He gives the efforts of his followers a direction and purpose by influencing their behaviour. Therefore, leadership may be defined as the quality of behaviour of a person by which he is able to persuade others to seek the goals enthusiastically. It is the force which binds a group together and motivates it towards certain goals. According to George R. Terry, "Leadership is the activity of influencing people to strive willingly for mutual objectives." Thus, leadership is a process involving two or more people in which one attempts to influence the other's behaviour towards the accomplishment of some goals.

DEFINITIONS

A few definitions of leadership may be helpful in clarifying the concept:

1. "Leadership is that combination of qualities by the possession of which one is able to get something done by others, chiefly because, through his influence, they become willing to do so."

   —Ordway Tead

2. 'Leadership can be defined as the process by which an executive imaginatively directs, guides and influences the work of others in choosing and attaining specific goals by mediating between the individual and the organisation in such a manner that both will obtain maximum satisfaction.'

—Haimann

3. "Leadership is the process of influence on a group in a specific set of circumstances that stimulates people to strive willingly to attain organisation objectives, giving them the experience of helping to attain the common objectives and satisfaction with the type of leadership provided."

—James Cribbin

4. "Leadership is the ability to persuade others to seek defined objectives enthusiastically. It is the human factor which binds a group together and motivates it towards goals."

—Keith Davis

5. "Leadership is the process of influencing others to work towards the attainment of specific goals."

—Pearce and Robinson

6. 'Leadership is the relationship in which the leader influences others to work together willingly no related tasks to attain goals desired by the leader and/or group."

—Terry and Franklin

TYPES OF POWERS

Power comes from specific and identifiable sources. The two major types of power, based on their sources, are (1) Position Powers and (2) Personal Powers. Position power is based on manager's rank in an organisation. Personal power is based on a person's individual characteristics.

1. Position Powers

The powers associated with a position, include legitimate power, reward power and coercive power.

(i) Legitimate power

Legitimate power is a type of position power granted to a person – for example, a manager – by the organisation. It is sometimes called formal authority. In the work setting, legitimate power is intended to give a manager the right to expect compliance by his employees.

(ii) Reward power

One of the strongest sources of position power for any manager is reward power, that is, the authority to give out rewards, especially differing amounts of highly valued rewards to different people. Exercising this power includes giving salary increases and recommending employees for promotion. Being wealthy leads to having considerable reward power, and being an extremely wealthy leader has become almost synonymous with power.

(iii) Coercive power

Coercive power is a leader's control over punishments. Organisational punishments include assignment to undersirable working hours, demotion and firing. Effective leaders generally avoid heavy reliance on coercive power because it creates resentment and sometimes retaliation.

2. Personal Powers

Personal powers are attached to a person and stay with that individual regardless of the position or the organisation. For those who want to be leaders, personal powers are especially valuable because they do not depend directly or only on the actions of others or of the organisation. The two major types are expert power and referent power.

(i) Expert Power

Expert power is based on specialised knowledge, not readily available to many people. It is potential source of power because other people depend on, or need advice from, those who have that expertise. For instances, an advertising copywriter with a proven record of writing winning and slogan has expert power, and so does a marketing manager who knows how to create demand for a product.

(ii) Referent Power

When people are attracted to, or identify with, someone, that person acquires what is called referent power. This power is gained because other people "refer" to that person. They want to please that person or in some way receive acceptance. A leader enjoys this power because of his skills and traits. People follow leaders because they like to associate themselves with them. They react favourably and behave the way their leader want them to behave.

NATURE OF LEADERSHIP

An analysis of the above definitions reveals the following characteristics of leadership:

1. There must be a group of followers, because leadership cannot flourish in a vacuum. Leadership cannot be imagined without followers.
2. Leadership is the ability to form a group of followers voluntarily without the use of coercion.
3. Leadership is a process of inter-personal influence by which leader influences the followers in a situation to strive willingly towards the realisation of common goals.
4. Leadership is a continuous process of influencing behaviour. An individual is said to be a leader only when he is accepted as a leader by a group of persons and there is communication between the leader and the group.
5. Leadership is basically a personal quality of character in a man who influences the behaviour of others. This quality motivates people to be with the leaders.
6. The objectives of both the leader and his men are one and the same. In the words of Terry, "Leadership is the activity of influencing people to strike willingly for mutual objectives."
7. The style of leadership is determined by the set of circumstances prevailing. Thus, there is no one style of leadership which can be applied in all situations.
8. Wherever a person influences the behaviour of others, he exercises leadership. A family, a hospital, business firm, a charitable organisation, etc. require leadership sometime or the other.
9. A good leader shares ideas, credits, experiences, etc. with his followers. He lets the subordinates to influence his behaviour so that they are satisfied with the type of leadership provided. A successful leader is one who influences the behaviour, attitudes and beliefs of his followers.

FUNCTIONS OF A LEADER

Some important functions of a leader are given below:

1. Team Work

One of the main functions of the leader is to develop and combine his followers as a team. A good leader, by his personal conduct and behaviours infuses confidence in his followers by directing them to work, giving them advice and getting through them good results in the organisation. Leader needs to create a congenial and healthy working environment for his team.

2. Integration of Teamwork

One of the main functions of a leader is to integrate the efforts of the followers and the organisational objectives. He directs the efforts of the group towards the attainment of the objectives of the organisation of which he is a part.

3. Managing of Time

Time is precious and vital but often overlooked by the management. The leader has a thorough knowledge of the principles of time management, he is in a position to monitor time in the interests of the organisation.

4. Communications

A leader must communicate the organisational policies, procedures and programmes, to the members of the organisation group; apart from informing the responsibility and authority.

5. Cooperation

A leader gets cooperation of his followers. He should be able in convincing his followers that success of enterprise is their own success. Establishment of coordination among different activities of the enterprise and the activities of different employees is another important function of a leader.

6. Use of Power

If a leader is to achieve the goals of the organisation expected of him, he must dominate his followers by using organisational power and authority. He must use power and authority in a manner that will elicit stimulate a positive response from the subordinates. A leader interprets the objectives of the group and lays down policies and programmes for attaining them. He acts as the planner and policy maker.

7. Discipline

Discipline is the force which directs, regulates and controls the activities of all enterprise. Therefore, the important function of a leader is to maintain discipline in the enterprise. If all the employees of an enterprise are disciplined, it becomes very easy for the enterprise to achieve its objects.

8. Motivating Followers

An important function of a leader is to motivate his subordinates to contribute their efforts to achieve the objects of enterprise. These motivation may be monetary or non-monetary.

9. Group Effectiveness

A leader provides an adequate reward structure to encourage the performance of employees, delegate authority wherever necessary and invite participation of employees in decision-making.

10. Representation

A leader is the representative of management and also the representative of subordinates. He takes initiative in all matters of interest to the group and strives to fulfil the psychological needs of his followers.

IMPORTANCE OF LEADERSHIP

Leadership is an indispensable factor in managing the affairs of an organisation successfully and effectively. Here, we are more concerned about the manager as a leader. An organisation, howsoever good it may be, cannot be run effectively without effective leadership. A leader has to create a sense of confidence in the minds of the employees and provide motive power to group efforts. It develops a coordinated network within the organisation, and directs people psychologically towards the accomplishment of group goals. A good manager achieves maximum cooperation from the group members by providing two-way communication and motivating them. He also coordinates the activities of the group members by reconciling their individual goals with the organisational goals.

Importance of leadership can be understood by the following functions which a leader generally performs:

1. Determination of Goals

A leader performs the creative function of laying down goals and policies for the followers. He acts as a guide in interpreting the goals and policies.

2. Develops Team Spirits

Leader inculcates a sense of collectivism in the employees and forces them to work as a team. Individuals within the group may possess varied interests and multiple goals. A leader has to reconcile their conflicting goals and restore equilibrium.

3. Inspiration to Employees

A leader creates a strong urge in employees for higher performance. He lifts a man's vision to higher sights. By showing the proper way to do a job, a leader helps employees to give their best to the organisation. The personal conduct and behaviour of a leader can direct others to achieve organisational goals. The main responsibility of a leader is to get the work done effectively by the followers. The followers cannot work hard and effectively without leadership. A good leader divides organisational activities among the employees in a systematic manner.

4. Organisation Structure

An organisation structure cannot provide for all kinds of relationships. That is why, informal relationships made to exist within the framework or formal organiation structure. But the organisation structure is complete or perfect with the help of an effective leadership. A leader guides the employees towards the achievement of organisational objectives. He is available for advice whenever an employee faces any problem.

5. Developing a Good Relation

Human relations represent the relations between the leaders and the followers. An efficient leader can develop the skill of the subordinates and promote self-confidence apart from motivation. The leader creates opportunities to show their abilities and induces the subordinates to work towards the accomplishment of goals. The leader promotes the cooperative attitude of workers and maintains better relations with them.

6. Creates Confidence

A good manager creates confidence in his subordinates by directing them, giving them advice and ensuring through them good results in the organisation- A confident employee proves to be an asset for the organisation. He provides psychological support and infuses the spirit of enthusiasm in subordinates by his conduct and discussion.

7. Spirit of Cooperation

A dynamic leader can coordinate the activities of the subordinates. In an organisation, workers are working in groups, therefore, there is a need for coordination among the group members. A leader promotes the spirits of coordination among the subordinates. Leadership is essential to group action. Without sound leadership, cooperative effort towards a goal is not possible.

8. Implementing Change

Leadership helps introducing changes in the organisation. The manager who has the qualities of leadership finds it easy to convince the employees about the positive effects of change to be introduced and thereby reduces their resistance to change.

9. Representing Members

A leader is a representative of members led by him. He makes all efforts for directing the behaviour of members towards the accomplishment of group goals. He takes initiative in all matters of interest to the group. He also attempts to fulfil the psychological needs of subordinates.

10. Utilisation of Manpower

The plans, policies and programmes of an organisation do not work themselves. There is a need for a leader. The leader implements the plans, policies and programmes to utilise the available manpower effectively and highest production with minimum cost. He delegates authority whenever needed and invites participation from the employees to achieve better results.

11. Appropriate Counsellor

Employees often suffer from emotional disequilibrium in organisation. Leader can render advice and can try to remove barriers, real or imaginary and instill confidence in the employees. Leadership creates a cooperative and wholesome attitude among employees for successful work accomplishment.

12. Builds Morale

By providing effective leadership, morale of employees is raised very high, ensuring high productivity and stability in the organisation. Higher productivity is the result of high morale. It can conclude that good leadership is indispensable in all managerial functions whether it is motivation, communication or direction.

Distinction Between a Manager and a Leader

Manager	*Leader*
1. A manager does things right.	1. A leader does the right thing.
2. He uses authority.	2. He uses power.
3. He manages subordinates.	3. He inspires people.
4. He may carry out the functions of leaders also.	4. Leader do not normally carry out the functions of managers.
5. He utilises material resources	5. He utilises human resources.
6. He performs organising and staffing functions.	6. He performs aligning functions.
7. He is concerned with controlling and problem solving.	7. He is concerned with motivating and inspiring.
8. "Planning and budgeting' are important to a manager.	8. 'Establishing direction" is important to a leader.
9. He has a short range view.	9. He has long range perspective.
10. He asks "how and why".	10. He asks "what and why".

QUALITIES OF A LEADER

Some of the qualities that make a good leader can be summarised as follows:

1. **Intelligence.** A leader must have above average knowledge and intelligence.
2. **Self-confidence.** He should have confidence in himself and strong will-power.
3. **Sound Physique.** Sound physical and mental health are essential to bear the burden of leadership.
4. **Maturity.** He should possess a high level of emotional stability and cool temperament.

5. **Empathy.** He should have the ability to see things from others' point of view.
6. **Decisiveness.** He should have sound judgement and ability to take quick action.
7. **Foresightedness and Vision.** He should have the capacity to look forward and anticipate the events.
8. **Motivation.** He should understand what motivates people.
9. **Responsibility.** He must be prepared to shoulder the responsibility for the consequence of any steps he takes.
10. **Open Mind.** He should absorb and adopt new ideas according to situations.
11. **Human Relation.** He must have the capacity to understand people and develop friendly relations with his subordinates.
12. **Communication Skills.** He should communicate clearly, precisely and completely.
13. **Decision Making Skills.** He must understand that "Leadership is a process of Decision-Making".
14. **Trustworthy.** He must be honest and trustworthy; and should be free from bias.
15. **Emotional Stability.** He should analyse problems rationally and take decision without bias and should not have short temper.

LEADERSHIP STYLE

The success of an organisation depends upon the leadership style followed by its leaders. That is, leadership style is defined as the manner in which the leader supervises and directs the members of the team. Different leadership styles exist among leaders in different situations. The style is the outcome of leader's personality, philosophy, experience and value system. This is the practical aspect of the leadership behaviour.

Leadership style describes how a leader has relationship with his group. Some of the leadership styles are discussed below:

1. Motivational Style (Rewards)	:	Positive Style Negative style
2. Power Style	:	Autocratic (Authoritarian) style Participative (Democratic) Style Laissez-faire (Free Rein) Style
3. Authority Style	:	Formal Leaders Informal Leaders
4. Orientation Style	:	Employee Oriented Style Task (Production) Oriented Style

The important styles are outlined below:

1. Positive Style

A leader motivates his employees to work hard by offering them rewards for better performance. The more the reward, the higher is the efficiency. Positive leaders promote industrial peace. Positive leadership results in high morale, high job satisfaction and his contribution to organisational productivity.

2. Negative Style

A leader forces his employees to work hard and penalises them if the work is not upto the organisation's standard. The penalty is given according to the performance. The penalty will be severe one if the performance has more short-comings. Negative style has high human cost.

3. Autocratic (Authoritarian) Style

In this style, the leaders have full power or authority to take a decision. The leaders create a work situation under which the employees are expected to work. The workers will obey the instructions of the leader; and the leaders have full responsibility. Subordinates are not aware of organisation goals. At the same time, the employees feel insecure and are afraid of the authority of the leader. The reason is that such leaders have the desire to wield loving for more powers.

Autocratic leader is completely opposite to democratic leader. Autocratic leadership is based on the principle of power. Such a leader wants to concentrate all the powers with himself.

Benefits of Autocratic Style

1. Subordinates need not take any decision.
2. Quick decision is possible.
3. It provides strong motivation to employees.
4. Less competent employees can perform their job effectively.

Drawback of Autocratic Style

1. Employees dislike the style.
2. Employees have no opportunity for development.
3. Workers feel frustrated and dissatisfied; therefore the productivity is affected.

4. Democratic (Participative) Style

This style is just opposite to autocratic style. The authority is decentralised. Thus the subordinates are permitted to take part in the decision-making. The decisions are taken wholeheartedly. The leader has consultation with his subordinates before taking a decision. The subordinates know the goals of the organisation. Therefore, they offer good ideas during discussions. Generally, most of the leaders follow this style. The democratic leader makes decisions by consulting his team whilst still maintaining control over the group.

Benefits of Democratic Style

1. Subordinates are aware of the goals of the organisation.
2. Workers get opportunity to show their talent.
3. Workers show more interest in increasing the productivity.
4. There is an increase in job satisfaction and cooperation of workers.
5. This style reduces absenteeism and labour turnover.

Drawbacks of Democratic Style

1. Making a decision and its implementation require more time.
2. Workers can easily dominate the leader.
3. Workers may not always willing to offer suggestions.

5. Laissez faire (Free Rein) Style

The leaders have no authority and responsibility under this style. The subordinates themselves take decisions for which they get authority. This style is employee-contred. Subordiantes are free to establish their own goals and chart out the course of action. They train themselves and are self motivated.

The leaders acts as a liason officer between the employees and the outside world. He brings the information which is needed to the employees. The information is utilised by the employees to do their job. The Laissez-faire is usually appropriate when leaders lead a team of highly motivated and skilled people, who have produced excellent work in the past. Once a leader has established that his team is confident, capable and motivated, it is often best to step back and let them get on with the task.

Benefits of Laissez-faire

1. The talent of the workers is properly utilised.
2. Workers get opportunity to develop their talent.
3. There is job satisfaction and high morale among employees.

Drawback of Laissez faire

1. The contribution of the leader is nothing.
2. The leader does not care to motivate the subordinates.
3. The leader does not support the subordinates.

6. Formal Leaders

Formal leaders have formal authority over their subordinates. They have authority by virtue of their position in the organisation. They are formally elected by management. They do not satisfy social and psychological needs of the subordinates. They are more of managers than leaders.

7. Informal Leaders

Informal leaders do not have formal authority over the workers. They enjoy the authority to issue orders and instructions because of their personal qualities, abilities, influential power, etc. and not because of their position in the hierarchy. They are not appointed by managers. If they have to choose between instructions issued by formal and informal leaders, they are more likely to follow the informal leaders. Generally, management is resistant to informal leaders.

8. Employee Oriented Leadership

Here, the leader is more concerned about their subordinates. Such leaders try to provide better working conditions and environment and satisfy the needs of workers and pay attention to interests and attitudes of employees.

9. Task (Production) Oriented Leadership

Leaders of this style believe that their interest is concerned with only to get the work done by subordinates. They keep subordinates busy all the times. They ignore the human aspects of subordinates.

A prudent manager must combine the two styles in varying degrees. He must think of higher production by improving men, machines, materials and methods but not at the cost of human values.

THEORIES OF LEADERSHIP

Leadership is complex and multidimensional in character what makes a leader effective is a question which cannot be answered easily. Leadership is one of the most fascinating and ancient subject. Leadership qualities are different and there are different behavioural theories of leadership depicting these varied qualities of leadership. The leadership concept has been supported by various theories. These theories have been developed through several stages of evolution. Early leadership theories focused more on qualities distinguishing between leaders and followers, whereas later theories looked at other variables such as skill level, and situational and circumstantial factors. Researches have led to various theories on leadership. The prominent among them are given below:

1. Personality Theories
2. Behaviour Theories
3. Situational (Contingency) Theories
4. The Followers' Acceptance Theory

1. Personality Theories

Personality theories can be classified into "Greatman Theory" and "Trait Theory"

(a) Greatman Theory (Charismatic)

Greatman theories assume that the capacity for leadership is inherent – that great leaders are born, not made. These theories often portray great leaders as heroic, mystic and destined to rise to leadership when needed. The "Greatman' was used because, at the time, leadership was thought of primarily as a male quality, especially in terms of military leadership. According to this theory, leaders are born and not made, and the various qualities which the leader is supposed to have, cannot be cultivated or developed because they are present and carried in genes. It was further supported by the fact that leadership emerged frequently within the same prominent families. Leaders, such as Alexander the Great, Napoleon, Mahatma Gandhi, etc. were said to have been blessed with an inborn ability to lead the masses.

(b) Trait Theory

One of the oldest and even popular theories was the trait approach. Trait means quality. According to this theory, leadership behaviour is influenced by certain qualities of a leader. That is, leadership behaviour is total traits. This theory seeks to determine the universal personal traits of effective leaders. Good personality, imagination, initiative, emotional stability, sincerity, mental ability, courage, persuasion, etc. are considered to be the traits of a successful leader.

The trait model of leadership focused on identifying the personal characteristics that cause effective leadership. Researchers thought effective leaders must have certain personal qualities that set them apart from ineffective leaders and from people who never become leaders. Hundreds of studies indicate that certain personal characteristics do appear to be associated with effective leadership.

Traits and Personal Characteristics (Effective Leadership)

Traits	*Description*
Intelligence:	helps managers to understand complex issues to solve problems.
Knowledge and experties:	helps managers to make good decisions and discover ways to increase efficiency and effectiveness.
Dominance:	helps managers to influence their subordinates to achieve organisational goals.
Self-confidence:	contributes to manager's effectively influencing subordinates and persisting when face with obstacles or difficulties.
High energy:	help managers deal with the many demand they face.
Tolerance for stress:	helps managers deal with uncertainty and make difficult decisions.
Integrity and honesty:	helps managers behave ethically and earn their subordinates' trust and confidence.
Maturity:	helps managers to avoid acting selfishly, control their feelings and admit when they have made a mistake.

Researchers have found out a number of qualities of leadership from their study. A successful leader has the following qualities:

1. Good personality
2. Ability to take quick decision

3. Persuasion
4. Intelligence
5. Reliability
6. Will power
7. Friendliness and Affection
8. Decisiveness
9. Teaching skill
10. Sense of Justice
11. Ability to understand
12. Tirelessness
13. Courage to face competitors
14. Different Thinking
15. Physical fitness
16. Communication skill
17. Motivation ability
18. Sense of humour
19. Empathy
20. Social skill
21. Technical competence
22. Moral qualities
23. Cost consciousness
24. Ability to get along
25. Moral courage

However, this theory has been criticised because of certain important defects: they are shown below:

1. Studies about the theory have not produced clear results.
2. The traits are not common and uniform.
3. The comparative importance of various qualities has not been properly understood and reported.
4. It does not recognize the influence of situational factors.
5. It fails to mention the traits which are necessary to maintain leadership.

2. Behaviour Theories

Traitists theory fails to explain the leadership phenomenon. The trait theory seeks to explain leadership on the basis of what leaders are and not what leaders do. The behaviourists, in contrast to traitists, attempt to explain effective leadership in terms of what leaders do. So, they emphasise that strong leadership is the result of effective role behaviour. Leadership is shown by a person's acts more than by his traits. The basis of this approach lies in how the management viewed the workers. Behaviour theory concentrated on explaining the behaviour of leaders. The behaviour of the followers changed according to the changes in the behaviour of the leaders. So, what the leader does is the main concern.

The behavioural approach is superior to trait approach in so far as it stresses upon what a leader does than what he is. The attention here is on leadership styles. Several research studies, for examples, Ohio State University, University of Michigan Blake, and Mouton's management Grid, etc., have been conducted to analyse leader's behaviour and its effect on leadership effectiveness. But no one style has been found normative or ideal. A particular behaviour may be effective in one situation but ineffective in another. The time factor becomes a vital element which has not been considered in this theory. Leadership style is a multi-dimensional concept and it is flexible.

3. Situational Theory

The situational theory states that there are certain situations in particular groups which can mould the leadership skills in a person. The work situation and its influence is a major factor in leadership. A leader, according to this concept, understands the needs of the situation and then acts accordingly.

The situational theory does not recognise the inborn qualities of leadership. This theory states that there is not one be "best style" of leadership universally applicable to all situations. A particular situation may create a new leader out of a person who was just a follower. The primary aspect of this theory is that leadership is the interaction between the leader and the group. But this theory states that the leadership style adopted for one particular situation may not be relevant in another situation. The situational theory rejects the "one best style" of leadership applicable to all situations.

The situational approach concentrates on the importance of the situation in the study of leadership. A variety of people with differing personalities and from different backgrounds have emerged as effective leaders in different situations. The person who becomes the leader of the work group is thought to be the person who knows best what to do and is seen by the group as the most suitable leader in the particular situation. The continuum of leadership behaviour draws attention to forces in the situation as one of the main forces influencing the nature of managerial behaviour. The situational approach emphasis the situation as the dominant feature in considering the characteristics of effective leadership.

Although number of situational theories have been developed so far, they all share one fundamental assumption that successful leadership occurs when the leader's style matches the situation. They emphasise need for greater degree of flexibility in leadership and reject the notion of universally applicable style of leadership.

4. The Followers' Acceptance Theory

The theory asserts that followers are important in deciding whether an individual is or is not their leader. If the followers recognise or accept him as their leader, he is the leader irrespective of his traits and behaviour. If the followers discard him or do not accept a person as leader, he cannot be their leader, no matter how strong he is. According to this theory, followers must form groups because a leader represents the group and not individuals. The theory assumes that the groups have certain basic needs which, they expect, shall be fulfilled by their leader.

Modern managers are of the opinion that acceptance theory plays a significant role in managing the people at present. Followers disown their leader when he fails to satisfy their needs. The needs of the group are the crucial and guiding factor in determining the leader.

The major weakness of this theory is that it completely ignores the qualities of the leader.

Transactional Leadership

Transactional leadership is based on legitimate authority within the bureaucratic structure of the organisation. The emphasis is on the clarification of goals and objectives, work task and outcomes and organisational rewards and punishments. Transactional leadership appeals to the self-interest of followers. It is based on a relationship of mutual dependence and an exchange process of: "I will give you this, if you do that."

Transformational Leadership

Transformational leadership, by contrast, is a process of engendering higher levels of motivation and commitment among followers. The emphasis is on generating a vision for the organisation and the leader's ability to appear to higher ideals and values of followers, and creating a feeling of justice, loyalty and trust. In the organisational sense, transformational leadership is about transforming the performance or fortunes of a business.

REVIEW QUESTIONS

1. What is leadership ? Describe the functions of a leader. (*B.Com., Madras*)
2. "Leaders are not born but made". Comment. (*B.Com., Jabalpur*)
3. Is leader the same as manager ? Discuss. (*B.Com., Calicut*)
4. Point out some important qualities that make for successful leadership. Define the concept of empathy. (*M.Com., MS*)
5. "Leadership is situational". Comment. (*B.Com., Bhopal*)
6. Define leadership. Are there any traits which seem to be common to all successful leaders ? (*M.Com., Banaras*)
7. What traits are necessary for a successful leader ? (*M.Com., Agra*)
8. A leader is not necessarily a good manager. Discuss. (*M.Com., Bangalore*)
9. How leadership is different from managership ? (*B.Com., Delhi*)
10. Critically examine the different theories of leadership. (*M.Com., Mysore*)
11. Discuss various leadership styles. How will you secure effective leadership in the management of an organisation ? (*M.Com., Bombay*)
12. Explain the qualities and functions of a leader. (*B.Com., Agra*)

21 CHAPTER

Communication

- Introduction
- Definitions
- Meaning
- Characteristics
- Process of Communication
- Importance of Communication
- Need for Communication
- Objectives of Communication
- Channels of Communication
- Downward Vs Upward
- Formal Vs Informal
- Verbal Communication
    - Oral Communication
    - Written Communication
- Non-verbal Communication
- Effective Communication
- Obstacles in Communication
- Overcoming Barriers to Communication
- Aims of good Communication
- Selection of Communication System
- Communication Network
- Review Questions.

INTRODUCTION

Communication is a natural instinct of all living creatures. It is the basic need of all human beings. It plays significant role in the present day organisations which are complex, dynamic and socially oriented. Effective communication keeps the organisation vital and smooth sailing. Communication is the oxygen of an organisational body. Hence, proper transference of communication from one part of the organisation to another part is essential for the survival and growth of an organisation.

The term "communication" is derived from the Latin word "communis" which means common. Thus, communication may be defined as an exchange of facts, ideas, opinions or emotions to create mutual understanding. It refers to various means of transmitting information from one place to another. Communication is one of the fundamental aspects of all human interaction. The ability to communicate effectively has enabled human beings to build organisations, societies and other social groups that make for survival and better living. "No business can exist without communication." Communication is a management skill and it is an indispensable part of any management. Communication plays the same role in a business organisation as the nervous system in a human body. It is a process of conveyance of information from one person to another. The term communication is used in a wider sense. Communication means not only letters, telegrams, telephone messages, but also transmission of reports, estimates, instructions, invoices, order, etc.

It is two-way exchange of ideas and information that leads to common understanding. In other words, communication means perfect identity of mind. Though the communication underlies all functions of management, it assumes greater importance in the function of directing. For the successful leadership and managership, communication is a must. Communication means and includes every device that may be used to convey meaning from one person to another.

DEFINITIONS

"People don't get along because they fear each other; people fear each other because they don't know each other; they don't know each other because they have not communicated with each other."

—Martin Luther King

"Managers tend to think that when their bulletins are sent they are communicated; but transmission of the message is only the beginning. A manager may send 100 bulletins, but there is no communication until each bulletin is received, read and understood. Communication is what the receiver understands, not what the sender says."

—Keith Davis

"Communication is intercourse by words, letters, symbols or messages and as a way that one organisation member shares meaning and understanding with another."

—Koontz and O'Donnell

"Communication is the process of meaningful interaction among human beings. It is a process by which, meanings are perceived and understandings are reached among human beings."

—McFarland

"Communication is the sum of all things that a person does when he wants to create an understanding in the minds of others. It is a bridge of meaning. It involves a systematic and continuous process of telling, listening and understanding"

—Allen

MEANING OF COMMUNICATION

Communication involves the act of imparting a common idea or understanding to another person and covers any behaviour that affects an exchange of meaning. Communication basically refers to the meaningful transmission of ideas to others, either orally or in writing. The communication can be defined as the process through which two or more persons come to exchange ideas and understanding among them. Communication is in fact a process of sharing information or ideas or the knowledge with others. It can be verbal and non-verbal. It is possible through one's expressions, attitude gestures, tones, words, writing, e-mails, etc. Eyes and nodding of head send speechless message.

CHARACTERISTICS OF COMMUNICATION

Communication is characterised by the following salient features:

1. There should be a sender and a receiver. The message should be interpreted by the receiver in the same sense as intended by the sender.
2. Communication is essentially a two-way process, involving a sender and a receiver.
3. Communication is an ongoing process.
4. Feedback is essential aspect of communication.
5. It pervades all human relationships. It is used by managers at all levels of organisation and in all areas of operations.
6. The purpose of communication is to create mutual understanding. Thus, communication is complete only when the message is correctly understood and the response to it becomes known to the sender.
7. The aim of communication is to elicit actions.
8. Communication is the process by which information is transmitted between individuals.
9. Communication is a goal-oriented process and there is congruence of their (sender and receiver) goals.
10. Communication is an exchange of facts, ideas, opinions or emotions by two or more persons.

PROCESS OF COMMUNICATION

The communication process consists of the following elements:

(1) *Message:* It is what is conveyed by the sender. That is, it is the information, written or spoken, which is to be sent from one person to another.

(2) *Sender*: Sender or communicator is the person who sends a message or an idea. He formulates the message which he wants to convey to others. He initiates the process of communication.

(3) *Encoding*: Sender translates the message into words, symbols or gesture, known to both the parties: that is, transmission of message in words or in any other way is called encoding.

(4) *Channel*: It is the medium or route through which the message is passed from the sender to the receiver. Channel may be formal or informal. The sender may use spoken or written methods.

(5) *Receiver*: The person who receives the message is known as receiver. He may be a reader or listener. Receiver is also known as communicates.

(6) *Decoding*: Decoding is a mental process by which the receiver draws meanings, from the words, symbols or pictures of the message. Receiver does decoding or understands it.

(7) *Feedback*: The effectiveness of communication is measured through feedback. When the sender receives the feedback, the process of communication is said to be completed.

IMPORTANCE OF COMMUNICATION

Communication is a vital tool of management. Communication is not a one way traffic. The process starts from the sender and proceeds to the receiver. But the effectiveness of communication process is further enhanced if the reaction of the 'receiver' to the communication moves in a reverse flow and reaches the 'sender'. This is known as 'feed-back' process. It is said that the success of an organisation depends on the adequacy of communication. The importance of communication is as follows:

1. Effective Functioning of the Organisation

The efficient functioning of the organisation totally depends on the effective communication system. A business organisation consists of people and network of decision affecting them. Managing an organisation is getting things done through others. Communication serves the management and makes everyone aware of what the organisation want to achieve.

2. Smooth Running of the Organisation

A smooth running of an organisation greatly depends on the effective system of communication. It is only through a good and effective office communication system that effective leadership, good human relations, high morale and motivation in the organisation can be maintained to ensure success of management objectives. Business is an open system which constantly interacts with its customers, suppliers, competitors, shareholders, etc. Communication enables an enterprise to satisfy the needs of various parties by interacting with them. When communication stops, organised activity ceases to exist.

3. Proper Planning and Co-ordination

Plans and decisions must be effectively conveyed to those who translate them into action. Effective communication is essential for quick and successful implementation of the management decisions. Good communications are essential to co-ordination. Effective communication is a pre-requisite for solving managerial problems.

4. Exchange of Information

Communication helps executives to acquire more knowledge. It also facilitates executives to share the acquired knowledge with their subordinates which results to increase in the overall managerial skill of people in the organisation. It also help in understanding the problems and offering solutions to them.

5. Human Relations

Most of the conflicts arise due to misunderstood motives and ignorance of facts. Proper communication helps to minimise friction and maximise mutual understanding, co-operation and goodwill. A good relation can be created with the help of an effective method of communication.

6. Basis of Decision-making

Communication is essential for decision-making and planning. The quality of managerial decisions depends on the quality of communication. Effective communication is helpful in the proper implementation of plans and policies of the management.

7. Promotes Industrial Peace

Communication is a two-way traffic which helps promoting cooperation and mutual understanding between both the parties - management and employees. An efficient downward communication helps the management to tell the workers what the organisation wants and how it can be performed. An upward communication helps the workers in putting their suggestions, reactions, etc, before the management. Thus, it promotes the industrial peace.

8. Essential for Planning

Planning, the most important function of management, require extensive communication among the executives and other staff. Similarly, communication is important to control the activities and to evaluate the performances of employees.

9. Leads to Efficient Operations

An effective communication system serves as a lubricant, fostering the smooth and efficient functioning of the enterprise. The achievement of enterprise goals is of paramount importance and communication is one of the important tools available to the manager seeking to attain them. It is through communication that a manager regulates the behaviour of subordinates in the desired direction.

10. Improved Public Relations

A business enterprise comes in contact with several groups - customers, public, Government, etc. Every business enterprise must create and maintain a good corporate image in the society. It is through communication that management can keep cordial relations with the groups. Public relations is mainly the job of effective communication with the external environment.

11. Enhances Motivation and Morale

Through communication, management can keep the employees fully informed of plans, job, changes, etc. The moral and motivation of employees tend to be high when they clearly understand what they are to do. Good communication improves good industrial relations and ensures participative and democratic pattern of management. Effective communication helps managers to know the needs of the workers and workers know the needs of the organisation and thus motivates workers to coordinate their needs with organisational needs.

12. Increases Managerial Efficiency

For the smooth running of the organisation, management conveys directions, goals, targets, instructions and responsibilities to managers. But all is not possible without effective system of communication. Effective leaders guide and inspire the employees to perform their individual and organisational goals. Communication process helps leaders to carry out the leadership functions.

NEED FOR COMMUNICATION

Good and effective communication has always been essential for success in business. Communication is intended to influence action in order to promote the common welfare of an organisation or a group. The purpose of all communication is to bring about a change for the better. Communication has become more important and essential for following reasons:

1. Effective communication between management and employees is necessary **to develop mutual trust and confidence.** Communication plays an important role in the improvement of management-employees relationship.

   A business concern can keep itself in close touch with its customers, investors, dealers and other sections of society through various forms of communication. It is through communication that the information of ideas, emotions, etc. to be conveyed from one person to another, from one person to a group or from one group to another. **Information is the life blood of business**. Organisation requires information, which has to be communicated. Information affects decisions. There is **no business without communication**.

2. Multinational Companies today employs many people and have offices in different parts of the world. Large business houses have a number of branches within the country and

even abroad. It is extremely important that the main office maintains a thorough and up-to-date activities at the branch, the offices with the activities at the main office and maintain some kind of relation among branches. This calls for **an effective and efficient system of communication**.

3. Today, public relations is an important ingredient of every organisation. Public relations is a management function that identifies, establishes and maintains usually beneficial relationships between an organisation and the various publics–its shareholders, its customers, its employees, its suppliers, etc. on which its success and failure depends. Society expects more and more information from organisation. Therefore, the society may be well informed about the company's contributions to the society. **Public relations help to improve its image in society.** For all these, **effective communication is necessary**.
4. Education involves formal communication so as to widen the knowledge and skills. It consists of both teaching and learning. **Education and training of workers are necessary to keep them abreast of new developments and to improve their efficiency.** Lectures, seminar, study tours, etc. are used for training. The main purpose of education is to widen knowledge for the management, for the employees and for the public. **All types of education takes place by means of communication.**
5. Good coordination solves problems as they arise. Excellent coordination anticipates problems and prevent their occurrence. **Effective communication is the essential tool of effective coordination**. Coordination cannot be achieved by an order from the top management. It is achieved only by an understanding of, and respect for, each other's talks. For instance, in a hospital, if the surgeon and the anaesthetist are failed to coordinate each other, the consequences will be fatal to the patient. Persuasive communication in the form of advertisement, personal contacts and publicity becomes essential to survive in the race of competition.
6. Nowadays, employees 'unions are very strong and powerful'. Management has to consult union leader on many matters. **Exchange of information and ideas between the company management and union leaders, through a good and effective communications help to maintain healthy relation between them.**
7. Today changes are common. When a new technology is adopted, training of staff becomes necessary in order to up-to-date their knowledge. **Communication skill is essential for success in every job**. Manager are required to deliver speeches, discussions, etc. and for all these a high degree of communication skill is needed. **The manager is constantly communicating with the man he manages, his superiors and with outsiders.** A recent survey pointed out that 80 – 90% of manager's time is spent in communicating, one way or the other. It is only through communication that he seeks to become a successful and effective manager.

OBJECTIVES OF COMMUNICATION

Communication is a means by which different persons are linked together in a group or organization to attain a common goal. No group activity is possible without communication. It enables the members to co-ordinate, to exchange and to make progress. A good communication should aim at making everyone concerned aware of the goal which the organisation wants to achieve. The two main objectives of communication are to inform and to persuade. A group of persons, whether a social community or a business firm, can pool their effort for a common goal only if all the members of the group know what they are working for and trying to achieve. Individuals and sections in a group will try to persuade one another to change one's attitudes, ideas, etc. so that the whole organisation may benefit. Effective and efficient performance of work in any office calls for providing convenient and efficient means of communication. The specific objective of each message may be to instruct, to advise, to request and so on, depending on the nature of relationship between the transmitter and the receiver. Communication may be downward-top to bottom, upward-bottom to top or horizontal-between persons of same status. Let us briefly look into the goals/objectives of communication.

Objectives of Communication

1. To give and receive information
2. To impart education and training
3. To motivate People
4. To provide counselling
5. To persuade people
6. To receive suggestion
7. To improve morale
8. To provide advice
9. To issue warning
10. To appreciate
11. To issue orders

1. **To Give and Receive Information:** Information may be given orally or in writing. The basic objective of communication is to turn the static into dynamic. Information affects decisions. Information needed for daily work can be given orally. If large groups have to be informed, a meeting may be called. Good management believes in keeping employees well informed about the company's aims, plans, progress and prospects, about working and service conditions, training and promotion opportunities and the benefits available to them. For instance, farmers in India have simple organisation. They need information about weather, prices, availability of seeds, facility of irrigation, market trend, etc. And these pieces of information are gathered from friends, relatives, through radio, television, etc. On the basis of the information gathered a farmer takes decisions: "what and when to sow?" "From where to get seeds?", "How to solve the problems of irrigation?" "How and from where to get financial assistance?", etc. Many companies circulate news about their employees, their achievements and even their family affairs so as to create an atmosphere of social friendliness. However, pointless communication is a waste of time. The purpose of all communication is to bring about change for the better. Communication is intended to influence action in order to promote the common welfare of an organisation or a group.
2. **To Impart Education and Training:** Education means imparting instruction, character building, enriching mental faculties, giving training to human beings, etc. Communication is vital in education. Education is achieved through communication. Employees are trained essentially by communication. Communication can be accomplished by means of lectures, discourses, books, cassettes, videos, seminars, conferences, study-tours, mock-sessions, case studies, etc. All education takes place by means of communication. A supervisor or any other person entrusted with the responsibility for training must have the ability to communicate.
3. **To Motivate People:** Motivation means getting people to give their best. The manager communicates with the people he manages and motivates them. He has to get people to work as a team. The motivation of the employees depends upon the patience and sympathy shown by the management. Motivation cannot be achieved by a single communication. It can be achieved only by a constant policy followed in all communications. Creations of healthy worker attitudes and good relations is a slow and continuous process, which takes

place through communication. It is always advisable to orientate the employees with the company's target, aim, object, etc. through communication.

4. **To Provide Counselling:** Companies which are concerned with employees' welfare have counselling centres for their employees. Services of specialists are engaged for the purpose: and employees receive free medical advice, legal advice and vocational guidance. Counselling can be successful if there is a two way communication.

5. **To Persuade People:** Inducing, compelling or prompting a person to do or to act, mostly in a positive way is persuasion. Managements try to persuade their workers to put in their best effort. Politicians persuade people to vote for them; teachers persuade their pupils to listen to them and study; sellers persuade customers to buy, etc. Persuasion is an important objective of communication. Sales letters, advertisements, etc. seek to persuade customers, When new policies or machineries are introduced, employees resist, fearing retrenchment. In order to accept the change, the managements must persuade them not to fear. Persuasion is more easily done by a person who enjoys respect and confidence of those whom he wishes to persuade. A good enunciation can make a person very persuasive.

6. **To Receive Suggestion:** Suggestions coming from employees are upward communication. The employees actually involved in the work have a better understanding of the shortcomings and can make useful suggestions for improvements. In big concerns suggestions are collected at regular intervals by means of a suggestion box. They are rejected or accepted or further clarification is asked for from the suggestor. Communication is used to convey suggestions or ideas. This is being constantly done in all human groups. Someone makes a suggestion and the others react to it. Such intercourse of ideas and suggestions is the moving force of all action in a society or in any social group like a family, office, factory. state, nation, etc. Effective communication promotes the acceptance. Suggestions and grievances from employees help managers to make necessary changes in disciplinary rules and procedures. Actions taken to enforce discipline become more acceptable to employees when the actions are properly explained.

7. **To Improve Morale:** Morale is the state of discipline and spirit in a body of works, army or nation. Morale must be kept high with constant effort and regular and consistent policy. Rumors of close-down, a take over, retrenchment, etc. cause anxiety and fear in the minds of employees. When morale falls, communication has to be stepped up. When employees are in fear, the top management has to reassure them and keep up their morale. Special morale boosting communications have to be well-timed, carefully planned and coordinated. They must fortify workers against debilitating frustration and inspire them to put in hard work that can produce good results.

8. **To Provide Advice:** Advice is opinion about what to do, how to behave, etc. Therefore it is a kind of information. Parents advise their children. Grown-ups advise young ones. Teachers advise pupils. Politicians advise everyone else. Advice means opinion given as to the action to be taken. Advice is most effective if it is oral-face to face. If the advice is on official matters, the senior can speak with authority. If the advice is on personal matters, it can be offered as a suggestion. However, good communication, in the form of advice facilitates the detection of defects and drawbacks and good results may be expected in a given situation. In any sense of the word, advice denotes some communication which is aimed at bringing about a change.

9. **To Issue Warning:** To warn means to give notice to. A warning may be given orally or in writing. A written warning is often called a memo. Warning may be given to an employee for his indiscipline. Groups may also be warned against activities that disrupt or obstruct smooth functioning or regular work. At first an attempt is made by advice, request,

suggestion, instruction, orders', etc. When all these fail, a warning is given.

We often see notices, such as "DANGER", "NO SMOKING", "BEWARE OF PICK-POCKETS", "UNGUARDED RAILWAY CROSSING", etc. All are warning. They are conveyed by some means of communication.

10. **To Appreciate:** Appreciation of initiative, good effort and work by employees is very useful for creating a good attitude. It may be conveyed orally. If given publicly, it has better effect. Letters of appreciation will certainly boost a flagging morale.

11. **To Issue Orders:** An order operates through communication. In order to get things done, a manager issues orders and instructions to his subordinates. For instances, **"Do that", "Don't do that"., "Sell this product", "Do not buy sub standard items"**, etc. Orders may be disobeyed or ignored. However, one of the objectives of communication is to convey orders, get them operated and receive a feedback. An order is a directive to do something whereas an instruction indicates how to carry out the order.

Man is a social animal. He fosters relation with his fellow-men by means of effective communications, such as listening, speaking and writing. The story of civilization and culture is, to a large extent, the story of man's advancement in the art of communication. The transformation of our planet into a global village owes much to modern communication systems such as the telegraph, the telephone, the television and the internet.

The life blood of a business organisation is purposeful communication. It transfers thought from one person to another. It directs, controls and evaluates each and every activity of the organisation. No group activity is possible without communication.

CHANNELS OF COMMUNICATION

A channel of communication is the path through which messages are transmitted from the sender to the receiver. The classification is on the following basis:

I. On the basis of Organisational Relationship

(A) Formal Communication

(B) Informal Communication

II. On the basis of Direction

(A) Upward communication

(B) Downward Communication

(C) Horizontal Communication (Lateral)

(D) Diagonal (Crosswise) Communication

III. On the basis of Medium of Communication

(A) Verbal Communication:

(a) Oral Communication

(b) Written Communication

(B) Non-verbal Communication

We will explain each of the above communication.

(A) **Formal Communication Channel:** Much of the communication in an organisation is what we call formal communication. It flows in formally established channels and is concerned with work-related matters. All orders, instructions, decisions, etc. are communicated to the subordinates through this channel.

Communication through the chain of command is known as formal communication. Formal communication is planned and established by management. It indicates clearly the authority responsibility relationships involved. It involves the transmission of official messages or information in the formal organisation structure. Such communications are generally in writing and they include transmission of orders, decisions, etc.

Formal Communications are in the following forms:

(a) Downward Communication
(b) Upward Communication
(c) Horizontal (Lateral) Communication
(d) Diagonal (Crosswise) Communication

(a) Downward Communication

It means the flow of communication from the top management downward to the operating level. It may also be called a communication from a superior to a subordinate. It follows the line of authority from the top to the bottom of the organisation hierarchy. Downward communication consists of plans, instructions, orders, rules, etc.

Downward communication can be oral or written. Oral communication can be through speeches, face-to-face interaction, meetings, etc. Written communication can be through letters, pamphlets, bulletins, posters, annual reports, etc.

(b) Upward Communication

Upward communication means the flow of information from the lower levels of the organisation to the higher levels of authority. It passes from subordinate to superior, for instances, from worker to foreman, from foreman to manager, from manager to General Manager, etc. Communication of this type includes ideas, suggestions, complaints, appeal, reports, etc. Upward communication is very important as it serves as the feedback on the effectiveness of downward communication. On the basis of upward communication, the management revises its plans, policies, etc. and makes further planning.

(c) Horizontal (Lateral) Communication

Communication between departments or people on the same level in the managerial hierarchy of an organisation can be termed as horizontal or lateral communication. It is most frequently used channel of communication. Worker communicating with other works; clerks exchanging information with one another; supervisors in a group, discussing some organisational problem at the tea-break, etc. are all engaged in horizontal communication. Functional managers operating at the same level, in different departments through their communication, present a good example of lateral communication. The main use of this dimension of communication is to maintain coordination and review the activities assigned to various subordinates. Further, occasions for lateral communication arise during committee meetings or conferences in which all members of the group mostly peers or equals, interacts.

(d) Diagonal (Cross-wise) communication

Flow of information amongst people of different departments at different levels is known as diagonal communication. When Regional Sales Manager talks to workers of finance or production department, diagonal communication is said to have taken place. This kind of communication is used to speed-up information flow, to improve understanding and to coordinate efforts for the achievement of organisational objectives. A great deal of communication does not follow the organisational hierarchy but cuts across the chain of command. The organisational environment provides many occasion for oral cross-communication.

(B) Informal Communication

There exists in every organisation an informal channel, often called the GRAPEVINE, that does not arise out of the organisational needs, but this is, nevertheless, an integral part of its communication system. Its source lies in man's compulsive instinct to communicate or talk out whatever he feels and thinks with his fellow beings and throw all norms to the wind. Man is gregarious by nature, that is, he likes to move about and form groups. Whenever the groups meet, there is bound to be talking on different subjects. This tendency is more visible in the low rung of the organisation. Informal communication is also known as GRAPEVINE. It represents the unofficial channels of communication which are created and controlled by people themselves rather than the management. This channel follows no definite rules but it spreads very fact and like the grapevine, in any direction.

Distinction Between Downward and Upward Communication

Downward Communication	*Upward Communication*
1. Travels fast	1. Travels slowly
2. Flow is downward	2. Flow is upward
3. From higher to lower levels	3. From lower to higher levels
4. Directive in nature	4. Non-directive
5. Order, manuals, handbook instructions, etc. are Examples.	5. Reports, grievances, protests, suggestions, etc. are examples.

Distinction Between Formal and Informal Communication Channels

Formal Communication Channels	*Informal CommunicationChannel*
1. It is rigid.	1. It is flexible
2. It can be oral and written	2. It is oral.
3. It is a slow means of communication	3. It is a fast means of communication.
4. It is task-oriented.	4. It is people-oriented.
5. Impersonal form	5. Personal and social
6. Official channels	6. Unofficial channels
7. It aims at achieving organisational goals	7. It aims at achieving personal goals.
8. Stable and rigid	8. Flexible and instable
9. It flows in vertical, horizontal and diagonal directions.	9. It flows in every direction.
10. Deliberately planned and systematic	10. Unplanned and spontaneous

VERBAL COMMUNICATION

Verbal Communication means communication through words. We use words to share our thoughts, feelings and ideas with others. Words are meaningless unless the receiver understands them in the same meaning as intended by the sender. When messages are sent through oral words it is known as oral communication and when they are sent through written words, it is known as written communication. Thus, verbal communication is two types: (*i*) Oral communication and (*ii*) Written Communication.

(*i*) Oral Communication

Oral communication may take place in face-to-face conversation or through mechanical devices. This is the most natural way of transmitting the message. Face-to-face communication is more successful because the communicator can make the listener to understand his message not only by the spoken words but also by the gestures he takes. Face-to-face conversation occurs in committee meetings, lectures, conferences, social gathering, interviews, etc.

Mechanical devices are gaining great popularity for communicating the messages in the modern business enterprises. The important devices used include signals, intercom, system, dictaphone, etc.

Merits of face-to-face communication

1. It is a time and money saving device.
2. It is more effective than any other method.
3. It is quicker.
4. It is more easy to measure the effect of communication.
5. It is the only way out during the periods of emergency.
6. It is more flexible.
7. It leads to greater understanding.
8. Doubts can be removed then and there.
9. It fosters a friendly and cooperative spirit.
10. Response of the receiver can be easily evaluated.
11. Secrecy can be maintained.
12. It conveys a personal warmth and friendliness.

Demerits of face-to-face communication

1. It is less reliable.
2. It provides no record for future reference.
3. It is unsuitable for lengthy messages.
4. It may be less accurate.
5. It may have less weight.
6. Poor listening on the part of receiver creates problems.
7. Oral communication is prone to noise.

(ii) Written communication

Written communication means transmission of messages, ideas, thoughts, etc. in writing with documentary proof in the form of notices, letters, hand-outs, circular, etc. Written communication can be used in formal and informal channels. When a message is communicated in writing, it is called written communication. Written Communication is generally used for communicating a message from the top management to the subordinates.

Merits of Written Communication

1. Written message are accurate and exact.
2. It carries greater weight than oral messages.
3. It serves as a permanent reference for future.
4. It is ideal way of sending lengthy messages.
5. It is a legal evidence in case of disputes.
6. It has the widest possible coverage.
7. It is suitable to convey messages to a large number of persons at one and the same time.
8. It is often less expensive than other media.
9. It tends to complete, clear, precise and correct.
10. It is good to send unpleasant messages.
11. Responsibility can be fixed in written communication.
12. It maintains uniformity of policies and procedures.
13. It is free from noise.

What makes a message/communication effective?

It is effective: When the writing is clear:
When the information is correct:
When the message is complete:
When the receiver understands the message at first reading:
When it is free from errors:
When it creates a good relationship. (goodwill)

Demerits of Written Communication

1. Writing is an art. Not everybody can put messages in writing.
2. Written messages lack flexibility.
3. Sender cannot read facial expression of the receiver.
4. It is a costly means of communication.
5. It is a time consuming means of communication.
6. Writing increases paper-work.
7. Secrecy cannot be maintained.

NON-VERBAL COMMUNICATION

Our gestures and facial expressions express what words cannot. We do not communicate through words alone. Expressions through body parts is known as gestural communication. If it is often used to supplement oral communication. Gestural communication is useful in conveying feelings, emotions, and attitudes. Non-verbal communication takes place without use of words. It conveys messages through body movements and audio visual signals. See the following examples:

Gesture	*Meaning*
Nodding the head up and down	Yes
Shaking the head side to side	No
Yawning	Tiredness or boredom
Hand clapping	Praise and appreciation
Biting nails	Insecurity, nervousness

PRINCIPLES OF EFFECTIVE COMMUNICATION

One of the important feature of communication is that it is a two-way traffic. It is very necessary to establish an effective machinery of communication to manage the affairs of the organisation effectively. The success of manager depends on how well he communicates. Therefore, communication is the most vital management tool. The effective system of communication should provide liberty to both parties – management and workers, to convey their ideas, opinions, facts, grievances, etc. to the other party, that is, it must establish a two-way traffic. The management, in order to have effective communication, should keep the following principles of communication in mind:

1. CLARITY: : Effective communication should be as clear as possible.
2. COMPLETENESS : Complete information makes communication effective.
3. BE BRIEF : Long messages become boring and may lose attentiveness of the receiver.
4. LISTENING HABITS : Some people are good speakers but bad listeners. They must develop listening skills also.

5. FOCUS ON NEEDS	:	Communication must satisfy the needs of its receivers.
6. FEEDBACK	:	Feedback is an important element of effective communication.
7. CONSISTENCY	:	The sender should not change his words and actions often.
8. AUTHENTICITY	:	Wrong information will result in wrong decisions.
9. SELF-CONTROL	:	The gestures of the sender should correspond with the message he send.
10. ADEQUACY	:	Inadequate information delays actions and destroys understanding and relations.
11. TIMELINESS	:	Information or ideas must be conveyed at the proper time.
12. ECONOMY	:	Clarity, adequacy and timeliness should not be sacrificed to achieve economy.
13. ATTENTION	:	A manager cannot enforce punctuality if he himself is not punctual. Actions speak louder than words.
14. ACCURACY	:	The communication medium should ensure accuracy in the transmission of messages.
15. SECRECY	:	The communication system should ensure secrecy.
16. SAFETY	:	The communication system should ensure guard against the risk of loss in transit.
17. CREDIBILITY	:	One should convey a message unless it is true and correct.
18. WRITING SKILL	:	Kiss principle to be followed in correspondence Keep it short and Simple. (Kiss)
19. COMPOSITION	:	The rules of grammar and composition must be followed.
20. SIMPLE WORDS	:	The message will be lost if the words are complex.

OBSTACLES (BARRIERS) IN COMMUNICATION

Communication is more effective when it move speedily and smoothly in an uninterrupted flow. Communication is the nerve system of an enterprise. It serves as the lubricant, fostering for the smooth operations of the management process. Despite the development of high speed electronic devices, communications are not successful in many cases. All messages are not effectively transmitted or received. Several obstructions, blockages, hurdles stoppages or bottlenecks, called barriers to communication, distort the message and make communication ineffective. Some of the barriers or obstacles to effective communication are given below:

1. Language Barriers

Words and symbols used to communicate facts and feelings may mean different things to different persons. This may act as a barrier to effective communication. The meaning intended by the sender may be quite different from the meaning followed by the receiver. The language of the sender may be very technical or incomprehensible to the receiver.

2. Inattention Barriers

When the receiver does not pay complete attention to the message, communication becomes ineffective. The efforts to communicate with someone not listening will fail. Generally, people are found paying half attention to what is being communicated orally.

3. Filtering

Filtering means manipulating information in a way that only favourable information is sent to the receiver. Information about failures and non-achievements is not sent upwards. Too many levels intervene causing delay in the transmission and distortion in the message. When the message has to pass through several hands, there is filtering.

4. Status Barriers

Every organisation has some kind of status system. Some individuals have higher status than others. A superior may give only selected information to his subordinates so as to maintain status difference. Subordinates, usually, tend to convey only those things which the superiors would appreciate. Such selective communication is also known as filtering. A subordinate may also feel reluctant to report his shortcomings or may not seek clarification on instructions which are subject to different interpretations for fear of loss of prestige in the eyes of superior.

5. Premature Evaluation

Some people have the tendency to form a judgement before listening to the entire message. This is known as premature evaluation. "Half listening is like racing your engine with the gears in neutral." Premature evaluation and response tend to stop the transfer of information.

6. Perpetual Barriers

Every individual has specific areas of interest. So, he may hear, read or see only that part of the message which is valuable to him. There may be deliberate filtering of the message by the sender.

7. Emotional Reaction

Barriers may also arise due to emotional attitude because when emotions are strong, it is difficult to know the frame of mind of other persons. Emotional attitudes of both, the sender as well as the receiver, obstruct free flow of transmission and understanding of messages.

8. Channel Distortions

Physical or mechanical barriers may also cause distortion of communication. A communication is a two-way process, distance between the sender and the receiver of the message is an important barrier to communication. Many people talking simultaneously, inaudible telephone lines, electronic disturbances, wrong transcriptions in telex massages, noise, etc. are examples of channels distortion.

9. Noise

Noise is quite often a barrier to communication. Noises, mechanical as well as natural, are a barrier to effective communication. They distract both sender and the receiver of the messages. For example, a factory that employs noisy machines hinder oral communication. Conversation becomes difficult due to physical noise and hence the messages get distorted and unclear.

10. Time and Distance

Smooth flow of communication is quite often affected by the time and distance. There is no doubt that the development of computer technology has made communication very fast and it has even overcome the space barrier. However, sometimes owing to the breakdown of modern equipment, communication is interrupted or delayed. Conveying a message at the right time to the right place is essential. Imperfect and delayed information is of little use and often creates confusion.

11. Interpretation of Words

Communication is carried on through words, whether spoken or written. Words are capable of communicating a variety of meanings. When the giver uses words or phrases which have a variety of meaning, the listener may not get the proper message or understand it in a different sense. It is possible that the receiver of a message does not assign the same meaning to a word that the sender has intended. This may lead to miscommunication.

12. Unclarified Assumptions

Many a time communication suffers because of vague or unclarified assumptions. When authority is delegated, it should be clear. One should know clearly what one is expected to do. It must be clear in the message itself. Unclarified assumptions lead to complications.

13. Closed Mind

A person who assumes that he knows everything will be rigid and dogmatic. Such a person is of limited intellectual acumen and narrow interests. When a junior comes to an executive with some new ideas, the executive should listen to him with an open mind. However, if he is closed minded, communication will breakdown as he is not prepared to consider his junior's ideas. The junior will lose the initiative to approach such an executive and his enthusiasm will wane. The firm, consequently, fails to take advantage of the junior's ideas which may be original, creative, brilliant.

14. Organisational Barrier

The classical organisational structure with a scalar chain of command restricts free and frequent communication. Within the organisation, orders and information have to pass through many levels of authority. Too many levels intervene causing delay in transmission and distortion of the message. The more complex the organisation, the more difficult it becomes to ensure that correct information is passed on to the right person at the right time thought the right medium.

15. Resistance to Change

The resistance to change is an important obstacle to effective communication. There is a general tendency among human beings to maintain statuesque. Change frightens them. They lack the spirit of adventure. They turn a deaf ear to new ideas and glorify the past. They cease to be receptive to communication. Their conservation thus becomes a barrier to communication.

16. Poor Messages

Clear ideas but wrong words and sentences are as bad as poor ideas. Wrong words and sentences can lead to misinterpretation of messages, words, sentences and paragraphs should be well connected and coherent to convey the right meaning.

17. Fear

Communication in an environment of threats, fear, punishment, etc. is a barrier to effective communication. There must be positive motivation for receivers to carry out sender's directions.

18. Poor Retention

Human mind cannot retain all that is communicated to him orally. He tends to forget a part of the information because of limited retention capacity. Therefore, it is suggested that the receiver repeat the message in more than one channel.

19. Empathy

In order to communicate effectively, the communicator should understand the receiver and develop better human relations with his subordinates. The language used in communication should not hurt the feelings or sentiments of the communicatees.

20. Economy

The communication system should be economical keeping in view its efficiency. The cost of communication should be kept under check by discouraging unnecessary messages and by avoiding the need for frequent clarifications or queries.

COMMUNICATION BARRIERS

1. Language Barriers
2. Inattention Barriers
3. Filtering

4. Status Barriers
5. Premature Evaluation
6. Perpetual Barriers
7. Emotional Reaction
8. Channel Distortions
9. Noise
10. Time and Distance
11. Interpretation of Words
12. Unclarified Assumptions
13. Closed Mind
14. Organisational Barriers
15. Resistance to Change
16. Poor Messages
17. Fear
18. Poor Retention
19. Empathy
20. Economy

FURTHER REASONS FOR COMMUNICATION BARRIERS

1. Badly expressed message are not read.
2. Inaccurate translation leads to inadequate understanding.
3. Fear results in poor communication.
4. Delayed messages are worthless
5. Words, in the messages, have different meaning.
6. Technical jargon, phrases, etc. sometimes create confusion.
7. Messages carry unfamiliar words.
8. Poor listening accounts for incomplete information.
9. Information often gets diluted when passes one person to another.
10. Poor retention may lead to imperfect responses.

OVERCOMING BARRIER TO COMMUNICATION

Communication is a major function office. The success of an organisation depends to a very large extent upon its ability to communicate effectively with its employees and customers. Effective communication takes place when a thing is understood in the sense in which it has been communicated. Effective communication is a good business and very essential for the success of an organisation. It is a two-way process. It may not be possible to achieve perfect communication. The following are some of the measures which may be adopted by the management to overcome the barriers and maintain the effectiveness of communication.

1. Proper Language

The message should be expressed in simple, brief and clear language. Use of technical terms should be minimised. The words or symbols selected for conveying the message must be appropriate to the reference and understanding of the receiver.

2. Clarity and Completeness

Clarity of thought is the first essential of good communication. The language used should be simple and precise which the receiver can understand easily. Technical jargons and high sounding words should be avoided. The contents of the communication should be adequate and complete. Incomplete message creates misunderstanding and delays in action. The message should be adequate and appropriate to the purpose of communication. The purpose of communication itself should be clearly defined.

3. Brevity

All communications should be brief. Unnecessary repetition and over elaboration should be avoided. The message should be concise and concrete. The communication must be well-planned and well-constructed. It is very essential for the management to maintain an efficient flow of communication in all directions. The flow of information should be regulated to avoid information overloaded.

4. Attention

Careful listening is essential for effective communication. The receiver should pay complete attention to the message so that communication becomes effective. The communicator should convey the message in such a way that the emotions and sentiments of the receiver are not hurt. Proper listening and open mind are necessary for this purpose.

5. Integrity

The message sent must be consistent with the objectives, policies and programmes of the organisation. Communication will be more effective if it is consistent than when it is varied. It is easier to follow consistent messages. To avoid credibility gap, management must ensure that their actions and deeds are in accordance with their communication.

6. Feedback

The effectiveness of communication is measured through feedback. Communication is a two-way process. The communication is complete when the receiver understand the message. In case of face to face communication, immediate feedback by seeing the emotions and expressions on the face of the listener can be of great help to the communicator. There should be a follow up action to ensure that the message is rightly understood. All communications should be followed up to generate feedback.

7. Media

The method of communication to be adopted should be in conformity with the nature and purpose of the message to be conveyed. The medium and method of communication should be chosen carefully to suit the particular communication needs. The equipment and mechanical devices to be used should be carefully selected and well maintained to prevent breakdowns.

8. Avoid Premature Evaluation

To communicate effectively, one should be a good listener. Superiors should develop a habit of patient listening and avoid premature evaluation of communication from their subordinates. This will encourage free flow of upward communication.

9. Developing Relations

Business requires joint efforts for accomplishing its goals. The need is, therefore, to develop proper relations among people working in the office. This will automatically reduce or eliminate behavioural barriers to communication by encouraging co-operation. An office manager should respect dignity and authority of his subordinates and be kind to them. Subordinates should also trust their superiors.

10. Gestures and Action

The way you say something is also very important alongwith the message for gestures such as twinkle of an eye, a smile, or a handshake, etc. convey sometimes more meaning then even words spoken or written. The main reason is that action and deeds often speak louder and clearer than words.

11. Proper Planning

Message should be planned before communicating to the receiver. In written communication, for example, the sender can read the message before transmitting it to the receiver. This enhances efficiency of the message.

12. Listening Skills

Receiver of information should develop his listening skills. He should conceptualise and listen to the message rather than simply hear it. Development of listening skills improves the communication process.

13. Empathy

Empathy mens the power of identifying oneself mentally with another person. Sender and receiver should identify each other's thoughts, feelings and needs before communication. This overcomes differences in perceptions.

14. Open Mind

We should be receptive to ideas, suggestions, etc. We learn from others. We must have open mind, invite and accept suggestions and improve our ability to communicate.

15. Overcoming Noise

Efficiency of message is greatly reduced by noise at the place where communication take place. If noise is made by a working machine, the machine should be switched off before passing the message. If it is not possible, the place of communication should be changed.

AIMS OF GOOD COMMUNICATION

Good communication aims at reaching the goals which the organisation wants to achieve. According to Scott, "Administrative communication is a process which involves the transmission and accurate replication of ideas ensued by feedback for the purpose of eliciting actions which will accomplish organisational goals." The message to be given is the information, which is to be transferred from one to another in an effective manner. If the message is understood by the reader, communication is said to have served the purpose. Our letter is our ambassador. It reaches where we cannot reach. A business letter represents the firm or the business house from it springs. The letter must strengthen the friendship between two business houses or the customer and the dealer.

SELECTION OF A COMMUNICATION SYSTEM

Office manager should be familiar with the various devices of communication and the different factors which should be considered before adopting a particular communication system. In order to get a good decision over the means of communication, the following factors may be considered:

1. Quickness/Speed

There are many types of transactions conducted during the business hours. One must speed up the transmission of message on the basis of importance and urgency of transaction. If the party is available in the transacted place, oral communication is enough. If the party is residing in the same city, telephonic message is good: if outside the city, message through Subscribers' Trunk Dialing (STD). If much distance is there, then telegram can also be sent. If the matter is not urgent, a mere letter will be sufficient.

2. Accuracy

If the accuracy of the message is the prime motive a letter will serve the purpose. Telephonic conversation might be misheard by the other party. Even telegrams, sometimes lead to wrong conclusion. Therefore, success can be reaped by a letter, provided the letter is properly written. Therefore, the communication medium which is selected should ensure accuracy in the transmission of messages.

3. Safety

There is always risk when valuables are sent by post. Therefore, for safety purposes, important documents may be sent by registered post; for further safety by registered and insured post.

4. Secrecy

In business field, certain transactions have to be kept confidential. When one aims at secrecy, letter will achieve the aim. In other communication systems, secrecy may leak out to unwanted persons.

5. Record

Record of the message is essential and is possible only if it is in writing. For this purpose, duplicate copies of the letters can be preserved and they are good proof against disputes, relating to the transaction, in future. There is no record for oral communication.

6. Cost

The cost of communication is also important. Before adopting any system, the expenses in different means may also be considered. The material cost (stationery) and labour cost in preparing the letter will also be considered.

7. Distance

Distance between the persons who are parties to communication is an important factor. If distance is too short, face to face communication is suitable. If there is distance, message can be transmitted through phone or telegram or letter.

COMMUNICATION NETWORK

A communication network reflects the interconnecting links or interaction among the members of an organisation. It provides channels or information to the organisational structure. There are five popular types of networks: Wheel Network, Circle Network, Free flow or All channel Network, Chain Network and Y Network.

1. Wheel Network

It is a network where all communication of subordinates must necessarily pass through the person at the centre. For instance, if there are five people in a structure, four people can communicate only with the fifth person at the centre. It does not provide any scope for interactions among the subordinate.

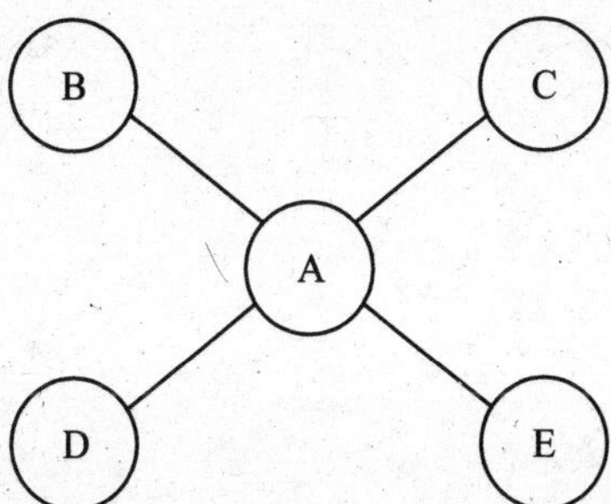

2. Circle Network

In case of circular network, the message moves in a circle. Each person can communicate with his two neighborhood colleagues only.

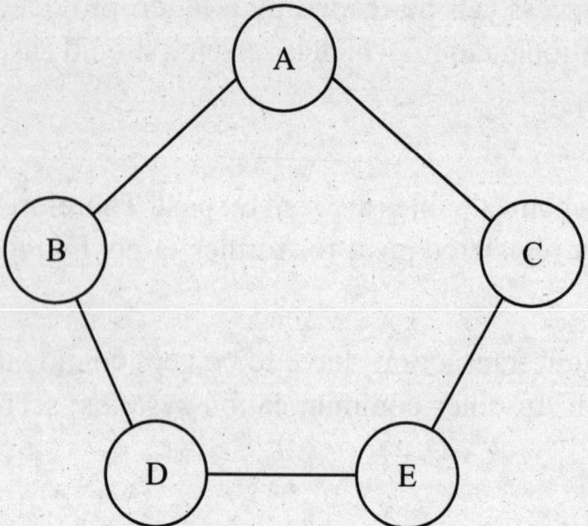

3. Free Flow or All-channel Network

In this network, all the subordinates in the structure are free to communicate with others. There is free flow of communication in all directions. This provides the maximum opportunity for free expression to everyone.

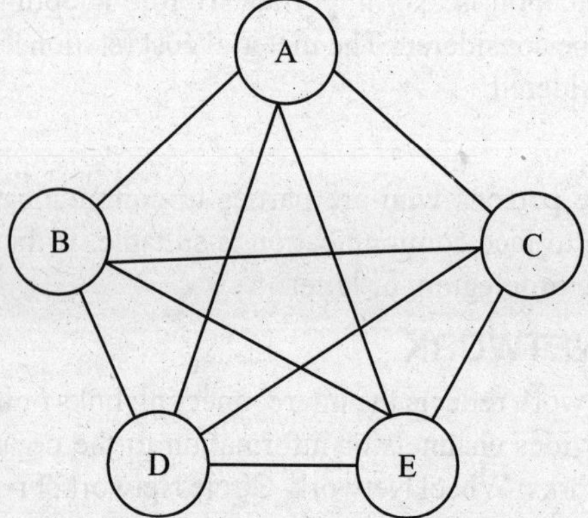

4. Chain Network

This types of network indicates one person communicates with one person only. It is a vertical type of network.

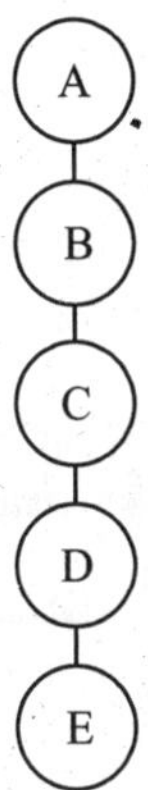

5. Y type Network

Here A is the central person who communicates with B, C, and D. It follows the formal chain of command where upward and downward communication takes place in the organisational hierarchy.

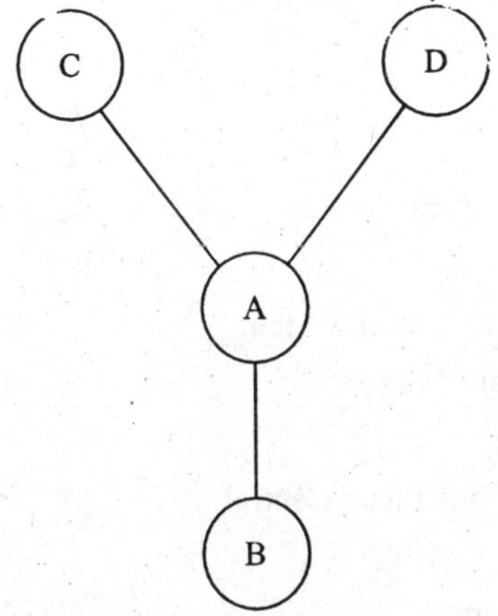

REVIEW QUESTIONS

1. State the common barriers to effective communication. *(B.Com., Madras)*
2. Discuss the importance of communication in an organisation. What guidelines will you suggest to make communication effective? *(M.Com., Andhra)*
3. Describe the various communication channels. *(M.Com., Utkal)*
4. What are the characteristics of a good communication system? *(B.Com., Bhopal)*
5. "Management is like a two-way traffic", it is based on an effective machinery of communication". Comment. *(M.Com., Jabalpur)*
6. Describe the various media of communication. Compare the merits and demerits of written and oral communication. *(M.Com., Bangalore)*
7. Explain the principal barriers to management communication and suggest measures for removing them. *(M.Com., Bombay)*
8. What is meant by communication ? Explain its characteristic and objectives. *(B.Com., MS)*
9. What are various principles consider for effective communication? *(B.Com., MS)*

CHAPTER 22

Process of Control

- Introduction
- Meaning of Control
- Definitions
- Nature of Control
- Importance of Control
- Relationship between Planning and Control
- Area of Control
- Control Process
- Benefits of Control System
- Types of Control
- Essentials of Effective Control System
- Limitations of Control
- Control by Exception
- Cybernetic and Non-Cybernetic Central
  - Cybernetic Control
  - Non–cybernetic Control
- Review Questions.

INTRODUCTION

Control is one of the basic managerial functions. It arises out of the character of organizations as purposeful, goal-oriented organisms. Management of all kinds of organisations determine goals and lay down plans for their achievements. Implementation of plans requires the performance of various functions and activities. It also involves expenditure of physical, financial and human resources. This makes control imperative in order to ascertain that the resources are being utilized most efficiently, the activities are contributing maximally to goal achievement, and the goals are being achieved so that corrective action may be taken for matching performance with goals. Controls are that aimed at identifying and bridging the gap between the actual and desired results. Planning, organizing, staffing and directing are aimed at making things happen and control is aimed at ensuring that things do happen as desired. Planning lays down the organisational objectives and means for their accomplishment. Organizing, staffing and directing provide resources, facilities, environment and mechanism for the implementation of plans, and achievement of the desired objectives. Controls ensure that plans are being implemented and goals are being achieved effectively and efficiently.

MEANING

Control is a basic managerial function which implies correction of performance of subordinates to ensure that the predetermined objectives are accomplished. To control means to check and ensure that each activity is performed in a planned manner as decided by the management. As a function of management the controlling is a process of taking necessary preventive and corrective actions which ensures that the resources of an organisation are being effectively and efficiently used for achieving organisational goals. The process of management starts with planning and terminates at controlling. With the help of controlling, the manager monitors the effectiveness of planning, organising, staffing and directing functions in terms of achievement of planned objectives. Controlling is the intergral part of managerial process. It is a monitoring function of ascertaining whether organisational efforts are heading towards the stated objectives or not. Controlling creates both positive and negative forces to keep the organisational efforts on the right track. The managerial function of controlling is mainly concerned with measuring and recording variations in performance and taking necessary corrective actions for the future.

The essence of control lies in checking progress against plans, setting up individual and organizational performance standard and seeing that they are achieved as per the plans. Henry Fayol states that in an undertaking, control consists of verifying whether everything occurs in conformity with the plan adopted, the instructions issued and the principles established. Its objective is to point out weaknesses and errors in order to rectify them and prevent their recurrence. It operates on everything — things, people and actions.

DEFINITIONS

The following are some important definitions of control: "In an undertaking control consists in verifying whether everything occurs in conformity with the plans adopted, the instructions issued and the principle established. Its object is to point out the weaknesses and errors in order to rectify them and prevent occurrence. It operates on everything — things, people and action."

— H. Fayol

"Control is checking current performance against predetermined standards constrained in the plans, with a view to ensuring adequate progress and satisfactory performance."

— Breach

"Control, in its managerial sense, can be defined as, the presence in a business of that force which guides it to a predetermined objective by means of predetermined policies and decisions."

— Mc Farland

Control stimulates action which will gear up all the departments. McFarland says that "Control is vital to the strength and morale of company employees." — workers will never like a situation to go out of control. Control will help in making correct and clear-cut decisions. It can make planning effective and meaningful.

RELATIONSHIP BETWEEN PLANNING AND CONTROL

Planning and controlling are closely related to each other. After a plan becomes operational, control is necessary to measure progress, in order to uncover deviations from the targets and to take corrective steps. It is also not possible to think of an effective system of control without the existence of good plans. According to Billy E. Goetz, "Managerial Planning seeks consistent, integrated and articulated programmes, while management control seeks to compel events conform to plans."

A plan without control is worthless and no controls can be enforced without plans. Planning is meaningless without control and control is blind without planning. Control makes planning a meaningful exercise and need for control arises only when there is a plan to be achieved. Planning sets the activities in motion and control keep them on the right track.

Planning starts the process of management and controlling completes that process. Controlling function is directly related to planning: managers monitor the results to achieve targets laid in the plans. Controlling provides feedback to the plans by pointing exceptions or variations in the planned performance.

Planning is an empty exercise without controlling. A good plan will not bring any concrete result if the management is lacking in controlling. Planning identifies the goals and determines the ways of achieving them. It is control which ensures attainment of goals by evaluating performance and taking corrective action. Control presupposes the existence of standards with which the actual performance is to be compared. If the standards of performance are not set in advance, the manager will have no idea of "what is control".

Plan provide the benchmarks to monitor, evaluate and regulate actual performance as it takes place. According to Robert Anthony, "Management control is a process carried out within the guidelines established by planning. The planning process is intended to make possible the achievement of planned objective effectively and efficiently. Planning involves a review of past events and control is also forward looking. The process of control makes the use of standards laid down by planning. The control process may in turn reveal deficiency of planning and may lead to revision of plans."

AREA OF CONTROL

A well designed control system covers almost all managerial activities. It is difficult to prescribe a precise list of areas where control should be exercised. In short, activities that affects the growth of organisation should be taken as area of control. Thus the main areas of control are as follow:

1. Control over Policies

The need of control over policies is self evident. In many enterprises, the policies are controlled through policy manuals.

2. Control over Costs

Cost control is exercised by the cost accountant by setting cost standards for materials, labour and over-heads and making comparison of cost data with standard cost.

3. Control over Methods

It is accomplished by conducting periodic analysis of activities of each department with a view to eliminate non-essential motions, functions and methods. A deep study is conducted to achieves all this.

4. Control over Organisation

It is accomplished through the development of organisation chart and manuals. Manual attempts at solving organisational problems and conflicts and helping in proper designing of organisation and its departments.

5. Control over Personnel

All employees working at different levels must perform their assigned duties and direct efforts towards the attainment of organisational goals. Control over their behaviour and efforts is the essence of control over personnel.

6. Control over Wages and Salaries

It is done by having programme of job evaluation and wage and salary analysis. Often, wage and salary committee is constituted to help these departments in the task of controlling wages and salaries.

7. Control over Capital Expenditures

Capital budgeting, project analysis, break even analysis, study of cost of capital, etc. are some of the popular techniques of control over capital expenditure.

8. Control over Research and Development

Such activities are highly technical in nature so no direct control is possible over them. Through training programmes and other devices, an indirect control is exercised on trained staff.

9. Control Over Production

It is effected through studies about market needs, attitudes of customers, revision in product lines, etc. Inventory control, inspection and quality control, etc. are some popular techniques of production control.

10. Control over External Relations

Public relations department is responsible for controlling the external relations of the enterprise.

CONTROL PROCESS

The processes or techniques of control wherever it is applied and whatever it controls, consists of the following steps:

1. Setting Standards
2. Measurement of Actual Performance
3. Compare Actual Performance with Standards
4. Taking Corrective Actions
5. Feedback

A brief explanation of the above steps are given below:

1. Setting Standards

A standard is a criterion against which future results can be measured. Many types of standards can be developed. The most common type includes time, quality, quantity and cost. The standards that are established must represent the objectives of the organisation and must be expressed in meaningful concrete terms. Obviously, for standards to be meaningful, they must be understood and accepted by individuals who are being controlled.

2. Measurement of Actual Performance

The very purpose of control is to check or measure the actual performance. If the standards prescribed are tangible, it is easy to measure the performance in similar units. If the standards are intangible, it is difficult to measure the performance. Work, operations and turnout should be observed, and facts collected. Statistical data, reports, opinions, accounting information, etc. will help in measuring the actual performance.

3. Compare Actual Performance with Standards

Whenever the actual performance is compared with standards, the deviations are known to the management. Then, the management may find the extent of deviations and identify the reasons for deviations. Comparison is very easy when standard is expressed in terms of quantity. If results are intangible or qualitative, personal observation will be used to find out the extent of deviation. When the actual performances are equal to the standards, there is no need for further action. Control process comes to an end with this state. However, if the standard is not achieved, the management has to decide the type of corrective action.

All the deviations need not be reported to the management. Deviations which are beyond the reasonable limits should be reported to the top management. Then, the reasons and causes for the deviations are analysed. The causes may be controllable or non-controllable. The management has to take necessary corrective action only in case the causes are controllable. However, no need will arise to the management to take corrective actions if the causes are uncontrollable.

4. Taking Corrective Action

Management has to find out the causes of deviation before taking corrective action. The causes of deviation may be due to ineffective and inadequate communication, defective system of wage payment, defective selection of personnel, lack of proper training, lack of motivation, ineffective supervisions and the like. The management has to take necessary corrective action on the basis of nature of causes of deviations.

5. Feedback

Feedback is an important element in the control process. It ties together all the elements of the control mechanism. The controller will receive feedback information regarding actual performance in comparison with the standards. If the feedback is positive and reveals accomplishment, the manager must encourage and appreciate the subordinates. If the feedback brings negative results, the manager has to take corrective action and alter the operations accordingly. Feedback will help in getting information well in time about the work performance, and it also motivates the workers.

BENEFITS OF CONTROL SYSTEM

A well developed control system has the following benefits:

1. It increases productivity
2. It reduces defects and mistakes
3. It facilitates communication
4. It improves safety
5. It lowers cost
6. It reduces the chances of errors

TYPES OF CONTROL

Depending on the time at which corrective action is taken, controls are of three kinds: (1) Feedback Control, (2) Concurrent Control and (3) Feedforward Control.

1. Feedback Control (Post Action Control)

Under feedback control, results are measured after the performance. Such measurement provides information about how goals have been achieved. This information is known as feedback and on this basis corrective action is taken. It involves checking a completed activity and learning from mistakes. For instance, by monitoring complaints from a discharged patients about billing errors, a hospital can learn about problems in the billing process. That is correction occurs after the event.

2. **Concurrent Control** (Real Time Control)

It involves monitoring and adjusting ongoing activities and processes to ensure compliance with standards. Concurrent control occurs while an activity is still taking place. For instance, the navigator of a ship adjusts its movements depending upon the direction of destination, obstacles and other factors. In industries, control chart is an example of concurrent control.

3. **Feedforward Control** (Pre-control)

This type of control is basically preventive in nature. The control takes place before work is performed. In this regard, management creates policies, procedures and rules aimed at eliminating behaviour that can cause undesirable work results. These controls are designed to eliminate the cause of any deviation that might occur later in the process. These controls are meant to make sure that performance objectives are clear and all resources are available at the time when needed in order to attain these objectives. For instance, Standard Cost Control techniques can be adopted to control the cost of a product before starting its commercial production.

ESSENTIALS OF EFFECTIVE CONTROL SYSTEM

A good system of control is one that makes the controlling function easy, effective and smooth. Therefore, it should contain the following features:

1. Objectives of the Organisation

Before planning a control system, it is essential to know clearly the objectives of the organisation. The control system should aim at accomplishing the organisation objectives. The control system should be both objective and understandable, objective controls specify the expected results in clear and definite terms.

2. Suitability

The control system should be appropriate to the nature and needs of the activity. Controls used in the sales department will be different from those used in finance or personnel. Hence, every concern should evolve such a control system as would serve its specific needs.

3. Flexibility

A good control system must keep pace with the continuously changing environment of business. It must be adaptable to new developments and responsive to changing conditions including revision of plans. Only a flexible system can pragmatic or practical.

4. Forward Looking

The control system ensures that mistakes made in the past are not repeated in future. A control system is ideal only when it points out deviations even before they take place. As far as possible it should seek to prevent deviations rather than remedy them after they have taken place.

5. Objective Standards

To have an effective control, there should be objective, precise and suitable standards. They should be definite and determinable. Standards of performance should as far as possible be objective and specific. They should be based on facts and participation so that control is acceptable and workable.

6. Economical

Economy is another requirement of every control system. The benefit derived from a control system should be more than the cost involved in implementing it. They must justify the expenses involved. A control system is justifiable if the savings anticipated from it exceed the expected costs on its working.

7. Control of Critical Points

Rather than controlling every activity, control system should focus on critical points only where deviations affect the organisational goals. Poor performance in these areas indicates deviations from the standards and requires corrective action.

8. Corrective Actions

A good control system should not only detects deviation, but also suggests practical corrective action. Koontz and O'Donnell state that an adequate system of control should disclose where failures are occurring, who is responsible for them, and what should be done about them.

9. Organisational Climate

In organisations where freedom is not given to workers, a tight control system will be successful and organisations where participative or democratic style of management prevails, a lenient control system should be adopted.

10. Human Factor

A good control system should be worker-centred than work-centred. Accountability for major deviations and assistance for improvement should be organised. Control system should not be viewed as a negative force that restricts workers' innovativeness and creativity. The focus should be on work and not on workers.

LIMITATIONS OF CONTROL

Control is essential for better performance and maintenance of good standards. However, there are certain limitations which are discussed below:

1. It is very difficult to establish standards for intangible activities.
2. Control cannot be effectively exercised over external factors which are basically uncontrollable. For instance, Government policies, changes in fashion, technological changes, etc.
3. The control system involves huge expenditure on its exercise. The performance of each and every person in the organisation will have to be measured and reported to higher authorities.
4. Control may not function effectively with untrained and unqualified subordinates.
5. Employees normally look upon the control techniques as an unwarranted interference in their work. Owing to this they may not fully cooperate with the persons operating the control system.

CONTROL BY EXCEPTION (MANAGEMENT BY EXCEPTION)

In controlling activities of subordinates, the superior may find that many of the activities have been performed as per standard so he can easily pass over these activities but he concentrates more on those activities which have been subject to major deviations from the standards.

According to L.R. Bittel, it is "a system of identification and communication that signals the manager when his attention is needed, conversely it remains silent when his attention is not required. The primary purpose of such a system is, of-course, to simplify the management process to permit a manager to find the problems that need his action and to avoid dealing with those that are better handled by his subordinates."

Advantages of Control by Exception

It provides the following advantages:

1. It saves the valuable time of busy executives.
2. It focuses managerial attention on major problems.
3. It widens the span of a manager, by freeing him from routine work,
4. It facilitates in effective decision-making through better judgement.
5. It is a technique of separating important information from unimportant one.

However, it suffers from the **following limitations:**

1. The paperwork increases.
2. It provides a false sense of security.
3. It is difficult to identify critical deviations.

CYBERNETIC AND NON-CYBERNETIC CONTROL

Cybernetic Control

Cybernetic control process refers to a system where control is automatic. The various operational activities are fed into computer and the moment deviation occurs, corrective measure is automatically taken by the system. That is cybernetic control is a system of control through which a critical resource is held at a desired level by a self-regulating mechanism. For cybernetic control to work, standards must be set, actual results must be reliably measured, standards and results must be compared and the resulting comparison must be feedback to management for action. For instance, fresh order for economic quantity should be made when the existing inventory reaches reorder point. Rather than human intervention to find when inventory reaches the reorder point, cybernetic control system provides for automatic ordering of inventory as soon as it reaches the reorder point. Minimum human effort is required in this system of control.

Non-cybernetic Control

This type of control system allows human discretion rather than leaving the business operations to be handled by machines. Future uncertainties allow changes in the existing pattern of working and therefore, human interference is advisable for taking the action. Moreover, machine is only an application of human. Non-cybernetic control system is more effective than the cybernetic system.

REVIEW QUESTIONS

1. Bring out the meaning and importance of control. (*B.Com., Madras*)
2. Explain the inter-relationship between planning and control. (*M.Com., MS*)
3. Explain the characteristics of an ideas control system. (*M.Com., Mysore*)
4. "Planning is looking ahead but controlling is looking back." Explain. (*M.Com., Bangalore*)
5. Suggest measures for making control effective in an organisation. (*M.Com., Bhopal*)
6. What is control? Examine the process of control. (*B.Com., Banaras*)
7. "Controlling ensures an efficient performance of other managerial functions." Comment. (*B.Com., MS*)
8. "Planning is meaningless without control and control is aimless without planning." Comment. (*M.Com., Mumbai*)
9. Explain the working of control processes. (*B.Com., MS*)
10. Briefly explain the principles of control. Also explain the importance and limitations of control to a business enterprise. (*B.Com., Delhi*)

Techniques of Managerial Control

23

CHAPTER

- Introduction

TRADITIONAL CONTROL OF TECHNIQUES

  - Personal Observation
  - Budgeting
  - Break Even Analysis
  - Cost Control
  - Financial Statement Analysis
  - Return on Investment
  - Statistical Reports
  - Quality Control

MODERN CONTROL OF TECHNIQUES

  - Management Information Systems
  - Management Audit
  - Responsibility Accounting
  - Network Techniques – PERT and CPM
  - Ratio Analysis
  - Economic Value Added
  - Market Value Added
  - Balanced Scorecard

- Review Questions

INTRODUCTION

To enable managers to control the organisational activities, a large number of controlling techniques are available. They help to produce right quantity and quality of goods at the right time. No single technique applies to control all organisational activities. There are a number of devices which help in controlling. These devices have been developed by various management experts and experienced factory managers. These devices are commonly known as control techniques. A variety of tools and techniques has been used over the years to help managers to control the activities in their organisations.

We may classify these techniques into two types:

I. Traditional Control Techniques

1. Personal Observation
2. Budgeting
3. Break-even Analysis
4. Cost Control
5. Financial Statement Analysis
6. Return on Investment
7. Statistical Report Analysis
8. Quality Control

II. Modern Control Techniques

1. Management Information System
2. Management Audit
3. Responsibility Accounting
4. Network Techniques – PERT and CPM
5. Ratio Analysis
6. Economic Value Added
7. Market Value Added
8. Balanced Scorecard

TRADITIONAL CONTROL OF TECHNIQUES

These techniques of control are being used by managers since long and, therefore, known as traditional techniques.

(1) Personal Observation

Observation of actual operations at the workplace is the most effective and the oldest method of control. Certain kinds of information and impression can be secured only through face-to-face contact. It helps the manager in taking corrective measures on the spot. Personal observation has also a psychological impact on the employees. They try to achieve better results when they know that they are being observed personally by their superior. Personal observation is the most direct and undistorted means of control. The observer exactly knows what is wrong and can take action forthwith.

However, this method demotivates the employees who work under psychological pressure of being constantly watched. It is also not suitable for large-scale organisations where managers cannot personally observe the performance of every worker. Small, medium and non-profit organisations can be benefited more by this technique of control than large-sized, and profit-making organisations.

(2) Budgeting

Introduction

Modern business world is full of competition, uncertainty and exposed to different types of risks. This complexity of managerial problems has led to the development of various managerial tools, techniques and procedures useful for the management in managing the business successfully. Budgeting is the most common, useful and widely used standard device of planning and control. The budgetary control has now become an essential tool of the management for controlling costs and maximising profit. Costs can be reduced, wastage can be prevented and proper relationship between costs and incomes can be established only when the various factors of production are combined in profitable way. The resources of a business can be effectively utilised by efficient conduct of its operations. This requires careful working out of proper plans in advance, co-ordination and control of activities on the part of management.

A proper planning and control are essential for an efficient management. A good number of tools and devices are available. Of all these, the most important device used is budget. Cost accounting aims not only at cost ascertainment, but also greatly at cost control and cost reduction. Thus the management aims at the proper and maximum utilisation of resources available. It is possible when there is a pre-planning. Modern management aims that all types of operations should be predetermined in advance, so that the cost can be controlled at every step. The more important point is that the actual programme is compared with the pre-planned programme and the variances are analysed and investigated. All are familiar with the idea of budget, at every walk of life — state, firm, business, etc.

Meaning

A budget is a detailed plan of operations for some specific future period. Many of us are familiar with the term 'Budget'. For instance, if we want to have a holiday trip of Kashmir, we are to estimate the cost of travelling, boarding, lodging, etc. so as to have sufficient amount for the trip. On return from the trip, we may like to compare the actual amount spent with the estimated or budgeted figures. Similarly we can know the importance of budgets even from the household management. The word 'budget' is derived from a French term "Bougette" which denotes a leather pouch in which funds are appropriated for meeting anticipated expenses. The same meaning applies to the business management. A budget is a numerical statement expressing the plans, policies and goals of the enterprise for a definite period in the future. It is a plan laying down the targets to be achieved within a specified period. It is a final and approved share of a forecast. When forecasts are approved by the management as a tentative plan for the future they become budget.

Definitions

The following are some of the important definitions:

1. "Budget is an estimate of future needs arranged according to an orderly basis, covering some or all of the activities of an enterprise for definite period of time".

   — George R. Terry

2. "A budget is a comprehensive and co-ordinated plan, expressed in financial terms, for the operations and resources of an enterprise for some specific period in the future."

   — James

3. "A budget is a pre-determined statement of management policy during a given period which provides a standard for comparison with the results actually achieved."

   — Brown and Howard

4. "A financial and/or quantitative statement, prepared prior to a defined period of time, of the policy to be pursued during that period for the purpose of a given objective."

   — ICMA, England

A study of the above definitions reveals the following basic elements of a budget:

1. Budget is a comprehensive plan of what the enterprise endeavours to achieve.
2. It is a statement in terms of money or quantity or both.
3. It is prepared for a definite future period.
4. It is prepared prior to the defined period.
5. It provides yardsticks and measures for the purpose of comparison.
6. It is prepared in advance and refers to the future course of action.
7. It indicates the business policy which has to be followed so as to achieve a given objective.

Forecast and Budget

Forecast is mainly concerned with probable events; but budget is concerned with planned events.

Forecast may be done for longer time; but budget is prepared for shorter periods.

Forecast is only a tentative estimate and can be revised; but budget remains unchanged for the budget period.

Forecast results in planning and the planning results in budgeting.

Forecast is a prediction or an estimate of changes, if any, in characteristics, economic phenomena which may affect one's business plans. It is a study into the future, when the forecasts are given a shape and approved by the management as a commitment, they become buaagets. For example, sales forecast is an estimate for future sales, while a sales budget is a commitment with an objective to reach certain sales figures.

Forecast is the base while a budget is the structure built on the base.

Forecast is not used for evaluating the efficiency of performance while a budget is always used for this purpose.

Forecast refers to the events over which there is no control, (for example, forecast of restricted import) while a budget is an endeavour to control the events.

Objectives of a Budget

1. It directs the attention of all concerned to the attainment of a common goal.
2. It leads to the disclosure of organisational weakness. The budgets are compare with actual performance; and variances, if any, are investigated. This step helps in taking corrective and remedial measures.
3. It aims at careful control over the performance and cost of every function.
4. It contributes to co-ordinated efforts of all departments in order to achieve an integrated goal. Budgets grow from bottom and are controlled from top-level.

Budgeting

A budget is essentially a statement of the intention of management. Budgeting refers to the management action of formulating budgets. Preparation of budgets involves study of business situations and understanding of management objectives as also the capacity of the enterprise. It includes the entire processing of making the budget plans. Preparation of budgets or budgeting is a planning function, and their application or implementation is a control function. When plans are embodied in a budget and the same is used as the basis for regulating operations, we have budgetary control. Budgetary control starts with budgeting and ends with control. Budgeting is defined as:

1. "The entire process of preparing the budgets is known as budgeting".

   — Batty

2. "Budgeting may be said to be the act of building budgets".

   — Rowland and Harr

Objectives of Budgeting

The main objectives of budgeting are:

1. To obtain more economical use of capital.
2. To prevent waste and reduce expenses.
3. To facilitate various departments to operate efficiently and economically.
4. To plan and control the income and expenditure of the firm.
5. To create a good business practice by planning for future.
6. To fix responsibilities on different departments or heads.
7. To co-ordinate the activities of various departments.
8. To ensure the availability of working capital.
9. To smooth out seasonal variations, by developing new products.
10. To ensure the matching of sales with productions.

What is a Budget?

1. Budgets are blueprint of the desired plan of action.
2. They are means of communications.
3. They indicate the business policies.
4. They serve as declaration of policies.
5. They provide a means of coordination of the business as a whole.
6. They are instruments of managerial control.
7. They are controlling tools.
8. They provide yardsticks for comparison.
9. They set definite goals.
10. They fix responsibilities and direct to profitable direction.

Budgetary Control

"Budgetary control means the establishment of budgets relating to the responsibilities of executives to the requirement of a policy, and continuous comparison of actuals with budgeted results either to secure by individual action the objective of that policy or to provide basis for its revision."

Budget, budgeting and budgetary control, according to Rowland and William H. Harr is that,

"Budgets are the individual objectives of a department, etc., whereas budgeting may be said to the act of building budgets. Budgetary control embraces all this and in addition includes the science of planning the budgets themselves and the utilisation of such budgets to effect an overall management for the business planning and control."

A budget is a numerical statement expressing the plans, policies and goals for a definite future period. Budgeting means the process of preparing budgets. Budgetary control is a system of controlling costs which includes the preparation of budgets, co-ordinating the departments and establishing responsibilities, comparing actual performance with the budgeted; and acting upon results to achieve maximum profitability.

Characteristics

1. *Establishment.* Budgets are prepared for each department and then the plans and objectives are presented before the management.
2. *Co-ordination.* The budgetary control co-ordinates the plans of various departments and the master budget is prepared.

3. *Continuous comparison.* The essential feature of budgetary control is to conduct continuous comparison of actual performance with budgeted figures, revealing the variations.
4. *Revision.* Budgets are revised, if necessary, according to changed conditions.

Advantages

The advantages and benefits of budgetary control are summarised below :–

1. Budgets fix the goals and targets, without which operation lacks direction.
2. Reduction in cost and elimination of inefficiency is achieved automatically.
3. The budget facilitates to maintain ordered effort and brings about efficiency in results.
4. An effective system of budgetary control results in co-ordinated effort of all persons involved.
5. Budgetary control enables the management to decentralise responsibility without losing control of the business since it pin-points inefficiency.
6. The budgetary control and standard costing go hand in hand and the combination of the two gives the most effective results. It promotes mutual co-operation and team spirits among the persons involved.
7. Budgetary control ensures that the capital employed at a particular level is kept at a minimum level.
8. It facilitates an intelligent and planned forecast for future.
9. It is a good guide to the management for making future plans. It is on the basis of budgetary control, realistic budgets can be drawn.
10. It aims at maximisation of profit, through cost control and proper utilisation of resources.
11. It brings to light the inefficiencies and weaknesses on comparing actual performance with budget. Thus management can take remedial measures.
12. It is a guide to the management in the field of research and development in future.
13. It evaluates the performance.
14. Since budget provides advance information, financial crises can be avoided.
15. It acts as a safety signal for the management. It prevents wastages of all types.

Essentials of a Successful Budgetary Control

A budget is both a plan as well as a control tool. A business budget is a plan covering all phases of operations for a definite period in future. It is a formal expression of policies, plans, objectives and goals laid down in advance by the top management for the concern as a whole and for every sub-division thereof. For an effective system of budgetary control, certain pre-requisites must be present. These essentials are:

1. The budgetary control system should have full support of top management.
2. There should be well-planned organisational set-up, with responsibility and authority clearly demarcated.
3. The accounting system should provide accurate and timely information.
4. Variations should be reported promptly and clearly to the appropriate levels of management.
5. Budgets have no meaning unless they lead to control action as a consequence of feed-back provided.
6. Staff should be strongly and properly motivated towards the system.
7. The budget should lay down the targets which are realistic and attainable.
8. It is most desirable that there is full and meaningful participation of all concerned.

9. Budgets should actually aim as a co-ordinating device rather than control device.
10. The budgets should be flexible enough to permit the adjustments in the light of changed operational circumstances.

Limitations of Budgetary Control

Budgetary control is a sound technique of control. But it is not a perfect tool. Despite the appreciation, it has its own limitations which are as follows:

1. Budgets deal with future. Forecasting is necessary for budgeting. Forecasts and estimates are rarely cent per cent accurate. The success largely depends upon the degree of accuracy of the estimates.
2. Budgeting is time-consuming process. During the preparation period, the business conditions may change and estimates may go wrong by that time.
3. The successful operation and execution of budgets depends upon the efficiency of the executive personnel.
4. Budgetary control is essentially a tool of decision-making and it helps the management in taking sound decisions. But it cannot replace the management.
5. Budgeting necessitates the employment of specialised staff and this involves expenditure which small concerns may not afford.
6. A budget programme should be dynamic, capable of being adapted to changing conditions. But when budgets are prepared with pre-determined targets, there is a feeling that the budgeted figures are final. Thus budgetary programme is bound to become rigid.
7. The success of the budgetary control largely depends upon willing co-operation or teamwork of all concerned. If there is no co-operation, the whole system collapses.

Organisation

The following are the essentials for a sound system of budgetary control:

1. **Chart.** There must be an organisational chart to show the authority and responsibility of each executive of the firm. This will enable him to know his relationship with other executives. The budget director derives power from the chief executive, helps in co-ordination and drawing up of all budgets and suggests changes, if necessary. The sales manager, production manager, purchasing manager, personnel manager and accountant will prepare their budgets.
2. **Budget Centre.** For the purpose of effective budgetary control, budget centres are defined. A budget centre may be a department or a section of the undertaking. Separate budgets are prepared for each department and the departmental head is responsible for carrying out budgets. Departmental heads should have effective control over the execution of the budget, to prevent unfavourable variation.
3. **Budget.** In small firms, the chief accountant prepares the budgets and co-ordinates various activities. In big concerns, a committee is appointed for this task. The committee consists of various section heads, the chief executive and the budget controller. The budgets are prepared by section heads and submitted to the committee for approval; changes are made, if necessary, and approved.
4. **Budget Manual.** It is a document which sets out the responsibilities of persons engaged in the routine work. Budget manual lays down the objectives of the organisation, responsibilities of all executives and the procedure to be followed for budgetary control. Duties, authorities, powers of each official of the different departments are clearly defined, so as to avoid conflicts among the personnel. It also specifies different forms and records to be used for the purpose of budgetary control.

5. **Budget Period.** This is the period or time for which the budget is prepared and remains in operation. The length of period depends on the nature of business, the production period, the control aspect, etc. There is no definite rule as regards the duration of a budget period. Generally, the budget is prepared for a year, which is preferred by most concerns. For example manufacturers of consumer goods may prepare budgets for a year, whereas in industries like shipbuilding the period of the budget may be 5 to 10 years.
6. **Key-Factor.** Key-factor is also known as 'limiting factor' or 'governing factor' which means this is the factor, the extent of whose influence must first be assessed, in order to ensure that the functional budgets are reasonably capable of fulfilment. The key factor may be, shortage of raw materials, non-availability of labour, limited sales, government restrictions, etc. The key-factor is a limitation on production or sales. First locate the key-factor, before preparing the budget, as it influences all other budgets. For examples, shortage of power supply leads to under-utilisation of plant capacity. Therefore, the concern will have to first prepare a budget for plant utilisation and later the other budgets say sales will be prepared.
7. **Master Budget.** A master budget is the summary budget for the entire enterprise and embodies the summarised figures for various activities. This is also known as summary budget or finalised profit plan. This budget includes the budgeted position of the profit and loss as well as balance sheet. Master budget is prepared by the committee and becomes a target for the company.

Classification of Budgets

On the basis of time	*On the basis of Flexibility*	*On the basis of Functions*
1. Long Term 2. Short Term 3. Current	1. Fixed 2. Flexible	1. Sales 2. Production 3. Materials 4. Labour 5. Overheads 6. Plant Utilisation 7. Cash 8. Capital expenditure.

There are various types of budgets. Some of the important budgets are discussed below:

Fixed and Flexible Budgets

Fixed Budget. This is a budget which is designed to remain unchanged irrespective of the level of activity actually attained. This is prepared for definite production and capacity level. It is not adjusted according to activity level attained. The fixed budgets are not effective tools of cost control. These types of budgets have limited use.

A fixed budget has been defined by ICMA, England as "A budget which is designed to remain unchanged irrespective of the level of activity actually attained."

However, in practical life, conditions do not remain static. The main reason is that actual output is often different from the budgeted output. In such a case the budget cannot be used for the purpose of cost control. There may be internal or external factors which force the level of activity to change.

Flexible Budget. This is a dynamic budget. It is a budget which is designed to change in accordance with the level of activity. Actual output may differ from the budgeted output; and as such, it is necessary to modify the budget on the basis of changed output. The budget is prepared in such a way as to present the budgeted cost for different levels of activity, it is more realistic and practical, because changes expected at different levels of activity are given due consideration. It is also called variable budget or sliding scale budget. The expenses are divided into three categories–fixed, variable and semivariable. It is an important tool of cost control, as it facilitates comparison of actual results with the budgeted figures.

ICWA, UK defines flexible budget as "a budget which, by recognising the difference between fixed, semi-fixed and variable costs, is designed to change in relation to the level of activity." Ascertainment of costs at various levels of activity becomes possible. Price fixation, sending quotations and tenders and finding out profit at changed capacities are facilitated.

Preparation of Flexible Budget

A budget prepared in a manner so as to give the budgeted cost for any level of activity is known as flexible budget. A flexible budget is the opposite of static budget. It is prepared for a range of activity instead of a single level. Fixed costs are related mostly to the period of time and are not concerned with the level of production or volume of sales. Variable costs vary directly and proportionately with the volume of activity. At zero level activity, the variable costs will not be in existence. The semi-variable costs occupy an "in-between" position between the fixed and variable costs. A part of these costs is variable and the rest is fixed. They are fixed to a certain level of activity and then rise with increase in the level of activity but not in the same proportion as the activity increases. As a matter of fact budget for each department can be prepared on the lines of flexible budget by classifying the costs into 'fixed' and 'variable'. In order to appropriately fix up the costs for different volumes, the degree of variability for each item cost at various levels of output could be evolved on the basis of past experience. This requires a close study of the individual items of expenditure, their nature and variability.

1. Decide the range of activity to develop a flexible budget.
2. Determine the cost behaviour—fixed, variable and semi-variable to each element of cost.
3. Select, the activity level (generally in terms of output)
4. Prepare the budget at each activity level.

Zero Base Budgeting

In common practice building the functional budgets is to base the budget year's figures on the previous year's budget. Taking the previous figures as the base, the required adjustments are made for the impact of inflation, proposed increased or decreased level of activity, etc. in the light of experience. Thus, in the traditional budgeting system, budgets are based on trends or historical level of expenditure. Thus a budget is developed on the concept of incremental basis. Mostly what is done is to add some percentage to the figures of previous year to determine the budget figures. That is, under the incremental budgeting system, the figures of the previous budget, on the basis of which future budget is drawn, are considered to be acceptable. It is the experience of many, particularly in the government departments and public undertakings that the actual expenditure should be in line with the budgeted amount otherwise the higher authorities will reduce the future budgeted and allocated amounts. The mangers justify the need to spend more than that of the previous budget. But they do not review their past activities and thus expenditure and inefficiencies are brought forward to the subsequent period *i.e.* the incremental budgeting perpetuates inefficiency instead of promoting operational efficiency.

In order, therefore, to streamline the allocation, to curb this tendency of equalising the expenditure with budgeted figures and to control the costs, a new technique called, "Zero Base Budgeting" or "Zero Based budgeting" emerged. Under this technique, no special budget is prepared but the approach is changed.

The use of Zero-base budgeting (ZBB) as a managerial tool has become increasingly popular since the early 1970's. It first came into being when Ex-President Jimmy Carter of the United States of America introduced it as a means of controlling state expenditure. The underlying idea of ZBB is that there is no given base figure for a budget. A fresh budgeted figure is to be determined keeping the circumstances and requirements. The basic concept of ZBB is simple: budgeting starts from scratch or zero. That is, every activity in an organisation must be examined and justified, any alternatives must be considered and the results evaluated. It is a method whereby all activities are re-evaluated each time when a budget is formulated.

It implies that:

1. Every budget starts with a zero base.
2. No previous figure is to be taken as a base figure for adjustments.
3. Each activity is to be examined afresh.
4. Every budget allocation is to be justified in the light of anticipated circumstances.
5. Alternatives are to be given due consideration.

Benefits

1. Effective cost control can be exercised.
2. Careful planning is facilitated.
3. Management by objectives becomes a reality.
4. Uneconomical activities are identified.
5. Inefficiencies are controlled.
6. Scare resources are allocated and used beneficially.
7. Each activity is thoroughly examined and justified.

(3) Break-even Analysis

The break-even point and break-even chart are two by-products of break-even analysis. In a narrow sense, it is concerned with the break-even point and in a broad sense, it is concerned with break-even chart. Break-even analysis is also known as cost volume profit analysis. The analysis is a tool of financial analysis whereby the impact on profit of the changes in volume, price, costs and mix can be estimated with reasonable accuracy. Break-even point is equilibrium point or balancing point of no-profit no-loss. This is a point at which loss ceases and profit begins. This is a point where income is exactly equal to expenditure.

Break-Even Point. Break-even point is a point where the total sales are equal to total cost. In this point there is no profit or no loss in the volume of sales. The formula to calculate break-even point is:

$$\text{B.E.P. (in units)} = \frac{\text{Total fixed cost}}{\text{Contribution per unit}}$$

or

$$= \frac{\text{Fixed cost}}{\text{Selling price per unit - Variables cost per unit}}$$

Illustration.

Find the profit from the following data:

	₹
Sales	80,000
Marginal Cost	60,000
Break-even point	60,000

(B.Com., MS)

Solution:

$$\text{P/V Ratio} = \frac{\text{Sales} - \text{Variable Cost}}{\text{Sales}} \times 100$$

$$= \frac{80{,}000 - 60{,}000}{80{,}000} \times 100$$

$$= 25\%$$

$$\text{B.E.P.} = \frac{\text{Fixed Cost}}{\text{P/ V Ratio}}$$

$$60{,}000 = \frac{\text{Fixed Cost}}{25\%}$$

$$\text{Fixed Cost} = 60{,}000 \times 25\% = ₹\ 15{,}000$$

$$\text{Profit} = (\text{Sales} \times \text{P/V Ratio}) - \text{Fixed Cost}$$

$$= (80{,}000 \times 25\%) - 15{,}000$$

$$= 20{,}000 - 15{,}000$$

$$= ₹\ 5{,}000$$

(4) Cost Control

Kohler defined the work "control" as "The process by which the activities of an organisation are conformed to a desired plan of action and the plan is confirmed to the organisations activities."

Cost control has been defined by kohler as "The employment of management devices in the performance of any necessary operation so that pre-established objectives of quality, quantity and time may be attained at the lowest possible outlay for goods and services. Such devices include a carefully prepared and reviewed bill of materials, instructions, standards of performance; competent supervision; cost limits on items and operations; and studies, interim reports and decisions based on these reports."

The techniques of cost control involves the determination of standards in respect of each item of cost, as ascertainment of actual costs regarding those very items, detection of variations of actuals from the standards laid down, analysis of these variances so as to determine the responsibility and the cause and cost of each variance, and then taking necessary action to ensure that actual costs conform to standard cost in future. The job of cost control is not so simple as a casual leader may suppose. There are a number of problems which have to be successfully solved if cost control is to be applied in any industrial unit.

The institute of Cost and Management Accountant. London defines cost control as: "The regulations by executive action of the cost of operating an undertaking particularly where such action is guided by cost accounting." The terms 'regulation' and 'executive' 'action' indicate conscious attempt of regulating the cost on the basis of predetermined ideas about that cost should be.

Essentials of Cost Control

The cost control process involves setting of cost centres (responsibility centres), both personal and impersonal, followed by pre-determination of costs function-wise or product-wise. This is followed by monitoring and control and by comparing actuals with standards. Standard costing is one of the techniques widely used for cost control purpose. In addition, budgetary control provides the basis for controlling expenditure and means to appraise the potential profitability of an alternative course of action.

The following key points are worth mentioning for exercising effective cost control:

1. Quantity and price standards should be set to, or be estimated for each physical unit. The factors influencing variances should not be ignored (inadequate facilities, poor organisation and poor materials).
2. To make the standards realistic, all concerned should be associated in determining standard costs.
3. The data collected should be kept to a minimum, and proper collection and processing of cost control data are important.
4. The different variances, price, usage, mix and efficiency should be considered, whether they are relating to material, labour or overheads.
5. No amount of detailed analysis of the cost of variances can undo what has already been done, however, control measures should ensure that such mistakes are not repeated. The only way to prevent excess costs in practice is for the manager to take action before the event.
6. The essentials of effective cost control not only include realistic targets (based on work study data) but also flexible attitudes regarding the standard set.

Cost control does not necessarily mean reducing the cost but its aim is to have the maximum utility of the cost incurred. In other words, the objective of cost control is the performance of the same job at a lower cost or a better performance for the same cost.

Advantages:

The advantages of cost control are given below:

1. Achieving the expected return of capital employed;
2. Increase in productivity of the available resources;
3. Reasonable price for the customers;
4. Continued employment for the workers;
5. Economic use of limited resources of production;
6. Increased credit-worthiness;
7. Prosperity and economic stability of the industry.

(5) Financial Statement Analysis

Financial statements are prepared primarily for decision-making. The statements are not an end in themselves, but are useful in decision making. Financial analysis is the process of determining the significant operating and financial characteristics of a firm form accounting data. The profit and Loss Account and Balance Sheet are indicators of two significant factors—Profitability and Financial Soundness. Analysis of statement means such a treatment of the information contained in the two statements as to afford a full diagnosis of the profitability and financial position of the firm concerned. Financial statement analysis is largely a study of relationship among the various financial factors in a business as disclosed by a single set of statements and a study of the trends of these factors as shown in a series of statements. The main function of financial analysis is the pinpointing of the strength and weakness of a business undertaking by regrouping and analysis of figures contained in the financial statements, by making comparisons of various components and examining their content. The financial statements are the best media of documenting the results of managerial efforts to the owners of the business, its employees, its customers and the public at large, and thus become excellent tools of the public relations.

Analysis and Interpretation

Analysis includes: (*a*) Breaking financial statements into simpler ones, (*b*) Regrouping, (*c*) Rearranging the figures given in financial statements and (*d*) Finding out ratios and percentages. Thus all process which help in drawing certain results from the financial statements are included in analysis. The data provided in the financial statements should be methodically classified and compared with figures of previous period or other similar firms. Thereafter, the significance of the figure is established. The work of an accountant in making analysis of financial statements is the same as that of a pathologist, who takes a drop of blood and analyse it to point out its various components and gives a report on the basis of this analysis. Similarly, an accountant makes analysis of each item appearing in financial statements and then gives a report on the basis of his analysis. Analysis only establishes a relationship between various amounts mentioned in Balance Sheet and Profit and Loss Account. After making analysis of the financial statements, the next step is to use mind for forming an opinion about the enterprise. This is the interpretation stage. The technique is called "Analysis and Interpretation" of financial statements. Analysis consists in breaking down a complex set of facts or figures into simple elements. Interpretation, on the other hand, consists in explaining the real significance of these simplified statements. Interpretation includes both analysis and criticism.

To interpret means to put the meaning of statement into simple terms for the benefit of a person. Interpretation is to explain in such a simple language the financial position and earning capacity of the company which may be understood even by a layman, who does not know accounting. The analysis and interpretation of financial statements requires a comprehensive and intelligent understanding of their nature and limitations as well as the determination of the monetary valuation of the items. The analyst must grasp what represent sound and unsound relationship reflected by the financial statements. Interpretation is impossible without analysis.

"Interpretation is not possible without analysis and without interpretation analysis has no value". Analysis and interpretation act as a bridge between the art of recording and reporting financial information and the act of using this information. Analysis refers to the process of fact finding and breaking down complex set of figures into simple components while interpretation stands for explaining the real significance of these simplified components. Interpretation is a mental process based on analysis and criticism.

George O. May points out the following uses of financial statements:

1. As a report of stewardship;
2. As a basis for fiscal policy;
3. To determine the legality of dividends;
4. As a guide to advise dividend action;
5. As a basis for granting of credit;
6. As informative for prospective investors in an enterprise;
7. As a guide to the value of investment already made;
8. As an aid to Government supervision;
9. As a basis for price or rate regulation;
10. As a basis for taxation.

(6) Return on Investment (ROI)

Return on investment is also known as return on the capital employed. Using this technique, the rate of profitability is identified by the management. The amount of profits earned by the company is different from the rate of profitability of the company. The difference between the cost and revenue is profit. The rate of profitability is the earning capacity of the company. Return on Investments is calculated by dividing the net profit with the total investment or capital employed in the organisation.

It measures the relationship between the amount of net profits and the size of investment in an organisation. It is a key measure of overall performance and an important technique of financial control.

Advantages of ROI

ROI is a tool of planning and control. It offers the following merits:

1. ROI reflects operating efficiency of business.
2. It offers a sound basis for interfirm comparisons.
3. It reflects the overall total control system.
4. It is a measure of overall performance.
5. It facilitates decentralisation of authority.

(7) Statistical Reports

According to Hauson, "Managerial statistics deal with data and methods which are useful to management executives in planning and controlling of organisation activities. Using the managerial statistics techniques, the manager compares the past results with current results in order to know the causes for changes. These are useful to the management in planning and decision-making for the future.

Statistical control reports are prepared and used in large organisations. Reports are prepared in quantitative terms. Therefore, the variations from standards are easily measured. Thus management exercises controls. Analysis is possible by means of comparison of ratios, percentages, trends, averages, correlation, regressions, etc. Statistical data and regular reporting system provide information about company's financial and non-financial performances. A look at the chart, histograms, pie diagrammes, bar graphs, etc. will give an idea to viewers. Therefore, statistical data analysis is a good device of control.

(8) Quality Control

Quality is a relative concept. It is related to certain predetermined characteristics such as shape, dimentions, composition, finish, colour, weight, etc. In simple words, quality is the performance of the product as per the commitment made by the producer to the consumer. In practice, when we say any product as a quality product, it means the product satisfies certain criteria for its functioning. For a quality product, it is necessary that it should satisfy the laid down criteria not only at the time of its manufacture, but also over a reasonable length of time.

Quality control is also a strategic decision. It can be defined as the systematic control of those variable which are encountered in the manufacturing process and which adversely affect the excellence of the final product in one way or other. Alfort and Beaty defined quality control as "Quality control is the mechanism by which products are made to measure up the specifications determined the customer's demands and transform into sales, engineering and manufacturing requirements. It is concerned with making things right rather than discovering and rejecting those made wrong. Quality is a technique by means of which products of uniform acceptable quality are manufactured."

Quality Circles

Quality circles is a small group of employees in the same works area or doing similar type of work who voluntarily for about an hour every week to identify, analyse and resolve work related problems not only to improve quality, productivity of the organisation but also to enrich the quality of work-life of employees.

Benefits of TQM

1. A satisfied customer will likely to recommend the product to other buyers.
2. Manufacturing cost is reduced by reducing wastes.
3. TQM increases employee productivity and equipment productivity.
4. TQM reduces mistakes, thus savings are increased.
5. TQM ensures better profitability for the organisation.
6. Better justification for budgets because efficient operations.

MODERN CONTROL OF TECHNIQUES

In addition to traditional techniques of control which are still being practised by managers, some of the modern techniques of control are discussed below:

1. Management Information System (MIS)

Information is the basis for decision-making in an organisation. The efficiency of management depends, to a larger extent, upon the availability of regular and relevant information to those who exercise the managerial function. A regular system of reporting is considered as a better guarantee of efficiency and operation than reliance on personal qualities. Thus it is essential that an effective and efficient reporting system is developed as part of accounting method. The main object of management reporting is to obtain the required information about the operating results of an organisation regularly in order to use them for future planning and control. The term 'report' normally refers to a formal communication which moves upward, *i.e.*, by a lower level to a higher level of authority in response to orders received from higher level. A person, who is issued with instructions to do certain things, should report back that he has done in compliance thereof.

The old techniques like intuition, rule of thumb, personal whim and prestige, etc. are now considered useless in the process of decision-taking. Modern management is constantly on the look out for such quantitative and other information which can help in analysing the proposed alternative actions and choosing one as its decision. Thus, modern management functions are information-oriented more popularly known as 'Management by information'. And the system through which necessary information is communicated to the management is known as "Management Information System (MIS)." The management needs full information before taking any decision. Good decisions can minimise costs and optimise returns. Management Information System can be helpful to the management in undertaking management functions smoothly and effectively.

Different authors define MIS as follows:

"MIS is a formal method of making available to management the accurate and timely information necessary of facilitate the decision-making process and enable the organisation's planning, control and operational functions to be carried out effectively."

—Stoner and Wankel

"MIS is a system that gathers comprehensive data, organises and summarises it in a form valuable to managers, and provides those managers with the information they need to do their work".

—R.W. Griffin

"MIS is a formal system of gathering, integrating, comparing, analysing and dispersing information internal and external to the enterprise in a timely, effective and efficient manner."

—Weihrich and Koontz

MIS provides information related to internal and external environmental factors to the organisation. Internal information relates to functional areas and external information relates to competitors, customers, suppliers, debtors, creditors, etc.

Advantages of MIS, in brief

1. Accurate and timely information helps managers to make scientific decisions.
2. MIS helps managers retrieve only relevant information.
3. Facilitates to managers in making optimum decisions.
4. MIS helps in coordinating activities of different section.

Generally the reporting levels in the internal management fall in the following three categories:

(A) Top Management Level: The top level management comprises of Board of Directors, General Manager, Assistant Managers, Finance Directors, Production Directors, Sales Directors, etc. The top management is primarily concerned with the policy formulations, planning and organisation. They are, therefore, interested in the overall efficiency or inefficiency of the business. Generally, the top management should receive the following reports at different intervals:

1. Periodic report about Profit & Loss Account and Balance Sheet.
2. Statement of Funds Flow and Cash Flow at regular interval.
3. Report on plant utilisation
4. Report of cost of production.
5. Report on research and development activities.
6. Periodic report on sales, credit collection, selling and distribution expenses, etc.

(B) Middle Management Level: This comprises the heads of various departments such as Sales Manager, Production Manager, etc. The report for this level should show the efficiency and cost data relating to respective areas or departments. The departmental managers are primarily concerned with the execution of plans, administration of policies, directing operating supervisors, etc. The work of co-ordinating activities of different departments is also undertaken by middle management. They receive the following reports: weekly or fortnightly.

1. Reports on material price and usage variances
2. Reports on labour rate and efficiency variances
3. Report on idle time, wastage of materials, etc.
4. Reports on stock levels
5. Reports on sales, production, etc.
6. Reports on orders booked, orders executed and orders still to be executed.

(C) Lower Management Level: The lower level management is assigned the work of executing various policies. They are in touch with the day-to-day performance of their section. They may need reports on daily or weekly basis. Supervisors, foremen, section-chief, sectional incharge, etc. come under this level. Reports are almost in the form of scrap of paper having no proper format. Reports are detailed and specific, restricted only to the activity with which they are concerned; Examples of such reports are:

1. Reports of over-time
2. Material usage variances
3. Labour efficiency variances
4. Material spoilage report
5. Accident report, etc.

(2) Management Audit

Management audit is a new concept in the sphere of auditing. The word 'Audit' takes its origin from Latin word 'audire' which means 'to hear'. The person who conducts audit is known as the auditor. In olden days, the original object of an audit was principally to see whether the Accountant had properly accounted for the receipts and payment of cash. In those days, audit was simply a comparison of records. That is, auditors are generally expected to detect errors and omissions in the books of accounts. In the context of financial accounting, the term auditing means examination of books of accounts to ensue that the financial statements are prepared in accordance with the statutory requirements and that they reflect a true and a fair view of the affairs of the concern. Cost audit which is concerned with the audit of cost accounts is a part of the work of the internal auditor. The principles underlying cost audit differs from financial audit not only in scope but objectives also. The term 'cost audit', according to ICWA, India, "It is an audit of efficiency of minute details of expenditure while the work is in progress and not a post-mortem examination. Financial audit is a *fait accompli.* Cost audit is mainly a preventive measure, a guide for management policy and decision, in addition to being a barometer of performance." The difference of the two is clear from the definition.

The management audit is an expansion of internal audit and which is now called Management Audit. It is the latest development of internal audit. Though, this concept is still in its infancy, yet it has caught world-wide attention of the Accountants, Management and Auditors. Management audit is concerned with management process as a whole. It covers review and appraisal of managerial policies and plans in comparison to pre-determined standards.

Definition

As its name signifies, the management audit means the audit of management process and functions. It is an independent appraisal activity for the review of control of managerial functions so as to ensure compliance with the organisational objectives, policies and procedures and the management methods and purposes.

William P. Leonard defines Management Audit, as "A comprehensive and constructive examination of an organisational structure of a company, institution or branch of Government, or of any component thereof, such as a division or department, and its plans and objectives, its means of operations, and its use of human and physical facilities".

Leslie R. Howard has given a comprehensive definition of Management Audit. According to him, "Management audit is an investigation of a business from the highest level downward in order to ascertain whether sound management prevails throughout, thus facilitating the most effective relationship with the outside world and the most efficient organisation and smooth running of internal organisation."

According to Bhandari, "Management audit is a comprehensive examination of an organisational system which comprises a review of final results and an intensive examination of objectives, programmes, policies, procedures, organisational structure, decisions and internal controls."

Taylor and Perry has given another definition. According to them, "Management auditing is a method to evaluate the efficiency of management at all levels throughout the organisation, or more specifically, it comprises the investigation of a business by an independent body from the highest executive level downwards, in order to ascertain whether sound management prevails throughout, and to report as to its efficiency or otherwise, with recommendations to ensure its effectiveness where such is not the case".

In this regard, George A. Terry states: "The periodic assessment of a company's managerial planning, organising, actuating and controlling compared to what might be called the norm of successful operation is the essential meaning of management audit. It reviews the company's past, present and future. The areas it covers are examined with a view to determine whether the company is receiving maximum results out of its endeavours."

Management audit may even be used to provide guidance on critical assessment of capital budgeting or profit performance, forecasting and planning activities on long-term and short-term basis. Management audit is thus concerned with evaluation of the control system and information system in various segments of the organisation. Thus it is clear that management audit is an evaluation, appraisal and review of managerial policies and programmes to ascertain whether they are carried out efficiently or not. If the work is not done satisfactorily then recommendations are made to take corrective actions.

Objectives of Management Audit

The basic objectives as contained in the above definitions are:

1. The management audit aims at achieving the efficiency of the management.

2. It suggests ways and means of increasing managerial efficiency.
3. It examines the organisational structure. If there are deficiencies then changes in organisations are suggested.
4. It studies the relationship of the concern with the outside world and the economic environment.
5. It is the main objective of management audit to see whether the business is managed efficiently or not.
6. It helps the management of all levels in the efficient discharge of duties and responsibilities.
7. It evaluates the performance of various management processes and functions.

Difference between Financial Audit and Management Audit

The following are the difference between the two, in brief:

Financial Audit	*Management Audit*
1. It is concerned with the certification of true and fair character of financial accounts.	1. It is not intended to certify the correctness of accounting data but is concerned with an appraisal of means and results.
2. It is simply a post mortem examination.	2. It is preventive as well as curative check up.
3. It requires accounting expertise.	3. It requires inter-disciplinary expertise.
4. It is mainly based on internal financial data.	4. It is based on financial and non-financial data obtained from internal as well as external.
5. It is statutory in case of Joint Stock Company.	5. It is still voluntary.
6. Scope of audit is determined by laws.	6. Scope of management audit is based on mutual agreement.
7. It is well developed and professionally controlled activity.	7. It is in its infancy stage.
8. Motivation for audit comes from tradition and law.	8. It depends upon the consciousness of management.
9. It is useful for shareholders and other external parties.	9. It is mainly useful for management itself.
10. It is an annual feature.	10. It depends on management and need not be annual - may be 2 or 3 or 4 yearly programme.

NEED FOR MANAGEMENT AUDIT

Financial audit is concerned with the certification of true and fair character of financial accounts. It is not concerned with evaluation of either 'means' or 'results'. The financial auditor does not report whether the policies laid down by the concern are carried out properly or not. He looks only at the history of financial transactions. He is concerned with financial aspects of the organisation. He does not suggest ways and means to eliminate wastage or reduce the cost of production.

The management of business at present is becoming more and more complex. The Directors are not experts in every field of management. Management audit is a kind of internal audit which reveals defects in the working of the organisation and suggests improvements to obtain best result of the operations of the concern. It is a comprehensive examination — an appraisal of all functions of management, viz., planning, organising, motivating, controlling and co-ordinating undertaken by management auditor.

Some of the uses of management audit, in brief, are:

1. Management audit makes substantial contribution to systems of goal setting in the organisation.
2. It helps to avoid wasteful, unnecessary and extravagant use of resources.
3. It is a kind of internal audit which reveals defects in the working of the concern and suggests improvements to obtain best results.
4. It helps in the improvement of Management Information System to expedite flow of information among responsibility centres.
5. It guides the management in pin-pointing key functions or operations in the profit-making process.
6. It helps in establishing, reviewing and improving the planning system.
7. It facilitates the management in getting the adequate information for correct decisions.
8. It sees whether the management is properly using the information that it is getting.
9. It enables appraisal of performance of various managers.
10. It assists all members of management to overcome delays, wasteful expenditure, recurring losses, gaps between budgeted and actual achievements, etc.

"Management Audit is performed with the object of examining the efficacy of the information control system, management procedures towards the achievement of enterprise goals."

"Management Audit can be defined as an objective and independent appraisal of the effectiveness of managers and the effectiveness of the corporate structure in the achievement of company objectives and policies. Its aim is to identify existing and potential management weaknesses within an organisation and to recommend ways to rectify these weaknesses."

3. Responsibility Accounting

The systems of costing like standard closing and budgetary control are useful to management for controlling the costs. In those systems the emphasis is on the devices of control and not on those who use such devices. Responsibility accounting is a system of control where responsibility is assigned for the control of costs. The persons are made responsible for the control of costs. Responsibility accounting implies a system of accounting whereby the performance of various people is judged by assessing how far they have achieved the predetermined targets set for the divisions, or sections for which they are responsible.

Definitions

Eric Kohier defines responsibility accounting as "a method of accounting in which costs are identified with persons assumed to be capable of controlling them, rather than with products or functions. It differs from activity accounting, in that it does not in itself require an organisational grouping by activities and sub-activities or provide a systematic criterion of system design."

Charles T. Horngreen defines, "Responsibility accounting is a system of accounting that recognizes various responsibility centres throughout the organisation and reflects the plans and action of each of these centres by assigning particular revenues and costs to the one having the pertinent responsibility. It is also called profitability accounting and activity accounting."

Responsibility Centres

Responsibility accounting focuses attention on responsibility centres. A responsibility centre is a sub-unit of an organisation under the supervision of a manager who has the responsibility for the activities of that responsibility centre. Each sub-unit has certain activities to perform and its manager is assigned the responsibility and / or authority to carry out those activities. Responsibility centre is the segment of business with reference to which information will be communicated to pin-point responsibilities.

Responsibility centres, for planning and control purposes, are classified into the following centres:

(*a*) **Expense Centre:** An expense centre is a responsibility centre in which inputs, but not outputs, are measured in monetary terms. Expense or cost centre is a segment of an organisation in which the managers are held responsible for the costs incurred in that segment. Responsibility accounting is based on financial information relating to input (costs) and outputs (revenues).

(*b*) **Revenue Centre**: A revenue centre is a segment of the organisation which is primarily responsible for generating sales revenue. A revenue centre manager does not possess control over cost, investment in assets, but usually has control over some of the expenses of marketing department. The performance of a revenue centre is evaluated by comparing the actual revenue with budgeted revenue.

(*c*) **Profit Centre**: A responsibility centre is called a profit centre when the manager is held responsible for both costs (inputs) and revenues (outputs) and thus for profit. A profit centre is a big segment of activity for which both revenues and costs are accumulated. A centre whose performance is measured in term of both - expense it incurs and revenue it earns, is termed as a profit centre.

(*d*) **Investment Centre:** It is defined as a responsibility centre in which inputs are measured in terms of cost/expenses and outputs are measured in terms of revenues and in which assets employed are also measured. A responsibility centre is called an investment centre, when its manager is responsible for costs and revenues as well as for the investment in assets used by his centre.

Advantages of Responsibility Accounting

Management uses responsibility accounting as a control device. The aim of responsibility accounting is to help management in achieving organisational goals. It is an invaluable support to modern management. It contributes to the firm's management by providing relevant information on a continuous basis. The following are some of the advantages of responsibility accounting.

1. It introduces sound system of control – a system of closer control.
2. Each and every individual in the organisation is assigned some responsibility and they are accountable for their work.
3. Everybody knows what is expected of him. Nobody can shift responsibility to anybody else if something goes wrong.
4. It is effective tool of cost control and cost reduction applied with budgetary control and standard costing.
5. It facilitate the management to set realistic plans and budgets.
6. It is only a control device but also facilitates decentralisation of decision-making.
7. It measures the performance of individuals in an objective manner.
8. It fosters a sense of cost-consciousness among managers and their subordinates.
9. It helps the management to make an effective delegation of authority and required responsibility as well.
10. Under the system of responsibility accounting, detailed information is collected about costs and revenues, on a continuous basis and the data is helpful in planning for future costs and revenues.
11. Timely corrective action can be taken and better control over costs can be achieved.

4. Network Techniques (PERT and CPM)

The two major techniques under this heading are PERT (Programme Evaluation and Review Technique) and CPM (Critical Path Method). Both techniques were developed independently, although virtually at the same time, around 1957-58. PERT was first developed for the US Navy in connection with the Polaris weapons system and is credited with reducing the completion time of the programme by two years. CPM was developed jointly by Du Pont and Remington Rand of USA in order to facilitate the control of large, complex industrial projects.

Both PERT and CPM are primarily oriented towards achieving better managerial control of times spent in completing a project. Under both the techniques a project is decomposed into activities and then all activities are integrated in a highly logical sequence to find the shortest time required to complete the entire project. The main difference between PERT and CPM lies in the treatment of time estimates. PERT was created primarily to handle research and development projects in which time spans are hard to estimate with any degree of accuracy. Consequently PERT time spans are based on probabilistic estimates. CPM, on the other hand, is usually concerned with projects that the organisation has had some previous experience with. Time estimates, therefore, can be relatively accurate.

The use of both PERT and CPM has spread rapidly today in controlling time-critical projects such as reinforcing a weak dam, constructing a building at an Olympic site or completing contracts that include penalty payment clauses. Many companies, make use of these techniques for working out the cost estimates of a project also.

Advantages:

The main advantages of PERT and CPM are as under:

1. It helps is avoiding waste of time energy and money on unimportant activities.
2. It enables managers to plan the time and cost estimates for completing a complex project.
3. It improves communication system in the organisation as people performing different events constantly interact with each other.
4. It helps to find deviations at the point of occurrence and take timely action to correct them.
5. It is more of a feed-forward controlling device than a feedback technique of control.

5. Ratio Analysis

The Balance Sheet and Profit and Loss Account are the basic financial statements of a business enterprise. They, undoubtedly, provide useful financial data regarding the operations of a firm. Financial statements contain a wealth of information which, if properly analysed and interpreted, can provide valuable insights into a firm's performance and position. The information contained in the financial statements is used by management, creditors, investors and others to form judgement about the operating performance and other financial position of the firm. Financial statement analysis may be done for a variety of purposes, which may range from a simple analysis of short-term liquidity of the firm to a comprehensive assessment of strength and weakness of the firm in various areas. However, they fail to present all the useful financial data required for decision making, specially financing decisions by the management. A Balance Sheet reports the firm's assets and liabilities at a point of time. The Profit and Loss Account presents the summary of items relating to the revenue and the expenses of a firm during a particular period of time. Neither of these shows the nature of the transactions entered into during the period to finance the firm's operations. Nevertheless, they provide some extremely useful information. *The Balance Sheet is a mirror of the financial position of a firm.* It reveals the assets the firm owns, the liabilities it is to pay to outsiders and the amount of internal liabilities in terms of capital supplied by the owners at a particular point of time. The *Profit and Loss Account shows the results of business activities or operations during a certain period of time, usually a year*. It presents the summary of income obtained and he costs incurred by the firm during a year. Thus, the financial statements provide a summarised view of the operations of a firm. Much can be learnt about a firm from careful examination of its financial statements. The analysis of financial statements is an important aid to financial analysis. Of the various methods of financial statement analysis, Ratio Analysis is by far the most widely used. Ratio analysis is based on different ratios which are calculated from the accounting data contained in the financial statements. Different ratios are used for different purposes. Financial analysis depends to a very large extent on the use of ratios though there are other equally important tools of such analysis.

Introduction

The company's financial information is contained in Balance Sheet and Profit and Loss Account The figures contained in these statements are absolute and sometimes unconnected with one another. An absolute figure does not convey much meaning. However, it is only in the light of other information that the significance of a figure is realised. For instance, Mr. X weights 50 Kg. Is he fat? We cannot give answer unless we know his age and height. Similarly a company's profitability cannot be known unless together with the amount of profit, the capital employed is also seen. The relationship of these two figures expressed mathematically is called a RATIO. The ratio refers to the numerical or quantitative relationship between two variables or items. A ratio is calculated by dividing one item of the relationship with the other. The ratio analysis is one of the most useful and common method of analysing financial statements. As compared to other tools of financial analysis, the ratio analysis provides very useful conclusions about various aspect of the working of an enterprise. The need for ratio arises due to the fact that absolute figures are often misleading. Absolute figures are certainly valuable but their value increases manifold if they are studied with another through ratio analysis. Ratios enable the mass of data to be summarised and simplified. Ratio analysis is an instrument for diagnosis of the financial health of an enterprise. Ratios, in fact, are full of meaning and communicate the relative importance of the various items appearing in the Balance Sheet and Profit and Loss Account.

Meaning of Ratio

A ratio is only a comparison of the numerator with the denominator. The term ratio refers to the numerical or quantitative relationship between two figures. A ratio is the relationship between two figures, and obtained by dividing the former by the latter. Ratios are designed to show how one number is related to another. It is worked out by dividing one number by another.

Ratio analysis is an important and age old technique of financial analysis. The data given in financial statements, in absolute form, are dump and are unable to communicate anything. Ratios are relative form of financial data and very useful technique to check upon the efficiency of a firm. Some ratios indicate the trend or progress or downfall of the firm.

Mode of Expression

(*i*) RATE, which is the ratio between the two numerical facts over a period of time, for example, stock turnover is three times a year.

(*ii*) PURE RATIO OR PROPORTION which is arrived at by the simple division of one number by another, for example, Current Asset to Current Liability ratio is 3 : 1.

(*iii*) PERCENTAGE which is a special type of rate expressing the relationship in hundred. It is arrived at by multiplying the quotient by 100, for example, gross profit is 30% of sales.

These alternative methods of expressing items which are related to each other are, for purposes of financial analysis, referred to as ratio analysis. In other words, ratios, as a tool of financial management, can be expressed as (*i*) Pure Ratio (*ii*) Percentage and (*iii*) a stated comparison between numbers. Each method of expression has a distinct advantage over the other. The analyst will elect that mode which will best suit his purpose and convenience.

It should be noted that computing ratios do not add any information not already inherent in figures. What the ratios do is that they reveal the relationship in a more meaningful way so as to enable us to draw conclusions from them. A single figure by itself has no meaning but when expressed in terms of a related figure it yields significant inferences. For instance, a firm earns ₹ 3,00,000 as net profit. This fact throws no light on its adequacy or otherwise. The figure of net profit has to be considered in relation to sales or capital employed or other variables. Then a meaningful conclusion can be drawn by converting the figures into meaningful comparable forms and removes the difficulty of drawing inferences on the basis of absolute figures. As a quantitative tool, it enables the analyst to draw conclusions or answers to questions such as : Are the net profit adequate? How does it stand in relation to capital? What does it represent by way of return on capital employed?, etc.

Steps in Ratio Analysis

The *first* task of the financial analyst is to select the information relevant to the decision under consideration from the statements and calculates appropriate ratios.

The *second* step is to compare the calculated ratios with the ratios of the same firm relating to past or with the industry ratios. This step facilitates in assessing success or failure of the firm.

The *third* step involves interpretation, drawing of inferences and report-writing. Conclusions are drawn after comparison in the shape of report or recommended course of action.

Importance of Ratio Analysis

The inter relationship that exists among the different items appeared in the financial statements, are revealed by accounting ratios. Ratio analysis of a firm's financial statements is of interest to a number of parties, mainly, shareholders, creditors, financial executives, etc. Shareholders are interested with earning capacity of the firm : creditors are interested in knowing the ability of firm to meet its financial obligations; and financial executives are concerned with evolving analytical tools that will measure and compare costs, efficiency, liquidity and profitability with a view to make intelligent decisions.

The importance of ratio analysis are discussed below, in brief:

1. **Aid to measure General Efficiency:** Ratios enable the mass of accounting data to be summarised and simplified. They act as an index of the efficiency of the enterprise. As such they serve as an instrument of management control.
2. **Aid to measure Financial Solvency:** Ratios are useful tools in the hands of management and other concerned to evaluate the firms performance over a period of time by comparing the present ratio with the past ones. They point out firm's liquidity position to meet its short term obligations and long term solvency.
3. **Aid in Forecasting and Planning:** Ratio analysis is an invaluable aid to management in the discharge of its basic function such as planning, forecasting, control, etc. The ratio, that are derived after analysing and scrutinising the past result, helps the management to prepare budgets to formulate policies and to prepare the future plan of action, etc.
4. **Facilitate decision-making:** It throws light on the degree of efficiency of the management and utilisation of the assets and that is why it is called surveyor of efficiency. They help management in decision-making.
5. **Aid in corrective Action:** Ratio analysis provides interfirm comparison. They highlight the factors associated with successful and unsuccessful firms. If comparison shows an unfavourable variance, corrective actions can be initiated. Thus, it helps the management to take corrective action.
6. **Aid in Intra Firm Comparison.** Intra firm comparisons are facilitated. It is an instrument for diagnosis of financial health of an enterprise. It facilitates the management to know

whether the firm's financial position is improving or deteriorating by setting a trend with the help of ratios.

7. **Act as a Good Communication:** Ratios are an effective means of communication and play a vital role in informing the position of and progress made by the business concern to the owners and other interested parties. The communications by the use of simplified and summarised ratios are more easy and understandable.
8. **Evaluation of Efficiency:** Ratios analysis is an effective instrument which when properly used, is useful to assess important characteristics of business—liquidity, solvency, profitability, etc. A study of these aspects may enable conclusions to be drawn relating to capabilities of business.
9. **Effective Tool.** Ratio analysis helps in making effective control of the business—measuring performance, control of cost, etc. Effective control is the keynote of better management. Ratio ensure secrecy.
10. **Act as a Barometer.** Ratios serve as barometer for the future. Ratios have predictory value. They are helpful in planning the business activities for a future. They·indicate direction in which adjustment should be made in budget or in performance to bring both closer to one another.

Figures, in their absolute forms, shown in the financial statements are neither significant nor able to be compared. In fact, they are dump. But ratios have power to speak.

Nature of Ratio Analysis

Ratio analysis is a powerful tool of financial analysis. A ratio is defined as "the indicated quotient of two mathematical expressions" and as "the relationship between two or more things". In financial analysis, a ratio is used as an index or yardstick for evaluating the financial position and performance of a firm. Analysis of financial statements is a process of evaluating relationship between component parts of financial statements to obtain a better understanding of the firm's position and performance. Financial analysis is used as a device to analyse and interpret the financial health of enterprise. The absolute accounting figures reported in the financial statements do not provide a meaningful understanding of the performance and financial performance of a firm. An accounting figure conveys meaning when it is related to some other relevant information. Just like a doctor examines his patient by recording his body temperature, blood pressure, etc., before making his conclusion regarding the illness and before giving his treatment, a financial analyst analyses the financial statements with various tools of analysis before commenting upon the financial health or weaknesses of an enterprise. A ratio is known as a symptom like blood pressure the pulse rate or the temperature of an individual. It is with the help of ratios that the financial statements can be analysed more clearly and decisions are drawn from such analysis. The point to note is that a ratio indicates a quantitative relationship, which can be, in turn, used to make a qualitative judgement. Such is the nature of all financial ratios.

Importance of Ratios

1. Ratios act as an index of *efficiency of a firm.*
2. They serve as an instrument of *management control.*
3. They are useful in *evaluating performance.*
4. They facilitate and help in *forecasting future events.*
5. They help management in exercising *effective decisions.*
6. They help management to take *corrective actions.*
7. They facilitate *intra firm comparisons.*

8. They play effective role for *easy and clear communications.*
9. They ensure *secrecy.*
10. They facilitate *inter-firm comparisons.*

(6) Economic Value Added (EVA)

Economic value added indicates how much economic value is added by the company to its assets. It measures economic value created by a company over and above its profits less any capital investments made to earn profits. EVA may be positive or negative. A positive EVA means company's returns are more than the cost of funds required to produce those returns. This means that company has created value for its shareholders. A negative EVA means company's returns are less than the cost of capital and it has lost value for the shareholders.

Corporate wealth (Investment is contributed by shareholders, debentureholders, creditors, financial institutions, etc.) It is necessary for corporate survival that it adds value to this wealth. Economic value added is "a financial tool for measuring corporate and divisional performance calculated by taking after-tax operating profit minus the total annual cost of capital." (Equity + Debt) It measures how much value is created by a business enterprise. Increase in value of investors' capital is value added.

As a performance tool, companies can improve EVA by earning more profits without using more capital or using less capital, or by investing capital in high-return projects, that is projects whose return are more than the cost of capital. It describes whether or not a business optimally utilises its assets to generate return and maximise shareholders' value.

7. Market Value Added (MVA)

Market value added is "a financial tool that measures the stock market's estimate of the value of firm's past and expected investment projects." In other words, it measures the market value of the firm's stock. If company's market value is more than capital invested in it (share capital, debentures and retained earnings), the company will have positive MVA. It means that managers have created wealth. If market value is less than capital invested in the firm. MVA will be negative which means wealth is destroyed.

EVA is value added to the shareholders by generating operating profit in excess of the cost of capital employed in business. It is the residual income after charging the cost of capital provided by shareholders and lenders. Several companies mention the EVA in their annual reports to show the extent to which they have been able to create shareholder value. Companies like Hindustan Liver, Bajaj Auto, Bharat Petroleum, etc. have scored high on EVA.

8. Balanced Scorecard

The **Balanced Scorecard** is a performance measurement tool that looks at four areas — financial, customer, internal processes and people/innovation/growth assets—that contribute to a company's performance. According to this approach, managers should develop goals in each of the four areas and then measure if the goals are being met. For instance, a company might include cash flow, quarterly sales growth, and ROI as measures for success in the financial area. or, it might include percentage of sales coming from new products as a measure of customer goals. The intent of the balanced scorecard is to emphasize that all of these areas are important to an organization's success and that there should be a balance among them.

One approach to determining the focus of control that has become popular in recent years is the **Balanced Scorecard.** Advocates of this approach argue that historically there has been an "over-focus" on financial ratios and budgetary controls and corresponding neglect of other important areas of measurement of a company's performance. To remedy this, the developers of the balanced scorecard approach proposed an integrated and "balanced" set of measures for four critical areas ("perspectives" as they called them).

1. The (traditional) financial perspective: How do shareholders perceive the company?
2. The customer perspective: How do customers perceive the company?
3. The internal business perspective: Does the company excel in its internal business operations and procedures?
4. The innovation and learning perspective: How well is the company doing at innovating, improving and creating value?

REVIEW QUESTIONS

1. What is budgetary control? What are the benefits and limitations ? *(M.Com., Karnataka)*
2. Briefly explain the traditional and modern techniques of control. *(M.Com., Mysore)*
3. State the meaning, process and benefits of budgeting as a technique of control. *(B.Com., MS)*
4. What is zero base budgeting? State its advantages and limitations. *(B.Com., Madras)*
5. How does break-even analysis help in controlling business activities? *(B.Com., Jabalpur)*
6. Explain the uses and limitations of ratio analysis as a technique of control. *(B.Com., Banaras)*
7. What do the network techniques of PERT and CPM help in controlling the business activities? *(M.Com., Bhopal)*
8. What do you mean by quality control? Explain the methods of quality control. *(M.Com., MS)*
9. Explain the concept of total quality management. How do quality circles enrich the quality of an organisation ? *(M.Com., Madras)*
10. Discuss management audit as a technique of control. *(B.Com., Calicut)*
11. What is budget? Explain budgeting as a tool of control. *(B.Com., MS)*
12. What do you mean by break-even analysis? *(B.Com., Madras)*
13. What is ratio analysis? Describe some important ratios used by organisations for the purpose of control. How for is ROI a measure of organisational efficiency ? *(M.Com., Bangalore)*
14. Explain fixed and flexible budgets. *(B.Com., MS)*
15. What is meant by a control process? Discuss its basic elements. *(B.Com., Madras)*

Organisational Conflicts and Grievances

24

CHAPTER

- Introduction
- Meaning
- Definitions of Conflicts
- Features of Conflicts
- Consequences of Conflicts
  - Positive consequences
  - Negative consequences
- Types of conflicts
- Methods of Handling Conflicts

MANAGEMENT OF GRIEVANCE

  - Introduction
  - Definitions
  - Features of Grievance
  - Causes of Grievance
  - Steps in Grievance Procedures
  - Pre-requisites
- Case Study - 1
- Review Questions.

INTRODUCTION

Conflict exists in all organisations and it takes many forms. Conflict is an inevitable part of organisational life because the goals of different stakeholders such as managers and workers are often incompatible. Organisational conflicts also can exist between departments and divisions that compete for resources or even between managers who may be competing for promotion to the next level in the organisational hierarchy.

Conflict is a state of discord caused by the actual or perceived opposition of needs, values and interests. A conflict can be internal (within oneself) or external (between two or more individuals). Conflict as a concept explains many aspects of social life such as social disagreement, conflict of interests, and fight between individuals, groups or organisations. In political terms "conflict can refer to wars, revolutions or other struggles, which may involve the use of force as in the term armed conflict. Without proper social arrangement or resolution, conflicts in social settings can result in stress or tensions amongst stake holders.

MEANING

The term conflict may mean different things to different persons. It may be regarded as the disagreement or hostility between individuals or groups in the organisation. It may even mean rivalry or competition or may be viewed as the perception of disagreement in the individuals. Pondy has described that the term conflict is used in four ways in the literature to describe:

(*i*) Antecedent conditions of conflictful behaviour, such as scarcity of resources or policy differences;

(*ii*) Affective states of individuals involved, such as stress, tension, hostility,, anxiety, etc.

(*iii*) Cognitive states of individuals, that is, their perception or awareness of conflictual situation; and

(*iv*) Conflictual behaviour, ranging from passive resistance to overt aggression.

When people work in organisations as individuals and group, their work and relationship may not always be smooth in conduct. Disagreements occur, there are differences in interpretations of facts, differences based on behavioural expectations, people compete with one another, protect their values and hold opinions different from others. This results in conflict. Conflict does not mean fight. It is only disagreement that arises due to opposing ideas and perceptions amongst individuals. It can take place between individuals, between members of the same group, between different groups and between organisations. It can arise between line and staff, different functional heads (production and sales manager) at different levels in different degrees.

DEFINITIONS

"Conflict is a process in which an effort is purposefully made by one person or unit to block another that results in frustrating the attainment of the other's goals or the furthering to accomplish those goals."

– Stephen P. Robbins

"Conflict is any situation in which two or more parties feel themselves in opposition. It is an interpersonal process that arises from disagreements over the goals or the furthering to accomplish those goals."

– Newstorm and Davis

"Conflict has been defined as the condition of objective incompatibility between values and goals; as the behaviour of deliberately interfering with another's goal achievement; and as emotionally in terms of hostility. Descriptive theorists have explained conflict behaviour in terms of objective conflict of interest, personal styles reactions to threats and cognitive distortions."

– Kilman and Thomas

FEATURES OF ORGANISATIONAL CONFLICTS

Analysis of the above definitions, reveals the following features of conflicts:

1. Conflict occurs when two or more parties pursue mutually exclusive goals, values or events. It is based on the assumption that there are two or more parties whose interests or goals appear to be incompatible.

2. Conflict occurs when an individual is not able to choose among the available courses of actions.
3. Conflict is different from competition. In conflict, one party sees an opportunity to interfere with the other's opportunity to acquire resources or perform activities. In competition both parties try to win but neither party actively interfere with the other.
4. "Conflict is opposite to cooperation". Cooperation implies mutual trust and confidence among employees in an organisation. Cooperation is essential for the successful functioning of every organisation. But conflict is detrimental to the survival and growth of an organisation.
5. Conflict is a dynamic process. It indicates a series of events. Each conflict is made up of a sequence of interlocking conflict episodes.

CAUSES OF CONFLICT

Conflicts arise due to the following reasons:

1. Different goals of different individuals or groups leads to conflict. That is, when the knowledge about facts is different, conflicts arise.
2. Organisational resources – mean, materials, etc. – are scarce and each unit wants maximum share of it. Competition amongst units for maximum share leads to conflict.
3. Differences of goals in groups leads to conflict between the two. For instance, production department may produce limited varieties in large volume in order to minimise cost. At the same time, sales department may feel that products of different sizes. colours, models, etc. may increase the sales.
4. When authority and responsibility of individuals and groups is not properly defined, people do not understand each other's role. This becomes a source of inter-group conflict.
5. Controversy and conflict are inherent in the concept of line and staff. Line managers dislike to take advice from younger staff specialists.
6. When work is passed from one unit to the other interdependence amongst units can lead to conflict. This is because the second unit will have to wait till it receive the output from first unit.
7. Some people like to argue and debate. They enjoy conflict as a matter of habit. It acts as a motivator for them to improve their performance.

CONSEQUENCES OF CONFLICTS

Conflict has both positive and negative consequences. Positive conflict is known as functional conflict and negative conflict is known as dysfunctional conflict.

Positive Consequences

The following are the positive consequences of conflicts:

1. Conflicts provide opportunities to individuals and groups to think again and take a more concrete view of the situation.
2. Group members unite together, take advantage of opportunities, overcome threats and take strong actions to resolve their problems. All members of the group work together for a common goal.
3. When conflict is developed, attention is immediately drawn to the malfunctioning parts of a system. It is an indication that the situation calls for improvement. Conflict is, therefore, an essential portion of a cybernatic system.
4. When group members face conflict, they think of all possible solution to the problem, evaluate their decisions and use their creative and innovative abilities to arrive at the best decisions.

5. Conflicts may be used as a device to overcome many frustrations and tensions. People may express their frustration and tension by means of conflicts. Thus they are relieved from utter mental tension.
6. It is empirically proved that productivity of conflicting groups is more than those which have close agreement amongst their members. Members with different perceptions and interests produce high-quality solutions to problems that improve productivity of the group.
7. It leads to innovation and at times to new direction. It is, therefore, even necessary for organisation's survival and growth.
8. Conflict signals something wrong with the present system of working and promotes group's ability to assess the present and desire for a better further.
9. Conflict is a test of the ability of people to learn and develop. It provides challenge to them. If they are able to meet the challenge, they feel satisfied and highly motivated.

Negative Consequences

Many times, conflicts may be detrimental and disastrous. Negative consequences of conflict are also known as its dysfunctions and these are:

1. When individuals or groups develop conflicting ideas, they avoid interacting with each other. This reduces communication amongst them leading to inter-group rivalry and loss of productive ideas.
2. Members promote their personal goals rather than group goals. They think of ways to promote their personal interests rather than organisational interests. This reduces organisational efficiency.
3. When conflict does not lead to solution of a problem, it is unproductive and investment of time and effort goes waste.
4. In the event of a conflict, there may be intensification of internalisation of sub-unit goals which may result in the neglect of overall organisational goals.
5. Groups hold strong perceptions about their activities and disregard those of the other groups. They highlight their strong points and competitors' weak points. This leads to deviation from organisation goals.
6. In an attempt to find as solution, management may gloss over serious differences and suppress certain feelings which may erupt at inappropriate moments and hit safe targets.
7. In extreme situations, members can stop working. This stops group's functioning and threatens its survival.
8. Conflict diverts efforts towards destructive activities. They spend more time on designing tactics to win the conflict rather than on pursuing organisational goals.
9. Conflict may weaken the organisations as a whole if the management is not able to handle it property. Some competent and dynamic executives may leave the organisation.
10. When management loses objectivity and treats disagreement as equivalent to disloyalty and rebellion, an opportunity for creativity should be deemed to have been lost.

TYPES OF ORGANISATIONAL CONFLICTS

Conflict may broadly be classified into the following categories:

1. Intra-personal conflict
2. Inter-personal conflict
3. Inter-group Conflict
4. Inter-organisation Conflict

Let us explain the above different conflicts:

1. Intra-personal conflict (Conflict within an Individual)

Intra-personal conflict arises inside an individual. A person joins an organisation basically to satisfy his varying needs. He faces a conflict within himself when he perceives that organisation is not satisfying his needs in accordance with his perceived standards. In the words of Keith Davis, "Organisations are the system of medieval torture which suppress and subjugate their victim individual. He lives in helpless confirmity, stripped challenge for psychological fulfilment". As a result, he becomes tension ridden and remains frustrated . Thus, there can be: (*i*) Goal Conflict and (*ii*) Role Conflict

(*i*) Goal conflict

Goal conflict occurs when an individual faces the problem of choosing among competing goals. There are three types of goal conflict:

(*a*) **Approach-approach Conflict:** A person wants two positive situations but can have only one. The person might be torn between two lucrative jobs (mutually exclusive goals).

(*b*) **Approach-Avoidance Conflict:** In this form of conflict, the person faces an alternative which has both positive and negative consequences. If he gets a job at the place he does not like, he faces both positive and negative consequences of the alternative and the conflict may affect his job performance.

(*c*) **Avoidance-Avoidance Conflict:** This conflict arises when a person has to choose betweer wo mutual goals each with negative aspects. For instance, a person may dislike his present job but the alternative of resigning and looking for another job is equally unattractive.

(*ii*) Role Conflict

Role conflict arises when a person has alternative ways of achieving organisational goals and he is asked to select a behaviour which may ensure the achievement of goals. A superior is expected to get things does but he is internally in tension whether to apply autocratic, participative or free rein technique of direction.

Role conflict arises because of the following reasons:

(*a*) When the organisational authority, duty and responsibility have not been properly defined and delegated to the individuals, the role conflict will arise due to ambiguity of role.

(*b*) When a person faces a predicament or contradiction between his cherished values and attitudes and those which are expected of him by his boss, peers or subordinates, the role conflict arise.

(*c*) When an individual is expected to play his role differently by his boss and by his subordinates, or by different groups having different values, goals and interest, he faces a serious role conflict. He does not want to displease his boss, nor his peers and subordinates.

According to R.H. Miles, "Role conflict is adversely related to job satisfaction and directly related low confidence and low morale on the job. It increases his tension, anxiety and frustration. It is cancerous but at the same time, it is exceedingly difficult to identify intra-personal role conflicts of a person. However, intra-personal role conflicts can be resolved by boosting morale, encouraging participations, avoiding ambiguity of roles and proper counselling and persuation."

2. Inter-personal Conflict (Conflict between individuals)

When conflict arises amongst people of different levels or functional areas, it is called inter-personal conflicts. The inter-personal conflicts can be of (*i*) Vertical Conflict and (*ii*) Horizontal Conflict.

***(i)* Vertical Conflict:** When conflict arises amongst superiors and subordinates in the chain of command or hierarchy, it is said to be vertical conflict. Subordinates resist controls or change and, therefore, do not always behave the way superiors want. Their goals may clash with organisational goals, their interests may clash with superiors' interests, they may not conform to rules and procedures, giving rise to conflicts.

***(ii)* Horizontal Conflict:** When people at the same level in the same functional area or different functional areas interact with each other, they share skills, resources and information which may not lead to desired outcomes. This can lead to clash of interests and interpersonal conflicts.

Inter-personal conflict arises on account of the following reasons:

(*a*) If people interacting with each other have different ego states, that is, they think and behave differently, there may be crossed transactions amongst them. Lack of complementary transations lead to interpersonal conflict.

(*b*) People coming from different socio-cultural backgrounds hold different perceptions. Such difference in perception may lead to interpersonal conflicts. Opinions may differ about task-related matters.

(*c*) Differences in value system and ego state may create misunderstanding leading to conflicts between individuals. For instance, one branch manager may favour price cutting to face competition while another branch manager may consider it unethical.

(*d*) When organisational situations force people to see things differently, they may think of their personal interests rather than organisational interests. Since people have different interests, their behaviour will be different which may lead to interpersonal conflict.

3. Intergroup Conflict

Conflict between groups is the most common type of organisational conflict. Groups exist in every organisation and when these groups interact with each other, intergroup conflicts may occur. Conflicts between lien and staff, between production and sales department, between union and management are examples of group conflict. Usual sources of inter-group conflicts are as follows:

(*a*) Each group tries to accomplish its own goals. Intergroup conflict arises when goals of two group are incompatible. Goal incompatibility implies that goals attainment by one group prevents or reduces goal attainment by the other group. For instance, labour wants more wages which means reduction in profits. At the same time, management wants more profit which means reduction in wages.

(*b*) Task interdependence refers to the dependence of one unit on another for resources or information. The relationship between mutual task dependence and conflict is not direct . But, in general, it can be said that as interdependence increases, the potential for conflict increases.

(*c*) Sometimes, two or more groups draw resources from a common pool which is inadequate to meet the total demand. Resources may be funds, personel, information or power. As each group attempts to get a bigger share, conflict arises between the groups.

(*d*) When two groups hold different attitudes, values and beliefs, they strongly work to promote their group interests. Promoting group interest may results in conflict amongst working of different groups.

(*e*) Conflict may arise when two groups compete over new responsibility,. Newcomers to organisations face ambiguity about job responsibilities. In some organisations, there are no clear job descriptions. Conflict may also arise due to problems in communication like noise, distortion, omission and overload.

METHODS OF HANDLING CONFLICTS

Constructive or functional conflict needs to be stimulated. But negative or destructive conflict must be eliminated through preventive and curative measures. Thus, there can be three different approaches to handling conflicts:

1. Conflict stimulation;
2. Conflict Prevention; and
3. Conflict Resolution.

1. Conflict Stimulation

Conflict may be stimulated when there is too much lethargy and conformity in an organisation. The following methods help to stimulate or encourage constructive conflict:

(*a*) **Reorganising:** Changing the structure of an organisation is effective method of stimulating conflict. When work groups and departments are reorganised, new entrants and responsibilities arise. Members try to read just themselves and in this process improved methods of operations may develop.

(*b*) **Communication:** Managers may manipulate messages in such a way as to stimulate conflict. Ambiguous or threatening messages, for example, a department is to be abolished can reduce apathy, stimulate new ideas and force revaluation of existing practices.

(*c*) **Encouraging Competition:** Foster competition by paying financial and non-financial incentives for good performance. This will promote conflict as each member will try to outperform others. That is, one group struggles hard to outperform the other, constructive conflict will occur.

(*d*) **Bringing in Outsiders:** Break old teams and departments and re-organise them. New work, members and responsibilities will be created requiring adjustment with each other. This will give rise to conflict and new and improved methods of operation.

2. Conflict Prevention

Following are the techniques employed to prevent conflict:

(*a*) **Reduction in Interdependence:** The basic reason in the intergroup conflict is interdependence among them. Departments may be provided with resources independent of other departments. Thus conflicts may be minimised by reducing interdependence among the departments.

(*b*) **Reduction in Shared Resources:** When two or more units are required to share resources, particularly scarce ones, the potential for conflict increases. The management of conflict suggests reducing such sharing. One technique for reducing such sharing is the increase in such resources so that each unit is independent in using them.

(*c*) **Exchange of personnel:** Personnel of the conflicting groups may be exchanged for a specified period as a way to reducing and managing conflict. An exchange of people is very similar to role reversal, which is aimed at greater understanding between people by forcing each to present and defend the others position.

(*d*) **Appeal to Higher Authority:** Conflicts may be resolved through the hierarchy. If resolution cannot be attained by two organisational members, they may take the issue to a common superior who resolves the conflict by making a decision.

(*e*) **Creation of Integrators:** To resolve conflict, organisation my create provisions for the appointment of special integrators who may manage the interdependence of various groups so that unsolved matters can be solved through them.

3. Conflict Resolution

The various measures, mentioned above, undoubtedly help in reducing the occurrence of conflicts in the organisation. As such, whenever conflicts arise, these have to be resolved by some specific actions, known as conflict resolution actions. Conflict resolution styles often can be well discussed through the Thompson model. According to him, there are five conflict resolution styles:

(*a*) Problem solving

(*b*) Avoidance (Withdrawal)

(*c*) Smoothing (Accommodating)

(*d*) Compromise

(*e*) Confrontation (Dominance)

A brief explanation is given below:

(*a*) **Problem Solving:** In this technique, an attempt is made to bring the conflicting parties together and to share the mutual problem. The focus is on sharing of information to avoid misunderstanding and to find out areas of common interest. Question of who is right or who is wrong is avoided. This method is suitable for resolving conflicts arising out of misunderstanding.

(*b*) **Avoidance (Withdrawal):** It involves withdrawal of parties from the scene of the conflict. When parties to the conflict fail to arrive at mutually agreed solution, they may detach themselves from the conflict believing that avoidance is more mature and reasonable then wasting time and energy on childish arguments.

(*c*) **Smoothing (Accommodating):** It is the process of suppressing differences existing between parties to the conflict and emphasising common interests. Sharing of opinions removes misunderstanding and both parties realise that they are not far apart. Smoothing or accommodating may be useful when the conflict is associated with aggressive feelings among the parties.

(*d*) **Compromising:** There is no distinct winner or loser because each party foregoes something. This technique is also know as lose-lose technique. The technique is commonly used to dissolve conflict which arises out because of differences in goals, attitudes or values. The technique is simple based on traditional give and take process and typically involves negotiation and a series of sacrifices. Labour conflicts are resolved by this technique.

(*e*) **Confrontation (Dominance):** In this technique, parties to the conflict are left free to settle their score by mobilising their strengths and capitalising on the weaknesses of others. Parties use weapons like fights, arguments and intimidation to win over each other. One party's gain in another party's loss. This technique is adopted when both the parties adopt a very rigid stand.

MANAGEMENT OF GRIEVANCE

INTRODUCTION

Emergence of grievance is a natural outcome of interaction among people, whether in organisational context or in other context. In the organisational context, employees may have grievances against management, in the same way, management may have grievances against employees. Grievance is a state of dissatisfaction over some issues related to employment. Generally, expression of this dissatisfaction in oral form is known as complaint while in written form, it is known as grievance.

DEFINITIONS OF GRIEVANCE

Grievance is defined as follows:

"A grievance is any discontent or dissatisfaction, whether expressed or not, whether valid or not, arising out of anything connected with the company which an employee thinks, believes or even feels to be unfair, unjust or inequitable." – *Michael Jucius*

"Grievance is any dissatisfaction or feeling of injustice in connection with one's employment situation that is brought to the attention of management" – *Dale S. Beach*

"A grievance is defined as anything that an employee thinks or feels is wrong, generally accomplished by an active disturbing feeling." – *Richard P. Colhoon*

FEATURES OF GRIEVANCE

From the above definitions, the features of grievance are:

(*a*) A grievance may be expressly stated by an employee.

(*b*) A grievance may be valid, untrue or rediculous.

(*c*) A grievance may be arisen out of something, connected with the organisation or work.

(*d*) A grievance may be written or verbal.

(*e*) A grievance give rise to frustration, indifference to work, poor morale, discontent; resulting inefficiency and low productivity.

CAUSES OF GRIEVANCE

Calhoon has observed that "Grievance exist in the minds of individuals, are produced and dissipated by situations, are fostered or healed by group pressures, are adjusted or made worse by supervisors, and are nourished or dissolved by the climate in the organisation which is affected by all the above factors and by the management."

The main causes of grievance may be classified under the following categories:

(1) Management policies

(2) Wages and working conditions

(3) Supervision, etc.

A brief explanation, is given below:

(1) **Management Policies:**

(*a*) Improper rules and regulations;

(*b*) Discrimination between union employees and non-union employees;

(*c*) Improper seniority, promotion transfer, etc.

(*d*) Lack of opportunities for career growth;

(*e*) Unfair penalties imposed for misconduct;

(*f*) Hostility towards trade union activities, etc.

(2) **Wages and Working Conditions:**

(*a*) Bad physical conditions of work place;

(*b*) Non-availability of proper tools, machines, etc;

(*c*) Poor relationship with the supervisor;

(*d*) Changes in schedules or procedures;

(*e*) Tight production standard, etc.

(3) **Supervision:**

(*a*) Unclear and vague job instructions:

(*b*) Poor supervision styles;

(*c*) Failure to maintain proper disciplines, etc.

More factors may operate in each category. However, the major reasons for workers' grievance are: Promotions, amenities, compensation, fines, increments, leave, medical benefits, safety appliances welfare arrangements, physical environment and working conditions, etc.

STEPS IN GRIEVANCE PROCEDURES

Whether the grievances are real or imaginary, unless these are handled promptly and resolved satisfactorily the employees will continue to nurse their dissatifaction which will ultimately have adverse effect on their morale. Even minor grievances, if not rectified promptly, may snowball into major fractions leading to major conflicts between management and employees. Steps involved in a grievance procedure depends upon the size of the organisation. In general, the following various steps in redressing grievances may be followed:

Stage I: The aggrieved Employee explains grievance to his immediate supervisor, who takes suitable action to overcome the grievance and inform the employee about the decision. Often the grievance is solved at this stage. In case, if the employee is not satisfied, he may go to next stage.

Stage II: In the second stage, the Sectional/Departmental head gather all relevant facts connected with the grievance. A union official may help the aggrieved employee to present the case. The departmental head gives his decision considering all relevant facts, within a reasonable time. If the aggrieved employee is satisfied, the matter is over. If not, he may go to the next stage or step.

Stage III: If the grievance is not redressed to the satisfaction of the aggrieved employee, the matter is referred to the Grievance Committee having members from both management and union. The committee examine the decisions arrived at the previous stages to arrive at the decision. The decision suggests the ways in which the grievance can be overcome. In case, the grievance is not redressed, the committee may recommend the matter to a higher level.

Stage IV: The executive or the committee should promptly take up the matter and discuss the grievance with the employee concerned and the immediate superior. If necessary, the grievance may be referred to higher management for settlement. The aim should always be to settle the grievances amicably and peacefully so that harmonious relationships within the organisation are not hampered. If the grievance is not redressed at the committee level, the committee recommends for arbitration.

Stage V: The final step is to submit the grievance to arbitration. An arbitrator is a labour law expert who is paid jointly by the union and the management. The arbitrator studies the case, hears both sides of the case, and renders a decision that both parties must obey. Both the parties agree that the decision of the arbitrator will be final and binding.

Stage VI: The both parties should not conclude that the grievance has been settled until a check is made to determine whether the employee's attitude has been favourably changed. Checking can be done through casual observation while the employee is working, decision taken favourably or unfavourably; the other method include to ask from the other employees about the aggrieved employee's reaction.

PRE-REQUISITES

The efficiency of grievance procedure depends upon the fulfilment of the following pre-requisite:

(1) There should be clarity regarding each and every aspect of grievance handling procedures.

(2) A grievance procedure should provide the way through which grievance can be redressed, to the satisfaction of both employees and management.

(3) Employees may have more faith in mutually agreed procedures.

(4) The employees are entitled to legislative and judicial protection and they get this protection from the grievance redressal procedure.

(5) Since justice delayed is justice denied, the processor should aim at rapid disposal of the grievance.

(6) The existing grievance machinery, as provided by law may be made use of.

(7) The grievance procedure should be simple.

(8) The success of the procedure also depends upon imparting training to the supervisors and union representatives in handling grievances.

(9) The successful working of a grievance procedure depends upon a proper follow up by the personal department.

(10) Grievance procedure, to be effective, must be acceptable to both management and employees and also to their union.

CASE STUDY - 1

The president of Simplex Mills sat at his desk in the hushed atmosphere, so typical of business offices, after the close of working hours. He was thinking about Rehman, the manager in-charge of purchasing, his ability to work with George, the production manager, and Vipulabh, the marketing and sales manager in the firm.

When the purchasing department was established two year ago, both George and Vipulabh agreed with the need to centralise this function and place a specialist in charge. George was of the view that this would free his supervisors from detailed ordering activities. Vipulabh opined that the flow of materials into the firm was important enough to warrant a specialised management assignment Yet since the purchasing department began operating it has been precisely these two managers who have had a number of confrontations with the new purchase manager, and occasionally with one another, in regard to the way the purchasing function is being carried out.

From George's point of view, instead of simplifying his job as production manager by taking care of purchasing for him, the purchasing department has developed a formal set of procedures that has resulted in as much time commitment on his part as he had previously spent in placing his orders directly with vendors. Further, he is specially irritated by the fact that his need for particular items or particular specifications is constantly being questioned by the purchasing department. When the department was established, George assumed that the purchasing manager was there to fill his needs, not to question them.

As Vipulabh sees it, the purchasing function is an integral part of the marketing function, and the two therefore need to be jointly managed as a unified process. Purchasing function cannot be separated from a firm's overall marketing strategy. However, Rehman has attempted to carry out the purchasing function without regard for this obvious relationship between his responsibilities and those of Vipulabh, thus making a unified marketing strategy impossible.

In his previous position, Rehman had worked in the purchasing department of a firm considerably large than Simplex. Before being hired, he was interviewed by all the top managers,including George and Vipulabh, but it was the president himself who negotiated the details of the job offer. As Rehman sees it, he was hired as a professional to do a professional job. Both George and Vipulabh have been distracting him from this goal by presuming that he is somehow subordinate to them, which he believes is not the case. The people in the production department, who use the purchasing function most, have complained about the detail that he requires on their requisitions. But he has documented proof that materials are now being purchased much more economically than they were under the former decentralised system. He find Vipulabh's interests more difficult to understand, since he sees no particular relationship between his responsibilities for efficient and effective procurement, and Vipulabh's responsibilities to market the firm's products.

The president has been aware of the continuing conflict among the three managers for some time, but on the theory that little rivalry is healthy and stimulating, he has felt that it was nothing to be unduly concerned about. But now that so much of his time is being taken up by much of what he considers to be petty bickering, the time has come positive action.

QUESTIONS

1. It George's view of the situation realistic?
2. How do you evaluate Vipulabh's position?
3. How might this conflict be associated with factors in the formal organisation?
4. What should the president of simplex mills do now?

REVIEW QUESTIONS

1. What do you mean by conflicts? Explain its causes. *(B. Com., Adhra)*
2. Explain the various types of conflict and the way to resolve them. *(B. Com., Bangalore)*
3. Is conflict always bad ? Explain in the light of its consequences. *(M. Com., Banaras)*
4. How should inter-group conflict be managed ? *(M. Com., MS)*
5. How can conflict be stimulated ? *(B. Com., Madras)*
6. Why do interpersonal conflict arise ? How should such conflicts be handled ? *(M. Com., Bhopal)*
7. Discuss how conflicts arise in organisations. *(B. Com., Agra)*
8. Discuss various types of organisational conflict. Distinguish between intra-individual and inter-individual conflicts. *(M. Com., Bangalore)*
9. Define grievance. Discuss it characteristics.
10. What is meant by grievance procedure ? Describe the steps taken by the manager of an enterprise in handling a grievance. *(M. Com., MS)*
11. What are the various forms of conflict that can occur within an organisation ? *(M. Com., Kerala)*
12. Discuss various group level conflicts. What are the main causes of such conflicts. *(B. Com., Mysore)*

25
CHAPTER

Organisational Change

- Introduction
- Meaning of Change
- Features of Organisational Change
- Factors for Organisational Change
  - Internal Factors
  - External Factors
- The Change Process
- What is Organisational Change ?
- Resistance to Change
- Overcoming Resistance to Change
- Types of Change
- Management of Change
- Case Study – 1
- Review Questions.

INTRODUCTION

Changing an organisation is the process of modifying an existing organisation to increase organisational effectiveness, that is the extent to which an organisation accomplishes its objectives. These modifications can involve virtually any organisation segment, but typically affect the lines of organisational authority, the levels of responsibility held by various organisation members, and the established lines of organisation communication. Driven by new technology, expanding global opportunities, and the trend towards organisational streamlining, almost all modern organisations are changing in some way.

Organisational change refers to the alteration of structural relationships and role of the people in the organisation. It is largely structural in nature. These changes may be pressurised by internal or external forces, may affect only one or all the levels and departments or may be related to organizational structure, people, technology, working or social environment. When any alteration in the organisational relationship takes place. It disturbs the exiting equilibrium. When an organisation goes on operating for sometime, and adjustment between its people, their structural relationship and technical set up is established. People get adjusted and get used to a set of working relationships, social groups and a set pattern of organisational and individual life. So long as this equilibrium exists, it is easier for the people to adjust in organisation. But when a change is introduced, the existing equilibrium of relationships is disturbed and the problem of new adjustment is created. The problem of readjustment creates various fears and apprehensions in the minds of the people and generates vivid problems and difficulties.

MEANING

Increasing competition in domestic and world markets requires business organisations to change their structures and work environment. The world is constantly changing and so are organisations. Business organisations are open systems. They interact with the environment and adapt to environmental changes. It is necessary for their survival and growth. Not only should enterprises adapt to the changes, they must also anticipate the changes and incorporate them in their plans and budgets. Change is essential for survival of business enterprises. "Change may be required for the organisation as a whole or for any part of the organisation; work force, basis of departmentation, span of control, machinery, technology, etc."

An organisation is an open system, which means that it is a constant interactional and interdependent relationship with its environment. Any change in its environment such as changes in consumer tastes and preferences, state of competition, economic policies of the Government, legal framework, etc, make it imperative for an organisation to make changes in its internal system. Further, organisation system if composed of a number of subsystems which are also in a dynamic relationship of interaction and interdependence with one another. Thus organisations are subject to constant pressures to change because of the dynamism in their internal and external environment.

FEATURES OF ORGANISATIONAL CHANGE

The main features of organisational changes are:

1. Change may be reactive or proactive. When change is brought about due to the pressure of external forces, it is called reactive change. But proactive change is initiated by the management on its own to increase organisational effectiveness.
2. Change is not a one-time process. Organisations continue to change their policies to survive, and
3. Organisational change disturbs the existing equilibrium of the enterprise and leads to a new equilibrium.
4. Change takes place in all organisations but at varying speeds and degrees.

5. An organisation may be changed in several ways.

Change may be made in its structure, its technology, its people or in other elements.

FACTORS FOR ORGANISATIONAL CHANGE

Pressure for change arise from both within and outside the organisation. The factors that necessitate change fall into two categories: (1) Internal Factors and (2) External Factors.

1. Internal Factors

Factors internal to organisation that cause change are as follows:

(a) Deficiency in the Existing System

Changes are necessary when the present structure or processes are not capable of achieving organisational objectives. For instances unnecessary lengthy chain of command, unmanageable span of control, lack of coordination among the departments, barriers in communication, disparity in authority and responsibility, lack of uniformity in policies, lack of cooperation between line and staff, etc. are main loopholes in an organisation, that is organisational deficiencies, which obviously call for their removal and hence necessitate changes in the existing organisational pattern.

(b) Changes in Managerial personnel

Change in the Managerial personnel in the organisation may take place on account of new appointments, transfers, promotion or may be caused by expansion and technological changes. Change in the top level managers involves certain organisational changes. Managers differ in their skills, styles, philosophies, etc. Whenever a manager is appointed, he favours his own organisational objectives, policies and style of functioning different from those of his predecessors. Dynamic managers introduce change because they want to lead the market. Thus introduces sweeping changes in the organisation to suit his style of working.

(c) Employees Pressures

Ever increasing demand of the employees for better job security, better working conditions, higher wages, participation in managerial process, better safety and welfare, etc. reflects negative behaviour towards manages which may force them to change their policies. Thus, change is enforced to develop cordial relationship in the organisation.

(d) Changes in Production Technology

Organisational structures change in response to changes in production technology. Technology is by far the most dynamic and significant factor forcing changes in organisational designs, goals, strategies, policies, etc. For instance, computer has revolutionized the organisational ways of doing things. Computerization has significantly affected managerial styles, communication systems and decision making processes by increasing the accuracy. Such a change involves the entire part of the organisation.

The introduction of new equipment represents another internal force for change. Employees may have their jobs redesigned, need to undergo training on how to operate the new equipment, or be required to establish new interaction patterns within their work group.

(e) Changes in work force

Changes in managerial personnel, due to appointment or retirement, require the organisation to change its values and philosophies. Changes in operative personnel also require the organisation to change its procedure to match those who join the organisation. There may be changes in leadership style and motivation systems.

2. External Factors

Changes occur frequently in the environment, for examples, economic, social, political changes, etc. An organisation must change in order to adapt itself to the new environment. Some of the external factors which affect change are as follows:

(a) Market Situations

Changing market conditions, say, changes in the nature and extent of demand, caused by varying consumer needs and preferences; changes in volume of supply; entry of new suppliers with new products; changes in the market conditions relating to price quality and packaging, etc. compel the organisation to go for changes in order to survive and grow in such market. Competitors introduce better services, improved advertising, etc. are also causes for changes.

(b) Technology

Technology also creates the need for change. For example, technological improvements in diagnostic equipment have created significant economies of scale for hospitals and medical centers. Assembly-line technology in other industries is changing dramatically as organisations replace human labour with robots. In the greeting card industry, e-mail and internet have changed the way people exchange greeting cards. Technology is changing at a rapid speed. Today's technology becomes obsolete tomorrow. Mechanization, computerization and automation have greatly affected the functioning of the modern organisations.

(c) Legal Requirements

Changes in Government and legal enactments forces organisations to incorporate necessary changes. Relations between business and Government are improving. International developments are forcing organisations to modify their structures and plans. Changes in taxation policies, new laws, court decisions, etc. require the organisations to change their policies.

(d) Economic Factors

Changes in economic conditions; exchange rate and interest rate fluctuations, changes in fiscal and monetary policies, inflation, cost of living, etc. necessitate changes in the organisational policies. For instance, global economic pressures force organisations to become more cost efficient. But even in a strong economy, uncertainties about interest rates, and currency exchange rates create conditions that may force organisations to change.

(e) Social Changes

Social changes reflect in terms of people's aspirations, their needs and their way of working. Social changes have taken place because of the several forces like, level of education, feeling of autonomy, international impact due to new information sources. Natural calamities like floods and earthquakes also require changes in the policies of the organisations.

THE CHANGE PROCESS

One of the most enduring, simple, and yet comprehensive frameworks of the change process was proposed by psychologist Kurt Lewin over 50 years ago. He argued that change went through three distinctive phases — unfreezing, movement and refreezing.

Phase I Unfreezing

Unfreezing makes the need for change so inevitable to members that they become ready to accept the change. It inculcates in people that the present system of working is undesirable and change is desirable. It motivates people to move from the old and traditional ways to new and modern ways of working. The driving forces overpower the restraining forces and people, therefore, do not resist change. Rather, they welcome change and participate in its implementation.

Phase II Changing (Moving)

Changing involves discovering and adopting new attitudes, values, and behaviours. A trained CHANGE AGENT leads individuals, groups or the entire organisation through the process. During this process, the change agent will foster new values, attitudes, and behaviour through the processes of identification and internalization. Organisation members will identify with the change agent's values, attitudes, and behaviour, internalizing them, once they perceive their effectiveness in performance.

Phase III Refreezing

Though change is desirable, people generally resist change. Despite learning new ways of doing things, they tend to revert to old behaviour after working in the changed environment for some time. Refreezing attempts to make change permanent till there is need to reintroduce change.

WHAT IS ORGANIZATIONAL CHANGE?

Most managers, at one point or another, will have to make changes in some aspects of their workplace. We classify these changes as ORGANISATIONAL CHANGE – which is any alteration of people, structure or technology. Organisational changes often need someone to act as a catalyst and assume the responsibility for managing the change process — that is, a CHANGE AGENT. Who can be change agent?

A professional process consultant may act as a change agent or a internal person may act as change agent. The change agent performs the following functions:

(a) He makes the client organisation to realize the need for change.

(b) He identifies and diagnoses the clients problems.

(c) He prepares the blue print for implementation of change.

(d) He makes himself acceptable to the client organisation.

(e) The client is made receptive to the change which is never thrust upon the client.

RESISTANCE TO CHANGE

Change is common. However, when change is introduced in an organisation, employees resist it. There may be resistance on the individual level as well as organisational level. Following are the reasons for resistance to change:

Reasons for Individual Resistance to Change

The following are the reasons for individual resistance to change:

(*i*) Economic Reasons

People resist change when they perceive that they will lose some economic benefits. These type of reasons include the fear of technological unemployment, fear of reduced working hours; consequently less pay, fear of demotion, obsolescence of skills, etc. Change from labour intensive to capital intensive techniques of production fear of loss of jobs among employees. Whenever people sense that new machinery pose a threatening challenge for their existence, they resist change. Thus people resist automation due to the fear of loss of job. The greater the expected loss, the greater the resistance.

(*ii*) Social Factors

When the friendship with fellow members is interrupted, they suffer from a psychological set back; and they find difficult to cope up with new environment. They form their own social groups at the workplace for the satisfaction of social needs. To the extent the satisfaction of these needs is affected by a change, people resist it. Change may involve risk and uncertainty and lower the happiness. People who are comfortable with *status quo* arrangement inevitably resist change unless strongly motivated.

(*iii*) Insecurity

When the employees from one post or location to the other, there is a sense of insecurity among the individuals. When employees are uncertain about new job, new environment and new work-groups, they resist change.

(iv) Fear of Unknown

Change causes uncertainty and risk during the transition period. The change will bring results in future which is always uncertain. Lack of certainty creates anxiety and stress in the minds of people and therefore they want to avoid it. Human beings are basically dislike uncertainty that change bring about.

(v) Peer Pressure

People may resist change because the group to which they belong oppose the change. Every group has its own norms. And this group pressure on its members to resist change. For instance, an employee feel that the proposed change is desirable. But he may resist the change because his trade union, where he is a member, is opposed to it.

(vi) Existing social Interaction

People desire to maintain existing social interaction since it is a satisfying one. When there is a change, their existing social interaction is likely to be changed which people do not want. Therefore, they resist change.

Reasons for Organisational Resistance to Change

Change is resisted at the organisational level also. Some of the reasons why organisations resist changes are:

(i) Fear of Loss of Investment

In case when organisations have invested a huge capital in their permanent assets and training of employees, they are afraid of their capital being sunk, if they introduce a new technology.

(ii) Threat to Power

Managers occupying top, key and prestigious positions resist change when they perceive that the change may threat their position, power or influence. Change may disrupt the power relationships and produce a new power equilibrium. This new equilibrium may reduce the power and prestige of some executives.

(iii) Interorganisational Agreement

Organisation interacts with its environment. In this interaction process, it may enter into agreement with other organisations over certain aspects of working. Thus, if any change is to be incorporated, the organisation has to take into account the wishes of other organisations too.

(iv) Organisation Structure

An autocratic or bureaucratic organisation structure where authority-responsibility relationships and work are divided into well-defined units, where employees' participation in decision making is minimum and information follow a vertical path is not responsive to change.

(v) Resource Constraints

Organisational change usually involves a huge expenditure and sufficiency of resources usually is a major constraint. In such situations, change is resisted by the departmental heads and employees.

OVERCOMING RESISTANCE TO CHANGE

Change is desirable for organisational development. Resistance to change should not be considered bad. It gives managers an opportunity to re-examine their proposals of change for their effective implementation. Following techniques are commonly employed by managers in order to overcome resistance to change:

(a) Education and communication

One of the simplest techniques to overcome resistance to change is to educate the people who resist change about the advantages of introducing change and the limitations of not having it. The manager should counsel them and train them to adopt change.

(*b*) Participation and Involvement

In this method, the change agent involves the resistors in the design and implementation of change so as to overcome resistance. When people are involved in designing the change, they can understand the need for change.

(*c*) Facilitation and support

If employee lack confidence about performing according to new procedures and method, managers should provide them moral support, advise them when necessary and create a cordial and friendly atmosphere of understanding. The change agent listens to the subordinates, provides emotional support and gives training in skills to cope with the change.

(*d*) Negotiation and Agreement

When the group is resisting change in a strong way, negotiation and agreement will be helpful. Another fruitful way of overcoming resistance to change is to offer incentive resistors

(*e*) Manipulation and cooperation

When people resist change, managers may adopt a manipulation policy. Cooperation involves giving individuals a meaningful role in designing and implementing change programmes.

(*f*) Explicit or implicit coercion

Under this method, the change agent threatens the resistors with the loss of job or status or promotion policies, etc. or by actually transferring them.

Hammer and Stanton have enumerated the following principles for overcoming resistance to change:

- Resistance is natural and inevitable: EXPECT IT.
- Resistance does not always show its face: FIND IT.
- Resistance has many motivations: UNDERSTAND IT.
- Deal with people's concerns rather than their arguments: CONFRONT IT.
- There is no one way to deal with resistance: MANAGE IT.

TYPES OF CHANGE

Effective management depends upon the way managers deal with different types of changes. There are two types of changes:

1. Reactive Change

Reactive change is undertaken when it is pressed by some factors, either external or internal, to the oganisation changes are made in response to a situation and are primarily unplanned in nature. Most of the organisations which believe in traditional pattern of working often go for reactive change. Managers make quick changes to deal with problems since they do not have time to analyse the situation and prepare a well-conceived plan. Changes are made in response to environmental events, threats and opportunities. For instance, many organisations which were in manufacturing business did not care to install pollution control devices; they did only when they were forced by the Government.

2. Planned Change

It is a systematic change and wider in scope than reactive change. It follows a proactive approach to change. Managers increase organisational effectiveness by anticipating the force causing change and plan ahead to deal with them. They anticipate environmental threats and opportunities and carry out the change process in phased manner. These changes are important for survival of the firm. They involve huge financial and non-financial resources and are planned in a scientific and systematic manner.

MANAGEMENT OF CHANGE

Management of organisational change is a complex process. Change in organisation does not occur instantaneously. It requires considerable planning and efforts on the part of the management. Main steps in the process of managing change are described below:

1. Identifying Need for Change

Major change decisions regarding new investment, technological change, changes in organization structure involving the creation of new positions and abolition of some existing ones, plans and strategies for implementing change, are ultimately top management decisions. The most information for identifying need for change comes from the organisation's feedback and control data. Some of the features of the organisation may indicate the need for change like cost of production, declining profit, employee turnover, role conflict, need for expansion and growth, etc. Such indicators may force management to analyse what actions can be undertaken to overcome these. The first step in the management of change is to feel the need for change, which is defined by the organisation's desire to move from the existing situation to the desired situation.

2. Analyse the Existing Situation

The most important step in managing change is the diagnosis. A manager may use various diagnostic techniques such as interviews, questionnaires, present observation, etc. Diagnosis helps the change agent to see what changes are needed in the structure, system or in people. The desire to reach a new state of equilibrium requires analysis of the organisation's existing goals, structure, technology and people. A careful analysis of the organisation's existing structure and its comparison with the planned situation helps managers in identifying the type of change to be made.

3. Prepare a plan for Change

This is perhaps the most crucial phase in the management of change. It involves finding answers to questions like when to bring change, how to bring change and who will bring change. When the existing situation is analysed and need for change is felt, managers prepare a plan for initiating the change. The kind of changes to be made in the organisation structure, development of new authority-responsibility relationships, new policies, procedures, market operations, and people help to make plans for change.

4. Try the Plan

A pilot run of the plan should be made by the organisation and if it is successful in one unit, it should be implemented in the entire organisation. Problem in the pilot run or pretesting of the plan should be corrected before the overall change of plan is implemented.

5. Implement the Change

While implementing change, several problems might have to be faced. *First*, resistance to change has to be overcome. *Secondly*, change may disrupt and undermine the existing control system. *Thirdly*, change might upset the balance of power in the organisation. It becomes, therefore, necessary to motivate change, to manage the transition and to shape the political dynamism. Change may invite resistance from members as it involves rearrangement of people and resources. There may be fear of insecurity, discontentment, loss of social interactions, position or status amongst members. Managers must, therefore, overcome the resistance. When resistance is overcome, people will willingly accept the change.

6. Follow up and Feedback

A successfully planned and implemented change may not always bring desired results. The change process should, therefore, be regularly monitored and reviewed to analyse the effect of change. Discrepancies or deviations should be taken to smoothen the process of change.

Without proper feedback, management of change is rendered incomplete and useless. A manager or change agent must compare the standards present during the pre-change period with actual performance after implementing the change and ensure whether the change has been fruitful or wasteful. The change agent in this last step should see that change is beneficial.

CASE STUDY – 1

It was with great enthusiasm that BEML made its move to employ an American consulting agency to stem the deterioration in quality and productivity of its employees and bring about change and organisation development. The consulting organisation was to stay in house for a period of two years during which time it was to study the organisation and come up with ways to bring about change in the organisation for the better.

During the first six months the agency received good response from the employees and management in terms of information and suggestions. These were assimilated and after interaction with the management, the consulting agency developed various methods to bring about change and organisation development. However things began to go wrong when the agency made attempts to implement its programmes and methods such as target setting, quality improvement measures, scheduling, etc. These measures had the type of American technology and work methods with 100 per cent accountability. Non-compliance and non-performance had negative impact on the employees' records.

Soon this manifested itself in the form of negative response and reaction contrary to the original enthusiasm and participation. The high point was the union raising objections to many of the measures initiated and suggested by the consulting firm. The end result was that the consulting firm had to be withdrawn.

QUESTIONS

1. Do you think the choice of consultant was wrong? Give reasons for your answer.
2. How would you have gone about to bring change at BEML?
3. Could you have avoided the problems faced by BEML? If yes, how?

REVIEW QUESTIONS

1. What is the role of the top management in bringing about organisational change? (*M.Com., Calicut*)
2. "Change is absolutely necessary; all resistance to change is bad." Do you agree? Give reasons. (*M.Com., Jabalpur*)
3. What do you understand by the term "change"? Why do people resist change in an organisation?
4. Discuss the causes and remedies for human resistance to change. (*B.Com., MS*)
5. Explain the nature and process of change. (*B.Com., MK*)
6. Discuss the process through which the whole problem of change can be managed. (*M.Com., Madras*)
7. Briefly explain the process through which management may try to overcome resistance to change. (*M.Com., Bhopal*)
8. Why is change resisted? How would you as a manager overcome people's resistance to change? (*B.C.A., Andhra*)
9. Who can be a change agent at the organisational level? What should be the method that a change agent should apply to make change acceptable? (*M.Com., Banaras*)
10. What is organisational change? Describe the reasons for change in organisations. (*B.Com., Kerala*)

Management by Objectives and Workstress

- Introduction
- Meaning
- Definition
- MBO Characteristics
- Steps in MBO Process
- Objectives of MBO
- Advantages of MBO
- Disadvantages of MBO
- Management by Exception (MBE)
- WORK STRESS
- Definition
- Importance of Stress
- Stress Management
- Case Study-1
- Review Questions.

INTRODUCTION

Management by objective or MBO refers to a formal set of procedures that begins with goal setting and continues through performance review. Managers and subordinates act together to set common goals. Each person's major areas of responsibility are clearly defined in terms of measurable expected results or "objectives" used by staff members in planning their work and by both staff members and their managers for monitoring progress. Performance appraisals are conducted jointly on a continuing basis, with provisions for regular periodic reviews.

The setting up of goals or objectives became so important in the business world that the concept of Management By Objectives (MBO) propounded by Peter F. Drucker came to limelight in the year 1954. It is also known as 'Results Management': 'Goals Management' : 'Work Planning Review'; 'Management by Results' : or 'management by Mission'. Basic principle underlying the theory of MBO is the participative style of management. It aims at setting goals through participation of superiors and subordinates. The heart of MBO is the objectives, which spell out the individual actions needed to fulfill the unit's functional strategy and objectives. MBO provides a way to integrate and focus the efforts of all organisation members on the goals of higher management and overall organisational strategy.'

MEANING

Odiorne has described "the system of management by objective as a process whereby superior and subordinate managers of an organisation jointly identify common goals, define each individual's major areas of responsibility in terms of results expected of him and use these measures as guides for the operating unit and assessing the contribution of each of its members."

MBO is considered a system and philosophy of management rather than simple technique. It is a goal oriented approach which facilitates performance of all management functions in a logical and effective manner for achieving goals.

MBO is as old as management itself. In fact, management has to be always with and by objectives. However, most managers are really not sure about their objectives. They are usually not clear as to what their organisation, department or section should achieve within a particular period of time. If properly implemented MBO can provide the dynamism, purposiveness and trust that are essential characteristics of effective management.

DEFINITIONS

A few definitions are given below:

1. Mc Conkey has defined it, "as an approach to management planning and evaluation in which specific target for a year or some other length of time are established for each manager on the basis of result which each must achieve, if the overall objectives of the company are to be realised. At the end of the period, the actual results achieved are measured against the original goals, that is, against the expected results which each manager knows, he is responsible for achieving."
2. "MBO is a comprehensive managerial system that integrates many key managerial activities in a systematic manner, consciously directed towards the effective and efficient achievement."
—Koontz and Weihrich
3. "MBO is a result-centred, non-specialist, operational managerial process for the effective utilisation of material, physical and human resources of the origanisation by integrating the individual with the organisation and organisation with the environment."
—SK. Chakraborty
4. Prof. Reddin, who has contributed significantly towards making MBO more operational, has the following to say, "Management by objectives the establishment of effectiveness

areas and effectiveness standards for managerial positions and the periodic conversion of these into measurable time bounded objective linked vertically and horizontally, and with future planning.

MBO CHARACTERISTICS

Based on the above definitions, MBO reveals the following features:

1. When goals are framed with participation of superiors and subordinates, it ensures integration of objectives across organisational levels and functional areas. This provides focus to all managerial activities and leads to effective attainment of goals.
2. The goals serve as standards of performance against which actual performance is measured. Discrepancy is removed through various techniques of control. Planning and control are the heart of MBO.
3. MBO is a continuous process or a never-ending process. The continuous nature of MBO process not only ensures sustained concentration of efforts toward organisational goals, it also helps in modifying the goals to suit changing conditions.
4. Performance of employees is periodically evaluated in the light of predetermined targets. Emphasis is put on improving future performance. Rewards are governed by the results achieved.
5. The basic emphasis of MBO is on objectives. Therefore, objectives are established for all the levels of the organisation, including the corporate level, all the units or departments and individual managers. Objectives provide the means for integrating the organisation with its environment, its subsystems and people.
6. Periodic review of performance is an important feature of MBO. The performance review is held regularly, normally once in a year. It emphasises initiative and active role by the manager who is responsible for achieving objectives. The review is future-oriented.
7. MBO recognizes the fact that the goal setting and achievement process is a cooperative and participative endeavour.
8. MBO aims at a radical realignment of relations between superior and subordinate managers. Superior managers are required to adopt a supportive stimulative role in relation to their subordinates.
9. Each manager sets his objectives and also evaluates his performance. He clarifies his job relationship with his superiors, peers and subordinates and the whole process of management revolves around the participative objective setting.
10. Objectives in MBO provide guidelines for appropriate system and procedures. Resource allocation, delegation of authority, etc. are determined on the basis of objectives. Similarly, reward and punishment system is attached with the achievement of the objectives.

STEPS IN MBO PROCESS

Setting objectives is the first task of management. Reaching the objectives (goals) is the very logic of the management process – through organising, directing and control. Most organisations which have seriously introduced MBO have reaped distinct improvement in their management.

The following sequence of steps is followed in the process of MBO.

1. Step I : Setting Overall Organisational Goals

The top management sets goals for the enterprise in key areas. The objectives for each department are laid down in consultation with the departmental heads. Then, the process - goal setting, is repeated at lower levels until goals for each and every individual are established. Superiors and subordinates discuss corporate objectives and drive individual performance target.

2. Step II Setting up subordinate's Goals

The process of objective setting begins with superior's proposed recommendations for his subordinate's objectives. In turn, the subordinate states his own objectives as perceived by him. Thereafter, the final objectives for the subordinate are set by the mutual negotiation between superior and subordinate. The goal setting process is complete when agreement is reached between superiors and subordinates as to what is to be accomplished. The subordinate goals are set at departmental level, section level and individual level, etc. Everyone in the organisation should know what is expected of him? These goals should aim at contributing towards the overall goal of the organisation. The objectives at all levels must be set out in concrete terms.

3. Step III Matching Goals and Resources

When the objectives are set carefully, they also indicate the resource requirements. In fact, resource availability becomes important aspect of objective setting because it is the proper application of resources which ensures objective achievement. Therefore, there should be matching between objectives and resources. The superior is better able to see the needs and allocates the resources. The allocation of resources should be done in consultation with the subordinates.

4. Step IV: Developing Action Plans

Specific key areas are determined which require more attention than others in terms of allocation of resources. These areas are (1) profitability, (2) Market standing (3) Innovation (4) Productivity (5) Worker performances (6) Manager Performance, (7) Public Responsibility, etc. These plans are usually formulated at lower levels in consultation with their superiors.

5. Step V: Periodic Meetings

At frequent intervals actual performance is reviewed jointly by the superior and the subordinates. The top level management will be able to know the views and difficulties faced by the staff in achieving the targets. If necessary, the goals are modified. Problems, if any, are identified and solutions are sort out. The success of plans is ensured through periodic review of performance.

6. Step VI: Appraisal of Performances

Evaluation of performance at the end of a period is essential to assess the work. The superior should evaluate the work of the subordinates and find out deviations, if any. The persons whose performance is below the standard performance are penalised and those whose perfomance is outstanding are rewarded. The process of appraisal will enable the management to take corrective measures if there are deviations in performance. Feedback promotes self-direction and control. It helps a person to know the direction in which he is going to improve his overall performance.

OBJECTIVES OF MBO

MBO aims at the following objectives

1. MBO promotes subordinate's participation in the goal setting process.
2. MBO is a goal oriented process and not work oriented process.
3. Superiors play a supportive role in guiding the subordinates.
4. Individual performance targets are derived from the overall objectives of the organisation.
5. Emphasis is put on improving future performance.
6. It is a continuous process, *i.e.* never ending process.
7. It facilitates fast and effective decision-making.
8. It serves as the basis of control.
9. Organisational efficiency is increased by picking out the key areas.
10. The programmes are designed to achieve the desired result.

ADVANTAGES OF MBO

MBO leads to the following benefits:

1. Clear Goals

MBO produces clear and measurable performance goals. The joint goal setting sessions are organised on a give and take basis. This enhances team spirits and better inter group communication. Goals are determined through employees' participation and therefore, they carry out their part of the job actively and willingly.

2. Result Oriented Planning

MBO results in verifiable goals which can easily be translated into action plans. The objective-setting process of MBO leads to an integrated hierarchy of objectives throughout the organisation.

3. Personnel Satisfaction

When the individuals are involved in objective-setting, they derive satisfaction because of the feeling that they are important to the organisation. They enjoy considerable authority which is a source of inspiration for better performance. Besides these, they are very sure that their performance will be measured in terms of their actual performance and will not be affected by managerial prejudices, biases and other personal factors.

4. Basis for Organisational Change

In any organisation, change is required because of change in external factors and in internal factors or change taking place in both the factors simultaneously. Therefore, to cope up with the change, the organisation has to change itself appropriately.

5. Motivation

Managers at all levels are involved in goal-setting. As a result they are more committed to the goals of the organisation. Rewards are linked with performance. Employees are allowed considerable discretion in setting individual targets which provides them psychological satisfaction.

6. Performance Appraisal

MBO provides objective yardsticks for systematic evaluation of performance. The performance of subordinates is monitored more effectively due to periodic review of progress. Measurable targets serve good standards for control.

7. Cooperation and coordination

Role of ambiguity and confusion are avoided. It helps to minimise duplication of efforts and overlapping authority. By clarifying the roles and responsibilities of each individual position, each individual knows what is expected of him. The subordinates are allowed to act upon their own initiative in deciding upon the ways of achieving their goals.

8. Improves Better Relationship

Setting of goals through MBO improves the relationship between employers and employees. This creates a healthy environment of cooperation, integration and coordination and organisational goals are achieved with zeal and enthusiasm.

9. Personality Development

When superiors have confidence in their subordinates it promotes a feeling of involvement, recognition and commitment amongst employees. Their behavioural attitude changes in a positive direction which leads to ego satisfaction and develops their personality.

10. Facilitates control

The self appraisal system promotes self-control by employees. Controlling aids can also used by superiors, through constant review of employees' performance, measuring it with planned performance and checking the deviations, to ensure that goals are effectively achieved.

DISADVANTAGES OF MBO

A number of problems are confronted while implementing this technique. The following are the weaknesses:

1. MBO emphasises on short-term goals. The long-term and quantitative objectives are not given proper attention.
2. The success of MBO will depend upon feedback system. But information is not properly conveyed to various levels.
3. The change in circumstances will necessitate a change in the objectives too. But the system is not rigidly followed.
4. MBO has been criticised as time-consuming and too pressure-oriented.
5. The traditional hierarchical organisation structure restricts involvement and participation of subordinates.
6. MBO generates paper work because large number of forms are to be designed and put into practice.
7. MBO is a philosophy of managing an organisation in a new way. However, managers fail to understand and appreciate this new approach.
8. Many managers often hesitate to change objectives during a period of time. Thus inflexibility created by applying MBO may cause harm than what it may contribute.

MANAGEMENT BY EXCEPTION (MBE)

The activities of a big organisation are so innumerable that it is neither feasible nor desirable for the management to exercise control over all minor or major deviations from the standards. "Trying to control everything may end up in controlling nothing." That is managers cannot control very organisational activity. When the deviation is not significant, the matter may not be reported to top managers. But if deviations are significant, they should be reported to manager. This is known as the management by exception (MBE). According to this principle, only exceptional (significant) deviations from the standards should be reported to the management.

The principle of MBE states that manages should concentrate only on significant deviations rather than each and every organisational activity.

BENEFITS OF MBE

Management by exception provides the following benefits:

1. It saves the time of managers because they deal only with exceptional matters.
2. Simple and routine problems are left to lower level managers.
3. It facilitate delegation of authority.
4. It separates important information from unimportance one.
5. It leads to optimum attainment of organisational goals by grouping the deviations between significant and insignificant.

WORK STRESS

People feel stress as they can no longer have complete control over what happens in life. There is no escape from stress in modern life. Hans Selye, an early authority on this subject, said that stress constitutes the factors affecting wear and tear on the body. In organisations, this wear and tear is caused primarily by the body's unconscious mobilization of energy when an individual is confronted with organisational or work demands.

Stress is the mental and physical condition that results from a perceived threat that cannot be dealt with readily. Stress is therefore an internal response to a state of activation. The stressed person is physically and mentally aroused. Stress ordinarily occurs in a threatening or negative situation, such as being fired. However, stress can also be caused by a positive situation, such as receiving a major promotion.

DEFINITIONS

"Stress is an adaptive response mediated by individual characteristics and / or psychological processes, that is, a consequence of any external action, situation, or event that places special physical and/or psychological demands upon a person."

—Ivancevich and Matteson.

"Job stress is a condition arising from the interaction of people and their jobs and characterised by changes within people that force them to deviate from their normal functioning."

—Beehr and Newman

Stress is an individual's response to a strong **stimulus**. This **stimulus** is called **a stressor**, that is, **any force creating the stress reaction.**

A person experiencing stress displays certain symptoms indicating that he is trying to cope with a stressor that is, any force creating the stress reaction. These symptoms can include a host of **physiological, emotional** and **behavioural** reactions.

Physiological symptoms of stress include increased heat rate, blood pressure, breathing rates and perspiration. Stress also leads to a chemical imbalance that adversely affects the body's immune system.

Emotional Symptoms of stress include anxiety, tension, depression, discouragement, boredom, prolonged fatigue, feelings of hopelessness and various kinds of defensive thinking.

Behavioural symptoms include nervous habits, such as twitching and sudden decreases in job performance due to forgetfulness and errors in concentration of judgement.

IMPORTANCE OF STUDYING STRESS

The study of stress is important for many reasons:

1. Stress can have damaging psychological and physiological effects on employees' health and on their contributions to organisational effectiveness. It can cause heart disease and it can prevent employees from concentrating of making decisions.
2. Stress is a major cause of employees absenteeism and turnover.
3. A stressed employee can affect the safety of other workers or even the public.
4. Stress represents a significant cost to organisations.

STRESS MANAGEMENT

Following approaches can be used to reduce the level of stress:

(A) Individual Approaches

An employee can take personal responsibility for reducing his stress level. Individual strategies that have proved effective are:

(1) Physical Exercise

Physical exercise is a good strategy to body fit and to overcome stress. Physical exercises of different types such as walking, jogging, swimming, playing, etc. are good methods of overcoming stress. The role of YOGA, a scientific technique of physical exercise to keep body fit and to overcome stress.

The benefits of physical exercise:

Increases energy

Reduces feeling of frequent fatigue

Improves sleep

Improves concentration

Helps to maintain a healthy body

Reduce the risk of heart disease

Improves cardiac function

So, you feel better and look better.

2. Relaxation

Impact of stress can be overcome by relaxation. The relaxation can be a simple one or some specific techniques of relaxation, such as bio-feedback and meditation. Meditation involves quiet concentrated inner thought in order to rest the body physically and emotionally. Meditation has been recognised as a powerful technique for reducing stress.

3. Social Support

Receiving social support – encouragement, understanding and friendship – from other people is an important strategy for coping successfully with job stress. A social support network can reduce the tension considerably.

(B) Organisational Approaches

The factors that cause stress are controlled by management. The following are the techniques:

(1) Job Enrichment

Redesigning jobs to give employees more responsibility, more meaningful work, more autonomy and increased feedback can reduce stress, because these factors give the employees greater control over work activities and lesser dependence on others.

(2) Goal Setting

Individuals perform better when they have specific and challenging goals and receive feedback on how well they are progressive towards these goals. The use of goals can reduce stress as well as provide motivation.

(3) Job Condition

With some jobs, the nature of the work can lead to stress. Management should ensure that workload is not too heavy, build in rests or breaks and avoid long working hours.

(4) Management Style

A great deal of stress at work can be a result of a manager's style in dealing with employees. Managers should have appropriate training or skills in dealing with others.

(5) Stress Control Workshops

The organisation can hold periodical workshops for control and reduction of stress. Such workshops may help individuals to learn the dynamic of stress and methods of overcoming its ill effects.

CASE STUDY - 1

Working for a Woman Boss

Mr Kapil Malhotra, a brand manager with a leading textile company in Calcutta, came to Mumbai to attend a seminar. Among other participants he met his old friend Anil Madan, currently with a pharmaceutical company in Bangalore and decided to spend a day with him.

As they discussed their office and work Kapil suddenly said, "Actually our biggest regret is that my sincere work and efforts are never appreciated nor my superior performance is given due credit. In our organisation, only the right connections can give you rewards. " Anil replied, "That happens in every organisation, though I am fortunate to have a boss, for whom the work and efforts are more important than our mere submission to her views. Our boss, Mrs. Reena Jain is one of the most capable person in the pharma industry today." Kapil was, however not impressed. He said, "I, for one, am sure that women at top positions are very demanding and complexed. Its quite strange that men in your organisation are comfortable with her, as men find it very humiliating and a blow to their ego to take orders from women bosses." Further, he added, "Not only men, even women prefer male bosses and find women bosses a pain in the neck". His opinion is neither unique nor isolated but a typical mindset of majority of professionals, who view women bosses as a direct threat and incompetent. Its so common a perception that often a woman has to prove at every step that she is capable and as competent as any man in her position.

Anil then shared his own experiences of having a female boss. "I feel she is as competent and capable as anybody else. She is highly qualified and mature with no over-zealous need to prove herself or outperform other men to prove a point. She is perhaps the best negotiator and has an amazing ability to see things from our perspective. She has promoted team-participation and involvement at all levels of the organisation. A stickier of quality and commitment herself, she impresses even her critics at senior levels. Empathy, listening and team-building comes naturally to her. One thing I, now, truly believe is that the fact that she is a woman has brought a unique perspective to her style."

Kapil remembered, an article on participative management, that says that autocratic managerial style is giving way to people oriented style. The article also said that women are more likely to succeed in the role of such leader.

QUESTIONS

1. What difference does it make, if you work under a female superior?
2. Abilities and not gender make a boss good or bad. Discuss.
3. What in your opinion, are unique and additional qualities a woman superior shows and brings in the organisation ?

REVIEW QUESTIONS

1. What do you understand by MBO? What steps can you suggest for effective implementation of MBO programme in an organisation? *(B.Com., Andhra)*
2. Explain the meaning and process of MBO. *(B.Com., MS)*
3. Define MBO. What are its benefits and limitations ? *(B.Com., Madras)*
4. Briefly explain the meaning and advantages of MBO. *(M.Com., Agra)*
5. Describe the steps involved in the MBO process. *(B.Com., Mysore)*
6. Discuss managing by objectives. *(B.Com., Madras)*
7. What do you understand by employees stress? *(M.Com., Andhra)*
8. Define stress. Discuss the sources of stress. *(M.Com., Mysore)*
9. What are the consequences of stress? *(B.Com., Jabalpur)*
10. Explain the strategies for managing stress. *(M.Com., Banaras)*

Total Quality Management

27
CHAPTER

- Introduction
- Quality
- Customer Satisfaction
- Customer Expectations
- Total Quality Management
- Quality Assurance
- Quality Circles
- Guidelines for Effective Problem Resolution
- Measuring Quality
  - Benefits of TQM
- Investors in People
- Review Questions.

INTRODUCTION

In recent years, many organisations have implemented **Total Quality Management** (TQM programmes. TQM entails not specific procedures, policies and practices but a philosophy that commits the organisation to continuous quality improvement in all of its activities. One of the major values customers expect from vendors is high product and service quality. Most buyers will no longer accept or tolerate average quality. If companies want to stay in the race, let alone be profitable, they have no choice but to adopt total quality management (TQM). Total Quality Management is an organisation wide approach to continuously improving the quality of all the organisation's processes, products and services.

For marketers, the best measure of quality is customer satisfaction. In a competitive environment, the ultimate indication of satisfaction is whether or not the customer returns to buy a second, third or fourth time. However, a firm can't afford to gamble that its marketing decisions are correct and then wait for repeat purchases to confirm or reject those judgements. Instead, managers realize that satisfaction is determined by how closely experience with a product meets or exceeds a customer's expectations. Therefore, marketers must do two things: (*a*) Ensure that all marketing activities, such as the price of a product, the claims made for it in advertising, and the places in which it is sold, contribute to creating reasonable expectations on the part of the customer. (*b*) Eliminate variations in customer's experiences in purchasing and consuming the product.

In business and management terms, there is an attempt to focus on a measurable concept of quality by concentrating on "fitness for purpose". A specification is supplied by the customer and the quality of the product is measured by how closely it conforms to this specification. It is based on the customer's perception of quality. In these terms quality can be defined as : "Continually meeting agreed customer needs" or "what it takes to satisfy the customer" or simply "FITNESS FOR PURPOSE".

In more general terms, quality is an elusive concept and the usual dictionary definition does not help to make it less so, that which makes a thing what it is, its attributes, its characteristics. The quality of a person may be measured by certain characteristics, such as honesty and courage.

One definition by the US Department of Defence is given below:

"Total Quality Management (TQM) is both a philosophy and a set of guiding principles that represent foundation of a continuously improving organisation. TQM is the application of quantitative method and human resources to improve the materials and services supplied to an organisation, all the process within an organisation, and the degree to which needs of customers are met, now and in future. TQM integrates fundamental management techniques existing improvement efforts, and technical tools under a disciplined approach focused on continuous improvement."

QUALITY

Quality can be seen as an attribute of a product or service which ensures that it is attractive in the eyes of the customer. It is a relative property rather than an absolute one, in that a given product or service will be attractive to customers if it fulfils their expectations more fully than any other product or service under consideration. It means delivering the right product of service, which is fit for the purposes required by the customer, at the right price, and at the right time and place. A company that produces and delivers a beautiful-looking car to a customer will not be considered to produce quality goods if the car does not work well. Whatever the costs involved, the materials used, or the care taken in manufacture, the quality of the car will be considered poor if it unreliable. A lawnmower that does not cut the lawn effectively is of no use to the customer whatever its price or however firmly the manufacturer describes it as a "quality" or "excellent" product.

There is no agreement on a definition of product quality, even though it is universally recognised as significant. One professional society defines 'product quality' as the set of features and characteristics of goods or service that determine its ability to satisfy needs. Despite what appears to be straight forward definition, consumers frequently disagree on what constitutes quality in a product — whether it be a cut of a meat or a performance by a rock musician. Personal tastes are deeply involved, what you like, another person may dislike. It is important to recognize, therefore, that quality—like beauty—is to a large extent 'in the eyes of the beholder.'

Besides personal tastes, individual expectations also affect judgements of quality. That is, a consumer brings certain expectations to a purchase situations. Sometimes you have high expectations, as with a movie about which a read rave reviews. Other times you have modes expectations, its with a course for next semester that is referred to as "not too boring". Your evaluation of a product's quality depends on whether the actual experience with the goods or service exceeds meets or falls short of your expectations.

CUSTOMER SATISFACTION

Whether the buyer is satisfied after purchase depends on the offer's performance in relation to the buyer's expectations. In general, satisfaction is a person's feelings of pleasure or disappointment resulting from comparing a product's perceived performance (or outcome) in relation to his expectations. If the performance falls short of expectations, the customer is dissatisfied. If the performance matches the expectations, the customer is satisfied. If the performance exceeds expectations, the customer is highly satisfied and delighted.

If it is accepted that high quality is a measure of excellence taken from the customer's point of view, then although producers may grade their goods in terms of quality, whether the producers; view of the grading is upheld will depend on customer perception. If customers like their strawberries to be large, firm, red and sweet, then fruit with those characteristics will be considered to be or the highest quality, and the producer of smaller, paler strawberries may not be able to convince customers of the high quality of their output, however, sweet they may taste.

The focus on the customer means that quality is conceptualised in terms of the customer's perceptions. The organisation's objective is to identify customer requirements so that both the customer's and the organisation's needs are met. It is also the intention to meet these requirements first time and thus avoid the cost of sorting out problems. The process involves : (a) Research; (b) specification and Planning, (c) Delivery and (d) Review. The process focuses on the customer at key points and returns constantly to research into changing customer needs. When customer needs are identified, planning can take place into exactly what has to be delivered. The specifications and standards are determined so priorities can be established to ensure that the product or service delivered is what the customer needs and that it meets customer perceptions. Although costs and price play an important part in this, most customers will pay what is necessary in order to receive what in their view is good quality. This in turn will generate profits as customers demand this product or service above others.

CUSTOMER EXPECTATIONS

How do buyers form their expectations? From past buying experience, friends, marketers, and competitors' information and promises. If marketers raise expectations too high, the buyer is likely to be disappointed. However, if the company sets expectations too low, it would not attract enough buyers, although it will satisfy those who do buy. Some of today's most successful companies are raising expectations and delivering performances to match. These companies are aiming "total customer satisfaction". Ram cycles, for example, guarantee "total satisfaction" and will replace at its expense any dissatisfied customer's cycle within a period of three years after purchase.

A customer can be defined as anyone who receives a product or service. This approach has been extended by many companies beyond the satisfaction of the external consumer in order also to include the internal customer. One department in an organisation receives products or services from another department and passes these on to a third group. On an assembly line a commodity is passed along the line from one individual or team to another, each dependent on the other for the receipt of the commodity at the correct quality at the correct time, and aiming to pass it on with the correct added value and again on time.

The concept of the internal customer means that each process is viewed as a product so that evaluation takes place at once by the immediate customer or by the processor. This system will help to eliminate waste and reduce cost, while the overall objective will remain the satisfaction of the external customer. The product or service will be 'right first time' so that errors will be prevented through the need to satisfy the internal customer at each stage rather than through a final inspection.

TOTAL QUALITY MANAGEMENT

Quality is never absolute—It is always relative to certain other considerations. The first consideration is that the word 'quality' is meaningless unless the ultimate use of the product is also stipulated. The term 'good quality' means the article is good for the purpose for which it was intended. An article may be good for one purpose, but may be unsuitable for another. For example thin papers – type-papers—may be suitable for taking carbon copies, but they cannot be utilised as wrappers, for which thick papers are used.

"Quality control refers to the systematic control of those variables encountered in a manufacturing process which affect the excellence of the end product. Such variables result from the application of materials, men, machines and manufacturing conditions. Only when these variables are regulated to the extent that they do not detract unnecessarily from the excellence of the manufacturing process as reflected in the quality of the finished product can the control of quality be said to exist." Bethel, etc.

As companies have made a conscious effort to focus on the customer', total quality management (TQM) and other methods have been introduced to implement this. It is possible to identify differences between total quality management (TQM) and titles such as strategic quality management (SQM). How important these are remains a matter of opinion. Total quality management is often described as 'value-based' approach to quality management; it may be seen either as a goal which an organisation aims to achieve, or the idea of a goal of total quality may be considered unattainable. On the other hand, strategic quality management can be described as both systematic and values based. It can be seen to suggest that the reason for improving quality is that it will have maximum strategic impact on the future of the organisation. Strategic quality management is designed as a practical and pragmatic framework in which the drive towards quality improvement can be sustained while not making claims on total quality. A counter-argument to this is to consider the word 'total' in the context of total quality management to mean that every part of an organisation is involved. The approach can be recognised, whatever its title, by its objectives. Total or strategic quality management can be defined as : "an intensive, long-term effort to transform all parts of the organisation in order to produce the best product and service possible to meet customer needs."

Product quality should be a primary consideration not only for manufacturers of goods but also for producers of services. It is virtually impossible for a services firm to achieve the same level of quality in all units of output. Quality varies because people, not just machines, are normally involved in producing services. In recent years, many organisations have implemented total quality management (TQM) programmes. TQM entails not just specific procedures, policies and practices, but a philosophy that commits the organisation to continuous quality improvement in all of its activities.

Total quality management is predicated on a commitment to customer interests, needs, requirements and expectations, and on the commitment of everyone to the constant improvement of the quality of everything that the organisation does and provide for its customers. Total quality management means an organisation culture to satisfy totally the customer needs and desires through an integrated system of tools, techniques and training. This involves reorganising management system, reengineering process of production and distribution radical changes in the organisation structure and processes. Such continuous improvements will give us high quality products/services. Effective management recognises productivity and quality as two sides of the same coin to increase profits and build customer patronage. An organisation that adopts TQM must implement changes in all areas of management. It must review its strategies, plans, policies, procedures and practices as per changing needs and desires of the market. The total quality is a way of life and not a magic formula. The management has to concentrate on achieving excellence in all areas of business and in all areas of management covering leadership, production process, distribution process, people management, resources management with continuous technological improvements, zero defects, ecology, social responsibility, etc.

QUALITY ASSURANCE

The quality assurance governs the ultimate fate of the enterprise in the market. No firm can really build up sustained bright product image merely through promotion. Only, through continuous managing for best quality—performance quality and market perceived quality—the firm can maintain bright product or brand image in the customer mind in a competitive market. Japan and Germany have emerged as business leaders today only through quality assurance and total quality management. If product features click with customer needs and expectations, even normal promotion is enough in a competitive market. Product becomes Unique Selling Point. Quality improvement is never ending. It is a relative value compared with the competition as perceived through the customer's eyes. It is an elusive concept because customer perception is itself difficult to predict.

Quality control often occurs at the end of the manufacturing process as a check to see if the commodity works. If it does not it is rejected and either scrapped or reworked. The problem with this approach is that there is heavy dependance on inspectors. This is expensive and obviously it is much better to identify the error at an earlier stage. Statistical process control (SPC) is a method of monitoring the conformity of a product to agreed specifications. By sampling units of the products, deviations from these specifications can be identified and adjustments made during the production process. Modern control techniques are based on the idea of an 'error-free' or 'zero-defect' approach or doing it 'right first time'. This concept arises because of the costs involved in correcting errors and the fact that the costs are usually greater the later they are identified. Under the TQM approach the team is made responsible for quality control, for reducing wastage and for ensuring that adjustments are made as soon as they are identified. Total Quality Management and Value Oriented Management are complementary and they must integrate in the management system to accomplish effective and efficient management. Indian Wisdom aims at maximum productivity and excellent quality and at the same time enrichment of minds of all employees.

Quality assurance provides a framework for quality control and quality improvement. Quality assurance supports teams of employees with systems, resources and discretion appropriate to their unique contribution to the organisation, to keep them in tune with progress of quality management and improvements.

QUALITY CIRCLES

Quality circle is a small group of employees in the same work area or doing similar type of work who voluntarily meet regularly for about an hour every week to identify, analyse and resolve work related problems not only to improve quality, productivity and total performance of the organisation but also to enrich the quality of work-life of employees.

Guidelines for Effective Problem Resolution

1. Admit mistakes and don't be defensive.
2. It is better if the organisation takes quick action.

3. Employees should avoid jumping to conclusion with their own interpretation.
4. Don't argue with the customers.
5. Deal customer's feeling tactically.
6. Clarify the steps needed to solve the problem.
7. Keep customers informed of the progress made on the complaint.
8. Consider remedial measures for inconveniences caused.
9. Give customers the benefit of the doubt.
10. Try to regain customer goodwill.

Dr. Deming opines that MNCs adopted quality circles without understanding what they are doing? He suggests 12 points for their successful functioning in the MNCs. They are:

1. Achieve consultancy of purpose
2. Learn a new philosophy
3. Do not depend on mass inspections
4. Reduce the number of vendors
5. Recognise two sources of faults: viz. management and production systems and production workers.
6. Improve on the job training
7. Drive out fear
8. Improve communication
9. Consider work standards carefully
10. Teach statistical methods
11. Encourage new skills
12. Use statistical knowledge

A quality circle is: "A group who meet voluntarily and regularly to identify and solve their own work related problems and implement their solutions with management approval." Small groups of employees, usually from the same work-place and under the same supervisor, volunteer to meet to identify problems and find solutions. They look at the problems that occur in their work area and that affect their own job. The group itself applies the solutions if it has the authority; otherwise management is presented with recommendations and decides on implementation. Team work and team spirit play a very important role in establishing quality management and quality environment. The total quality mission will fulfil the needs and desires of our customers, both internal and external. The mission can be achieved only through teamwork *i.e.* doing together. Only togetherness or unity or our efforts will create and sustain an environment, where all the self-activated towards the total satisfaction of customer needs and expectations, each one contributing his own special talents and abilities to the process. Through mutual trust, mutual respect, personal pride and above all through genuine team work, we will try utmost for excellence or perfection. This involves constant improvements in offering our services, products and processes. Team work does not happen by command at a moment's notice. It requires collaboration and spirit of cooperation. It needs action plan directed towards its accomplishment. Management's commitment, support and encouragement will be absolutely necessary.

MEASURING QUALITY

A simple indication such as profit growth, market shares or the return on capital invested can be used to judge how well a quality management system has worked, and these certainly should be among the measures used. A manager needs to be both a problem solver and planner and to be able to communicate the importance of medium and long term objectives to employees at all level so as to support the attainment of objectives and targets and measure performance against these. In Thriving on Chaos Tom Peters identifies 12 attributes of a quality system, which in themselves represent a check-list against which an organisation's management can assess the stage it has reached in the development of such a system.

1. Management is obsessed with quality;
2. The company has a guiding system or ideology;
3. Quality is measured;
4. Quality is rewarded;
5. Everyone is trained in techniques for assessing quality;
6. There is a shift of managerial philosophy from adversaria to co-operative;
7. It is recognised that there is no such thing as an insignificant improvement;
8. There is constant stimulation to improve quality;
9. There is a structure within the company dedicated to quality improvement.
10. Everybody is involved in quality management, including suppliers, distributors, customers;
11. It is understood that costs decline as quality increases;
12. It is recognised that quality is relative and improvement is never ending.

BENEFITS OF TQM

1. A satisfied customer will likely to recommend the product to other buyers.
2. Manufacturing cost is reduced by reducing wastes.
3. TQM increases employee productivity and equipment productivity.
4. TQM reduces mistakes, thus savings are increased.
5. Increased pride of workmanship among individual workers.
6. Better justification for budgets because of efficient operations.
7. TQM ensures better profitability for the organisation
8. Improved sustainability caused by extended time between equipment failures.
9. Streamlined maintenance and production processes.

INVESTORS IN PEOPLE

For many organisations people represent their largest cost, often 70 or 80 per cent of the total. In the U.K., an initiative which recognises this fact and has the goal of attaining quality in organisations is "Investors in People". This rests on the premise that companies which have developed, or are developing, an awareness of quality acknowledge that people are the real key to achieving improvements. In a "quality" culture, people take ownership of their work and responsibility for the quality of their work.

"Investors in People" arose from the U.K. Government White Paper Employment for the 1990s which launched a partnership between business and Government. The National Training Task Force was established and the Training and Enterprise Councils and Local Enterprise Councils (in Scotland) were launched. A major priority of this initiative was to raise employer, commitment to training, hence the "Investors in People". The approach was to listen to businesses' ideas and needs, and look at the people factors which make one organisation more successful than another.

In all these practices, people are understood to be the key to achieving total quality and there is an emphasis on teams and seeing colleagues as internal customers, while being genuinely motivated to develop existing skills, develop new ones, accept the devolution of responsibility, make the best use of current or new resources, and if required, acquiring new managerial skills. Organisations need to recognise people as a valuable business resource, which can be used to create, protect or waste assets; that there are investment costs as well as benefits in this process; that the benefits will be greater than the costs; and that organisations will only benefit fully from investing in people if they start with clearly defined objectives and actions. It is recognised that the foundation TQM is the human response and human efforts which can give extra-ordinary results with available material resources and achieve total quality. Japan is the pioneer in TQM.

The "Investors in People" programme aims to help organisations to improve performance through a planned approach that is,

(*a*) Makes a public commitment from the top to develop all employees to achieve its business objectives;

(*b*) Regularly reviews the training and development needs of all employees;

(*c*) Takes action to train and develop individuals on recruitment and throughout their employment;

(*d*) Evaluates the investment in training and developing to assess achievement and improve future effectiveness.

REVIEW QUESTIONS

1. Define Total Quality.

2. What is meant by strategic management?

3. What is TQM?

4. How important is participative management for a total quality programme?

5. What part can management play in quality circles?

6. Explain "Investor in People". Summarise the benefit of it.

28 CHAPTER

Case Study Method

- Introduction
- Objectives of Case Method
- Guidelines

EXAMPLES

- Case Study – 1
- Case Study – 2
- Case Study – 3
- Case Study – 4
- Case Study – 5
- Case Study – 6

INTRODUCTION

Case study method has become quite popular in management education and occupy a significant place. A person cannot expect to become a successful manager just by studying books on management. A case study presents data, information and situational contact pertaining to an organisation with a simple, medium or complex set of difficulties, problems, constraints or dilemmas faced by the manager in a particular organisation. At the end, a case provides questions to be effectively and efficiently tackled by the case analyst. That is, a case is a description of a situation-real or hypothetical-involving some problems to be solved. It means, the case analyst is required to propose a suitable solution or make an appropriate decision

OBJECTIVES OF CASE METHOD

The case method is widely used to impart knowledge and develop strategic management and marketing skills. A good case should present to the students a realistic situation by which they are exposed to decision making practices. The quantum of information available in a case varies widely. It should be realized that there is nothing like a complete case. Managers face the problem of decision making under uncertainty and, often, inadequate information.

Unlike textbooks and lecture notes, managerial cases do not provide definite answers. Rather the pros and cons of issues involved in a case are discussed. Various alternatives and approaches are evaluated. The purpose of case analysis is not to learn authoritative answers to specific managerial problems. But it is to develop skill in the process of designing workable plan of action through evaluation of the prevailing situation. Students should understand it is the managerial exercise of identifying, diagnosing and deciding that counts in case analysis. The objective should be to develop the ability of thinking managerially and exercising responsible judgement.

The case study method is aimed at:

1. Helping participants to acquire the skills of applying concepts and principles of management.
2. Training the participants to workout answers and solutions themselves.
3. Developing the ability and skills of diagnosing problems, analyising, evaluating and decision-making.
4. Facilitating the participants meaning analysis and interpretation.
5. Acquiring skills to apply theoretical knowledge to practice.
6. Cultivating the habit of analysis and formulation of plan of actions.
7. Training the participants of practice independently.

There is no single approach or one best way of analysing a case. Hence, the quality of case analysis largely depends upon the imaginative, creative innovative ability of the case analyst in analysing and interpreting the context and the content of the case on the one hand , and one the other hand, interpreting results of the analysis and recommeding appropriate solutions.

GUIDELINES

There is no proven procedure that can be recommended for case analysis. Each case is a unique situation and requires suggestions accordingly. However, case analysis typically involves the following steps:

1. **Identify the Problems:** Every case contains a problem or number of problems which reflects the gap between desired and actual situations. In order to identify the problem it is necessary to read and reread the case carefully and thoroughly. Important points may be underlined.
2. **Diagnosis:** Having formulated the problem, the analyst should elaborate on the problem statement by focusing on what, where, when, who and how part of the issues involved in

the case study. Everything should revolve around the problem statement. The case analyst will develop meaningful alternative solutions as many as possible.

3. **Evaluation of Alternatives:** The financial statements, tables, etc. given in the case are analysed and summarised carefully. Ratios may be calculated. The factors underlying the firm's successes and failures are evaluated. The competitive position is judged. The alternative solutions to the problem are then identified and compared. Relevant information is separated from the irrelevant. A reasonable and objective interpretation of facts is necessary. The analyst will thoroughly and completely evaluate the pros and cons of each alternative decision or course of action. The analyst, at this state, evaluate each alternative. Thus, by weighing the relative strengths and weaknesses of each alternative, it will be possible to arrive at a logical decision. The case analyst will have to organise systematically the convincing evidence so as a substantiate a specific recommendation, while stating conclusions clearly.
4. **Recommendation:** Normally, there is no single solution to a case. Two managers of equal ability may select different alternatives. In some cases, it is possible to say that certain recommendations are superior to others but quite often it may be difficult to say that one alternative is better than the other. The case analyst must nevertheless decide. In deciding an alternative, it is to be seen whether it is based on the particular facts of the situation and is really workable under the circumstances.

A plan of action, which is workable, is recommended. It is necessary to support your views or judgement by necessary evidence. Recommendations should be stated in sufficient detail so as to be meaningful. These should be so organised and written that they communicate particularly what you want to say. Written presentation of analysis calls for writing skills on the part of the analyst; the skills are briefly highlighted below:

1. Use simple and short sentences in the recommendation.
2. Avoid using passive voice.
3. Avoid vague statements.
4. Be specific and precise in the approach.
5. Various points raise in the suggestion must be analysed carefully.

The case study method has large education value. The class-room discussion of case studies helps the management trainees in developing necessary skills for successful decision-making in real business situations. It is also found useful to training programmes for working executives. The trainees use their own experience in analysing the cases and derive management principles from the discussion of their analysis.

CASE STUDY – 1

Suvidha Private Limited was a Cricket ball manufacturing company employing about 100 persons including persons at various levels of management. Because of increasing business, the company needed to strengthen accounting procedure particularly through computerization. For this purpose, the company decided to hire a new manager, designated as assistant business manager. The company invited application through press advertisement. After receiving the applications, it appointed a selection committee consisting of members of top management including business manager Atul Mohan. The committee interviewed several candidates and finally selected Mahesh as new Assistant Business Manager. Mahesh was neat, well dressed, and quite articulate.

Mahesh joined the company immediately and started working very hard. He used to put extra efforts and even worked during holidays, as he did not have any family responsibility. He gained the reputation of being a dedicated and competent employee, his strong point being his knowledge of accounting and computer system. He was reporting to Atul Mohan, the business manager who was quite impressed with his working.

At that time, the company had no computer system, and its accounting procedures were in need of considerable improvement. Anil Kumar, the managing director of the company, directed Atul Mohan to get the needful done. Since most of accounting work related to sales, no separate accounting department existed and the work was performed under the direction of the business manager. Mahesh was asked to prepare a project report so that necessary changes could be made. In order to get the first hand information about the problem, Mahesh began meeting regularly with Lokesh Kumar without the knowledge of Atul Mohan. There was no attempt to have secret meeting; Lokesh kumar would just call Mahesh in for a report without bothering to tell Atul Mohan. The management team, whose members were with the company for a quite long period had formed a tight-knit group and appeared satisfied with the company. They all worked together and the company prospered in spite of fierce competition.

The meetings between Lokesh Kumar and Mahesh continued and Atul Mohan was gradually losing contact with the project and its progress. In fact Mahesh was almost reporting directly the managing director though he was placed under business manager and retained his title of assistant business manager. Atul mohan was no visibly upset over the development and was also concerned about Mahesh's spreading share of influence. He started feeling down in the company

QUESTIONS

1. What is the nature of problem in this case?
2. Could Atual Mohan have prevented Mahesh's assumption of power? If so, how specifically could it have been done?
3. Suggest the courses of action now available to Anil kumar, Atul and Mahesh.

CASE STUDY – 2

Electra Electricals Limited was engaged in manufacturing and selling electrical goods of high quality. It believed in introduction of new and sophisticated products in the market. Mr. Piyush Mohan, previously the Corporate Development Manager, was promoted to the rank of general manager in the company. In his new position, he needed a bright manager to serve as his deputy to assist in carrying out his day-to-day activities and coordinating marketing, manufacturing, research and development and finance functions. There were three candidates available who could be considered to the position of Mr. Mohan's deputy. All of them had very good academic background and successful careers of varying lengths with the company.

The first candidate Mr. Akhilesh was with the company for the last three years. He had engineering and MBA degrees from reputed universities. He believed in high achievement. He used to perform assigned tasks very quickly and accurately. He performed well when he has complete control over the situation. Many critical tasks he preferred to do himself and accomplished in much shorter time.

The second candidate for the position was Mr. Vikrant. He has Ph.D degree in quantitative analysis with engineering background. He joined the company about a year back. His performance in the previous job was rated to be of high standard and he got quick promotion with wider responsibilities at each promotion. He developed good understanding of the company's working though he was somewhat reserved in staff meetings.

The third candidate was Mr. Rakesh; he did not have any engineering or management degree but attained good marks in his arts degree. He had been with the company for the last fifteen years. He was quire good in his work and has good knowledge of the company's operations. He enjoyed working with most key managers and did not have confrontation or disagreement with any manager of the company. However, he was not aggressive and had difficult time in examining criticaly new ideas and proposals.

QUESTIONS

1. Assuming that you have to select one of the above candidates, whom will you prefer ?
2. If you have to conduct interview for the selection of the candidates, what types of questions will you ask ?

CASE STUDY – 3

Kailash Milk Products Limited is engaged in collecting, processing, and distributing milk and milk products in a large city in North India. Most of the products of the company are such that these have to be distributed on daily basis. The company has a crew of distributors who approach the fixed customers, both bulk buyers and individual. Mr. K. Dubey joined the crew of distributors after graduating in-Commerce. The distribution manager was quite impressed by Mr. Dubey but initially could not offer him a better job than that of a distributor. However, he promised to give him better opportunity whenever available. Mr. Dubey joined gladly.

The distributors are employed on monthly salary basis. In order to ensure distribution of the products, the company has a provision of over time pay. Normally, crew members work slowly in the beginning just to accumulate over-time pay. The pace becomes hectic towards the end of the day with some over time to meet the distribution schedule. There is no group leader but there are several old-timers who influence newcomers regarding the work rules. Mr. Dubey did not like this method of working but had to follow the group to be a good teammate. He gathered that over the years, the company had paid around sixty per cent overtime unnecessarily.

After a year, impressed by the work of Mr. Dubey and his overall suitability, the Distribution Manager offered him the position of distribution supervisor. The basic duty of supervisor was to look after the distribution system and to develop new customers in a given area. Beside Mr. Dubey, there were four other supervisors also. Dubey was sure of making distribution system effective, as he was aware about the delaying tactics of the crew. He was quite sure about cutting the overtime cost and impressing upon the manager about fixing the quota of work per day in two parts before lunch and after lunch. The distribution manager left convinced and introduced the system. However, the efficiency dropped down considerably and no crew member was near the target.

QUESTIONS

1. What were the reasons for decreased efficiency in the new system?
2. Advise Mr. Dubey and distributions manager about the future course of action.

CASE STUDY – 4

The very validity of management education is being questioned these days, when business houses find that it is inadequate and those countries like Japan who do not have formal managment education are overtaking many western economies. Success in business no doubt is due to a leader who work in an exemplary manner, inspiring others in the process. Knowing things does help but to limited extent. To a large extent, dealing appropriately with people is what matters. And dealing with people appropriately is an ingredient of leadership.

Whether the group of people we deal with is large or small it needs the caressing hand of a leader, the leader about whom all of us know is the head of a family on whose qualities the well being of the family depends.

In today's organizations we have so many managers we are expected to be leader. It is their leadership quality which makes a society what it is and effective leader is always a force multiplier.

We have to view leadership in a holistic manner. Leaders become the change agents. Though leadership cannot be taught it is possible for a man with capability to transform him into a leader. Leadership is ultimately an issue of self development. The very fact that you are reading this chapter to study the chemistry of leadership is proof of your motivation to develop yourself.

What role a leader is expected to perform? In a country like India keeping other resources like finance and technology constant we can improve productivity by 30 to 40% by improving our leadership abilities. Leadership theories are not of much help. Leadership is to be improved by taking a practical approach.

It is reasonable to think in terms of improving the leadership potential of those who are already in the fray and are shouldering responsibilities, and also of those who are about to enter the fray. This is the crux of the matter. The message we want to convey is that you can improve yourself and you can improve other by setting a personal example only.

QUESTION

1. What leadership styles are adopted by the Indian Managers?

CASE STUDY – 5

The New Manager

Mr.Avinash was appointed as general manager, administration in Phoenix Industries Limited. He joined the company only about two years back. Prior to joining this company, he served another company for two years. He did his M.B.A. from a reputed institution. He considered himself as a high flier. After getting promotion as general manager, administration, he felt quite excited and was quite enthusiastic about his new job. The post of general manager was sufficiently at high level. However, because of young age and lack of adequate experience, Mr. Avinash was considered as junior executive by most of his subordinates.

The administration department of the company had four major sub-units: purchasing, record maintenance, printing, and secretarial services. Each sub-unit was headed by a manager. These four managers were directly reporting to Mr. Avinash. They had combined experience of over 80 years with an average age of 45 years. Most of them had been with the company for a fairly long period of time and that too with their present units. Since Mr. Avinash was quite less experienced and young, these four managers viewed his appointment with hesitancy and suspicion. Also, they had liking for the previous general manager and were sorry to see him leave the company.

The new general manager. Mr. Avinash, started holding weekly meetings of the department. However, he noticed that managers were hesitant to speak in the meetings; he was the only one to speak. He made some changes in the operating procedures that he felt would increase efficiency and announced them in a weekly departmental meeting. There were no reactions to the changes, but later he noticed that the managers continued to follow the old procedures. He talked to them individually but felt that they were not opening up to him. The problem continued.

After about two months, Mr. Avinash started receiving complaints from other departments about the services they received from the administration department. The complaints mostly related to printing and purchasing. Avinash believed that his department should provide the best possible services and, therefore, admonished his managers in a weekly departmental meeting. He still received little response from them. He continued to receive complaints and was becoming increasingly frustrated. On one day, he became very upset at the third complaint that week over jobs done in the printing unit. He stormed out of his office down to the printing unit. The manager of the printing unit was out. Avinash called over the chief print operator, chewed him out, and told him to redo the job on the same day. When printing unit manager returned and learned what happened, he immediately called a meeting with the three other managers and described events to them. On this, commented the manager-purchasing unit, "We have to do something. Avinash is too young, incompetent, and is a tyrant". I agree, he dictates to us in departmental meetings, and now he goes behind our back to our employees. He shows no confidence in us. I am fed up with this situation," said manager-secretarial services. Finally, the manager-maintenance chimed in, "I don't think we have much choice. Avinash is regarded high by top-level management. We can't talk to him and higher up, and if we continue doing things this way, our careers will be ruined. Therefore, I think that we should look for some other job opportunitie." They all reluctantly agreed with this statement and the meeting ended.

QUESTIONS

1. Describe the nature of the problems in this case.
2. Explain what could have been done to prevent the problems.
3. Outline the means you would propose to solve the problems.

CASE STUDY – 6

The Assistant Business Manager

Ice Cool Private Limited was an ice-cream manufacturing company employing about 100 persons including persons at various level of management. Because of increasing business, the company needed to strengthen its accounting procedure, particularly through computerisation. For this purpose, the company decided to hire a new manager, designated as assistant business manager. The company invited applications through press advertisement. After receiving the applications, it appointed a selection committee consisting of members of top management including business manager Rakesh Mohan. The committee interviewed several candidates and finally selected Bishwash as new assistant business manager. Bishwash was neat, well dressed, and quite articulate.

Bishwash joined the company immediately and started working very hard. He used to put extra efforts and even worked during holidays as he did not have any family responsibility. He gained the reputation of being a dedicated and competent employee, his strong point being his knowledge of accounting and computer system. He was reporting to Rakesh Mohan, the business manager who was quire impressed with his working.

At that time, the company had no computer system, and its accounting procedures were in need of considerable improvement. Anil Kumar, the managing director of the company, directed Rakesh Mohan to get the needful done. Since most of accounting work related to sales, no separate accounting department existed and the work was performed under the direction of the business manager. Bishwash was mainly appointed to strengthen the accounting aspects of the business. He was asked to prepare a project so that necessary changes can be made. In order to get the first hand information about the problem. Bishwash began meeting regularly with Anil Kumar without the knowledge of Rakesh Mohan. There was no attempt to have secret meeting: Anil Kumar would just call Bishwash in for a report without bothering to tell Rakesh Mohan. The management team, whose members were with the company for a quite long period had formed a tight-knit group and appeared satisfied with the company. They all worked together and the company prospered in spite of fierce competition.

The meetings between Anil Kumar and Bishwash continued and Rakesh Mohan was gradually losing contact with the project and its progress. In fact, Bishwash was almost reporting directly to the managing director though he was placed under business manager and retained his title of assistant business manager. Rakesh Mohan was now visibly upset over the development and was also concerned about Bishwash's spreading share of influence. He started feeling down in the company.

QUESTIONS

1. What is the nature of problem in this case?
2. Could Rakesh Mohan have prevented Bishwash's assumption of power? If so, how specifically, could it have been done?
3. Suggest the courses of action now available to Anil Kumar, Rakesh Mohan, and Bishwash?